Urban Life

and

Urban Landscape Series

# Lancaster,

# Ohio, 1800–2000

## Frontier Town to Edge City

DAVID R. CONTOSTA

OHIO STATE UNIVERSITY PRESS
Columbus

Copyright © 1999 by The Ohio State University.
All rights reserved.

Library of Congress Cataloging-in-Publication Data

Contosta, David R.
    Lancaster, Ohio, 1800–2000 : frontier town to edge city / David R. Contosta.
       p.   cm. — (Urban life and urban landscape series)
    Includes bibliographical references and index.
    ISBN 0-8142-0825-8 (cloth : alk. paper). — ISBN 0-8142-5027-0 (pbk. : alk. paper)
    1. Lancaster (Ohio)—History. I. Title. II. Series.
F499.L2C66   1999
977.1'58—dc21                                                      99-21549
                                                                                                       CIP

Designed and typeset by Pelican Street Studio, Inc.
Type set in Dante and Castellar.

9 8 7 6 5 4 3 2

IN MEMORY OF

My grandparents
    Ercole "Frank" Contosta (1883–1960)
    Bertha Hartman Contosta (1890–1984)
    Bert B. Mowry (1881–1948)
    Mary A. Jenkins Mowry (1885–1946)

My grandparents in wish
    Edson B. Olds Smith (1868–1961)
    Alice M. Stover Smith (1878–1966)

My parents
    Miles R. Contosta (1920–1997)
    Betty J. Mowry Contosta (1920–1992)

My brother
    Thomas H. Contosta (1948–1967)

# Contents

List of Illustrations, ix

List of Maps, xiii

Foreword, xv

Preface, xvii

List of Abbreviations, xxi

**Introduction:** The Town and American Life, 1

1. **Frontier Lancaster:** The Town Emerges, 9
2. **Heroic Age:** A Town Divided, 33
3. **Victorian Lancaster:** Town Improvement, 69
4. **Boom Town:** Industrial Lancaster, 125
5. **Turmoil, Depression, and War:** The Town Endures, 167
6. **The Town at High Noon:** Postwar Lancaster, 201
7. **Suburban Lancaster:** Toward the Edge City, 230

   **Conclusion:** Into the Future, 269

Notes, 275

Bibliographic Essay, 313

Index, 321

# Illustrations

Early Fairfield County log cabin,   17
Newspaper advertisement for Jesse Woltz, cabinetmaker,   20
First Fairfield County Courthouse, 1807,   24
Matlack House, 1807,   25
Ewing House, 1824,   26
Garaghty-Mumaugh House, 1824,   27
Sherman House, 1811,   28
Ferguson-Furniss House, 1833,   28
Canal in Lancaster,   38
Maccracken House (The Georgian), 1832,   41
DeVol—Dallow—Anchor Hocking Guest House, 1834,   43
Stanbery-Rising House, 1834,   43
View of Lancaster's Main Street by Henry Howe, 1846,   44
Lancaster's first city hall, 1859,   52
Fairfield County Fairgrounds, 1875,   53
William Tecumseh Sherman,   62
Hocking Valley Manufacturing Company,   73
Shimp's Hill with horse and carriage,   74
Becker Brewery letterhead,   77
Houses on North High Street between Sixth and Allen,   80
Residence with porch, 1880s,   81
Smith residence, North Columbus Street, c. 1860,   82
Second Fairfield County Courthouse, 1872,   85
Andy Bauman letterhead,   88
Lancaster's fountain and Fountain Square, 1890s,   89
Lancaster's second city hall,   90

## ILLUSTRATIONS

The Opera House, 1883, 91
Hotel Martens, 1883, 92
Passengers disembarking from horsecars, 1890s, 93
Lancaster's Union Station, 1900, 94
South School, 1875, 95
Segregated elementary school for Lancaster's
 African Americans, 1875, 96
Boys' Industrial School (BIS), 99
Fairfield County Infirmary, 100
Forest Rose Cemetery, 101
Engine House 1, 1899, 103
St. Peter's Lutheran Church, 1875-1882, 104
Methodist campground, 105
Masonic Temple interior, 108
Cattle barn, Fairfield County Fair, 109
Apples and fruits at Fairfield County Fair, 110
Hillside Hotel, 112
Smith family at Christmas Rocks, 1880s, 113
Soda fountain, Reed and Walters Drug Store, 114
Baseball team, 1890s, 115
African Methodist Episcopal (AME) Church, 119
Oil well at Bremen, 126
Isaac J. Collins, 129
Interurban car, 1930, 131
Owners of a new automobile, c. 1910, 132
Main Street, early twentieth century, 134
Effinger House and Broad Street, 1920s, 135
Colonial Revival houses, East Fifth Avenue, 136
West Side houses, Harrison Avenue, 138
Lancaster High School, Mulberry Street, 140
St. Mary Schools, 143
Lancaster Athletic Club, 146
Hippodrome movie theater, 148
Air show, 1912, 150
Buckeye Lake Park, 1920s, 152

Mount Pleasant and Rising Park, 158
Rising Park, stone shelter house, 159
Anti-Prohibition cartoon, 1928, 162
Hospital, Park Street, 164
Hospital, Ewing Street, 165
Captain William Belhorn and victory parade, 1919, 170
Epstein's Shoes, 176
Godman shoe factory, Columbus and Mulberry Streets, 181
Thomas "Tom" Joyce, 183
R. Kenneth Kerr, 186
Anchor Hocking corporate headquarters, 189
"Last roundup" of trolleys, 1937, 190
New buses arrive, 1937, 191
Hotel Lancaster, 192
The Contosta family, World War II, 199
*Green Grass of Wyoming:* cast and local dignitaries, 202
*Green Grass of Wyoming:* filming and stars, 204
"Etta Kett Day," sesquicentennial celebration, 1950, 206
Perrin "Pel" Hazelton and Virginia Mowry Hazelton at
    Sesquicentennial Ball, 1950, 207
Sesquicentennial parade, 1950, 208
Main Street, 1950s, 212
Salesgirl Marilyn Miller, 216
Football at North Field, 1950s, 220
Fairfield County Fair, 1965, 221
Ladies' luncheon, First Presbyterian Church, 1950s, 223
Strip shopping center, Memorial Drive, 233
Lancaster High School, Route 37, 235
Lancaster High School, Mulberry Street, 235
Ohio University at Lancaster, 237
Parking lots, West Wheeling Street, 242
Ruth Wolfley Drinkle and Charles Drinkle, 244
The Georgian, restoration of 1970s, 248
Bandstand, Zane Square, 250
Anchor Hocking's Plant 1, 255

AEP clock tower, 257
River Valley Mall and Lancaster's edge city, 259
River Valley Highlands development, 260
Restored shop fronts, Main Street, 265
Reese-Peters House, 1834, 267
East Allen Street, 400 block, 272

# Maps

Original town of Lancaster, with squares, 1800,   9
Zane's Trace and Fairfield County,   13
Boundaries of Zane's square mile,   21
The Carpenter Addition, 1814,   23
Ohio's canal system and the National Road,   36
Early gas wells in Lancaster,   75
Lancaster in 1866,   78
Aerial lithograph of Lancaster, 1885,   83
Highways of Fairfield County, 1950s,   238
Lancaster, 1950s,   239
Lancaster, 1998,   261

# Foreword

DAVID CONTOSTA'S HISTORY OF Lancaster is a sensible, well-written, and generously illustrated volume. It is informed by professional scholarship but aimed at a broad audience, including young and older people with little or no practice in the serious study of American or urban history. And Contosta, who grew up in Lancaster, writes with an ex-resident's personal interest from a perspective that yields an affectionate yet critical account of his hometown's past and present.

But Contosta also wrote this book as part of his continuing effort as a historian and citizen to make sense out of American civilization, a task he approaches by defining Lancaster as a town, a place that by conventional definition falls in size somewhere between a village and a city. Here he reminds us that there have been and still are lots of such places, and that a very large percentage of Americans still reside in towns, many of them, like Lancaster, sitting in the shadow of a much larger city (like Columbus). But he conceives of Lancaster's history neither as a unique story nor as one typical of American towns generally. Instead, he tells it as a story both like and unlike those one might tell about other towns and therefore makes it a story useful to non-Lancastrians in thinking comparatively and critically about their own towns.

This book will also help residents of other kinds of urban places make sense out of their past and present, for Contosta highlights themes in Lancaster's experience that recur in American urban history generally. One of these themes is the idea of the urban frontier, the notion that cities spearheaded the spread of Western civilization across America. When we think of the urban frontier, we tend to concentrate on rapidly growing villages and towns that became major American cities. But that frontier also consisted of less dynamic but very important outposts, including a host of waterfront towns that filled gaps between larger cities, such as Boston, New York, and Philadelphia on the East Coast; Baltimore, Charleston, and

New Orleans in the South; Pittsburgh, Cincinnati, Louisville, and St. Louis in the Ohio and Mississippi River valleys; Buffalo, Cleveland, Detroit, and Chicago along the Great Lakes corridor; and San Diego, Los Angeles, San Francisco, and Seattle in the Far West.

To these gap-filling waterfront frontier towns, Contosta adds another category, "inland" towns like Lancaster that served as the cutting extensions of the urban frontier. He argues, moreover, that Lancaster's subsequent stages of city and suburban growth very much resembled those we tend to associate only with big cities, although Lancaster never became one. But it too developed a mixed socioeconomic structure and municipal social services characteristic of mid-nineteenth-century big cities, and displayed also the "walking city" social and economic geography that marked bigger places in that period. To be sure, Lancaster's population did not in the late nineteenth and early twentieth century diversify as intensely as Cleveland's, or even Cincinnati's, but it spread out like the two Ohio metropolises and went through social, economic, and political growing pains familiar to contemporary Clevelanders and Cincinnatians. And not only did Lancaster sprout in the last half of the twentieth century a suburban "edge city" that competed with downtown Lancaster for residents, stores, offices, and factories, but it also became itself an edge city of Columbus, a competitor with the larger place for residents, stores, offices, and industries.

Contosta, of course, might have written a different book, one that focused less on Lancaster as a place and a civic entity. He could, for example, have used Lancaster as a setting for the exploration of translocal events, such as the social and physical mobility of Americans, or the formation and conflicts of various social, economic, or cultural groups. But he chose instead to leave those studies to other historians, and to prepare a story that encourages in Lancastrians and other readers the cultivation of a concern for place and a sense of civic loyalty and responsibility that might mitigate their single-minded pursuit of their particular group interests.

In this spirit I think it appropriate to acknowledge that the appearance of this book coincides intentionally with Lancaster's bicentennial in 2000 and also (almost) with the bicentennial of the state of Ohio in 2003. Such occasions elicit in their celebrants an increased curiosity about the past, an interest this history hopes to steer toward the town's future as a place and civic entity. This kind of book presents the past as liberation history, as a legacy that town dwellers today and in the future may accept, reject, or modify, if and as they choose.

ZANE L. MILLER

# Preface

I GREW UP IN LANCASTER, OHIO, during the two decades after World War II. One of my earliest images of Lancaster was its sesquicentennial celebration, held during June of 1950 when I was not quite five and a half years old. Although I was more excited about the amusement rides in the middle of Main Street than anything else, the sights of so many men with mustaches and beards, grown especially for the big event, and the delivery of the huge sesquicentennial edition of the local newspaper have also stayed with me. When the celebrating was over, I asked my parents when we could "do it all again," and was more than disappointed to hear that it would take another fifty years, when Lancaster held its next big birthday. This possibility seemed eons away—in the year 2000, I figured out with some help from adult arithmetic, when I would be an "old man" of fifty-five.

I gave up on seeing another town anniversary anytime soon, but found myself surrounded by reminders of the past—human and otherwise. Our next-door neighbor, Mrs. Black, who lived to be 103, had been born all the way back in 1860 and could even remember the end of the Civil War. Across the street there were Pop and Mom Smith. Pop was born in 1868 and Mom ten years later. My grandfather, born in 1883, and my grandmother, born in 1890, lived several blocks away and were youngsters compared to our most senior neighbors. Yet all of them had lived through a great transformation in history: the movement from a world of horses, oil and gas lamps, and face-to-face conversation to an era of automobiles, electric lights, and telephones. Repeated over and over again, stories of their first ride in a car or that maiden conversation over the telephone made the past come alive and added to my curiosity about local history.

Then there were the several dozen large and attractive pre–Civil War houses that stood on the hill just north and east of downtown, silent testaments to a vibrant past. Lessons to be learned from these houses were not so obvious as stories about the horse-and-buggy days, and it would take years for me to figure out what they had to say about Lancaster.

At college I decided to become a professional historian, and my continuing interest in the town where I grew up eventually suggested a focus on urban history. An opportunity to live in France and subsequent travels abroad offered many grounds for comparison among towns and cities. My life for the past twenty-five years in Philadelphia and its suburbs has added to this store of comparisons.

The inspiration for this book came out of these experiences, and from a desire to know more about the place where I was born and spent my childhood years. I hope that this self-discovery will help others to understand the complex evolution of American cities and towns, and above all the residents of Lancaster and communities like it. Professional historians may also find the book of interest and be stimulated to probe particular aspects of Lancaster's past, and of the nation's other towns and smaller cities. That Lancaster is now two hundred years old, with a history that is richly documented, has made the story a practical as well as immensely self-fulfilling journey.

Readers will notice that I have followed a basic chronology in presenting the history of Lancaster. Within each period, however, I have tried to emphasize a certain theme or themes. This decision has resulted in some overlap in chronology between chapters. For example, I did not deal with Lancaster's suburbs in chapter 6, which concerns the immediate post–World War II period, but placed the topic in chapter 7, which takes the story of suburbanization and of Lancaster's movement toward an edge city from the late 1940s to the end of the twentieth century. Such an organization should help readers to grasp these and other important movements far better than if they had been fragmented into a strict chronological presentation of the community's past, with each person, fact, or event coming in exact sequence.

For the sake of consistency and in order to avoid confusion, I have used the Lancaster street names as they existed in the late 1990s, unless otherwise indicated.

I am grateful to those local historians who have gone before me and to the dozens of individuals in Lancaster who have helped me with the project and extended their hospitality. Many of their names and contributions appear in the notes and in the bibliographic essay.

I wish to thank the staffs of several libraries who were generous in their assistance: the Fairfield County District Library, the Ohio University Library–Lancaster, the Ohio State University Cartoon Research Library, the Columbus Public Library, the Public Library of Cincinnati, the Chestnut Hill College Library in Philadelphia, and the St. Joseph's University Library, also in Philadelphia. Gene Matheny, executive director of the Fairfield County Visitors and Convention Bureau was helpful in numerous ways. The Lancaster Fairfield County Chamber of Commerce kindly supplied many facts and figures.

Among those individuals who assisted me at the Lancaster City Hall were Mayor Arthur Wallace, Law Director Terre Vandervoort, City Treasurer Gene Ash, Assistant City Engineer Richard L. Mark, and Engineering Specialist Jeff Gawell. Franklin B. Melick, community development director, also provided an abundance of helpful information. In addition to sharing his own wide knowledge of Lancaster, Gene Ash gave me the use of a beautifully carved Victorian desk in his office at city hall as a base of operations while I pored over dozens of volumes of city records and historic maps.

I am indebted to Jean (Mrs. Lloyd) Tobias, who allowed me to select and publish a number of photographs from the Tobias Studio collections. Charles E. "Chuck" Reed generously researched the I. J. Collins will for me and William H. Schroer took time at my request to research the Prohibition question in Lancaster. I also owe much to Philip M. Hazelton, with whom I have written a yet unpublished memoir about growing up in Lancaster during the post–World War II era.

Several persons who are well acquainted with Lancaster read the manuscript and provided much appreciated corrections and suggestions: Gene Ash, Jack Furniss, Virginia Hazelton, Jo and Don Libert, and Caroline Peters Rockwood.

Zane Miller, editor of the Urban Life and Urban Landscape Series of the Ohio State University Press, offered many insights and suggestions and was enthusiastic about the project from beginning to end. Charlotte Dihoff, acquisitions editor at the press, believed strongly in the book from our earliest discussions and, with the cooperation of her staff, made it a reality. Barbara Hanrahan, director of the press, has been helpful and encouraging in many ways. I am also obliged to the care and craftsmanship of John Delaine and Ruth Melville at the press, and to copy editor Colleen Romick.

I want to thank my wife, Mary, and our two boys, David and Johnnie, for understanding my need to spend long hours in my study and for the many summer research trips back to Ohio.

# Abbreviations

These abbreviations are used in the captions for the illustrations and maps and in the notes and bibliographic essay.

| | |
|---:|---|
| BIS | Boys' Industrial School |
| *DAB* | *Dictionary of American Biography* |
| *Eagle* | *Ohio Eagle* and later *Lancaster Eagle* |
| *E-G* | *Lancaster Eagle-Gazette* |
| *E-G Sesqui* | *Eagle-Gazette, Sesquicentennial Edition,* June 3, 1950 |
| FCDL | Fairfield County District Library |
| FHA | Fairfield Heritage Association |
| FHQ | *Fairfield Heritage Quarterly* |
| *Gazette* | *Lancaster Gazette* |
| OSU | Ohio State University |

# Introduction
## The Town and American Life

EVEN AS THE TWENTIETH CENTURY comes to an end, the majority of Americans do not live in large cities, despite an intense urbanization that began over a hundred years before. Fully 44 percent of the nation's urban population reside in communities of fewer than 50,000 people, while 41 percent come from cities of 100,000 or more.[1] Rather than declining over the last few decades, the percentages of people living in smaller communities have held steady, and in the case of those with 25,000 to 50,000 inhabitants, they have risen slightly.[2]

A century ago, small and modest-sized towns were even more typical of community life in America. Such towns were often the settings for novels and short stories, and until the 1920s they were generally seen in a positive light.[3] They were "good communities" in a nation undergoing rapid industrialization and urbanization, standing in contrast to the greed, crime, disease, and social strife of big cities. Women writers in particular—Harriet Beecher Stowe, Edith Wharton, and Willa Cather, among others—frequently used the small town as an idyllic setting for their novels and short stories.[4]

During the 1920s, most writers turned against the town as part of a wider critique of Victorian, middle-class values that were thought to persist most alarmingly in smaller communities, and especially in the Midwest. For these writers, the town was a place of intolerance and mindless conformity that lacked artistic interest or intellectual stimulation. The big city, by contrast, was an ideal setting for freedom, diversity, and creative ferment. Novelists such as Zona Gale, Sinclair Lewis, and Sherwood Anderson all attacked the small town in their novels, though their fictional towns were never without a few redeeming graces.[5]

When sociologists began to study towns in the 1920s, most shared these negative views about smaller communities.⁶ This attitude would persist for the next three or four decades in studies like Robert S. and Helen M. Lynd's *Middletown* (actually Muncie, Indiana) and William Lloyd Warner's accounts of Newburyport, Massachusetts. For such authors, small-town Americans were clinging to outmoded values that, because of the inescapable demands of modern life, they applied inconsistently and often hypocritically. In *Middletown,* the Lynds reported that Muncie's professed values of female chastity and sexual fidelity were mocked by the realities of prostitution, adultery, divorce, and loveless unions. In like manner, Middletowners contradicted an oft-professed faith in education by their failure to give students the social and intellectual tools necessary to cope with a rapidly changing world.⁷

In contrast to sociologists, historians in the United States paid little attention to particular towns or cities until the middle of the twentieth century. And when historians did turn to urban topics, they tended to join with the sociologists (who had, by then, abandoned their interests in towns) in emphasizing the nation's largest cities and their multifaceted problems: poverty, racism, shrinking employment and populations, and budgetary crises. Urban studies, whether undertaken by historians, sociologists, or geographers, were now defined as the examination of the country's largest cities—which, while deeply troubled, were still thought to be the most important centers of culture and civilization.⁸

As the large cities lurched from crisis to crisis, millions of Americans fled into the new automobile suburbs of the post–World War II period, a phenomenon that would eventually raise many questions about suburbs and their effects on American life.⁹ Most studies were critical of the suburban trend. They castigated suburbs as boring, isolated enclaves of largely white Americans who had fled various ethnic and racial minorities, taking their middle-class tax dollars with them. Most suburbanites, however, were blissfully unaware of these accounts, and the suburban tide has continued as the twentieth century comes to an end. By this time, however, many suburbs face the same kinds of traffic congestion, intense development, and crime that their residents sought to leave behind in the cities. For some, neither the city nor the suburb offers a satisfactory way of life, and there has been a perceptible moving out and beyond the suburbs to long-settled towns on the far edges of the metropolitan fringe. At the same time, a nostalgia for the supposed simplicities and traditional values of small-town America has found powerful echoes in Disney World's "Main Street" and in Garrison Keillor's long-running radio program, *A Prairie Home Companion,* and his book *Lake Wobegon Days.*[10]

In this atmosphere of renewed interest in smaller communities, some historians have begun to pay more attention to individual towns and villages, with a few studies starting to appear in the late 1960s.[11] Some of the communities studied are important in their own right because of some dramatic or spectacular episode in their pasts, or for some notoriety of lifestyle: Salem, Massachusetts, because of the witchcraft trials; Pullman, Illinois, because of its fame as a carefully planned company town and the labor strife that erupted there; or Scarsdale, New York, because of its reputation as a wealthy and flamboyant suburb.[12] Historians have also examined less-famous towns as case studies to illuminate larger forces and trends on a regional or national scale.[13]

This renewed interest in towns during the latter decades of the twentieth century—both by their new residents and by urban scholars—happily coincides with the two-hundredth anniversary of the founding of Lancaster, Ohio. First settled in 1800, Lancaster reached a population of just under 3,500 people in 1850, was incorporated as a city the following year, and has enjoyed the official designation of a city ever since. Yet "town," defined by the *American Heritage Dictionary* as "a population center . . . larger than a village and smaller than a city," would seem more appropriate as a description of this community that has grown slowly over the decades, achieving a population of only 9,000 in 1900, 22,000 in 1940, and about 40,000 at the end of the twentieth century.

This two-hundred-year study reveals that Lancaster was never the sort of idyllic community that late-nineteenth- and early-twentieth-century novelists liked to imagine. Nor has it been the social and cultural wasteland that writers and scholars portrayed for towns during the three or four decades beginning in the 1920s.

During its early years, Lancaster was one of the largest and most important towns in what would later be called the Midwest. As such, it offers an excellent example, in its formative life, of the thesis put forth in the now classic work by Richard C. Wade, *The Urban Frontier.* Wade held that towns and cities in the trans-Appalachian West were the spearheads of settlement, contradicting the long-held belief that rural activity preceded towns and cities and that farming had actually paved the way for urban life.[14] As a frontier town, Lancaster provided supplies for the outlying populace, markets for agricultural goods, capital for town residents and rural dwellers alike, political leadership and local government, and the beginnings of higher culture, with many of the physical comforts and amenities of eastern cities appearing with remarkable speed.

In addition, Lancaster has been home to talented individuals who made their mark on the national and international scene. Among the notables who grew up in Lancaster—or who spent some portion of their careers in town—were Civil War general William Tecumseh Sherman and his brother, U.S. Senator John Sherman; Richard Outcault, creator of the newspaper comic strip and the cartoon character *Buster Brown;* Lloyd C. Douglas, the immensely successful religious novelist; and Malcolm Forbes, who began his publishing career in Lancaster and later devoted an entire issue of *Forbes* magazine to the town.

Though such men have made their mark in the wider world, neither they nor any local happenings would place Lancaster in the category of a famous town. Instead, a study of Lancaster will be of interest beyond its own boundaries precisely because it fails to qualify for great fame, a characteristic that it shares with hundreds of other places, making it symptomatic of so many localities neglected by historians. Lancaster is also of interest because of what it has to reveal, on an intimate scale, about problems, issues, and trends in American civilization as a whole.

Seen in this light, all history is local history, as past events—however earth-shattering they might be—necessarily unfold at a particular place.[15] And often it is "place" that makes all the difference: the outcomes of numerous military engagements have turned on the slightest degree of location, just as the economic and social fortunes of individuals often depend on being at the "right place" in history. Remove the Kennedys from Boston and Hyannis Port, or the British royal family from London and Balmoral, and they become very different people, while the locales so closely associated with them become less interesting and important.

Several factors are of major significance in Lancaster's evolution. One has been its location near the entrance to the Hocking River valley. Although the river has never been navigable for most of its length, the valley has provided a pathway for various forms of transportation, beginning with pack trails and wagon roads, later with canals and railroads, and still later with motor highways. Yet unlike communities on major waterways such as the Ohio River or Lake Erie, Lancaster's position in transportation and trade has been more modest, giving rise to an equally modest prosperity and growth and, in the process, preserving its status as a town rather than making it into a large city.

A modest but consistent supply of natural resources has reinforced Lancaster's standing as a town, including rich farmland north, east, and west of town, coal and oil deposits south of town, stands of hardwood forests in every direction (particularly in the early decades), and a once substantial supply of natural gas in and around Lancaster. Though a gas boom during the late 1880s and early 1890s produced rapid growth for several decades, these deposits were not large enough to create a great city; nor was the discovery of oil in surrounding Fairfield County of such lasting magnitude as to touch off a sustained boom in the population.

The sort of people who have made Lancaster their home have also been an important force in shaping the town. From the beginning, the vast majority of residents have been of white European ancestry, overwhelmingly from the British Isles and from Germany. This fact of local life has lessened the incidence of ethnic or racial strife, though episodes of religious, racial, and ethnic prejudice have periodically erupted into public view (as witnessed in a strong showing by the Ku Klux Klan in the 1920s) and have certainly been part of local belief systems and conversational life. The large numbers of residents whose families came to town from the Upper South is also significant, explaining the strong Southern sympathies of many Lancastrians during the Civil War (flaring into several violent episodes) and probably contributing to an ongoing belief in states' rights and a suspicion of government regulation. Reinforcing these conservative sentiments have been consistent levels of prosperity in Lancaster and freedom from most urban problems that have made other Americans more sympathetic to government intervention.

Important, too, has been the impact of surrounding Fairfield County, of which Lancaster has always been the county seat. While this study is not a combined history of Lancaster and Fairfield County, it takes up county matters, including some attention to county politics and the development of several county villages, to the extent that these topics illuminate the Lancaster story. As the "biography" of a place, the book does not attempt to be an encyclopedia of almost every person, place, organization, or event that might have been recorded during the course of two centuries. Nor does it attempt detailed explorations of any one group in local history, though such approaches may be suggested for other researchers.

A consciousness of the local past, especially during the twentieth century, forms another consistent theme in Lancaster's development. Proud references to General Sherman and other early citizens of note, along with a growing dedication to preserving the town's many beautiful houses and other historic structures, have created emotional rallying points as well as an inspiration for social and civic activity. Although understandings of the local past have sometimes been distorted, particularly when it came to the Civil War period, this strong interest in local history has been an important factor in creating and sustaining a sense of community.

Throughout its history, technology—especially transportation technology—has been a crucial force in molding Lancaster. Canals, railroads, and then the internal combustion engine (powering cars, trucks, and buses) have kept Lancaster connected to its markets and sources of raw materials, and have helped to assure its material well being. But as Lancaster neared its two-hundredth birthday, technology was changing the town in ways that no one could have anticipated fifty years before. Until the end of World War II, the physical and economic expansion of Lancaster had reinforced rather than undermined the central role of its downtown as a business and merchandising hub and as the major scene of social and cultural activity. But an upsurge in motor vehicles since the war, and the need to provide vast expanses of parking for them, has undermined Lancaster's downtown as a focus of civic, social, and economic life. Meanwhile, the movement of homes, offices, shopping centers, churches, and industries into what must be called Lancaster's suburbs produced numerous points of activity and interchange, and the increasing destruction of irreplaceable farm land. At the same time, a modern highway from Lancaster to Columbus, some thirty miles to the northwest, led many local inhabitants to find employment in the capital city, while residents of Columbus have taken to buying homes in and around Lancaster.

One consequence of these patterns has been the beginnings, in and around the River Valley Mall north of town, of what the journalist Joel Garreau has called an *edge city*. This is a group of offices and commercial establishments that has become a demographic and economic center in its own right.[16] The mall complex—along with Lancaster as a whole—has become something of an edge city on the far fringes of the Columbus metropolitan area.

Revealingly, this movement in Lancaster to the suburbs and then toward the edge city has had nothing to do with race, for Lancaster's minority population is so small as to be almost nonexistent. Instead, the major reason for such changes has been an increased accommodation to the automobile and its demands for highways and parking spaces. While not denying the reality of "white flight" in many communities, this finding may suggest that the movement out of America's cities has had more to do with technology than it has with race, and that massive suburbanization would have taken place even without racial divisions in the United States.

Although Lancaster is in transition, it also appears to have moved into a period of sustained growth, economically and demographically, as it celebrates its bicentennial. In this respect it is one of the nation's more fortunate towns, unlike the hundreds of small communities throughout America that have stagnated or declined at the end of the twentieth century.[17] In fact, through its entire two hundred years of existence, Lancaster has declined in population during just one ten-year census period, from 1980 to 1990, and then by only 1 percent. Lancaster's problem in the foreseeable future is not lack of growth but how to channel that growth in the most positive directions.

At a time of transition for Lancaster and for many towns throughout the United States, the author hopes that this history will be a source of pleasure and understanding. For those who study American towns, the author hopes that this book will reinforce a renewed interest in the nation's smaller communities.

ONE

# Frontier Lancaster
## The Town Emerges

In the late autumn of 1800, on November 14 to be precise, the first lots in the settlement of New Lancaster went up for sale. Although there is no record of the weather, one can imagine that this November day two centuries ago was not unlike mid-Novembers of living memory—a cool and partly cloudy day with brown leaves clinging stubbornly to a few trees and wild vines.

Lancaster was fortunate not to remain just an idea on paper, as did so many other speculative ventures in town and city planning in the frontier

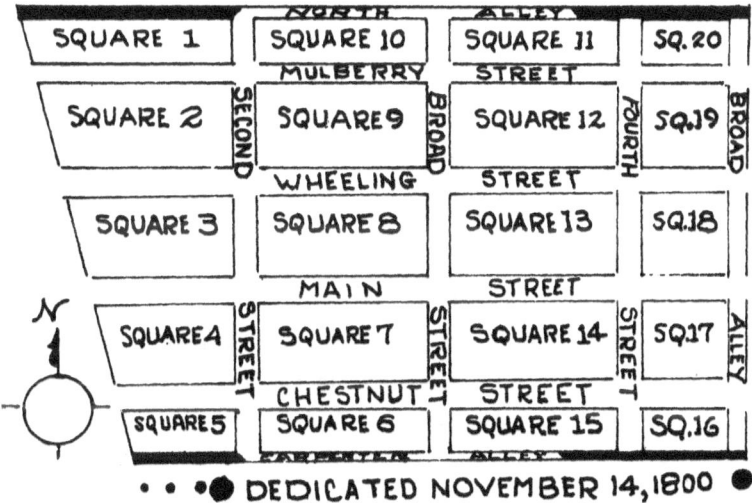

Original town of Lancaster, with squares, as laid out in 1800. Map by Charles Goslin, *Crossroads and Fence Corners*, 2:12.

areas west of the Appalachians during the early years of the nineteenth century.[1] A variety of forces, most of them natural, saved Lancaster from that fate, allowing it to become a flourishing frontier town that provided opportunities for merchants, craftsmen, unskilled workers, and professionals, and that organized the surrounding area politically, economically, and socially.

Many thousands of years before the first lots were sold in Lancaster, a welter of geological forces had been shaping a likely site for the town. Today there are abundant clues to these evolutionary changes: the low hills surrounding Lancaster and the much flatter terrain just a few miles north of town, for instance, offer visual indications of the varied effects of geological time.[2] An even more dramatic reminder of these ancient upheavals is Lancaster's Mount Pleasant, a sandstone cliff that towers some 250 feet above the northeast corner of town.

Producing these upheavals were a series of glaciers that advanced and receded over the area, carving out the natural landscape that the first pioneers beheld and that remains two centuries later. As the North American continent cooled and then warmed, these glaciers came and went through Lancaster and surrounding Fairfield County, the last of them known as the Wisconsin Glacier, so named because its effects were first discovered in the present-day state of Wisconsin. This glacier entered Ohio about 25,000 years ago and covered about two-thirds of the state for some sixty centuries. Although earlier glaciers had penetrated into the southern corners of Fairfield County, the Wisconsin halted just south and east of Lancaster.

Besides carving out a picturesque landscape, these mountains of ice left a rich natural bounty to Lancaster and its vicinity. Indeed, without the effects of glaciation, the town would not exist, for the runoff from these glaciers gouged out the Hocking River and cut this river valley through to the mighty Ohio. Although the Hocking River was never navigable as far as Lancaster, which lies only a few miles south of its source, the Hocking Valley has provided a convenient pathway—first for a canal, later for a railroad, and still later for a motor highway.

The glaciers also left rich deposits of gravel, known as glacial outwashes and end moraines. Hemlock forests, which were pushed forward by the glaciers, remain in deep gorges south of town. Residents of Lancaster and Fairfield County also owe portions of nearby Buckeye Lake, a favorite summer resort for over a century now, to the gouging effects of glaciation and the collection of melting waters.

Far more significant for the town's economic success is the fact that

Lancaster lies toward the southern end of a zone known as the glaciated portion of the Allegheny Plateau, a geological formation that extends from western Pennsylvania into Ohio's northeast corner and then continues into Ross County in the south-central part of the Buckeye state. This area contained rich farmland and valuable natural resources, such as oil and natural gas, that would contribute significantly to the growth and prosperity of Lancaster, as well as other towns and cities in this glaciated region.

It was after the last ice age, with the disappearance of the Wisconsin Glacier, that the first human inhabitants came, perhaps as early as 13,000 B.C., to settle in what would become Lancaster and Fairfield County. Later named the Paleo-Indian people by anthropologists, these first inhabitants probably disappeared from the area when the large mammals that they hunted migrated northward as the climate warmed in central Ohio. Over the centuries other inhabitants replaced them, including the Hopewell people, who flourished from about 100 B.C. to A.D. 600. The Hopewell were known for their elaborate burial mounds, several of which have been found in Fairfield County; but far more impressive are the mounds they built in concentric rings at Circleville, about fifteen miles west of Lancaster in neighboring Pickaway County.[3]

The Hopewell vanished, too, for reasons that are still unclear. After the Hopewell came the Fort Ancient people, so-called for the stockades that they built to protect their villages. They lasted into the period of European exploration and may have died of diseases introduced by European explorers; and they doubtless suffered heavy losses during repeated raids of the Five Nations of the Iroquois Confederacy, based in central and western New York. Just exactly which of these earlier groups may have lived in what became Lancaster and Fairfield County is uncertain, but it is clear that none was present when the first white settlers arrived there.

In fact, the "Ohio Country" was largely uninhabited during the late seventeenth and early eighteenth centuries. During the 1730s, however, the Wyandot (also known as the Huron) began to move into Ohio from the north, a group of them settling in and around what would later become Lancaster. By then the Wyandot were familiar with European ways and depended upon whites for certain trade goods. Such were the Native Americans whom Lancaster's first settlers encountered. They were not a native people in their original state, utterly innocent of Europeans and their ways.

Although the Wyandot often moved from place to place, they established semipermanent villages, most of them along rivers or streams where they could easily clear and plant rich bottomlands, and where such waterways offered convenient transportation. There they built "longhouses," dwellings that consisted of sheets of bark lashed to a frame of wooden poles. Their diet featured mainly game and cultivated vegetables, such as squash, gourds, and pumpkins, which the women planted and tended. In addition, the women gathered roots, berries, and nuts, and made medicines from various wild plants.[4]

One Wyandot village resting within the future boundaries of Lancaster contained some five hundred inhabitants, according to early sources. It stood along the north bank of the Hocking River at the end of South High Street, where a strong spring entered the river. The settlement was named for Chief Tarhe, or "the Crane," as he was known in English. All traces of Tarhe Town (or Cranetown) have disappeared, but the name *Tarhe* would later be given to an elementary school as well as to the main trail up Mount Pleasant.[5] In addition to the Wyandot, there were small bands of Delaware (or Lenni-Lenape) Indians in the northeast portion of Fairfield County, and of Shawnee in the southern part of the county.[6]

Chief Tarhe's people, like all other native tribes within the future state of Ohio, had to surrender their lands throughout southern and eastern Ohio as a consequence of the Treaty of Greenville, signed in the summer of 1795, following the Battle of Fallen Timbers a year before. By the time lots went up for sale in Lancaster, Tarhe Town had been abandoned, though a few stray Wyandot lingered for several years until their supplies of game disappeared and they had to move on. They made no trouble for the white settlers, who in turn saw no reason to drive them out.

Thus, early Lancastrians had no harrowing tales to tell about fighting Indians around the old hometown, though the story of the Wyandot abduction of a white woman and her recapture in 1790 proved grist for a romantic saga about Lancaster and another historic place name. This was the story of Forest Rose, the name given to the kidnapped woman by Emerson Bennet, who published the novel *Forest Rose* in 1848. Set in Tarhe's village and on scenic Mount Pleasant (called Standing Stone by the Wyandot), as well as on Cold Spring Hill, a mile or so west of the mount, the story included colorful descriptions of nature, star-crossed lovers, and a fierce but ultimately successful fight between the two rescuers and some one hundred Wyandot braves. The romantic account of Forest Rose would be echoed in numerous ways over the decades: Lancaster has a Forest Rose Cemetery and a Forest Rose Avenue, and the name has turned up on a number of local products,

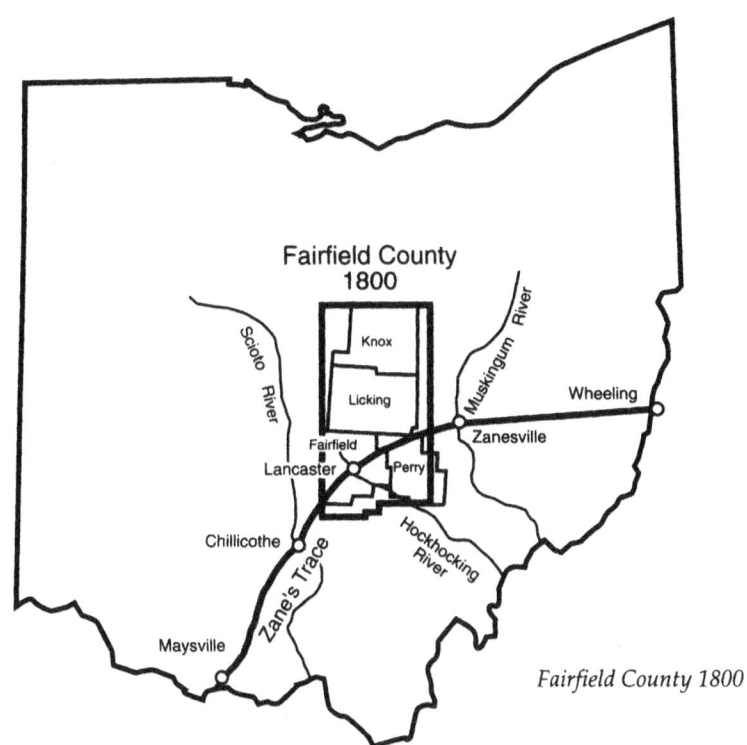

Map of Ohio showing the route of Zane's Trace, as well as the present and original boundaries of Fairfield County. Drinkle, *Heritage of Architecture and Arts*, p. 3.

including Forest Rose Beer and Forest Rose Flour.[7] Generations of local children would reenact the rescue by scrambling up the sandstone cliffs of Mount Pleasant in mock battles against the Indians.[8]

Far less exciting is the account of Lancaster's actual founding, which had its most immediate origins in a trailblazing expedition. The undertaking began when Ebenezer Zane (1747–1811) successfully petitioned the United States Congress in 1796 to open a trail—or trace, as it was then called—from Wheeling, Virginia (later West Virginia), to Maysville (then Limestone), Kentucky, with both its beginning and ending points on the Ohio River.[9] Largely following the contours of an earlier Indian trail, the trace cut a somewhat irregular ninety-degree arc from the eastern border of what is now the state of Ohio to the state's southwestern boundary. The trailblazers—Zane's brother Jonathan and his son-in-law John McIntire—

did little more than clear away brush and dead trees from the route, making a passage wide enough for packhorses, but this laid the basis for a wagon road only a few years later.

In payment for his efforts, Zane claimed three square-mile sites along the trace, all at places where the trace intersected waterways: Zanesville (named for Ebenezer Zane), along the Muskingum River; Lancaster, along the Hocking River; and Chillicothe, along the Scioto River.[10]

Ebenezer Zane's two sons, John and Noah Zane, acting under a power of attorney from their father, offered the first lots for sale in Lancaster in mid-November of 1800. In this sense, Lancaster was truly a frontier town, as were Zanesville and Chillicothe, for it was established and divided into lots before most of the surrounding countryside had been inhabited or put to the plow.[11] The Zanes can be seen as town speculators who, like many others east of the Appalachians, searched out strategic points in the West where they hoped to make money by laying out a frontier town.[12]

Zane's Trace, which was completed to Maysville, Kentucky, in 1797, opened up the southern half of Ohio, with settlers coming into the future site of Lancaster and Fairfield County from both the Virginia and Kentucky ends of the route. Since both entrances to the trace were in what might be called the Upper South, it is understandable that large numbers of Lancaster's settlers would associate themselves with that region of the country for many years to come. Although no federal census before 1860 listed places of birth, other evidence suggests that about half of Lancaster's early residents hailed from the Upper South.[13]

A list of 100 prominent early residents sheds light on these early Southern origins.[14] According to this list, 49 (or 49 percent) of these came from Virginia, Maryland, or Kentucky, with Virginia's 26 leading the list. Next were the 39 persons from the Middle Atlantic states of Pennsylvania, Delaware, and New York. Because of its close proximity to Ohio and the eastern end of Zane's Trace, Pennsylvania accounted for 33 of this number. In last place were the New Englanders, hailing from Connecticut, Vermont, Rhode Island, and Massachusetts. Connecticut, with 4 individuals on the list, contributed nearly half the number of New Englanders. If one considers the figures from individual states rather than those from broader regions, Pennsylvania, with 33, led as a source of immigration among the 100 prominent citizens. Virginia was second with 26, and Maryland third with 16.

A study by genealogist Patsy Kishler of early immigration to both Lancaster and Fairfield County reveals somewhat similar figures.[15] From the

661 male heads of households included in this study, the following numbers and percentages can be calculated for Fairfield County as a whole: Upper South, 299 (45 percent); Middle Atlantic, 296 (45 percent); and New England, 66 (10 percent).[16] The individual state rankings show Pennsylvania as first with 271, Virginia as second with 175, and Maryland as third with 108.

The considerable number of people from Lancaster County, Pennsylvania—more than from any other single county in Pennsylvania—explains the decision to name the town Lancaster, Ohio, after both the county and county seat back in Pennsylvania. According to early accounts, Emanuel Carpenter Sr. (d. 1822), formerly a resident of Lancaster County, Pennsylvania, prevailed upon John and Noah Zane to name the town *New Lancaster,* a designation that was simplified in 1805 to simply *Lancaster.*[17]

The second-largest group of Pennsylvanians (31) came from Berks County, which, like adjoining Lancaster County, was in the heart of the Pennsylvania Dutch (that is, the Pennsylvania German) region.[18] Thus, a significant number of early settlers in Lancaster, Ohio, spoke German. Later immigrants arriving directly from Germany would help to keep the German language alive in Lancaster for several generations. Without doubt, Lancaster was a bilingual community during its early decades. When the Duke of Saxe-Weimar visited the town in May of 1826, he remarked in his journal that virtually all the businesses in Lancaster had signs in both English and German over their shops and that a number of German-speaking residents called on him at his lodgings. One of them, Judge Jacob Deitrich, who had earlier founded Lancaster's first newspaper, *Der Ohio Adler,* served as the duke's guide and principal interpreter while he was in town.[19] In the years ahead, Lancaster's German population would leave a lasting legacy in certain manners of speech, in hundreds of surnames, and in the abundance of Lutheran churches in town.

The large numbers of migrants from the Upper South would produce considerable sympathy in Lancaster and Fairfield County for the Confederacy during the Civil War and would influence race relations in the county and the town long after the war had ended. The New Englanders who came to Lancaster, though small in numbers, would become some of the most important early leaders locally and in the nation at large, with strong Calvinist beliefs in elitism and civic duty. All three regions—New England, the Middle Atlantic states (mainly Pennsylvania), and the Upper South—would leave their mark on the early architecture of Lancaster.

There were also African American residents in Lancaster from a very early date. All these early black residents were recently freed slaves (or the children of slaves) whose Southern owners were forced to free them upon moving into Ohio, where slavery had been outlawed by the Northwest Ordinance of 1787.[20] The first blacks to settle in what would soon become Fairfield County arrived in 1799, both young former slaves, brought from the Upper South by their owners.[21]

The most successful of these manumitted blacks was Scipio Smith (or "Scipio Africanus," as he renamed himself), a tin- and coppersmith who came to Lancaster in 1810. He worked at first for tin- and coppersmith Samuel Effinger before operating his own business. Scipio Smith went on to found Lancaster's African Methodist Episcopal (AME) Church around 1825, serving as its first minister.[22] The church was erected on land between what are now South High Street and Pearl Avenue that had been given to the black community by Emanuel Carpenter Jr. for this purpose.[23] Just why Carpenter did this is uncertain. In any case, many of Lancaster's African Americans settled near the church in the south end of town. The emergence of a black community in this area, later known as the South End, was doubtless one reason that many white residents viewed this part of Lancaster as "undesirable."

The first of those who actually settled in or around Lancaster were Captain Joseph Hunter and his family. They emigrated from Kentucky in the spring of 1798 and erected a log cabin just west of the Hocking River, not far from the present intersection of Lincoln Avenue and Memorial Drive. Later that same year several other families joined the Hunters. In the following year, according to George Sanderson (c. 1790–1872), a prominent early citizen and Lancaster's first historian, "The tide of emigration [sic] set in with great force," increasing still more during the next three years. The newcomers raised cabins, cleared land, and planted crops as soon as possible.[24] In Sanderson's words, "These settlers subsisted principally on corn-bread, potatoes, milk and butter, and wild meats."[25]

"Subsisted" is an accurate description for the early settlers' way of life, for without a large local market or any cheap or convenient way to send their crops out of the immediate area, they were largely reduced to subsistence agriculture, and this continued until improvements in transportation linked them to wider markets.[26] Even the opening of roads north to Lithopolis in 1802 (later extended to Columbus, some thirty miles northwest of Lancaster), west to Circleville in 1811, and south to Logan in 1823 gave little boost to local agriculture, since these roads were quite primi-

An early Fairfield County log cabin that once stood on Bauman Hill Road. Drinkle, *Heritage of Architecture and Arts*, p. 7.

tive.[27] In fact, as late as 1850 Lancaster would have a reputation for some of the worst roads in Ohio. The road to Columbus was described as so "wretched" that travelers avoided it altogether during the winter months, except for the most serious emergencies.[28]

Zane's Trace was often in bad condition, too, but Lancaster's location almost midway along the trace still made it a good place to settle. It also allowed Lancaster to become an economic base for surrounding farms and villages, a relationship to the countryside that was typical of frontier towns in Ohio and further west.[29] Because of its central location along the trace and its near central location in the state, there were early and oft-repeated hopes that Lancaster might become Ohio's capital. Although this did not come to pass, Lancaster was the county seat of Fairfield County from the very beginning. For all these reasons Lancaster was a logical place to set up a legal or medical practice, to ply a skilled craft, or to offer a variety of wares to local residents and area farmers. For such men it was the economic opportunities of town life, and not farming, that attracted them to Lancaster, as it was for other frontier towns and cities of the early nineteenth century.[30]

For these reasons Lancaster experienced a rapid growth during its first three decades, reaching an estimated 400 people by 1810 and some 800 inhabitants in 1815.[31] The U.S. Census for 1830, the first to report figures on Lancaster, gave an official count of 1,530 residents for that year.[32]

A journal entry of one Josiah Epsy, who visited the town in October 1805, conveys some idea of Lancaster's early growth: "The soil around New Lancaster is exceedingly rich and productive and that neighborhood is filling and improving more rapidly at present than any in the state."[33] As for the origins of the residents, Epsy wrote, "[They] are chiefly married Germans from Lancaster [County] and other eastern counties of Pennsylvania."[34] A half dozen years later, in 1811, another visitor named John Melish wrote, "Lancaster is a handsome little town . . . [and] now counts about 100 homes."[35]

In reality, only five other Ohio towns or cities had populations larger than Lancaster's in 1830. These were, in descending order, Cincinnati (24,831), Zanesville (3,094), Dayton (2,950), Chillicothe (2,846), and Columbus (2,435).[36] That Lancaster ranked sixth, just behind Columbus—which would later become many times larger than Lancaster—is impressive, as is the fact that Lancaster could boast a greater population in 1830 than Cleveland, Akron, or Mansfield.

It is also significant that Lancaster, Zanesville, and Chillicothe were all located along a much improved Zane's Trace, the only road across Ohio until 1838 and one of the principal routes west of the Appalachians. It is not surprising that Lancaster attracted a number of enterprising individuals who established prosperous professions and flourishing businesses in the frontier town.

Indications of Lancaster's economic activity can be gleaned from the advertisements that appeared in the *Ohio Eagle,* published weekly in Lancaster in both German and English, the German edition being known as *Der Ohio Adler.*[37] Advertisements from the years 1816, 1817, and 1818 show that new enterprises were cropping up almost every month. This flurry of economic activity may have stemmed partly from improvements on Zane's Trace undertaken by the new Chillicothe Turnpike Company, whose articles of association were drawn up in April 1817.[38] Also playing a part in this economic expansion was the Lancaster Ohio Bank, the town's first financial institution, which opened its doors on August 30, 1816.[39]

The bank assisted merchants who needed capital to start their businesses or a loan to increase their inventories.[40] Of special importance was the bank's authority to issue paper currency. This alleviated the shortage of money in the local economy, which had relied considerably on silver coins and often on Spanish silver dollars minted in Mexico, a coin that continued to circulate in Lancaster and Fairfield County as late as 1820.[41]

In any case, readers of the *Eagle* on April 3, 1817, learned that John E. Kridelbaugh was opening a new shop for "earthen ware," presumably various objects made of fired and glazed clay.[42] In September of the same year, Samuel Effinger was announcing himself as a "coppersmith and tin manufacturer," who provided such items as kettles and stew pans, as well as sheet iron for stoves and stove pipes—all made to order.[43]

That October, Samuel F. Maccracken opened a dry goods store where he sold groceries, hardware, and other assorted items.[44] Effinger and Maccracken would go on to become two of the most prosperous citizens of Lancaster and the founders of socially prominent families.

Similar advertising continued into 1818. The *Eagle* of January 29 contained a list of items sold by saddler John Noble, including bridles, collars, harnesses, reins, and, of course, saddles. In March, John Stallsmith invited readers to visit his bootery and shoemaking shop.[45] In April, cabinetmaker Jesse Woltz (1792–1839) used the handsome woodcut of a chest of drawers to draw attention to the fine furniture he was prepared to make for order. Besides chests, Woltz would fashion, from either cherry or walnut, "Sideboards; Secretar[ies] and Common Desks; Clock Cases; Knife Cases; Circular, Strait, Front & Panel-end Bureaus; Tables of every Description; Square, Round, & Oval Candle Stands; Wash Stands: High and Low-Post Beds, &c., all of which he will varnish off in style."[46] Nearly two centuries later, some of Woltz's finest pieces remain in Lancaster, including several tall clock cases. The works for many of these clocks were assembled and installed by Timothy Sturgeon (1778–1826), a silversmith and clock maker who had come from Lancaster, Pennsylvania, sometime between 1800 and 1802.[47] Other early businesses in Lancaster included several makers of spinning wheels, led by craftsmen William Bodenheimer, also a wheelwright and later a gunsmith.[48] Joseph Work was a well-known Lancaster shoemaker during this period, while Robert Claspill, a plow maker, became known for his craft throughout the region.[49] Several of these men, such as Woltz and Sturgeon, were among the most skilled artisans west of the Alleghenies, and their finely crafted pieces are coveted as much at the end of the twentieth century as then.[50] For these men it was the frontier town of Lancaster, and not farming possibilities in surrounding Fairfield County, that attracted them to the area and kept them in town.

In addition to independent craftsmen and merchants, there was a spa-

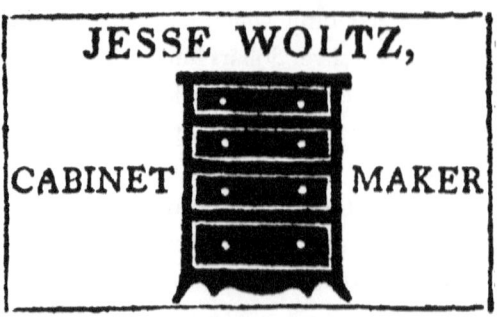

Newspaper advertisement for Jesse Woltz, cabinet-maker. *Eagle,* April 23, 1818.

cious market house, built about 1820 (demolished in 1883), with booths and stalls that vendors could rent. The market house stood in Lancaster's central square, at the southwest corner of Main and Broad Streets, a site later occupied by the town's Victorian fountain. Built of brick on the bottom story and wood above, the market house contained a large meeting room on the second floor, where numerous religious, civic, and fraternal groups assembled.[51] Surviving images, including a photograph, show the market house to be an attractive structure, with two well-shaped Palladian windows at either end of the wooden second story.[52]

The market house was just one example of the many fine buildings that began to appear in Lancaster about 1810, made possible by the town's growing prosperity. Many of these, like the market house, faced the central square. The square itself, known at first as the "Public Grounds," probably took its inspiration from the center squares seen throughout southern and eastern Pennsylvania, the model of which was Philadelphia's central square, as designated in William Penn's plan for the Quaker city.[53] As in cities and towns throughout southeastern and south-central Pennsylvania, Lancaster's square was fashioned out of the four corner lots that abutted the intersection of the two main streets (Main and Broad Streets to future generations).

Beyond this central square, Lancaster's other streets formed a checkerboard pattern, again like the plan in Philadelphia, similar even to the point of copying the exact sequence of Philadelphia street names for east and west thoroughfares—that is, Chestnut, Walnut, and Locust.[54] Streets running north and south in Lancaster originally had numbers for names, as they also did in Philadelphia and in Lancaster, Pennsylvania. These were

Boundaries of Zane's square mile, showing town square and street grid as they appeared in the mid-twentieth century. Schneider and Stebbens, *Zane's Trace*, p. 23.

First (Front Street/Memorial Drive), Second (Columbus Street), Third (Broad Street), and Fourth (High Street).[55] Although these number designations have not survived for the north-south thoroughfares, the tree names for three of the east-west streets have remained up to the time of this writing. Just who named the original streets is unclear. It may have been the Zanes themselves, or it may have been Emanuel Carpenter Sr., an original purchaser of land in Lancaster, the first judge in Fairfield County, and the individual who had suggested the name "Lancaster" for the new settlement.[56]

Whoever the author of local street names may have been, Lancaster's original gridiron contained some twenty square blocks, each with lots that were 82 feet wide and 164 feet deep.[57] Alleys (yet another Philadelphia feature) ran midway between each block, giving access to the back of shops along the main street and to barns and stables behind residences elsewhere. In some cases, property owners would sell off plots along the alleys (yet another Philadelphia practice), where purchasers erected small houses, resulting in a mixture of income levels throughout much of the old town.[58]

Although modeled after eastern city plans, Lancaster's checkerboard street pattern was typical of other frontier towns and cities west of the Appalachians because of its obvious advantages: it made surveying easier and thereby minimized boundary disputes among lot owners. It also suggested a sense of orderliness and big-city pretensions as towns were getting under way. Just as important, the pattern of intersecting streets immediately announced that one was "in town" and not out in the country, where roads might follow the contours of the land. But there was a price to pay for the rigid gridiron of intersecting streets, which ignored the beauty of the natural landscape and made it difficult to set aside large parcels of land for public use and recreation.[59] Lancaster's small public square and the failure for over a century to provide substantial park land were partly due to the town's rigid checkerboard pattern.

But the grid pattern did facilitate land sales, and within fifteen years of Lancaster's founding, most of the land in the squares closest to the center of town had been purchased. In 1814, Emanuel Carpenter Jr. bought 437 acres of the remaining unsold land from the Zanes, lying south of Chestnut Street, for $6,782.[60] Carpenter's Addition, as it was called, departed from the checkerboard pattern, with two diagonal streets (the present South Columbus and Perry Streets) intersecting the Carpenter plat. These diagonals, along with South Broad and Lawrence Streets, were supposed to converge at a circle in the middle of the addition. The plan, with lots in the shape of trapezoids and wedges, was advanced for its day, and in certain ways would seem to resemble the plans for several early suburban communities in England and the eastern United States.[61] The sources of Carpenter's scheme are unknown, and it may well be that he had no intention of creating an early "suburb." Nearly two centuries later, the result is an area of jagged streets and odd-shaped lots that has never appealed to Lancaster's more prosperous families, perhaps because of its location in a low-lying area not far from the Hocking River, near where a portion of

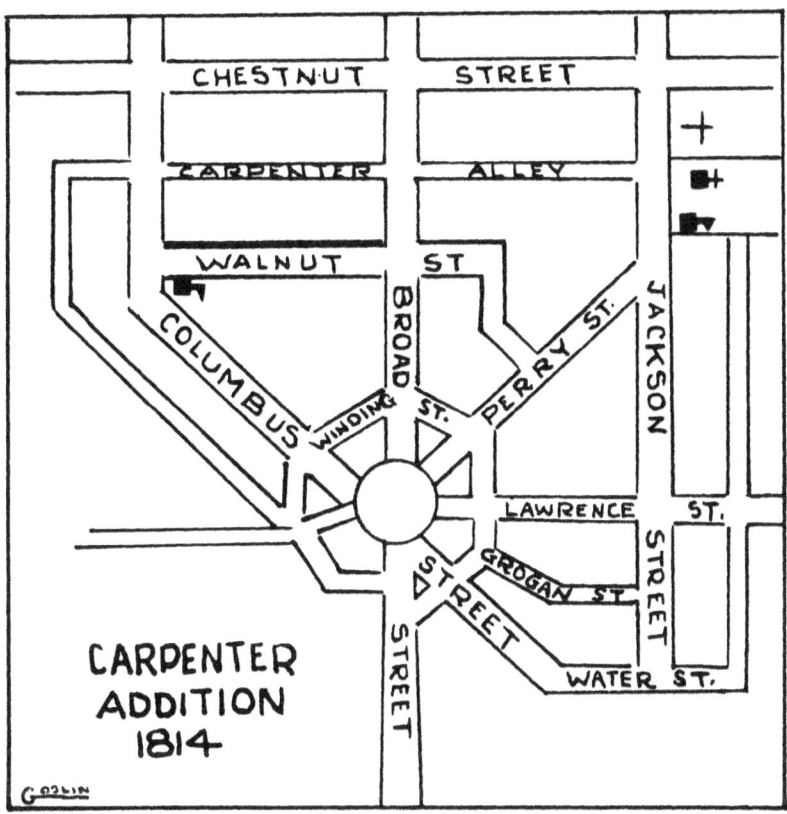

The Carpenter Addition, 1814, the first housing addition in Lancaster, characterized by its break from the original street grid. Map by Charles Goslin, *Crossroads and Fence Corners*, 2:108.

Lancaster's African American community was concentrating. It is also probable that this sharp "break" from Lancaster's original grids repelled buyers as such breaks have done in many other communities throughout the United States, in part because they are difficult to survey.[62] Later, the Carpenter Addition would simply become part of the "South End," one of the least desirable places to live in Lancaster, a reputation later reinforced by its bordering a canal and still later the railroad station and its yards.

Far more successful was Lancaster's public square, however small. In its center stood the first Fairfield County Courthouse, completed in 1807 and demolished just after the Civil War.[63] But unlike the layout of the

The first Fairfield County Courthouse, completed in 1807 and demolished in 1867, stood in the middle of the town square. This photograph, taken c. 1865, also shows St. John's Episcopal Church (with the two towers) and the Maccracken House (later known as The Georgian), just beyond St. John's. Tobias Studio Collection, FCDL.

square, which echoed its Pennsylvania origins, the courthouse at once announced its Virginia roots. Its model was probably Ohio's first statehouse at Chillicothe, a town that lay well within the so-called Virginia Military Reserve and that had been settled mainly by men and women from Virginia and Kentucky.[64] The Chillicothe statehouse was itself based upon a familiar courthouse design in Virginia, whose prototype may have been the Governor's Palace at Williamsburg. As such, the first Fairfield County Courthouse in Lancaster had a square floor plan and projecting front gable, common features in Virginia public architecture. Crowning the square hip roof was an octagonal cupola and double concave dome.[65]

Several early residences in Lancaster likewise suggested Southern influences. These featured wide central hallways and large open porches, both responses to warm summers in the Upper South. One of these was a

Matlack House, 1807. Photo by author, 1980.

brick house built about 1807 by Kentuckian Samuel Matlack, probably as housing for servants. Standing in the rear of the much larger Reese-Peters House on Main Hill (about a half block east of the square), this small, two-story residence featured a long, open front porch.[66] Far more elegant was the residence of Virginia-born Thomas Ewing, one of Lancaster's wealthiest and most famous citizens. Constructed in 1824 (with several later additions), the house's most striking features were the wide central entrance with an elliptical fanlight and matching Palladian window directly above on the second floor.[67]

Although a large number of Pennsylvanians settled in Lancaster, their influence on the town's architecture was much more elusive than the Southern. For instance, there were none of the familiar stone houses and barns that dotted the countryside of eastern Pennsylvania, mainly because the only available building stone in the area was a soft, and not very attractive, sandstone. Emigrants from Pennsylvania therefore turned to brick for more substantial houses, a building material that was available in Lancaster and Fairfield County because of abundant deposits of clay and limestone (for mortar) in the area. But since Virginians and Kentuckians also

Ewing House, 1824. Photo by author, 1997.

used brick for building, what distinguished the Pennsylvania-style dwelling were the narrow widths and plain dimensions, which reflected the simplicity of both Quaker and Pennsylvania German traditions.[68]

Two of Lancaster's early dwellings in particular suggested Pennsylvania influences. One was the Garaghty-Mumaugh House of 1824, built for Michael Garaghty, a dry goods merchant and cashier of the Lancaster Ohio Bank, and designed by cabinetmaker and master builder Isaiah Vorys Sr. (1796–1866).[69] Also Pennsylvanian in appearance was the Effinger House, built in 1823 (demolished 1929) for copper- and tinsmith Samuel Effinger. A fan-lighted doorway, with a matching Palladian window above, highlighted the exterior of the Effinger House. (The doorway and window

Garaghty-Mumaugh House, 1824. Photo by author, 1997.

have survived and are now installed in the Fairfield County District Library.) Following Samuel Effinger's death, the house passed to his son, Michael, who would become one of Lancaster's most prominent medical doctors. The Effinger House stood immediately north of the square on a property occupied after 1940 by the Hotel Lancaster (known at the time of this writing as Shaw's Restaurant and Inn).[70]

Although New Englanders represented the smallest regional group in Lancaster's population, houses influenced by New England prototypes are the easiest to recognize.[71] A good example is the birthplace of General William T. Sherman and his brother, Senator John Sherman, located just above the public square on East Main Street. The Sherman House, as it would be known to later generations, was begun in 1811 by their father, Charles Robert Sherman, who had emigrated from Norwalk, Connecticut.[72] Because there was no available limestone for mortar in most of New England, stone or brick construction was rare in that region, resulting in the frequent use of heavy wooden frames covered by clapboards, the same method used for constructing the original Sherman House in Lancaster. The "lean-to" kitchen and partly enclosed side porch also belonged to the New England tradition. Another residence of apparent New England design was the Ferguson-Furniss House of 1833. Owner William Ferguson's origins are unknown, but he was a skilled bricklayer, who neverthe-

The Sherman House, birthplace of General William Tecumseh Sherman and of U.S. Senator John Sherman, 1811. *FHQ*, Fall 1984, p. 2.

Ferguson-Furniss House, 1833. Photo by author, 1997.

less chose to build his own house of wood. Both the entrance on one side and the central chimneys of the Ferguson-Furniss House were characteristic of New England construction, features calculated to conserve heat.[73]

Besides echoing the regional origins of early inhabitants, the high quality of Lancaster's architecture during the first decades of the nineteenth century reflects the town's continuing prosperity.[74] These spacious and attractive buildings also help to demonstrate that Lancaster's pioneer days were in fact short-lived, as they were in other successful frontier towns and cities in the Midwest.[75] Because they were erected over a period of about twenty-five years, most of these early structures were in what might be called a late Federal style. These, along with a number of fine houses that would be built during the 1830s and early 1840s in a combination of late Federal and Greek Revival styles, lent a distinct neoclassical flavor to Lancaster's best residences, what one architectural historian has called an "Indian Summer of Colonial architecture." This late flowering of Colonial styles, or more properly of English Georgian motifs, existed in many communities west of the Appalachians, where older designs lingered long after newer forms had conquered the Atlantic seaboard.[76] (This atmosphere of late Colonial architecture would be reinforced in Lancaster around 1900 by a national trend in architecture and decoration known as the Colonial Revival.)

Meanwhile, in surrounding Fairfield County, several small villages grew up to serve local farmers who found the trip into Lancaster, some twelve to fifteen miles from the far corners of the county, much too difficult. The most important of these early villages were Rushville (1808), Lithopolis (1815), Pickerington (1815), and Amanda (1819).[77] Many village merchants depended upon Lancaster as a source of merchandise, banking, and other commercial services, yet another characteristic of frontier towns that organized and dominated the economy of outlying communities and farms. Other frontier towns in the central Ohio region played the same role, including Zanesville, Newark, Chillicothe (which also served as Ohio's first capital), Circleville, and Columbus.

There are only scant indications of what the early residents of Lancaster and these other communities did for recreation or just how they socialized with one another.[78] One can imagine the men gathering in taverns and inns to share gossip and learn the latest news from travelers, just as one can imagine meals and entertainments in private homes. It is clear that celebrating the Fourth of July was a big event in Lancaster from the beginning. According to George Sanderson, the first such observance took place on Independence Day of 1800 on what is now the West Side of Lancaster, probably near the intersection of Lincoln Avenue and Memorial Drive.[79] A participant that day, Sanderson recalled that the small group of revelers shouted "Hurrah for America," fired their muskets into the air, and "shot target," after which they devoured a large midday meal. "Although they had neither tables, benches, dishes, plates or forks," Sanderson wrote, "every[thing] substantial in the way of a feast . . . was amply provided, such as baked pone and johny-cake, roasted bear's meat, jerk[y], turkey, &c."[80] By the early 1830s the celebration of Washington's birthday was also an annual event. On February 22, 1833, according to the *Eagle*, citizens assembled in the courthouse "at early candle light" (that is, about dusk) to honor the father of their country.[81]

Worship in the various churches likewise brought groups of citizens together, who doubtless took advantage of the time before and after services to talk and catch up on the latest gossip.[82] By the middle 1830s, the Presbyterians, Methodists, Baptists, Roman Catholics, Lutherans, German Reformed, and Episcopalians all had established congregations in Lancaster.[83] More exciting for some than the regular Sunday church services were the outdoor revival meetings, held as early as 1816 in the area.[84]

This period also saw the establishment of Lancaster's Masonic Lodge in 1820, the first of many lodges in town that would become a major facet of social life for local men, especially in the late nineteenth and early twentieth centuries.[85]

But long before that, townsmen found comradeship in a succession of militia units such as the Greenfield Volunteers. An item in the *Eagle* for April 17, 1830, announced that the Greenfield men should assemble on Saturday morning at 10:00, armed, equipped, and ready for drill.[86] Just where they would meet, the newspaper did not say.

All schooling was "private" in this period. The earliest schools operated out of private homes, as individuals set themselves up as schoolmasters or schoolmistresses and charged a fee for each pupil, often advertising their services in the local newspaper.[87] It was not unusual for these arrangements to last for only a year or two, as the teachers married or moved on to other enterprises. In 1820, however, the more permanent Lancaster Academy, likewise a private school charging tuition, opened in a two-story brick structure on West Wheeling Street (on a site later occupied by the local telephone building). By 1830 it was known as Howe's

Academy, under the direction of brothers Samuel and Mark Howe. The first public schools opened in Lancaster in 1830, as required by an act of the Ohio state legislature. The public schools were poorly funded for several decades, with the result that private and public schools coexisted for another generation, until more adequate funding for the public schools caused the private school market to collapse during the 1850s.[88]

Programs put on in the schools received extensive coverage in the local press. But far more absorbing to most readers were newspaper accounts of immoral or criminal behavior. The *Eagle* carried numerous divorce notices during the early nineteenth century, usually for adultery, desertion, or bigamy, with all the salacious details spelled out for readers.[89]

In July 1816, one Elizabeth M'Crellis used a personal notice in the *Eagle* to warn other women against her shiftless husband: "Whereas my husband, Thomas M'Crellis, enlisted about two years ago and left me with three children to maintain; since which time I have never received a line from him . . . and having lately understood that he has married another woman at New Orleans, this is to caution all women to beware of such an abandoned wrench [sic], who may endeavor to deceive them."[90] At the end of this warning, the *Eagle*'s publisher requested that the item be reprinted in the New Orleans newspapers should a copy of the issue find its way into that Southern city.

Then there were the stories in the local press detailing various robberies, murders, and other acts of violence. On May 25, 1833, readers of the *Eagle* learned that one James Turner had been convicted of murdering his brother and had been sentenced to the penitentiary for life. Four months later the same newspaper told how the stage coach from Lancaster to Zanesville had been held up, the robbers absconding with two trunks containing clothes and valuable papers.[91] Although there are no figures on the incidence of such crimes in and around Lancaster during the early decades of the nineteenth century, such accounts should put into question the commonly held belief that men and women were essentially more moral in the past than they were two centuries later.[92]

Those accused of crime in Lancaster stood trial at the Fairfield County Courthouse in the town square. As a legal entity, Fairfield County had been created on December 9, 1800, by an order of Arthur St. Clair, the governor of the Northwest Territory, a little more than two years before Ohio became a state. That Lancaster and several other frontier towns in the southern half of Ohio—Cincinnati, Zanesville, and Chillicothe among them—predated the state of Ohio itself emphasizes their role as spearheads of settlement.

Originally Fairfield County included nearly all of Licking and Knox Counties, as well as portions of Perry, Hocking, and Pickaway Counties. As this larger area became populated, new counties were carved out of the original boundaries of Fairfield County, and by 1818 it would assume its present size, with the exception of some minor alterations in 1850 and 1851.[93] Officers of the county government included the county commissioners, a sheriff and his deputies, treasurer, clerk of courts, surveyor, recorder, and auditor.[94] From their base in Lancaster they provided a legal and governmental system for Lancaster and the surrounding hinterland.

Lancaster itself did not appear to have a government separate from that of the county until 1831, when it became an incorporated village by an act of the state legislature.[95] However, there is evidence of a village council before this date, which apparently functioned as an extralegal instrument of government, an arrangement that was fairly common throughout Ohio at the time.[96] This early council as well as the first chartered government used the second floor of the market house as a meeting place and town hall.[97] There was no mayor under the village government, with the president of the village council serving as the nearest thing to a chief executive. Under the village charter, the main officers were, in addition to the mayor, the recorder, treasurer, surveyor, and assessor. There were also fire wardens and a board of health. In charge of enforcing law and order was the "property guard," a rudimentary police force headed by a captain and three subordinates.[98] Unfortunately, the council minutes and ordinance records have not survived for this early period of local government.

Lancaster's incorporation was just one sign that its frontier days were passing. This new status came just as Lancaster was entering upon one of its most prosperous and dramatic periods. An economic boom, the erection of handsome residences, political and social turmoil, the Civil War, and the emergence of the town's most famous men would all become part of the Lancaster scene over the next three and a half decades. And with improved transportation, Lancaster would become even more of an economic, political, and social center for an area that extended ten or twelve miles in every direction.

TWO

# Heroic Age
## A Town Divided

Whenever Lancaster residents begin talking about their collective past, they invariably turn to the town's most famous sons, and particularly William Tecumseh Sherman, the great Civil War general who was born and grew up in Lancaster. If the conversation shifts to historical landmarks, it is the elegant antebellum houses lining Wheeling or Main Hills that come to mind.

Such emphasis on the local past is understandable, since it was during the three decades or so preceding the end of the Civil War that Lancaster reached a peak of prominence that, in certain respects, it has never again equaled. Many residents have wondered why Lancaster has failed to produce a "second Sherman" or another hillside of dwellings that can match those of the pre–Civil War period. The answer to this puzzle lies in the special combination of economic and strategic forces that came together between the 1830s and the 1860s to produce what might be called Lancaster's heroic age.

Among these were improved transportation systems, first a canal and then a railroad, which brought increased prosperity and access to far-flung markets. These allowed Lancastrians most of the comforts—and even many of the luxuries—enjoyed by residents of the eastern United States and marked an end to the town's frontier period. But even more than during frontier days, Lancaster continued to be the economic, political, and cultural center of its hinterland, composed mainly of surrounding Fairfield County.

Yet some of the same energies that gave rise to increased wealth, great men, and beautiful houses led to political and social conflict in Lancaster, as throughout the nation, during the three and a half decades before and during the Civil War. Arguments over tariffs, the financing of canals and other "internal improvements," and the economic future of the United States led to bitter divisions between North and South, as did differences over the nature of the federal union, the right of the South to secede, and the abolition of slavery. These same issues revealed deep divisions among the residents of Lancaster. In the decade before the Civil War there were also powerful blasts in Lancaster's press against Roman Catholics and against immigrants in general, echoes of a national debate over immigration and religion.

For the most part, late-twentieth-century residents of Lancaster have remained unaware of this uglier but very significant aspect of their community's history, which has been ignored and then forgotten out of a desire to extol the more positive aspects of the local past. In reality, Lancaster represented a microcosm of those issues that divided many American towns during this period, and particularly in areas populated from both the North and South.

The most important economic force during the first part of this antebellum period was the construction of an ambitious network of canals in Ohio, which allowed Lancaster to continue playing its role as an economic and cultural center for the immediate region, as it had since the frontier period. Both the idea and the reality of artificial inland waterways dated back to ancient times, but beginning in the seventeenth century the French, the Dutch, and then the English had successfully completed numerous canal projects. During the course of these undertakings the engineering principles and construction techniques of canal building had been well developed. Even before the American Revolution, far-sighted individuals began to envision a system of canals that would improve the navigation of eastern rivers and, eventually, penetrate the interior of the continent. After gaining independence, enterprising Americans embraced with even more enthusiasm the idea of canals as a way of developing the nation's economy and of joining the various regions of the country into a closer economic and political union. But it was the inauguration of the Erie Canal by New York State in 1817 that touched off canal fever in Ohio—and elsewhere in the United States.[1]

Completed in the fall of 1825, the Erie Canal cut a 44-foot-wide waterway that ran 363 miles from Albany on the Hudson River to Buffalo on Lake Erie. The canal was an immediate success. The tolls collected provided more than enough for the state of New York, which had undertaken the canal as a public works project, to pay the interest on its canal bonds and eventually to retire the debt altogether. New York City, in particular, benefited from the canal, for it could now tap the trade of upper New York State, northern Pennsylvania, and northeastern Ohio. More than anything else, the completion of the Erie Canal allowed New York City to replace Philadelphia as the principal city of the United States. Desperate to compete with New York for the trade of the west, Pennsylvania launched an audacious plan to build a canal from Philadelphia to Pittsburgh, known officially as the Main Line of Public Works, that would cross the Appalachian wall by hauling canal boats up the mountainsides on inclined planes powered by stationary steam engines at the top.

Ohio sought to become part of this burgeoning canal network by linking Lake Erie to the Ohio River, giving citizens of the Buckeye State access to both the Pennsylvania and New York systems, but especially to the Erie Canal. At the same time, a system of canals connecting the interior of the state would give landlocked Ohioans a convenient water route all the way to New Orleans (by way of the Ohio and Mississippi Rivers) and to New York (by way of Lake Erie, the Erie Canal, and the Hudson River). Farmers, townspeople, bankers, and speculators throughout Ohio dreamed of new opportunity and wealth.

The first serious move toward creating a system of Ohio canals came in 1818, when the newly elected governor of the state, Ethan Allen Brown, asked the legislature to appropriate funds for a survey of possible routes. The wrangling over canal routes, spurred by fierce local jealousies, kept the legislature from approving a canal project for nearly seven years. Finally, an act passed on February 3, 1825, authorized the building of two canals, both undertaken and financed as state projects.

No matter how much each city, town, and village in the state wanted the canal to pass through its community, the availability of sufficient water to keep the canals full at all seasons of the year dictated the possible routes.[2] This meant that the canal builders had to construct huge reservoirs, feed water into the canal ditch, and run canals parallel to major rivers and their tributaries. With this factor uppermost in their minds, surveyors determined that the most feasible route for the first of the two projects, to be known as the Ohio and Erie Canal, was from Cleveland through the Cuyahoga River valley and from there down the valleys of the Tuscarawas, Muskingum, and Licking Rivers. The canal would then turn east to join the Scioto River valley just below Columbus and then continue

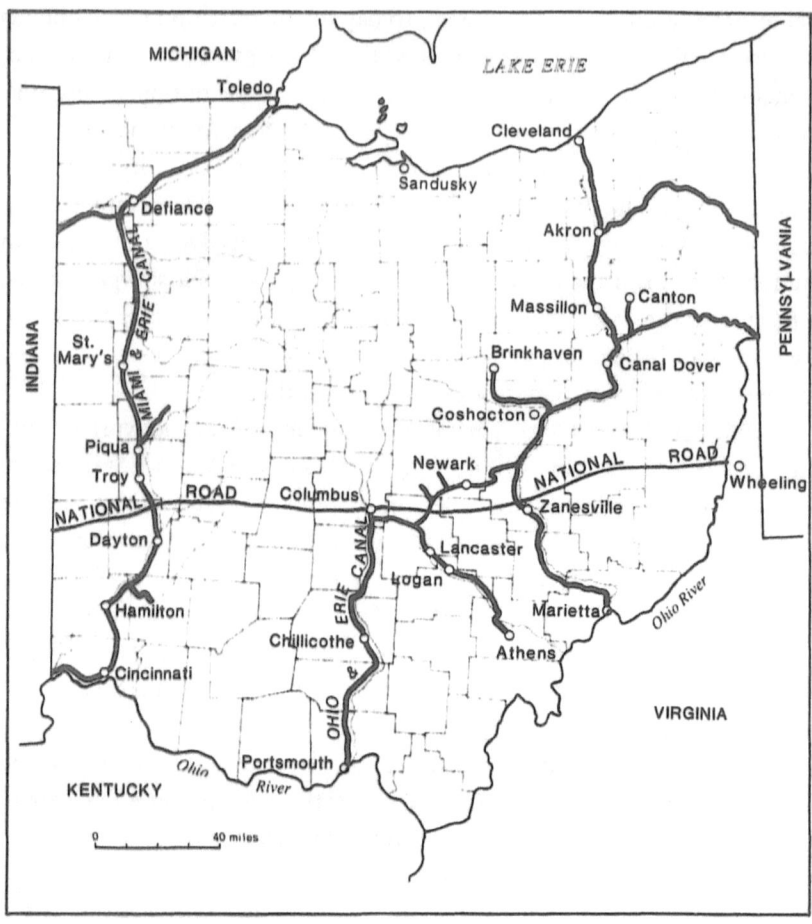

Ohio's canal system and the National Road. Knepper, *Ohio and Its People*, p. 152.

nearly due south to the Ohio River at Portsmouth, for a total distance of 308 miles. In order to secure the votes of the heavily populated Miami Valley in southwestern Ohio, the legislature approved a second canal that paralleled the Miami River from Cincinnati to Dayton. This canal later extended to Toledo on Lake Erie (completed in 1845) and was known as the Miami and Erie Canal.[3]

In order to provide enough water for the Ohio and Erie system as it crossed from the Licking River to the Scioto, the state constructed a reservoir of 2,500 acres at the high point between the two valleys, called the

Licking Summit. This body of water, designated for many years as the Licking Reservoir, was formed by enlarging the preexisting Buffalo Swamp with a long earthen dam along the north side. At the west end of the reservoir it was necessary to cut a three-mile channel some sixty feet deep in order to break through the edge of the summit. This project, called the Deep Cut, took seven years to complete and was an engineering wonder of the nineteenth century that remains as an unmistakable feature of the landscape just west of Millersport.[4]

It was at the Licking Summit on July 4, 1825, that New York governor DeWitt Clinton, known as the "Father of the Erie Canal," turned the first spadeful of earth. Among the speakers that day was Lancaster's Thomas Ewing, then the twenty-eight-year-old Fairfield County prosecutor who would later occupy several high national offices. (Three quarters of a century later, after the canal had been abandoned, the reservoir would be renamed Buckeye Lake and would become a favorite summer resort for the residents of Lancaster, Fairfield County, and other nearby areas.)[5]

However excited Lancastrians might have been to hear of the groundbreaking for the Ohio and Erie Canal, they were disappointed that it would run through rival towns such as Newark, Circleville, and Chillicothe, yet pass some four miles to the north of Lancaster itself. There was also considerable fear that smaller settlements in Fairfield County, such as Millersport and Carroll, would reap the economic benefits of the canal while Lancaster stagnated. Determined not to be left out of the canal bonanza, a group of Lancaster merchants obtained a charter in 1825 to construct the Lancaster Lateral Canal, which would connect the town with the Ohio and Erie at Carroll. The directors of this venture were dry goods merchant Samuel F. Maccracken; entrepreneur and mill owner Jacob Greene; merchant, judge, and state legislator Elnathan Schofield; merchant and mill owner Benjamin Connell; and merchant Frederick A. Foster (who also served as secretary of the local canal company).[6] Given their business interests, all these men stood to benefit from a spur canal into Lancaster. But it was not until 1831 that they raised sufficient funds, through the sale of stock and loans from the Lancaster Bank, to begin work on the lateral project. The drive for funds received strong support from the *Lancaster Gazette*, a rival to the *Eagle* since 1826. In May of 1831 the *Gazette* warned that without the lateral canal, Lancaster would lose most of its commerce to nearby Newark, the county seat of Licking County, located along the main route of the Ohio and Erie. Without the short

The canal in Lancaster lined with warehouses and wharfs, date unknown. Tobias Studio Collection, FCDL.

extension into Lancaster, the *Gazette* asserted, the town would soon know only "decay, ruins, and desolation."[7]

Fortunately, the Lancaster Lateral was completed in 1834, at a cost of $37,000, just as the Ohio and Erie Canal went into full operation.[8] Lancaster held its official celebration for the canal on July 4, 1834.[9] According to a reminiscence some years later from an eyewitness to the event, thousands of spectators assembled on Cold Spring Hill just north of Lancaster, where boats moved along the canal "amidst the booming of cannons, beating of drums, and the wafting to the breeze of flags and banners." The crowd then feasted on a roasted ox, after which there were several bare-knuckled fistfights.[10]

The Lancaster Lateral project almost immediately gave rise to a plan to extend the canal down the Hocking River valley. Finished in 1843 and known as the Hocking Valley Canal, its route ran for 56 miles from Carroll (through Lancaster) to Athens and provided cheap transportation for the coal and salt mined in Hocking and Athens Counties. This canal became possible in large part because of the Loan Law of 1837, passed by the Ohio legislature, which allowed the state to lend money to private canal companies. In the process of organizing the Hocking Valley Canal, the new company purchased the Lancaster Lateral for a little over $61,000 and made it an integral part of the Hocking Valley Canal.[11]

Lancaster now had water connections to New Orleans, New York City, and from there to ports all over the world. One gauge of how these connections affected Lancaster was the dramatic growth in its population between 1830 and 1840—from 1,530 to 3,272, for an increase of 114 percent, the largest 10-year percentage gain in its entire 200-year history.[12] This was not as impressive as the increase for Newark, on the main line of the canal, which grew from 999 in 1830 to 2,705 in 1840 (or 171 percent).[13] But Lancaster's growth during the decade was greater than that of Circleville (the county seat of adjacent Pickaway County), which, like Newark, was on the main canal. In Circleville the population rose 101 percent, from 1,136 to 2,329.[14] Chillicothe, also on the canal, saw an increase from 2,846 people to 3,977—or slightly under 40 percent.[15] Of all the neighboring towns of substantial size, only Newark had a larger percentage increase in its population than Lancaster, in part because Newark had been smaller and much less developed than Lancaster in 1830. Lancaster's better showing than Circleville may have been due to its location at the entrance to the Hocking Valley as well as its occupying a point where the Lancaster Lateral (and subsequently the Hocking Valley Canal) crossed the Chillicothe Turnpike (or the improved Zane's Trace). The explanation for Chillicothe's smaller percentage increase stemmed partly from the fact that the town was larger than Lancaster at the beginning of the canal era.

In Fairfield County itself, several new villages appeared at strategic points along the canal. These were Millersport (founded 1827) at the entrance to the deep cut on the Licking Summit; Baltimore (founded 1825), situated along several locks west of Millersport; and Carroll (founded 1829), further west and likewise the location of canal locks. Carroll was also the place where the Lancaster Lateral/Hocking Valley Canal branched off from the Ohio and Erie. The building of the Hocking Valley Canal produced yet another village, namely Sugar Grove (1836), some half-dozen miles south of Lancaster.[16]

While the canals gave life to these communities, they destroyed the Fairfield County village of Monticello, so named by a group of Virginia settlers in honor of the Virginia home of Thomas Jefferson. Monticello once lay near the intersection of Route 204 (at one time the main road between Columbus and Zanesville) and Route 37 (the principal route from Lancaster to the north) and flourished initially because of these intersecting roads. But the Deep Cut interrupted the old Columbus-Zanesville Road at the same time that the canal bypassed Monticello in favor of Millersport. Thus, Millersport prospered as Monticello declined and eventually disappeared. At the end of the twentieth century, only a stone marker in the center of a farmer's field marked the former site of Monticello.[17]

In Lancaster itself, the Hocking Valley/Lateral Canal roughly paralleled the Hocking River along a site later occupied by Memorial Drive (U.S. Route 33), with a tow path on the west side of the waterway. There were a number of warehouses along its way through town, as well as several iron foundries that utilized the canal to receive raw materials and ship out finished goods. These foundries, along with several mills, used the canal spillways, or overflows, as sources of power for water wheels.[18] Yet another physical feature of the canal system was the twelve-acre Cold Spring Reservoir above what were then the northern limits of Lancaster. The reservoir's boundaries corresponded roughly with Markwood Avenue on the east, Cold Spring Hill on the West (later the site of the Plaza Shopping Center), Arlington Avenue on the north, and Fair Avenue on the south. In winter the frozen waters of the reservoir supplied a commercial ice business. Workers cut ice from the surface and then preserved it in double-walled ice houses, with sawdust as insulation. (This once flourishing ice business disappeared with the drainage of the reservoir in 1898.)[19]

Though more indirect, another impressive consequence of Lancaster's prosperous canal days was the number of large and elegant houses constructed during the 1830s. Virtually all of these were built on a steep rise just east of the town square along Main and Wheeling Streets, which ran parallel up the hill, and then along High Street at the crest of this rise. Residents of a later time, long used to automobiles and suburban housing, who might wonder why such attractive residences would be built so close to "downtown," should keep in mind that the inhabitants of Lancaster in the 1830s (and also of large cities like Philadelphia and New York) needed to be within easy walking distance of their employment. For even those who could afford to keep horses and carriages preferred not to drive them to work, given the time and effort that it took to hitch them up in addition to the care and attention that horses required throughout the day. Unlike automobiles, horses could not be left unattended in the street for hours on end while their owners were at work.

Maccracken House (The Georgian), 1832. Photo by author, 1997.

For several reasons, then, the "Hill" overlooking Lancaster's small mercantile center was an obvious place to build an imposing house. Besides their proximity to the business and shopping district, these hillside residences were valued for healthfulness at a time when many men and women rightly associated low-lying land with waterborne diseases. What is more, homeowners prized their view of the rolling terrain just outside town.[20] Because these coveted sites were more expensive than lower-lying areas, only Lancaster's professional and business elite could afford them. As a result, the Hill became home to the town's "upper class," a status that it maintains, to varying degrees, nearly two centuries later.

These houses on the Hill, erected between 1830 and 1840, represented a cross between late Federal and Greek Revival styles. The most impressive of these was the so-called Georgian, the residence of Samuel F. Maccracken (1785–1857), built in 1832 on the northeast corner of Broad and Wheeling Streets. At one time or another, Maccracken's varied business enterprises included a tan yard, a general store (including a branch store in Newark), and an insurance agency. He was also a director of the Lancaster Lateral Canal, and in 1830 he became a member of the Ohio Canal Fund

Commission. In the latter capacity he was responsible, as were the other commissioners, for selling bonds to finance construction of Ohio's canals.[21] This was a lucrative appointment: Maccracken and the other six commissioners received generous compensation for their work, and Maccracken probably used his income to build his fine house in Lancaster.[22]

The designer of Maccracken's large, two-story brick home (known only in the twentieth century as The Georgian) was the most accomplished of Lancaster's master builders, Daniel Sifford, who came to town from Frederick, Maryland, in 1827. In addition to designing The Georgian, Sifford was the builder/architect for Lancaster's St. John's Episcopal Church, the English Lutheran Church, the city hall of 1859, and the American Legion home, once the private residence of Sifford himself.[23]

With the assistance of Asher Benjamin's *Handbook for Carpenters*, Sifford spent three years building the Maccracken residence. It featured a serpentine wall, a common characteristic of the late Federal style, on the Broad Street facade. Oval-ended rooms and floor-to-ceiling windows on the Broad Street side opened onto a two-story, Greek Revival portico with five Ionic columns. The entrance on the Wheeling Street side of the house was also Greek Revival in style, with a small square portico supported by Ionic columns. Directly above the door on the second floor was a wide Palladian window with an elliptical fan light that was Federal in flavor. In this house the Maccrackens entertained many guests of national prominence, including Henry Clay, Daniel Webster, John Marshall, and DeWitt Clinton.[24]

Although not as impressive as the Maccracken House, there are a half dozen other beautiful Federal and Greek Revival residences on Wheeling, Main, and High Streets, built in the decade between 1830 and 1840. These include the Matlack-Burns-Roche House (1830); the Stanbery-Rising House (1834); the Reese-Peters House (1834); the DeVol–Dallow–Anchor Hocking House (1834), yet another Sifford commission; the Reese-Mattox-Rockwood House (1840); and the Cox-Hunter-Welsh House (1840).[25]

Beyond the category of these impressive structures, dozens of other dwellings went up in Lancaster during the 1830s, as residential development spread north and east. In 1835, for instance, lots went on sale in the so-called Northwestern Addition, bounded by the canal on the west, Columbus Street on the east, Union Street on the south, and Sixth Avenue on the north. Two years later lots were offered in the Eastern Addition, a tract extending from Maple to Cherry Streets and from Chestnut to Mul-

DeVol–Dallow–Anchor Hocking Guest House, 1834. Photo by author, 1997.

Stanbery-Rising House, 1834. Photo by author, 1997.

View of Lancaster's Main Street, 1846, by Henry Howe, *Historical Collections of Ohio*, p. 591.

berry Streets.²⁶ As with the Carpenter Addition a generation earlier, individuals purchased lots and arranged to have their own houses built, with the result that dwellings varied somewhat in size and style, though none of them radically so.

In each case the new houses, with few exceptions, went up on streets directly abutting built-up sections that were slightly closer to the town center. Although Lancaster was spreading out from the center, it was an orderly progression that did not leapfrog over earlier built-up areas (as developers would do in the latter half of the twentieth century). This was because Lancaster remained a walking town, with nearly everyone going on foot to work, to shop, or to socialize.

Other manifestations of the canal boom were the many new businesses in Lancaster, in addition to a greater variety of items for sale, many of which came from long distances by canal. The Lancaster Drug Store, for instance, advertised "Nine Tons of Drugs, Medicines, Paints, Dye-Stuffs, Oils, Glass, and Groceries," while the Lancaster Coffee House offered everything from New Orleans molasses, cinnamon, allspice, and pepper, to a selection of "fine engravings, Chinese tea," "Spanish cigars," and fancy snuff boxes.²⁷

Weary travelers could rest at the well-appointed Phoenix Hotel downtown, located on the south side of Main Street between Center Alley and the public square. The Phoenix was later renamed the Tallmadge House by proprietor Darius Tallmadge, also owner of the Ohio Stage Company, which ran coaches to Wheeling, Columbus, Cincinnati, Portsmouth, and points in between.[28] The Tallmadge House was a popular spot for local dining and banquets. During the 1840s gentlemen of the town also gathered across the street at Giani's wine house (pronounced "Guy Anna's" by the local residents), where they could enjoy a variety of fine imports.[29] For those wanting milder fare, there was the Kelly and Bush Ice Cream Saloon on the south side of Main Street, where patrons could consume their "luxuries of the season in 'grand style' in two airy rooms."[30]

The canal brought new creature comforts, too. In the fall of 1840, the same year that the Hocking Valley Canal extended as far south as Nelsonville, the first barge loads of coal reached Lancaster. Many citizens soon abandoned wood as a heating fuel in favor of coal, prompting several small iron foundries in Lancaster to go into the business of producing coal-burning grates that fitted into open fireplaces, as well as more efficient coal-burning stoves. In addition, the abundant coal supply from the Hocking Valley provided the raw material for making coal gas. A works for producing this kind of gas opened in Lancaster in 1855. The gas was piped into some businesses and homes for lighting purposes, and the town installed gas street lamps on the main street. Coal gas was very expensive to manufacture, however, and it found only a limited market.[31]

The canal also brought a new form of entertainment, holiday excursions by canal boat. On the Fourth of July 1836, a number of citizens walked in a procession down Main Street in the early evening to the canal docks, where they boarded boats for a leisurely ride on the Lancaster Lateral.[32]

But the canal also brought death—in the form of Asiatic cholera. Infected passengers on British ships had brought the disease from India, and from the British Isles it had spread to various seaports in the eastern United States. From there it traveled with canal boat passengers into the interior of the country. In order to keep the fatal disease out of Lancaster, the council passed an ordinance in July 1849 forbidding canal boats to pass through town with any persons on board who were infected or who had died of cholera. Despite such precautions, which were probably impossible to enforce with any great effectiveness, some nineteen deaths in Fairfield County during 1850 were attributed to the dread disease, including seven in Lancaster.[33] Progress exacted a price.

Meanwhile, Lancaster's new prosperity was helping its lawyers to continue to build their reputations throughout the state.[34] According to *Ohio Jurisprudence*, described as the first legal encyclopedia of Ohio law, "The

Fairfield County bar of this period was . . . by common consent . . . the most eminent array of lawyers ever gathered in one community."[35] The preeminence of Lancaster's bar during the first half of the nineteenth century can be attributed, in large part, to the town's central location in the southern half of Ohio, then the most populous part of the state. Lancaster's location along the midpoint of Zane's Trace (and successor roads) and later near the main line of the Ohio and Erie Canal enabled local lawyers to travel the "judicial circuit" and ply their legal skills throughout the region.[36] (The young Abraham Lincoln had pursued this same method of itinerant legal work out in central Illinois; and, like Lancaster's attorneys, he made numerous political contacts on the circuit who later helped him win elective office.)[37]

Individual ability was an additional factor in the success of the Lancaster bar, since several pioneer attorneys were exceptionally well versed and skilled in the law and passed their knowledge on to others who "read law" under them. Among these legal "masters" was Philemon Beecher (1775–1839), who came to Lancaster in 1801 from Virginia, where he had already been admitted to the bar. Beecher was soon elected to the Ohio House of Representatives, becoming speaker in 1807. He was then elected to the U.S. House of Representatives and served in that body from about 1819 to 1829, with the exception of one term. Beecher was also a major general in the state militia, the first president of the Lancaster Ohio Bank, and a businessman who invested widely in local real estate.[38]

Thomas Ewing (1789–1871), Beecher's most successful student, formed a legal partnership with Beecher. Born in what would later become West Virginia, Ewing was elected to the United States Senate in 1830 and again in 1850. He served as secretary of the treasury under President William Henry Harrison and then as secretary of the interior under President Zachary Taylor. Ewing also had numerous investments and business interests and was probably Lancaster's wealthiest citizen throughout the mid-nineteenth century.[39] Both of Beecher's sons-in-law, Henry Stanbery and Philadelphus Van Trump, became prosperous and successful lawyers in Lancaster. Later in life, Stanbery (1803–83) was the attorney general of Ohio and then the attorney general of the United States under President Andrew Johnson. In this capacity, Stanbery played a crucial and successful role in defending Johnson during his impeachment and attempted expulsion from the presidency.[40]

Another important member of the legal community was Charles

Sherman (1788–1829), a native of Norwalk, Connecticut (and father of William T. and John Sherman), who came to Lancaster in 1811. Besides a flourishing legal practice, Sherman was famous for his oratory and served as a justice of the Ohio Supreme Court from 1823 to 1829. It was Charles Sherman who had urged his friend Thomas Ewing to settle in Lancaster.

Other local lawyers and politicians of distinction during this period were Hocking H. Hunter, William W. Irvin, William J. Reese, John T. Brasse, Thomas Ewing Jr., John D. Martin, John M. Creed, William Medill, and John Brough. Medill (1802–65) was governor of Ohio in 1854, president of the Ohio Constitutional Convention in 1850, and a member of the Ohio legislature, as well as a U.S. congressman. Thomas Ewing Jr. (1829–96) went on to become the chief justice of the Kansas Supreme Court, and following the Lincoln assassination, would serve as defense counsel for Dr. Samuel Mudd and two others accused of conspiring in the crime.[41] Lancaster's John Brough (1811–65), one-time publisher of the *Eagle*, served as governor of Ohio during the crucial years of 1864–65.[42]

Three of Lancaster's early- and mid-nineteenth-century lawyers—Thomas Ewing, Charles Sherman, and Henry Stanbery—were later included in the prestigious *Dictionary of American Biography*, a further indication of the status of Lancaster's legal profession. In addition, four other Lancastrians from this period appeared in the *Dictionary*: William T. Sherman and John Sherman; Hugh Ewing, U.S. Minister to the Hague; and John W. Noble, U.S. Secretary of the Interior. Seven such entries are impressive for any town of several thousand people.

Besides making names for themselves in the state and nation, Lancaster's lawyers joined with the town's most successful merchants to form a social and civic elite. At a time when local governments did little more than maintain courts, keep the peace, and register property transactions, these men took the lead in promoting better transportation systems, such as the Lancaster Lateral Canal.

This same group stepped forward, like their counterparts in other Midwestern communities, to sponsor organizations to promote the higher culture of the town. In February 1830, they established the Lancaster Institute, probably modeled after similar literary societies back east. Among its founders were Samuel F. Maccracken, Samuel Effinger, Elnathan Schofield, John Noble, Thomas Ewing, Hocking Hunter, Philemon Beecher, John Creed, Dr. Robert McNeil, and the Reverend John Wright. With the exceptions of Wright (the minister of the First Presbyterian Church),

McNeil (a medical doctor), and Nobel (then a hotel keeper), the founders of the Lancaster Institute were either prominent lawyers or successful merchants. They dedicated their new organization to "the promotion of Literature and Science," and in meetings held in the hall over the market house, they sponsored debates and heard lectures from members as well as guest speakers.[43] It was before this body that George Sanderson, one of Lancaster's original settlers, local hero of the War of 1812, state militia officer, Ohio legislator, justice of the peace, and newspaper publisher, lectured on the early history of Fairfield County.[44] Later expanded and issued as *A Brief History of the Early Settlement of Fairfield County* (1851), Sanderson's account became the first published history of Lancaster and Fairfield County and a valuable source for local historians in the future.[45]

It was essentially this same group of men that established the Lancaster Library Association in early 1833.[46] Joining them were William J. Reese, lawyer and husband of Mary Elizabeth Sherman; Michael Garaghty, banker and dry goods merchant; James Gates, jeweler; Joseph Grubb, chair maker and portrait painter; Dr. James White, medical doctor; Gotlieb Steinman, hotel keeper and bank director; and Joseph Work Sr., shoemaker. These associations of lawyers, doctors, merchants, and, later, industrialists would dominate the social and cultural life of Lancaster throughout much of its two-hundred-year history, as they have in other towns and cities in the United States.[47]

Yet even this resourceful group of business and professional leaders could not shield Lancaster from wider economic and technological forces that began to threaten the town's economic boom during the latter 1830s. The first of these was a nationwide economic depression, or panic as it was called in those days, that began in 1837 and lasted well into the early 1840s. There were heated arguments at the time over what caused the economic decline, but most economic historians would agree that it resulted from speculation and overexpansion encouraged by the easy-credit practices of an unregulated banking system. One victim of this general collapse in the credit system was the Lancaster Ohio Bank, which was forced to close in 1842.[48]

Just how this panic affected living and working conditions in Lancaster is unknown, but an almost complete halt in the town's population growth would indicate that it suffered significantly from the depression. Between 1840 and 1850, for example, Lancaster's population rose by only 211 people —from 3,272 to 3,483.[49] This was an increase of just 6 percent for the entire decade, as compared to a dramatic increase of 114 percent in the previous ten years (1830 to 1840). Yet other communities in what might be called south-central Ohio fared better than Lancaster during the 1840s. The population of Newark grew by 35 percent, Circleville by 46 percent, Chillicothe by 79 percent, Zanesville by 100 percent, and Columbus by a huge 196 percent.[50]

One reason for Columbus's great surge was its status, since 1816, as the state capital. An equally important reason was its location at a very important crossroad of transportation and trade, for it was at Columbus that the National Road (completed across Ohio in 1838) intersected with the Ohio and Erie Canal. Although the National Road (superseded in the twentieth century by U.S. Route 40 and then by Interstate 70) passed through the northern part of Fairfield County, it did so at a distance of approximately sixteen miles from Lancaster, and thus had no appreciable effect on the town. The National Road also bypassed Newark, running about five miles south. But Newark's relative proximity to the new road, combined with its location on the Ohio and Erie Canal, probably explains its healthy growth during the 1840s. Zanesville's impressive increase during the same decade doubtless resulted from having the National Road pass directly through town, where it intersected with the "Muskingum Improvement," a canal that branched off from the Ohio and Erie Canal and ran parallel to the Muskingum River through Zanesville and down to Marietta on the Ohio.[51] Both Circleville and Chillicothe did well during the 1840s, because the tremendous growth of Columbus at the head of the southern branch of the Ohio and Erie Canal probably attracted a large volume of traffic through these two towns. Lancaster, by contrast, struggled for several years to recover.

Confidence had seemingly returned to Lancaster by 1844 when application was made to the state legislature for the incorporation of a financial institution, to be known as the Hocking Valley Bank. A charter was secured in 1847 and the Hocking Valley Bank became a Lancaster landmark that would endure (though under a different name) up to the time of this writing.[52] The new bank, and the end of the panic, helped Lancaster to recover somewhat during the remainder of the decade.

Despite the arrival of better times and continued access to the canal system, communication beyond Lancaster could be slow and undependable. As late as 1847 there was no daily mail delivery to Lancaster from Columbus or from other towns and villages in the area.[53] Two years later

Lancaster received its first telegraph service when lines were strung from Columbus along the canal bank, with the first telegraphic message received from the capital on the evening of October 19, 1847. For the first time in their history, Lancastrians could receive nearly instantaneous news and correspondence over large distances, but for most residents telegraphic messages were prohibitively expensive, except in the greatest of emergencies.[54]

Far more significant in providing rapid communications and transportation than either the telegraph or the canal was the arrival of Lancaster's first railroad in 1854. Ironically, the initial wave of railroad enthusiasm had occurred in the area at the very time that the canals were opening in Ohio, and within a generation the railroads would make the canals nearly obsolete. Enterprising Lancastrians seemed to have realized the importance of railroads very early, as evidenced by their successful effort in 1833 to obtain a charter from the state to build a railroad down the Hocking Valley to the Ohio River. This line would have had its terminus at Lancaster, where it would have connected with the Lancaster Lateral Canal. This proposal fell through when the state decided to finance the Hocking Valley Canal instead of supporting a railroad down the valley.[55] Such a railroad would eventually be built, but not for another generation.

As it turned out, the first railroad to pass through Lancaster was the Cincinnati, Wilmington, and Zanesville line (later known as the Cincinnati and Muskingum Railroad and still later as a branch line of the Pennsylvania Railroad). It was incorporated in early 1851 and opened to Lancaster three years later. In order to bring the railroad through the area, Fairfield County purchased $250,000 in stock, paid for by selling county bonds.[56] The first passenger train pulled into Lancaster on April 11, 1854, at about 4:30 in the afternoon. According to the *Gazette*, approximately 8,000 celebrants (probably an exaggeration, given that the population of the entire town at the time was only 3,500) turned out at the foot of South Broad Street to welcome in the railroad age. Cannon fire announced the train from Circleville as a brass band filled the air with popular tunes. Upon disembarking, the passengers joined a procession led by the band in a "gaily festooned wagon, drawn by 10 prize gray horses." That evening there was a supper at the station house attended by some 800 guests, at which there were more than a dozen toasts. The evening ended with a dance at the Temperance Hall, an ironic location given the many enthusiastic toasts earlier that evening.[57]

No doubt this first railroad into town, coupled with a more general recovery, helped Lancaster to grow by 820 people during the 1850s, for an increase of 24 percent. Though this was better than its showing for the decade earlier, it was small in contrast to the great spurt of the 1830s.[58] A comparison of the census counts in south-central Ohio communities show that Lancaster fared about as well—and in several cases better—than the others during the 1850s: Circleville and Newark both increased by 28 percent, while Zanesville grew at a rate of 16 percent for the decade, Chillicothe at 7 percent, and Columbus at just 4 percent. The last three fared worse than Lancaster in percentage terms, though all were larger than Lancaster in actual numbers of residents.[59]

Another economic panic in 1857 may have accounted for some of the slackening of growth throughout the region during the 1850s. But it is more likely that a fairly mature economy, at least in the context of the times, would explain the slowing of population growth in all these south-central towns. By 1860, for example, most of the usable land in the area had been cleared and planted, and until significant amounts of mechanized equipment emerged some decades later, there would be little increase in agricultural productivity. Meanwhile, the roads, canals, and railroads in place by 1860 were more than sufficient to carry the region's agricultural produce to the most advantageous markets, making additional transportation systems redundant as well as counterproductive. And as yet there were no signs of a true industrial revolution in the region. Until significant industry began to appear in Lancaster and the other towns during the late nineteenth century, population growth rates would not begin to rival those of the 1830s.

Thus, if population is any indication, Lancaster declined in importance between 1830 and 1860, sliding from the sixth largest community in the state to the twentieth. This relative decline should not be taken as a sign that Lancaster's economy was in a shambles or that many of its inhabitants were mired in poverty. On the contrary, Lancaster remained a basically prosperous community with a good deal of civic pride. Its rise in 1851 from an incorporated village, which it had been since 1831, to a "city of the third class" (that is, the smallest category of incorporated Ohio cities) boosted this pride. For the first time, Lancaster had a mayor, as well as a city council, though its modest size meant that it continued to be a town in every sense but the state's legal definition of a city (having a population of at least 2,500).

Despite the change in status, Lancaster's government continued to use

Lancaster's first city hall, 1859. To the right of the city hall is the market house, c. 1820. Leonard Hajost Collection.

the upper floor of the market house as its headquarters until 1859, when a new city hall opened on the southeast corner of the central square, designed by Lancaster's master builder, Daniel Sifford.[60] Besides the mayor's chamber and other offices, the building provided housing for the fire department, a jail, and the Lancaster post office. The second-floor council chamber doubled as an all-purpose assembly room for social gatherings as well as for church services. Another large room on the third floor accommodated the meetings of various lodges and other organizations.[61]

Yet another sign of prosperity was the first Fairfield County Fair, which took place in Lancaster in 1851. Its sponsor was the Fairfield County Agricultural Society, founded in 1850 "for the improvement of agriculture and domestic manufacture." The site of this first fair was a field north of town belonging to the Agricultural Society's president, John Reber, that lay just west of the intersection of Columbus Street and Reber Avenue (so named in honor of John Reber). This exhibition was so successful that the society purchased a fourteen-acre tract across Columbus Street and just east of the original site. The fair for 1852 opened on these new grounds, and has taken place there every year since (though on an expanded acreage)—always during the second week in October. This site, which spreads out below picturesque Mount Pleasant, the Wyandot's Standing Stone, remains one of the most attractive fairgrounds in the nation.[62]

The Fairfield County Fairgrounds at Lancaster as depicted in an 1875 lithograph. Tobias Studio Collection, FCDL.

For generations many of Lancaster's residents have taken satisfaction in seeing the season's bounty fill the fairgrounds, in much the same way as they have enjoyed leisurely drives into the rich farmland surrounding the town. Surveying such a rural scene in the midsummer of 1860, a writer for the *Lancaster Gazette* commented: "A ride into the country adjacent to Lancaster, at this season of the year, is most delightful. The richness and healthy appearance of the cornfields, with all other growing crops, gives promises of abundant supply; and cannot fail to elevate aspirations of thanks to our heavenly father, who has assured us, that seed time and harvest time shall not fail."[63] The writer could not know that the next growing season would bring a bloody civil war that would preoccupy Lancaster and Fairfield County like no other event thus far in their history.

Though the Civil War seemed to come suddenly after the fall of Fort Sumter in April 1861, its causes had been festering for decades. Slavery and states' rights, as nearly all historians agree, were at the heart of the conflict, but it was also a breakdown of the American political system that plunged the nation into the maelstrom of civil war. This political failure had a long history, too, with numerous reverberations in Lancaster and

Fairfield County. A brief look at antebellum politics helps to explain how and why local residents were so divided over the war itself, and gives some insights into certain cultural divisions that would continue to exist for years to come.

As students of politics have known for some time, political preferences and party affiliations have much to do with a person's overall cultural identity, including regional ties, ethnic background, and religious affiliation. In the first six decades of the nineteenth century, such factors made most Lancaster and Fairfield County residents powerful supporters of the Democratic Party and its forerunner, the Jeffersonian Republicans (not to be confused with the later Republican Party of Abraham Lincoln and his party successors).

These strong ties to the Democratic Party were rooted in the Jeffersonian Republicans'—and later the Democrats'—stress on states' rights, an emphasis that held great appeal among Southerners who feared that a strong central government might attempt to interfere with slavery. As a largely rural and agricultural section of the country, the South also applauded Jefferson's preference for an agrarian society over one dominated by cities and commerce. The large number of men and women who came to Lancaster from the Upper South tended to share these views and continued to favor the Democratic Party, as did most other residents of southern Ohio throughout the nineteenth century, and into the first decades of the twentieth. Rural Pennsylvanians, the Pennsylvania Germans included, likewise tended to favor the Democrats and had brought these preferences with them when they moved west.[64] Given Lancaster's and Fairfield County's great influx of persons from Virginia and Pennsylvania (who represented over 70 percent of early settlers), it is no surprise that the Jeffersonian Republicans and then the Democrats drew overwhelming support from the local population.[65]

Although a majority of the native-born residents in Lancaster at the time of the 1860 federal census reported that they were natives of Ohio, 36 percent of those born out of state (but not of foreign birth) came from somewhere in the Upper South, with Virginia leading the list as it had in earlier decades. Residents from the Middle Atlantic states, with Pennsylvania again in the vanguard, made up some 53 percent of the 1860 "out-of-staters," with the New England region representing only 8 percent of inhabitants born outside Ohio. The remaining 3 percent of this group came from an assortment of states, most of them just north or west of Ohio.[66]

In Lancaster, as everywhere else in the nineteenth century, the newspapers served as the principal means of communication for political parties—so much so that nearly all newspapers affiliated themselves with one party or another. Even in modest-sized towns it was not unusual to have two newspapers, one for each of the major parties. In Lancaster the Jeffersonians/Democrats enjoyed a monopoly of support from the local press for some two decades. Their newspaper was the *Ohio Eagle*, established about 1807.[67]

To compete with the *Eagle*, Colonel George Sanderson established the *Lancaster Gazette* in 1826 at a time when the American party system was undergoing one of its periodic transitions. The Federalist Party, which had never enjoyed any significant support in Lancaster and Fairfield County, had disintegrated by 1816, and virtually all its candidates had taken to calling themselves Jeffersonian Republicans. However, between 1824 and 1828 a serious split had occurred within party ranks between the followers of John Quincy Adams and Andrew Jackson. The Jacksonians would soon begin calling themselves Democrats, while Jackson's opponents would form the Whig Party. The northern Whigs would later help to launch the Republican Party of Lincoln; the Democrats would maintain their name to the present time.[68] The *Lancaster Gazette* was founded to support the reelection of John Quincy Adams in 1828 in a bitter rematch against Andrew Jackson, whom Adams had defeated four years earlier. The *Gazette* would continue to be a loyal voice for the Whigs and then for the Republicans, while the *Eagle* upheld the Democratic standard. Not until 1936, when the two newspapers merged as the *Lancaster Eagle-Gazette*, would their partisan battles come to an end.[69]

An examination of the two newspapers reveals that the partisanship was often heated, and that it helped to fuel social and political animosities in Lancaster and surrounding Fairfield County. In June of 1832, for example, the *Eagle* urged the "Democratic Young Men of Fairfield County" to a rally in the hall above the market house to call for the reelection of President Jackson and to preserve the nation "from war, pestilence and ruin."[70] A little over a year later the *Eagle* described certain political claims made by the *Gazette* the previous week as "the ravings of a distempered and diseased mind."[71]

Despite its efforts on behalf of Whig candidates, the *Gazette* failed to make much of a dent in the local Democratic vote, with the Democrats sweeping election after election. Every Democratic candidate for the presidency was victorious in Fairfield County during the pre–Civil War period, at the same time that the Democrats maintained a hold on local offices. During the presidential election of 1840 the *Gazette* complained that the local Democrats, who controlled the county government, had refused to allow the Whigs to use the courthouse for their meetings.[72] Even the appearance of Whig candidate Henry Clay in Lancaster during August 1844 had little or no effect on the local vote for him.[73]

It was also during the 1840s that the *Gazette* espoused strong feeling against foreigners, which often manifested itself in strident anti-Catholicism.[74] The Whigs had adopted this position in reaction to the preference of a good many recent immigrants for the Democratic Party—especially Irish Catholics, who began arriving in the United States in large numbers because of the deadly potato famine of the 1840s. Anti-Irish and anti-Catholic sentiment among the Whigs also stemmed from the Whigs' strong following among persons of Protestant British backgrounds.[75]

The Whig Party had disintegrated by the 1850s, but some of those who believed that Catholic immigrants posed a threat to the United States formed a new group called the American Party. In 1854 the *Gazette*, which had been affiliated with the Whigs, cast its lot with the outspokenly nativist American Party.[76]

In its issue for September 20 of that year, for example, the *Gazette* published a long diatribe against the Pope, against the rising tide of Catholicism in the United States generally, and against the plans of Lancaster's Catholics to build a new church. The Pope, it charged, was a foreign ruler, as well as "the most complete tyrant on the face of the earth"—to whom all bishops and priests in the United States owed absolute obedience. Under the circumstances, the *Gazette* asked its readers to consider the intentions of local Catholics to erect a new church:

> It becomes the Protestant Freemen of Fairfield County seriously to consider whether they will ever permit the soil of this county to be contaminated by such a nefarious institution. We do not advise a resort to violent means—far from it. We wish the Protestant feeling of the county fully aroused, in order that public opinion may, if possible, prevent the establishment of a Nunnery in this enlightened county—an institution suited only to the darkness of the middle ages, and the latitude of Spain and Italy.[77]

There had been a time, the *Gazette* lamented, when local Protestants had not dared to vocalize their "abhorrence of the doctrines and practicers of the Romish Church, for fear of the social influence of a few Catholic families." That day, the *Gazette* exulted, had passed: "The man who should now dare to bow obsequiously to Romanism for Catholic patronage or good will, would be marked by his fellow citizens as equally an enemy of God and true religion, and a traitor to his country. If Catholics wish to proscribe those who express their religious opinions without reserve, they must do it at their own risk."[78]

In 1856 the *Gazette* followed most other newspapers affiliated with the American Party in adhering to the new Republican organization, which espoused Northern interests as well as a nativist agenda.[79] The *Gazette* had already published numerous criticisms of the South and its low-tariff position. Although critical of slavery, the *Gazette* and the vast majority of Republicans in Lancaster and Fairfield County were far from being extreme abolitionists. Rather, they supported a moderate antislavery policy, which opposed the spread of slavery into the western territories, the same position that Abraham Lincoln held during the campaign of 1860. Thus on April 5, 1860, the *Gazette* vehemently denied charges by the rival Democrats that it favored the abolitionist camp: "The charges of . . . black Republican, negro equality, negro suffrage, woolly head, abolitionism, we repeat, . . . are as false and ridiculous, as they are unworthy of the great Democratic party." In contrast to their own moderation, the *Gazette* charged, the Democrats had become totally subservient to the South: "Body, boots, and brains [the Democrats have] gone over to the South, [and are] devoted exclusively to the interests of that section."[80]

What is clear from these charges is that there was considerable prejudice against African Americans in Lancaster and Fairfield County in the years leading up to the Civil War. According to the federal census of 1860, the year before the war began, there were 141 blacks living in Lancaster, representing slightly over 3 percent of a total population of 4,303.[81] Just twelve years before, prejudice against this minority group had erupted in an episode of mob violence on the night of July 31, 1848, the eve of a celebration by local African Americans of the anniversary of emancipation in the West Indies. To help celebrate this event, the Lancaster sponsors had invited approximately one hundred black residents of neighboring Chillicothe and Circleville. The prospect of such a meeting angered a number of local whites, who attacked the home of Nelson Smith—described as "the headquarters of the colored people"—where they destroyed all his furniture and did much damage to the house itself.[82] The out-of-town celebrants fled, and observances for the following day were canceled.

Despite the great prejudice against blacks locally, some inhabitants of Lancaster and Fairfield County sympathized with African Americans and participated in the network known as the underground railroad, which helped slaves escape from bondage. Because of the fugitive slave clause in the United States Constitution and the Fugitive Slave Act of 1850, slave owners could pursue runaways into the North and take them back into slavery. Legislation required Northern law-enforcement agents to assist in the return of runaway slaves, and anyone who helped them to make their way to freedom in Canada could be judged guilty of a serious crime. Because of these circumstances, much secrecy surrounded the operation of the underground railroad, making it extremely difficult for historians to document either its activities or the hiding places for runaways, known as "stations." It seems clear, however, that one of the escape routes ran from the Ohio River through Athens and then into Fairfield County, where it branched in several directions, depending upon which way was considered safest at a given time. In Lancaster one of the "conductors"—that is, people who guided, hid, and otherwise aided runaways—was Dr. Michael Effinger, who as a medical doctor had a good excuse for being almost anywhere day or night. The Effinger family had been sympathetic toward African Americans at least since the period when Dr. Effinger's father, Samuel, had employed Scipio Africanus Smith. Besides concealing runaways in his own "Effinger House," slaves were allegedly hidden in the Maccracken residence (The Georgian), though there is no documented evidence for either site.[83]

More widely known as a stop on the underground railroad was the Fairfield County village of Rushville, some fifteen miles east and slightly north of Lancaster. There another medical doctor, Simon Hyde, hid and otherwise assisted runaways. Aiding him for a time in Rushville was the Reverend William Hanby. Hanby's son, Benjamin, was deeply moved in 1842 by the story of a dying runaway named Joseph Selby, who told of his beloved Nelly Gray, whose freedom he wished to buy once he was safely across the border in Canada. Inspired by this tragic story, Benjamin Hanby wrote the immensely successful ballad "Darling Nelly Gray," which was credited with turning many Americans against slavery.[84]

Despite such opponents of slavery in Lancaster and its vicinity, Lincoln and the antislavery Republican Party lost Lancaster and Fairfield County with a total of just 2,278 votes out of the 5,883 votes cast, or 39 percent of the total. The Democratic candidate, Stephen A. Douglas, received 3,249 votes locally, or 55 percent. The remaining votes went to the two minor party candidates: the Constitutional Unionist John Bell, 155 votes, and the Southern Democrat John C. Breckinridge, 201 votes.[85]

Lincoln's election that November was unmistakable proof for many Southerners that the North had won control of the federal government and that Southern interests were now in great danger. South Carolina led the way and seceded toward the end of December, and by April ten other states had joined it. The residents of Lancaster and Fairfield County followed the breakup of the union in the local newspapers, culminating as it did in the firing on Fort Sumter in Charleston Harbor on April 12, 1861, and Major Robert Anderson's surrender of the fort the following day. Responding to President Lincoln's call for 75,000 troops to put down the rebellion, Lancaster's militia company, founded in 1859 by Captain Joab A. Stafford and known as the Lancaster Guards, received orders on April 16 to report to Columbus. That evening a large citizens' meeting took place at city hall, where they collected $1,000 to assist the soldiers and their families.[86] Lancaster's city council sold several thousand dollars worth of bonds in order to defray the costs of enlisting men and providing them food and shelter until they went into official state service.[87]

This action by town fathers to finance the raising and maintaining of troops might seem odd to citizens of a later time, used to a powerful central government, who would assume that national authorities would have handled such matters from the beginning. But when the Civil War began, the United States was in many respects not a complete nation. The fact that Lancaster's council had to go out and buy an American flag to fly over city hall following the attack on Fort Sumter underscores the extreme localism that characterized virtually all American communities at the outbreak of the Civil War, a condition which itself had contributed to the disintegration of the Union.[88]

Nevertheless, great excitement accompanied the Lancaster Guards' departure from town on April 17, 1861, as reported in full by the *Gazette*:

> Yesterday from dawn till 5 P.M. . . . the military paraded the streets [of Lancaster], the stars and stripes floating proudly above them

to the music of the Union. The enthusiasm was unbounded. More than 3,000 persons, men, women, and children assembled in the streets and the public square. . . . At about 4 o'clock [the guards] . . . made [their] appearance. . . . The company [of one hundred men] formed into line on Broadway [known to later generations as Broad Street], and was escorted to the depot by an immense throng of citizens, led by the Lancaster Brass Band.[89]

Captain Stafford's Lancaster Guard was the first militia unit to report to Columbus in response to the call for troops, becoming Company A, First Ohio Volunteer Infantry.[90]

The departure of the Lancaster Guard was followed by hundreds of men volunteering throughout the area. These became the Seventeenth Ohio Regiment, quartered in the county fairgrounds at Lancaster (temporarily designated as Camp Anderson) at the foot of beautiful Mount Pleasant. The men seem to have been housed in hastily built wooden barracks on the grounds. After two months of training, under the command of Major H. H. Giesy, the Seventeenth left Lancaster on June 14 for western Virginia (now West Virginia), where they fought with other Ohio units under the command of General George McClellan to secure the western counties of the Old Dominion from the Confederacy.[91] This early Union victory, which kept the Confederacy from reaching all the way to the Ohio River, has been described as one of the crucial engagements of the Civil War.[92]

A month later Lancaster and Fairfield County men—members of the Lancaster Guard who had been the first Ohioans to report for war—were not so fortunate as the Seventeenth had been in western Virginia. For on July 21, they and 30,000 other Union troops were routed at the Battle of Bull Run, one of the greatest humiliations for the North during the entire Civil War.[93] Trying to put the best face on the defeat, the *Gazette* welcomed the Lancaster Guard back to town in early August. The newspaper also glossed over their panic-stricken retreat as best it could by insisting, no doubt incorrectly, that the men had fallen back "only to cover the retreat of a beaten and retiring army."[94]

In addition to the Lancaster Guard (Company A) and the Ohio Seventeenth, over a dozen other companies came from Fairfield County. Fairfield men also made up segments of other units that contained men from other parts of the state. About 88 local men died as a direct result of battle, while an additional 143 lost their lives from disease, accident, or other causes. Another 101 received wounds but survived.[95]

Men from Lancaster and Fairfield County saw action in virtually every theater of the war and were present at many crucial battles. Whenever news of Northern victories reached Lancaster, pro-Union citizens shouted through the streets and organized celebrations. During the early months of 1862 they rejoiced at the capture of Fort Donelson in Kentucky and the Union success at Pittsburg Landing, Tennessee (more popularly known as Shiloh). The Forty-sixth Ohio, which had been organized by Lancaster's Captain Giesy following his return from western Virginia, participated in the fierce and bloody battle of Shiloh.[96] Word of Union victories at Gettysburg and Vicksburg in early July 1863 touched off an explosion of joy among Union supporters in Lancaster on July 7 and 8. On the evening of the 8th, according to the *Gazette,* "loyal people of the county began to pour into [Lancaster], and at dark the streets were overflowing with surging and roaring floods of people. Rockets, Roman candles, fire-crackers, fiery serpents, pyrotechnic wind-mills, muskets, cannon and bonfires filled the [town] and the sky with noise and splendor."[97]

Just two weeks after this celebration, Lancaster was rife with rumors that Colonel John Hunt Morgan and his Confederate cavalry, popularly known as Morgan's Raiders, were headed for Lancaster. In fact, they passed through the southern corner of Fairfield County at New Straitsville. In reaction to telegraphic messages about Morgan's movements, Lancaster's council, on July 22, ordered all businesses closed, with permission for store owners to open only in order "to sell powder, shot, percussion caps and such other ammunition as may be necessary for the occasion."[98] Fortunately, Morgan did not head toward Lancaster and was captured near East Liverpool, Ohio. Incarcerated in the Ohio State Penitentiary at Columbus, Morgan and six of his officers tunneled their way out of prison and escaped back to the Confederacy.

In November, following the dedication of the cemetery at Gettysburg, the *Gazette* published the text of Lincoln's short but moving Gettysburg address.[99] On Christmas Day of 1863 many Lancastrians thrilled at the arrival in town of General William Tecumseh Sherman, who was beginning to emerge as one of the most brilliant and successful of the Union commanders. Sherman had been born in Lancaster on February 8, 1820, the son of Charles Robert and Mary Hoyt Sherman. Following Charles Sherman's unexpected death at Lebanon, Ohio, while riding the judicial

William Tecumseh Sherman in 1875, the famous Civil War general born and reared in Lancaster, FCDL.

circuit of the Ohio Supreme Court, young "Cump" had been taken in by his father's good friend and neighbor, Thomas Ewing. Cump thus moved a half block up Main Hill to the imposing Ewing residence at the northwest corner of Main and High Streets.[100] Mrs. Thomas (Maria Boyle) Ewing, a devout Catholic, was concerned that Sherman, who had been named for the great Indian chief Tecumseh, did not have a Christian name and had him christened William by a Catholic priest.[101]

Although baptized by a priest, Sherman did not convert to the Catholic faith. According to one of his recent biographers, this resistance was partly in reaction to the sense of abandonment that Sherman felt after his father's death and of the consequent ambivalence that he held toward the Ewings.[102] His marriage in 1850 to Ellen Ewing, the daughter of

Thomas and Maria Boyle Ewing, may have complicated his feelings toward the Ewing family. He and Ellen, a devout Catholic like her mother, quarreled over religion throughout their marriage.[103] In addition, Sherman had often felt intimidated by his highly successful father-in-law, Thomas Ewing, especially before the Civil War when Sherman had a lackluster career as a low-ranking army officer and as an unsuccessful businessman. Sherman's Christmas visit to the Ewing home in 1863 may have been as uncomfortable as all his other trips back to Lancaster over the years, even though he was well on his way to becoming Lancaster's most famous son. But this was not apparent on the evening of December 28 when a throng of local well-wishers assembled outside the Ewing residence to welcome Sherman home and to congratulate him for his great achievements. Attorney John D. Martin spoke briefly on behalf of his fellow townsmen and Sherman responded in kind.[104]

Understandably, Sherman's supporters back in Lancaster were euphoric over his capture of Atlanta on September 2, 1864. "All honor to Major General W. T. Sherman," wrote the *Gazette*, "Lancaster's most distinguished son."[105] Yet the campaign through Georgia had cost Lancaster one of its early leaders in the war, Major H. H. Giesy, who had formed the Seventeenth Ohio Regiment and had gone on to raise and then lead the Forty-sixth Ohio. Giesy was mortally wounded in an engagement near Dallas, Georgia, and died on May 29, 1864.[106]

Although Giesy's profile as an officer made him one of the better known casualties of the time, dozens of other families in Lancaster and Fairfield County were already mourning the loss of fathers, sons, and husbands. In early 1863, for example, the wife of Nimrod Webb received a letter from her husband's commander near Murfreesboro, Tennessee, informing her of Nimrod's death in combat. It read in part:

> Mrs. Webb:
> It is with a heavy heart that I write to inform you that your husband Nimrod A. Webb is no more. [H]e fell mortally wounded at the battle of Stone River on the 31st day of Dec. last and died on the 11th inst[.] in the hospital at Murfreesboro[,] Tenn. [F]rom a long and close intimacy with your departed husband I can say without reserve that he was a kind friend[,] a true Soldier[,] and a brave man. . . . I feel that there is nothing that I can say that would afford consolation in this your great day of sorrow, but be assured

that I sincerely sympathize with you and your family in your great affliction. . . .

> With many regards Yours[,]
> E. T. Hooker
> Capt Comdg. Compy.
> A 1st Regt. Ohio Vol. Inft[.][107]

Nimrod Webb, like the other 230 local men who lost their lives in the Civil War, would not return home to be a father and husband and to grow old and die among familiar surroundings.

As local men were falling on the battlefields and in the camps, there was continuing contention back home about the war and the issues that it raised. Although the staunchly Republican *Gazette* missed no opportunity to boast of Union victories, it mustered only faint enthusiasm for Lincoln's Emancipation Proclamation. Accordingly, in an editorial on May 23, 1863, the *Gazette* lent its support to emancipation only as a means of defeating the South and not as an act of simple justice or morality toward the slaves: "Therefore, we say if slavery stands in the way of suppressing the rebellion, run over it and crush it, or pluck it up by the roots; if the wealth of the South sustains the rebellion, confiscate the property [in slaves] and impoverish the rich rebels."[108] As for "negro equality," the *Gazette* left no doubt in readers' minds that the slaves, freed or not, would never be the equal of whites: "For our part we don't believe our children will ever need to be taught that they are better than a negro. Nor do we believe it will ever be necessary to pass laws to prevent them from associating and amalgamating with blacks."[109]

Although there were some War Democrats in Lancaster and surrounding Fairfield County, it is clear that the *Eagle*, long affiliated with the Democratic Party, was a major antiwar newspaper from the very outset of the conflict. Typical of its views was an editorial that appeared on June 13, 1861, which read in part, "The [Democrats] of Old Fairfield believe this an unholy war, fruitless for good, certain in its results to add to the estrangement and bitter hatred of the [two] sections."[110]

Throughout the war, the *Eagle* blamed all the violence and death entirely on the Republican Party, denounced President Lincoln as a dictator, usurper, and tyrant—worse even than Napoleon Bonaparte—and compared the subjugation of the South to England's bloody conquest of Ireland in the seventeenth century.[111]

Later the *Eagle* excoriated Lincoln's Emancipation Proclamation, and had especially bitter words to say about the Union's decision to recruit African American soldiers.[112] On the issue of sending black men into battle, the *Eagle*'s editor wrote, "The negro is a barbarian. His method of making war is by the destruction and massacre of women and children, as well as men, by the perpetuation of atrocities that makes humanity shudder."[113]

According to the *Gazette*, much of what appeared in the *Eagle* about the war was simply treason: "The last number of [the *Eagle*] was as dirty, mean and treasonable as any of its predecessors, containing no word of encouragement for those who are striving to maintain the government, but laboring by its tone and sentiment to divide the North, encourage the South and drive from the government its legitimate support."[114]

In the late spring of 1863, accusations by the *Gazette* against the *Eagle* reached new heights: "There is in Lancaster, a political sewer, called the *Ohio Eagle*. . . . Through this sewer, at weekly intervals, there flows into the homes of the people whatever literary filth and moral and political venom [that] may have accumulated during the week. . . . The nature of this being is a pond covered with a moral scum and filled with moral frogs, lizards, snakes, and slimy reptiles."[115] The *Eagle* frequently responded in kind. About the editor of the opposition newspaper it wrote, "We are convinced that his ravings are unworthy of notice, and that his corrupt, malicious spirit, and rotten carcass is not worth the powder that would be required to blow out of existence a *skunk* or any other *stinking thing!*" [emphasis in the original].

Unfortunately, the fighting between these rival newspapers went beyond words. On the night of June 1, 1863, a mob broke into the *Gazette*, where they seized twelve cases of composed type and scattered them into the street, besides tearing up every copy of the newspaper that had already been printed. There was no doubt at the *Gazette* that this attack had been the work of the *Eagle* and its Democratic minions.[116] The *Eagle* charged that the attack had been faked by the *Gazette* itself, whose editor had merely thrown some wornout type into the alley.[117]

Eight months later, in February 1864, it was the *Eagle* that was attacked, in broad daylight by about a dozen Union soldiers who were being applauded by a number of Republicans assembled on the street outside. The office escaped total destruction, it seemed, when the town marshal and several deputies arrived and persuaded the mob to disperse. Later that same week solders ransacked several grocery stores belonging to Democrats, kicking and beating at least one proprietor.[118]

Lancaster's Democrats, like those elsewhere who were highly critical of the war, were called Copperheads (that is, poisonous snakes) by their Republican opponents.[119] Throughout the combat between local Democrats and Republicans, Lancaster resident Dr. Edson B. Olds was frequently an object of heated argument.[120] For next to Clement L. Vallandingham of Dayton, Olds was the most notorious Copperhead in the state of Ohio. A druggist rather than a trained medical doctor, Dr. Olds (c. 1802–69) had moved to Lancaster in 1858 from Circleville (located in the old Virginia Military District and thus home to many men and women of Southern descent). While in Circleville, Olds had served two terms in the Ohio House of Representatives (1842–46) and one in the Ohio Senate (1846–48), as well as three terms in the U.S. House of Representatives (1849–55)—all as a Democrat.

Olds believed that the South should be permitted to keep its slaves, upheld Southern secession, and charged that President Lincoln had usurped the Constitution on many occasions. Olds also led a campaign in 1863 to found an "anti-Abolitionist church" in Lancaster, unsuccessfully it would seem, where the minister would stick to preaching the "gospel of Our Lord Jesus Christ unmixed with politics."[121]

When military conscription was introduced in the North in 1862, Olds denounced the draft in speech after speech. On August 12, 1862, federal officers arrested him on the orders of Secretary of War Edwin M. Stanton and imprisoned him at Fort Lafayette, Indiana. In the words of the antiwar *Eagle*, Olds had been kidnapped and "dragged from his bed" by "hired tools of the . . . unscrupulous and despotic [Lincoln] administration."[122]

While in prison at Fort Lafayette, Olds was overwhelmingly elected to the Ohio legislature in November 1862.[123] When Olds was released in December of that year a crowd of several thousand people met him at the train station, where jubilant Democrats carried him on their shoulders to his residence at the northwest corner of Columbus and Wheeling Streets (later the site of the Stewart Brothers–Alban furniture store).[124] No Civil War hero from Lancaster enjoyed such a reception at any time during the conflict.

Though the *Gazette* raged against Olds and his Copperhead supporters, Republicans continued to lose every local election during the Civil War, including the presidential contest of 1864, when both Lancaster and

Fairfield County cast a large majority of their votes for Democrat George B. McClellan, who defeated Lincoln locally by over 1,300 votes.[125] A victory for McClellan—who had advocated a negotiated peace with the South, even if it left slavery intact—would have been disastrous for the Union cause.[126] Thus, by voting for McClellan in large numbers the majority of men in Lancaster and Fairfield County registered their disapproval of emancipation and of President Lincoln's conduct of the war. Fortunately for the Unionists, the Copperhead Clement Vallandingham did not succeed in his bid for the Ohio governorship in a race against John Brough of Lancaster, a Republican who ran on the Union ticket.[127]

By the late twentieth century, Edson B. Olds was forgotten as a historical figure, at least until an article in the quarterly magazine published by the Fairfield Heritage Association brought his story to light. Even Olds's grandson, Edson B. Olds Smith (1868–1961), an elderly neighbor of this author in my childhood, never alluded to his notorious grandfather's activities during the Civil War in his frequent reminiscences about the local past.[128] In its collective consciousness Lancaster has chosen to remember William Tecumseh Sherman—and not Edson B. Olds, whose local following was probably far greater than Sherman's. Lancaster's Olds Avenue in the North End bears the name of this outspoken Copperhead, so designated by his grandchildren, who once owned the land around Olds Avenue. The name Sherman, by contrast, has been honored by a street on the West Side of Lancaster, by a junior high school in the same part of town, and for several decades by a national guard armory (now demolished). For many years, too, Sherman's birthplace has been a house museum in Lancaster, while Olds's residence has long since disappeared. Sherman, of course, was on the winning side and Olds on the losing side of the Civil War; moreover, Sherman had won lasting fame on the world stage as a brilliant military mind.

Beyond the Civil War itself, the heated disputes between Republicans and Democrats revealed two very different views of the world—in Lancaster and in the nation at large. The Democrats represented an earlier vision of a rural America, where citizens depended upon decentralized government and local control to manage their public affairs. The Republicans, by contrast, were looking toward an industrial, urban America, where an increasingly powerful central government could be used to help finance transportation systems and assist business enterprises in various ways. Even the Republican tendency to oppose Catholic immigrants stemmed partly from the belief that Catholics were likely to be antimodern in both religious and secular concerns. In Lancaster, this tension between the two worldviews would remain into the late twentieth century, even after the two political parties had changed places in the ideological spectrum, with Democrats favoring strong central government and the Republicans tilting more toward state and local initiative.[129] Ironically, this change in attitudes would eventually cause a majority of voters in Lancaster and Fairfield County to switch their allegiance to the once widely despised party of Lincoln.

Both Republicans and Copperheads were doubtless relieved when the war finally ended. The news of Lee's surrender to Grant at Appomattox Court House, Virginia, on April 9, 1865, produced peal after peal of bells from the churches in Lancaster—and throughout the county—while bonfires and pyrotechnic displays illuminated the night sky.[130] Only six days later, on April 15, Lancaster plunged into another emotional turmoil at the news of Lincoln's assassination at Ford's Theater in Washington. On Wednesday, April 18th, the day of Lincoln's funeral, buildings throughout downtown were draped in black and bells tolled from ten in the morning till noon, as many residents assembled in their respective churches for services. At two in the afternoon a large procession walked up Main Hill to the Thomas Ewing residence, where Ewing had been scheduled to address the crowd. Ewing was unable to appear because of illness, so the assemblage listened as Hocking H. Hunter, the "first white child born in Lancaster," offered a few words of lament for the slain president.[131]

What Dr. Olds and the other Copperheads may have felt and thought on this day went unrecorded. Whatever their reactions, any public expression of their disappointment would have been inappropriate, politically self-defeating, and probably dangerous. Thus those April days of celebration and then of sorrow over a slain president gave the appearance of local solidarity. As in the past, these special occasions took the form of communal rites in which virtually anyone in town could participate through processions in the street, bonfires, and out-of-doors speeches—in the public square or on the front lawn of an important civic leader. In this age, before movies, radio, and television, Lancastrians experienced both the excitement and sorrow of great events collectively. Despite the passions that rent Lancaster during its heroic age, the era closed with a solemn sense of having passed through a terrible ordeal together.

THREE

# Victorian Lancaster
## Town Improvement

FOR MANY AMERICANS THE word *Victorian* still evokes images of ugly houses and even uglier furniture, combined with a prudish attitude toward manners and morals and a generally old-fashioned way of life. In reality, the Victorian age in Lancaster, and in most other communities throughout the United States, was a time of transformation, when many aspects of modern life were taking form. It was also a time of optimism and a widespread belief in progress.[1]

The term *Victorian* applies to certain social, cultural, and intellectual trends that characterized both the British Isles and the United States during the era of Great Britain's Queen Victoria, who reigned from 1837 to 1901. Chief among these were evangelical religion, rapid industrialization, increased wealth, and improved transportation systems; the beginnings of consumerism; a stress on personal morality and self-discipline as a way to achieve individual and communal well-being; the creation of new institutions as a vehicle for social order at a time of rapid change; cultural self-consciousness and boosterism; an emphasis upon the home and family life, including a belief in women as guardians of hearth and home; and a preoccupation with time economy. Most of all this was an age of improvement, when men and women on both sides of the Atlantic believed in the possibility and the reality of progress on almost every level, with the moral and the material going hand in hand.

Between the end of the Civil War and the beginning of the twentieth century, many facets of Victorian life were evident in Lancaster. These included frequent religious revivals and an array of activities sponsored by local churches; an impassioned crusade against alcohol; an expanded and improved downtown shopping district; the establishment of lodges and other fraternal organizations; the erection of new schools, an opera house, fashionable new residences, an ornate county courthouse, and a large cemetery in the late romantic style; the founding of a public library and municipal waterworks; an increase of industrialization on the local scene; a doubling of the town's population; and endless words of praise from local boosters about Lancaster's numerous advantages.

As in the past, the forces that shaped Lancaster during its Victorian age were local, regional, national, and even international. By 1900 the interplay of such forces had given rise to certain physical features of the town that are recognizable a century later as the twentieth century comes to a close—convincing proof that Lancaster's Victorian age was as much a conduit to the present as it is a vanished era. Studying these forces as they played themselves out in an American town offers vivid and concrete examples of how they affected life in the nation at large.

As in the past, Lancaster's location was a major factor in determining the pace of economic change. Since it was not located along the most important routes of transportation and trade, like Pittsburgh or Cincinnati on the Ohio River or Cleveland and Chicago on the Great Lakes, Lancaster did not enjoy the strategic advantages of these cities. And because it was not on an important river, lake, or ocean port, the trunk lines of the major railroads also passed it by. Yet railroad connections remained key to Lancaster's prosperity in the late nineteenth century and for many years thereafter.

Lancaster had received its first rail connection in 1854, when the Cincinnati, Wilmington, and Zanesville Road (later part of the Pennsylvania Railroad network) began operating through the town. In the immediate post–Civil War period, Lancaster gained a second rail line that connected it with Columbus to the north and with the coal fields of the Hocking Valley to the south, with the line running as far as Athens.[2]

Renewed efforts to launch what became the Hocking Valley Railroad had begun in 1848 when a group of prominent Lancaster citizens successfully petitioned the Ohio legislature to allow Fairfield County to subscribe $500,000 for such a road. Despite a vigorous campaign by a local railroad committee, a countywide vote on the issue, held April 7, 1848, failed to authorize the subscription. Some voters objected because they believed that the money was a public gift to wealthy businessmen; others opposed the one-mill increase in property taxes to support the railroad bonds; and still others rejected the measure because there was no mention of railroads in the Bible.[3]

Sixteen years later, this enterprise received new life when the state granted a charter in 1864 for the Mineral Railroad Company. In 1867 the name was changed to the Columbus and Hocking Valley Railroad. (Much later the road would be acquired by the Chesapeake and Ohio system.) This time the Lancaster council acted on its own to issue $20,000 in 7 percent bonds to assist the railroad company in purchasing property for the right of way through the south end of town, provoking a public outcry that the council had acted without authorization, though there were no legal actions taken to overturn the decision.[4] The company sold most of its stock in Columbus and southeastern Ohio, with the largest purchasers of shares in Lancaster being Thomas Ewing and the attorney/entrepreneur John D. Martin, both of whom owned considerable amounts of land in the Hocking Valley. Other significant investors in Lancaster were George Mithoff, president of the Hocking Valley Bank; John R. Mumaugh, a real-estate agent and bank director; and attorney Hocking H. Hunter.[5]

Despite long opposition to public funding for the railroad, some 1,800 residents of Lancaster and the surrounding area made a celebratory excursion to Columbus on the new Hocking Valley line on June 14, 1869. It took them two hours to travel the thirty miles to the state capital, where members of the Lancaster City Council, railroad officers, and other dignitaries sat down to a midday dinner at the Neil House, compliments of Columbus's city council. Other excursionists had their meals, presumably at their own expense, at other hotels in Columbus. Afterwards, the visitors toured the statehouse and various points of interest, returning to the train station around 3:30 in the afternoon for the return trip to Lancaster, where they arrived at about 5:30.[6] Though the train might appear slow by late-twentieth-century standards, the trip from Lancaster to Columbus by canal had taken all day, and by stagecoach—depending upon the condition of the roads—it might take even longer. Thus, the railroad meant that Columbus was approximately six times closer to Lancaster, when measured in time traveled, than it had been before.

Lancastrians could also take the Hocking Valley route south to Athens after the line reached that destination in July 1870.[7] The road went through coal-mining country on its way south, and the railroad sponsored special excursions from Columbus and Lancaster down to the mines around Nelsonville. In the words of the *Gazette*, "Such an excursion is just the thing for this hot weather. The coal mines are full of novelty and interest, and the surrounding scenery [of the Hocking hills] is as beautiful as can be found anywhere."[8]

For those who chose to go farther afield, the direct train route to Columbus offered convenient connections to Cincinnati, Cleveland, Chicago, and New York City. The Lancaster traveler could leave town on the 7:15 A.M. train for Columbus and arrive in New York (via Cleveland) at noon the next day. Or the traveler might head west from Columbus and reach Chicago at 8:00 the next morning.[9] Journeys that had required weeks only a few decades before now took just a day or day and a half to complete. (Such a rapid means of transportation for both passengers and freight doomed the local canal network. By the end of the century the canals had ceased to function through Lancaster, and in 1898 even the reservoir at Cold Spring Hill was drained.)[10] All at once, the world was becoming much smaller—even for Lancaster.

The construction of the Hocking Valley Railroad also gave a real boost to Lancaster's economy, as noted by a reporter for the Columbus *News*, who had ridden the train through Lancaster in July 1869. "New buildings are going up on almost every street [in town]," he wrote.[11] This pace of growth also preoccupied city council, with many a meeting devoted to the opening of new streets, the accepting of plats for new additions, and the annexation of property. In May 1867, for example, the council authorized the extension of High Street to Fair Avenue (then known as Lundy's Lane), and in January 1869 it approved the laying out of Mulberry Street as far east as High Street.[12] Later in 1869 council voted to open Union Street between Broad and Columbus Streets.[13]

In addition to providing Lancaster and Fairfield County with rapid access to far-flung markets and giving a great boost to real estate in town, the Hocking Valley Railroad allowed for the opening of new and more abundant coal fields, such as the mines around New Straitsville in adjoining Perry County. Connecting these mines with the Hocking Valley Railroad was a spur line of some twelve miles, completed in 1871 between Logan (on the main line) and New Straitsville.[14] Lancaster's John D. Martin, who had invested in the rail line and who owned large amounts of property in the New Straitsville coal fields, made a considerable fortune there over the next few years.[15]

These new sources of fuel and transportation would shake off the "death-like lethargy"—in the words of the *Gazette* in March 1873—for which Lancaster had come to be known in the area of industrial enterprise.[16] Six years earlier, the *Gazette* had expressed similar hopes for enlivening the town through new enterprises: "What [Lancaster] now

Hocking Valley Manufacturing Company about 1900. Ebbert, *Lancaster and Fairfield County*, p. 178.

most needs is the addition of first class manufacturing establishments of various kinds. . . . This is what will bring accessions to our population, infuse fresh vigor into the old residents, make times lively, increase and diversify the current of cash and impart a powerful impulse to business of all kinds."[17] In fact, the coming of the Hocking Valley line did bring new manufacturing firms and did contribute to the expansion of preexisting establishments. Among these were the Lancaster Iron and Shovel Works, the J. H. Arney Foundry and Machine Shop, the Eagle Machine Works, the Hocking Valley Bridge Works, and Hocking Valley Manufacturing.[18]

Besides the new railroad, many coach and wagon roads out of Lancaster were upgraded during the latter half of the nineteenth century by private turnpike companies, which received the right to charge tolls in exchange for improving and maintaining the routes. A hinged board or gate, called a pike, barred access to the road until users paid the fee, at which time the toll collector would "turn the pike" and allow horse-drawn vehicles to pass through—a process that gave the name turnpike, or "pike" for short, to these improved roads. By the late 1880s there was a Cedar Hill

Horse and carriage coming through Shimp's Hill on the Baltimore Pike (later Ohio Route 158). Photo by Edson B. Olds Smith, 1880s. Author's collection.

Pike, a Baltimore Pike, an Amanda Pike, a Lithopolis Pike, and a Zanesville Pike.[19] Long after these turnpikes had been turned over to the county or the state and became public thoroughfares with numbered routes, some old-timers continued to refer to these roads as pikes—in some cases, well past the middle of the twentieth century.

In addition to better transportation systems, the arrival of a new energy supply in the late 1880s—namely, the discovery of natural gas under Lancaster—held promise for a great new wave of prosperity. The decision to drill was stimulated by the discovery of gas in Findlay, Ohio, in

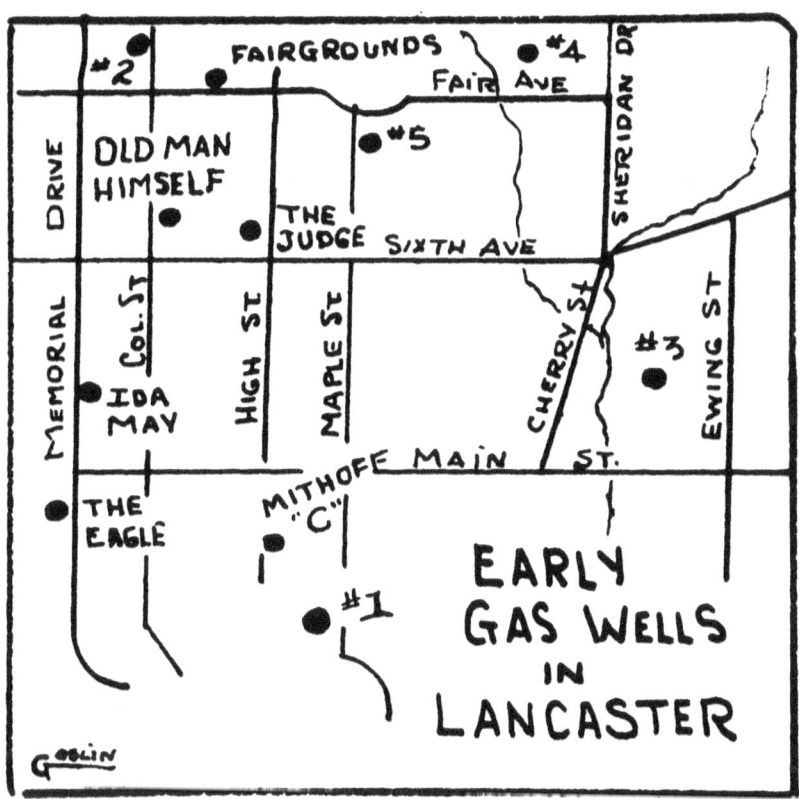

Locations of early gas wells in Lancaster. Map by Charles Goslin, *Crossroads and Fence Corners*, 1:63.

1884. Responding to reports from Findlay, a group of local men organized the Lancaster Natural Gas Company on December 2, 1885. On February 1, 1887, the company struck gas from a well near where South Maple Street intersects with the railroad tracks. This success led to the formation of two more companies in the spring of 1887, the Mount Pleasant Natural Gas Company and the East End Natural Gas Company. Both brought in wells in October of the same year. At the end of 1887 the three firms agreed to merge under the name Lancaster Gas and Oil Company, and gained authorization from mayor and council to lay pipes to supply homes and businesses throughout the town.[20]

The most dramatic event of the gas boom came on March 4, 1888, when a well drilled by Theodore Mithoff on his property, at the southeast corner of Columbus and Allen Streets, hit a huge pocket of gas, which at first spewed out eight million cubic feet a day and became the largest producing well in the world at that time.[21] Born in Germany, Mithoff (d. 1894) was already Victorian Lancaster's most successful entrepreneur, being the president and principal stockholder of both the Hocking Valley Manufacturing Company and the Hocking Valley Bank, as well as owner of the Mithoff House, a hotel built in 1866 on the southeast corner of Main and Columbus Streets.[22]

Mithoff dubbed his gusher "the Old Man Himself," an affectionate name that various friends and family members had called Mithoff for many years.[23] News of Mithoff's spectacular success spread all over town on the morning of March 4, and by two o'clock in the afternoon a parade had formed in the town square and proceeded to march out to the Mithoff home. At seven that evening a large crowd gathered at the well, which was then ignited (in order to reduce the pressure), sending a gigantic flame leaping hundreds of feet into the air. The whole town was illuminated: according to eyewitnesses, the light was so intense, one could read fine print a mile away from the site, and the glow was visible as far as Columbus, thirty miles to the northwest.[24] Present that evening was twenty-year-old Edson B. Olds Smith. Decades later, Smith recounted more than once his memories of excitement and terror during that evening at "the Old Man Himself."[25]

The Mithoff well came none too soon, because the Natural Gas Company was having trouble meeting a growing demand. The company offered the gasworks to the city, which obtained permission from the state legislature to place a $50,000 bond issue on the ballot in order to raise the necessary funds. There was considerable opposition to the bond issue, but the huge Mithoff well, which came in less than two months before the vote, seemed to assuage most doubts about the likely success of the municipal gas venture. The bond issue passed by a large margin on April 30, 1888, an event celebrated with bonfires, rockets, and Roman candles. Any lingering doubts about the municipal gasworks dissipated entirely when Lancaster paid off the last of the bonded indebtedness at the end of 1895. By 1900, the gasworks was showing a profit of $45,000 annually.[26]

Gas officials immediately drilled more wells, including one in the county fairgrounds. This well came in on July 4, 1889. The fair board quickly laid pipes around the racetrack and held the world's first horse race by gaslight. That same year, the gasworks erected a gas-illuminated

Letterhead of an invoice from the Becker Brewery in 1898. Kevin Rosier Collection.

arch near the railroad station at the foot of South Broad Street in order to advertise free fuel for any company that would locate in Lancaster.[27] Unfortunately, this profligate use of gas contributed to an early depletion of municipal wells, and by the mid-1890s the gasworks had to turn to a series of privately owned companies to augment its supplies, including the Logan Gas Company and later Ohio Fuel Gas. (Lancaster's gasworks would drill its last wells in the early 1950s and would sell its last field in 1972, though at the time of this writing, the municipal gasworks itself remained in business by purchasing supplies in bulk from private utilities.)[28]

Among the first enterprises responding to the free gas was Alten's Foundry, established in 1889 by Henry Alten (d. 1911), who was, like Theodore Mithoff, a German immigrant. Taking advantage of both the fuel and the need for special tools, Alten initially specialized in the making of oil and gas-drilling equipment.[29] Another was the Getz Shoe Factory, founded by Colonel Albert Getz (1844–1935), likewise an immigrant from Germany and a Civil War veteran.[30] Preexisting enterprises in Lancaster also turned to gas as a way of lowering their fuel costs. One of these was the brewery of Ernest Becker (1822–92), yet another German immigrant who operated his plant at the southwest corner of Forest Rose Avenue and Union Street. There he made his locally famous Bismark Beer, named for Germany's "iron chancellor," Otto von Bismark. In January 1888 Becker drilled his own well next to the brewery and named it "the Ida May."[31] Just as such ventures were popping up all over town, the worldwide economic depression that struck the United States in 1893 dampened economic

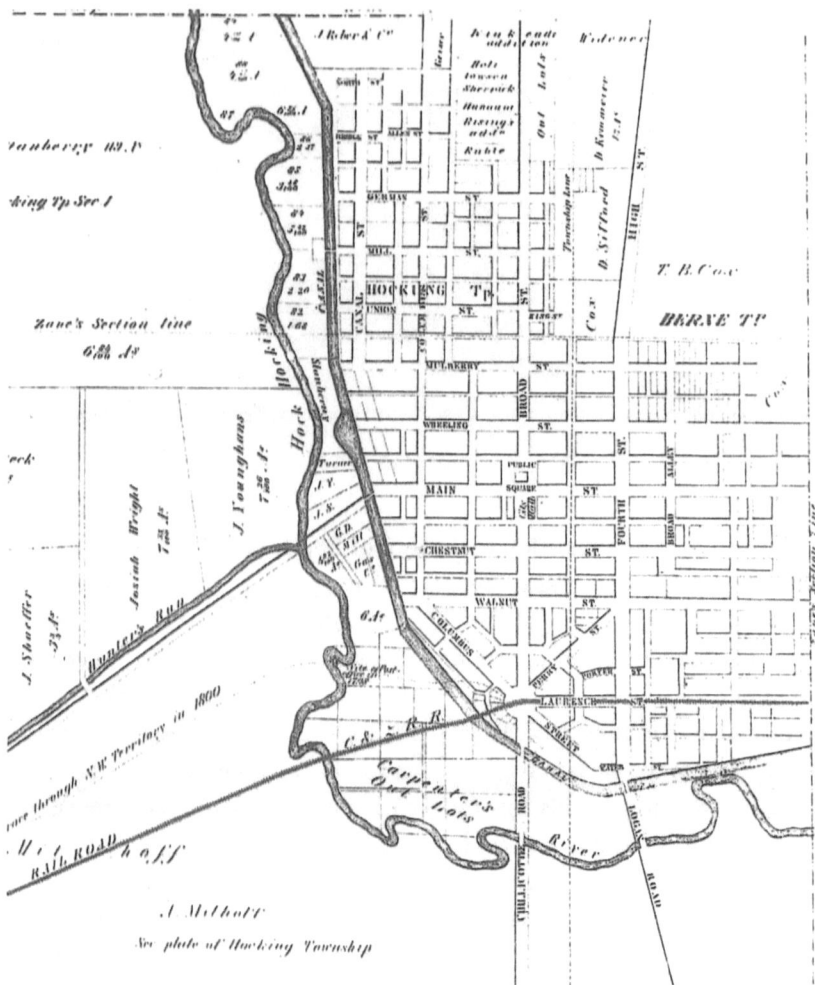

Lancaster in 1866, showing Hocking River, canal, and Cincinnati and Zanesville Railroad. The map appears to designate several dozen new building lots just east of Wheeling and High Streets. *Hannum's Atlas of Fairfield County*, p. 15, FCDL.

growth in Lancaster for the rest of the decade; thus, the full effects of the local gas boom would not be felt until early in the next century.

One indication of the relatively modest growth of Lancaster immediately after the gas discoveries was its change in population between 1890 and 1900, during which time it grew from 7,555 to 8,991, for an increase of 19 percent. This was more impressive than the numbers for the decade just before, when Lancaster went from 6,803 in 1880 to 7,555 in 1890, for a difference of 11 percent. But the increase in both decades pales in comparison to Lancaster's growth between 1870 and 1880, when the town's population rose from 4,725 to 6,803, for an impressive jump of 44 percent. It would appear that the effects of the Hocking Valley Railroad, completed in the late 1860s, had a more powerful effect on the local economy than the discovery of gas—at least initially.[32]

Population figures for towns and cities within a 45-mile radius would seem to bear out such a conclusion. Athens and Columbus, both located along the Hocking Valley Railroad, also experienced their largest spurts of growth for the latter third of the nineteenth century during the period from 1870 to 1880: Columbus grew by 65 percent (31,274 to 51,647), while Athens increased by 45 percent (1,696 to 2,457). Circleville, which was not on the Hocking Valley line, grew by only 12 percent (5,407 to 6,046) during the same decade. Chillicothe, also not on the Hocking Valley route, did better than Circleville, with a 23 percent increase (8,920 to 10,938); but this was just over half the rate of growth for Lancaster during the same period. Two cities within the 45-mile radius that were not on the Hocking Valley line but that did as well as or even better than Lancaster in population growth between 1870 and 1880 were Newark (6,698 to 9,600—or 43 percent) and Zanesville (10,011 to 18,113—or 80 percent). In both cases, these impressive rates during the 1870s may have been due to the cities' locations along the main line of the Pennsylvania Railroad through the center of Ohio.[33]

As might be expected, Lancaster's population growth led to another surge in the construction of new housing. In March 1871 the *Gazette* reported that thirty new dwellings were already under way and that several more were under consideration.[34] Two years later, in the spring of 1873, the *Gazette* carried an enthusiastic article about a housing development in the fields just east of Mulberry Hill, until recently under cultivation by the Lancaster Hop Company. (The company, which had acted as developers for the new housing, had moved its hop fields, essential for the brewing of local beer, several blocks to the east, in the vicinity of Mount Pleasant Avenue.)[35] As the *Gazette* reporter descended Mulberry Street one April morning in the carriage of hop company president T. W. Tallmadge, he found spread out before them "a village . . . of some fifteen or twenty houses, nestling upon the plateau below; which had sprung up there in a way not unlike those magical towns along the line of the Union

Modest late-nineteenth-century houses on the west side of North High Street between Sixth Avenue and Allen Street. These were part of a development by J. W. Hall, a resident of Cincinnati. Ebbert, *Lancaster and Fairfield County*, p. 200.

Pacific Railroad."[36] These modest houses, located just below the east slope of Mulberry Hill and largely intact at the end of the twentieth century, were built for "laboring men" and their families.[37]

A decade and a half later, in 1888, there were notices in the local newspapers for lots in what was being called the Maple Street Addition (probably the first block or two of North Maple, just above Main Street) and in the West Allen Street Addition. The lots on Maple Street sold for $50 to $150 and those on Allen, which were probably larger, from $200 to $300. Buyers had to put down one-third of the price, with the remainder to be made in two annual payments.[38] Responding to this expansion, the city council voted in June 1888 to annex Maple Street from Main Street to Fair Avenue.[39]

Assisting purchasers in buying lots and erecting homes by the 1870s and 1880s were several "building associations," forerunners of what would later be called building and loans, and still later savings and loans. The first

Unidentified Lancaster residence, but possibly a house in the Maple Street Addition of the 1880s. Tobias Studio Collection, Cartoon Research Library, OSU.

of these associations in Lancaster was established in 1867 by German immigrants who had brought the concept from their homeland, where building associations had originated.[40] Two such institutions have survived from the late nineteenth century to the time of this writing: the Fairfield Federal Savings and Loan (1895) and the Equitable Federal Savings and Loan (1899), the latter a branch of Bank One.[41]

As in earlier decades, these small housing developments were contiguous to older, built-up portions of Lancaster, resulting in an orderly and compact physical growth of the town. And in a time before zoning ordinances, grocery stores and other business opened in or near these new neighborhoods to cater to a population that still preferred, whenever possible, to travel on foot.

A few of the wealthier residents constructed large and beautiful resi-

# CHAPTER THREE

Smith residence on North Columbus Street, c. 1860, the childhood home of Edson B. Olds Smith. Photo by Edson B. Olds Smith, 1880s. Author's collection.

dences, often beyond the more built-up areas of town. The most impressive of these were in the so-called Italianate mode, a romantic style that flourished in England and the United States during the middle of the nineteenth century. Lancaster's best examples of the Italianate style are the Smith-Van Gundy, Brock-Utley, McNeil-Peters-Reynolds, and Creed-Tallmadge-Nusser Houses.[42] The last of these was begun, probably about 1840, by John Creed, longtime president of the Lancaster Ohio Bank. Darius Tallmadge, owner of the Tallmadge House hotel and numerous other enterprises in Lancaster, purchased the house upon Creed's death in 1847 and made it into a full-scale Tuscan villa, perhaps with the help of designs from the copybooks of architects Richard Upjohn and Andrew Jackson Downing. Located about a mile west of downtown Lancaster, just off Lincoln Avenue (U.S. Route 22), the house was surrounded in Tallmadge's day by beautiful gardens. A path leading up from the Hocking Canal that skirted the property was lined with ever-blooming roses, giving rise to the

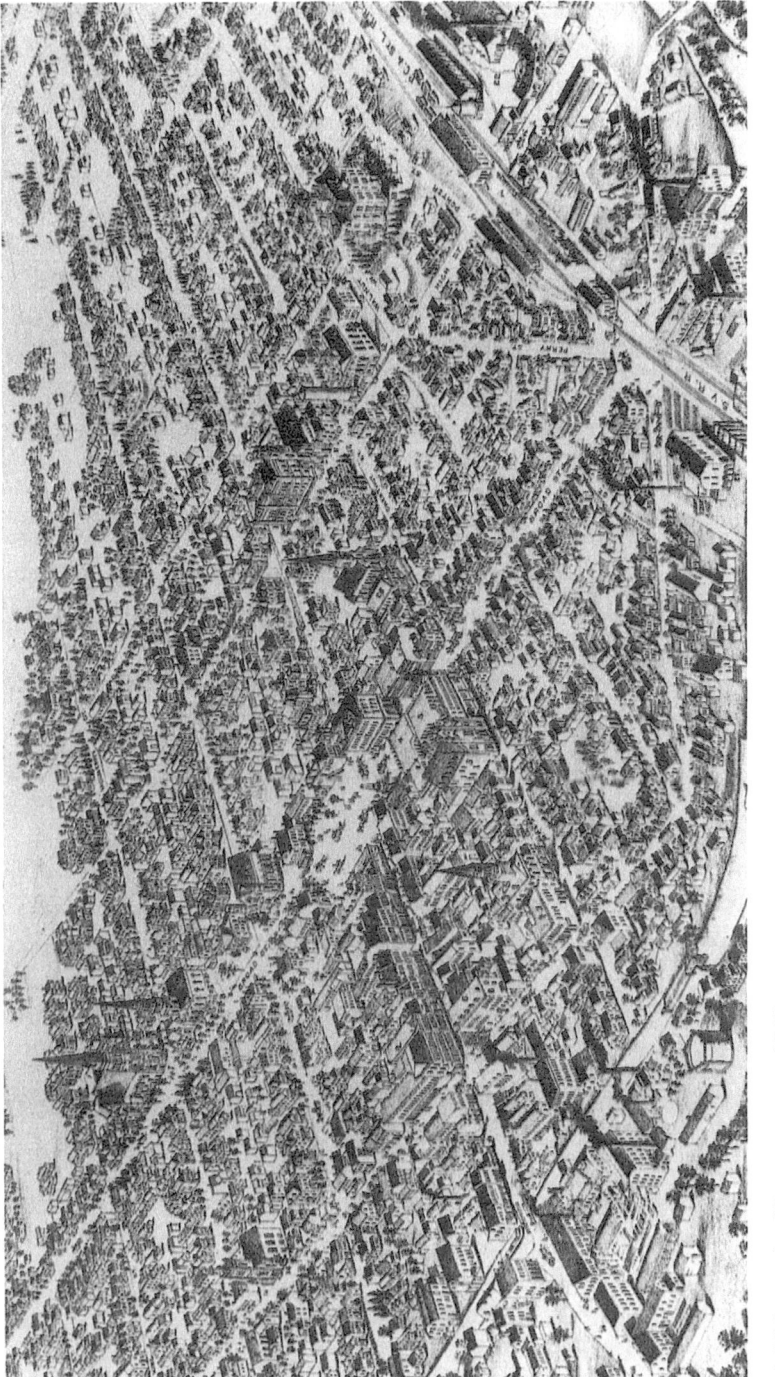

Aerial lithograph of Lancaster, 1885, FHA.

name *Rosebank* for the entire area around the Tallmadge residence.[43] Beginning in 1890, after several dozen acres of land were offered for sale as the Rosebank Addition, this area became the most coveted local address after Wheeling and Mulberry Hills in the center of town.[44]

With the exception of outlying Rosebank and a few other "country houses," residential development tended to follow the principal, intersecting roadways through town (Columbus, Broad, and Main Streets), as is evident from an 1885 aerial lithograph of Lancaster, doubtless adapted from a photograph taken out of a hot-air balloon.[45] At the time of this lithograph, residential development along the north-south Columbus Street and Broad Street corridors had crept as far north as Fair Avenue, while development along Main Street had reached as far east as Cherry Street. Residential development halted abruptly on the west at the canal and the Hocking River, and on the south where the river and canal turned eastward.

The 1885 lithograph shows that most of Lancaster's industries were along the canal banks. Here was what might be described as an industrial "crescent" that followed the canal bed as it turned north (or south—depending upon one's direction of approach), and ran more or less parallel to the Hocking River. A counting of smokestacks on the lithograph revealed some fifteen factories or mills, all modest-sized. Throughout the rest of the nineteenth century, this canal-river corridor along what were then the western and southern edges of the town would remain Lancaster's industrial district.

The lithograph also indicates that the downtown shopping district continued to occupy one block of Main Street between Columbus Street on the west and Broad Street on the east, though by 1885 there would seem to have been some continuation of shops along both Broad and Columbus Streets—from a quarter to a half block in either direction. Over the next several decades this extension of the downtown would push a block or two farther along each of these cross-streets and, in the process, would form what might be described as an H-shaped pattern.

As both the lithograph and photographs from the 1880s and 1890s demonstrate, many of the older, essentially Federal-style downtown buildings had been made over with Italianate and Mansard (or Second Empire) facades. In any case, the businesses operating on Main Street in 1890 consisted of four drugstores, one tailor shop, three shoe stores, two dry goods establishments, a jewelry store, six grocery stores, one bakery and ice cream parlor, a saddlery shop, four barbershops, three hardware stores,

Second (and present) Fairfield County Courthouse, 1872. Photo 1920s. Tobias Studio Collection, FCDL.

three banks, three bookstores, a chinaware shop, three hotels, two furniture stores, a harness shop, a Singer Sewing Machine agency, three millinery shops, a butcher shop, a café, two billiard parlors, a bowling alley, a funeral parlor, and seven saloons—the drinking establishments outnumbering any other single type of business in the downtown.[46]

If someone had returned to downtown Lancaster in 1890 after an absence of twenty years, he or she would have taken immediate notice of a greatly changed public square, an indication of the drive for improvement that had taken hold in Lancaster during its Victorian age. Instead of the old brick courthouse at its center, there was now an open space through which horses, carriages, and pedestrians could pass without having to go around the courthouse, which had been demolished in 1867 by order of the county commissioners. The old building, having been put up in 1807, was now too small for county government and was considered antiquated by the standards of the day, with only candlelight to pierce winter gloom or dark of night and coal stoves to ward off the cold.[47]

Accordingly, in the spring of 1867 the commissioners voted to erect a new courthouse one block east of the town square, on the southeast corner of Main and High Streets—at the very summit of Main Hill. The new structure was built and designed by Henry Orman (1804–1900), a skilled local cabinetmaker and builder who had no formal training as an architect.[48] Constructed of local sandstone, the new courthouse was ready for business in March 1872.[49] Rendered in what might be described as the Italian palazzo style, it featured a bracketed hipped roof, stone coins at each corner, large roundheaded windows, and a Palladian entrance on the Main Street side. More severe than fanciful in its overall appearance, the building nevertheless exuded some of the richness of the Italian Renaissance, a grand gesture in this Victorian age, which used art and architecture to make associations with other times and places. For Lancaster and Fairfield County, the new courthouse was a means of proclaiming their prosperity and good taste.[50]

Yet the courthouse site deprived the building of any visual prominence. Tucked into a corner lot and flanked by buildings on the other three corners, it could not be seen or admired at a distance like the earlier courthouse, or like many other courthouses in town squares that would continue to grace county seats in central Ohio, such as the Licking County Courthouse at Newark.[51] There is no surviving explanation as to why the commissioners did not simply build a new courthouse on Lancaster's town square, but it is probable that the relatively small size of the square rendered it unsuitable for the new and much larger courthouse. The siting of Lancaster's city hall, which had occupied the whole southeast portion of the square since its construction in 1859, also made a new courthouse in the square unfeasible.

If the new courthouse did not offer grand vistas, Lancaster's Main Street, which passed through the town square and then up the hill to the courthouse, was often an unattractive sight during the years just after the Civil War, as the *Gazette* frequently pointed out in its campaign for aesthetic improvement. One of the newspaper's worst complaints about the filthy and unsightly state of this thoroughfare appeared in the issue for September 17, 1874: "The gutters are choked up with watermelon rinds, waste paper and rubbish from stores, and the accumulation of filth and refuse generally. . . . The inevitable picture presented on Main Street, on these sweltering afternoons, has been a battalion of geese marching down the sidewalk with exasperating impunity, a cow or so, a half dozen dogs before every basement entrance, and every corner festooned with a brigade of swine."⁵² If nothing else, this description of livestock running the streets was a reminder that Lancaster remained very much a small town, where many residents kept cows, pigs, ducks, geese, and assorted other animals on their properties and where the open countryside was never more than a brief walk from the center of town. But for local boosters, who had imbibed the Victorian values of improvement and beautification, such conditions were intolerable.

Although Lancaster had many civic-minded boosters during its Victorian age, the most outstanding of these was A. "Andy" Bauman (1840–1919).⁵³ Like so many of the town's other Victorian entrepreneurs, Bauman was a German immigrant who had settled in Lancaster with his family in 1855 at the age of fifteen. By the 1880s Bauman was operating a bakery, grocery store, and ice cream parlor from a three-story Italianate building on the north side of Main Street (west of Center Alley), as well as a variety store across the street, known as Bauman's Fair.⁵⁴

Perhaps the most visible and longest-lasting Victorian improvement in Lancaster was one in which Bauman played a crucial role. This was the ornate fountain that stands in the town square more than a century after its dedication in 1890.

The idea of a fountain did not originate with Bauman, having been proposed to the city council in 1881 by banker Henry B. Peters, attorney and businessman John D. Martin, and several other leading residents. The old market house on the southwest corner of the public square was scheduled for demolition, and the men believed that the site would be ideal for a fountain. In response to the market house's demolition in late 1883, this same group of men donated $1,000 to Lancaster's treasury for such a fountain, but withdrew it in the spring of 1885 because of council's failure to move ahead on the project.⁵⁵

According to local tradition, it was Andy Bauman who reinvigorated the fountain movement. Bauman, it seems, had admired a small fountain in a restaurant that he visited during one of his many trips to New York City and had ordered a smaller version of this fountain for his bakery and ice-cream parlor back in Lancaster, later removing it from his downtown establishment to the front yard of his house at 152 West Wheeling Street (a site earlier occupied by the Lancaster Academy and later by the telephone company). After admiring this front-yard fountain, a group of local women decided about 1888 that their town square should have such a water feature, and formed themselves into the Fountain Committee. They

Andy Bauman's grocery store, bakery, and ice cream parlor at 149 West Main Street, as depicted on this 1901 letterhead. Kevin Rosier Collection.

asked Bauman to go to New York and purchase a suitable fountain for Lancaster, a commission that he happily carried out. Meanwhile, the women held a variety of fund-raising events. The fountain was installed on the southwest corner of the square, where the old market house had stood, and was formally dedicated on July 23, 1890. A parade, speeches, and fireworks marked the grand occasion.[56]

Soon joining the fountain on the list of civic improvements was a new city hall, erected directly across the street from the fountain and on the same lot as the 1859 structure. Lancaster's gas discoveries financed the building, with council approving a bond issue for $75,000 in early 1896, the bonds to be retired from profits of the municipal gasworks. Later that

Lancaster's public fountain, early 1890s, with horsecars in the intersection of Main and Broad Streets. The Effinger House is visible beyond and across Main Street from the fountain. The "temporary" wooden Civil War monument appears on the far right. Tobias Studio Collection, FCDL.

year, council engaged Henry Ives Cobb, a prominent Chicago architect of the day who had designed many public buildings throughout the Midwest. Completed in the spring of 1898, the city hall was best described as Richardson Romanesque in style, a popular design for public buildings in the 1880s and 1890s that takes its name from the late-nineteenth-century architect Henry Hobson Richardson. Though not as accomplished as a genuine Richardson design, Lancaster's city hall featured characteristically large Romanesque entrances and roundheaded windows throughout the building. It was built with sandstone from the Allegheny Quarry, just east of Lancaster. But the most notable aspect of the structure was the imposing clock tower and belfry rising from the west facade, or Broad Street side, of the building, its clock originally illuminated by four gas flames. Soon discolored by coal soot, Lancaster's new city hall exuded a medieval look that would appear somewhat forbidding to future generations. The major offices were on the ground floor of this Romanesque pile; the jail was in the basement; and a new public auditorium and public library chamber were on the second floor.[57]

One block south of the new city hall, standing just west of the corner

Lancaster's second (and present) city hall, completed 1898. Photo 1925. Tobias Studio Collection, FCDL.

The Opera House, 1883. Photo 1941, after the building had been taken over by the Vlerebome wholesale grocery firm. Leonard Hajost Collection.

Hotel Martens, on right, 1883. Photo 1910. Tobias Studio Collection, Cartoon Research Library, OSU.

of Broad and Chestnut Streets, was another proud monument to Lancaster's Victorian age, the Opera House.[58] Built in 1883 by John D. Martin, the two-story, red-brick building with Romanesque doors and windows was the scene of many plays and musical entertainments, most of them staged by itinerant troupes.[59] Next door, on the northwest corner of Broad and Chestnut, was the Martin Hotel, also erected in 1883. (In 1905 both the hotel and opera house were purchased by two brothers, McClelland and Charles Martens, and the Martin Hotel became the Hotel Martens, a confusing change given the similarity of the two names.) Best known for its ornate Mansard roof and Mansard tower above the corner entrance of the building, the hotel (demolished in 1971) boasted some seventy guest rooms and fine dining facilities.[60]

In order to provide a convenient means of reaching the downtown, a group of entrepreneurs, led by the redoubtable Andy Bauman, established a street railway system in 1889, which began operation the following year.[61] The first vehicles to ply this line were horsecars, pulled by two horses along rails set into the street and operated by the Lancaster Street

Passengers disembarking from horsecars at the Fairfield County Fair, early 1890s. Tobias Studio Collection, FCDL.

Railroad. In the summer of 1896 the horsecars gave way to electrified trolleys, under the aegis of what was now called the Lancaster Electric Railway, reputed to be the smallest trolley system in the United States at the time. The trolley routes were identical to those of the horsecars and used the same rails as the earlier cars, running east and west on Main Street and north and south on both Columbus and Broad Streets, the latter being parallel thoroughfares that were a wide block apart. The cars were apparently the same, too, having been refitted with electric motors. Trolley fare was five cents, but riders could economize by purchasing thirty-three tokens for a dollar.[62]

Because the horsecars and the electric trolleys that replaced them converged on Lancaster's downtown, they made this commercial district even more vital as a center of social, economic, and civic life. In this sense their effect was very different from the automotive revolution several decades later, which would disperse such activities over a far wider area and eventually threaten to destroy the downtown itself. The horsecars and trolleys strengthened the pattern of residential development along the principal corridors of Main, Broad, and Columbus Streets and the various side streets connecting to them. These vehicles also provided a convenient link to the railroad station in the South End. And in 1900, passengers could board trains from the handsome new Union Station.[63]

Lancaster's Union Station, opened in 1900. Leonard Hajost Collection.

Besides the street railway, there were other signs of improvement during this Victorian age. Among them was Lancaster's first public, or "free," library, established by a vote of council in 1878. The library found quarters on the second floor of two different commercial buildings downtown before moving, in 1889, to the city hall. In 1898 the library occupied much of the second floor of the new city hall, where it would remain for more than eight decades.[64]

Victorian Lancaster also saw the construction of three new public elementary schools, at a time when prominent and well-appointed structures were being employed throughout the United States to announce a town's prosperity and the permanence of its institutions during a time of constant change. In 1873 the Lancaster school board erected a new North School at the northeast corner of Broad and Allen Streets. Two years later, in 1875, the board built a new South School at Walnut and Maple Streets. The last educational structure to go up during this period was a new East School, situated along the present Madison Avenue between Mulberry and Wheeling Streets. Both the North and South Schools had elaborate Man-

South School, erected 1875. Photo 1930, shortly before the school's demolition. Tobias Studio Collection, FCDL.

sard cupolas rising from the center of their hipped roofs. East School, only two stories in height, had a small square cupola that was somewhat Colonial in flavor.[65]

Lancaster's public high school, which first opened in 1849, did not enjoy its own building but operated from two different elementary schools. (Relatively low enrollments, at a time when most youngsters attended school only through the eighth grade, made the building of a separate high school impractical, and doubtless unacceptable to local taxpayers.) The first home of Lancaster High School had been the second floor of the North elementary, which in 1849 stood on the northeast corner of Broad and Mulberry Streets, later the location of St. Peter's Lutheran Church. When North School moved to Broad and Allen Streets in 1851, the

CHAPTER THREE

96

The former black elementary school, erected in 1875 on the North School grounds and demolished in 1968. For several decades in the twentieth century, this structure was used as a locker room for the high school football teams, who played on adjoining North Field (seen in the background). Photo 1968. Courtesy Mrs. Perrin Hazelton.

high school filled its third floor and continued to occupy a similar part of the subsequent North School building erected on the same property in 1873. Two years later, when a new South School opened, the high school relocated there. High school graduation rates grew slowly but steadily during the Victorian period, from just 3 in 1863, to 9 in 1873, to 22 in 1893.[66]

As was typical in most communities across America, at a time before movies, radio, or television, high school graduations were occasions for civic entertainment as well as a chance to show off the work of the schools. In 1867 graduation ceremonies took place in the public auditorium before a large crowd, with the reading of literary works by the graduates, a student oration, and vocal music.[67] By 1889 there were enough high school graduates to launch an alumni association, with an annual reunion and banquet.[68] By then the alumni of the Lancaster school system had already begun the habit of looking back nostalgically on their school days at a time when middle-class Americans, who could afford to forgo their children's labor in a town setting, were beginning to see childhood as a time of special innocence and joy. Thus, when the North School building of 1851 was about to fall to a wrecking crew in the late summer of 1878, a writer for the *Gazette* offered readers a feast of memories:

> We took a look through the old educational temple . . . , and viewed over the scenes of many a stirring event of our boyhood. . . . With tears and sighs we gazed upon our old seat, where we used to sit . . . , with one eye on the well attrited page, and the other askant upon the teacher, a glimpse of whose classical back was the signal for a soggy paper wad to plaster itself against the ceiling, blackboard, or the back of some girl's head![69]

As the memory of landing spitballs on a schoolgirl's head suggests, Lancaster's public schools were coeducational from the beginning.

Until the late 1880s, however, there was racial segregation in the public system, with African American students attending a small brick schoolhouse, erected in 1875 (demolished 1968) and located on the southeast side of the North School property at Broad and Allen Streets.[70] African Americans had been admitted to the town's one high school in 1878. Integration of the elementary schools probably occurred because of Ohio's repeal, in 1887, of an 1848 law that had required separate schools for blacks who numbered more than twenty in a given community.[71] Though there is no reason to believe that coeducation and racial integration reflected a widespread local belief in gender and racial equality, Lancaster's youth in the late Victorian period did escape the sorts of educational divisions that typified schools on the East Coast, where there were continuing prejudices against public education as well as coeducation, or in the South, where legally mandated racial segregation would prevail for many decades more.

The only children in Lancaster who did not participate in the public experience were those from Roman Catholic families who attended their own parish school. Lancaster's St. Mary parish had opened an elementary school in 1841 on the third floor of its church building, then at the northeast corner of High and Chestnut Streets. When a new St. Mary Church was finished next door in 1864, the old building was taken over completely by the school, with convent rooms for the Dominican sisters who taught there. In 1891 the parish added a high school department to its curriculum.[72]

Local Catholics had decided to create their own school system because religion was not taught systematically in the public schools and because any sort of religious observance in the public schools, as in opening prayers or Bible readings, was likely to be Protestant in form and substance. Yet public school graduates for generations to come would use the phrase "He/she went to St. Mary's" as a way of suggesting that the individual in question had somehow missed out on an important vehicle of community membership and identity—not understanding that many Catholics looked upon public education as an extension of the Protestant worldview. In the opinion of Catholic school alumni, it was the public school children who had missed out—on the close-knit atmosphere of their small parochial school.

If public school alumni felt vaguely sorry for Catholics (and the Catholics for the public school students) who had not participated in their common experience, both groups could agree on feeling themselves lucky not to have grown up at the Fairfield County Orphans Home (later known as the Children's Home). Established in 1882 and built in 1885, the home was located east of town along what became U.S. Route 22. As such, the home was another example of the Victorian age's emphasis upon building institutions to bring rationality and order to fulfill a civic responsibility or need.[73] The pride that Lancastrians felt toward these physical manifestations of local solicitude is evident in the large number of local newspaper articles about such institutions and in the great amount of space devoted to them in an account of the community published under the title *Lancaster and Fairfield County*, issued by the Lancaster Board of Trade and City Council in 1901.

One institution that had received and would continue to receive extensive newspaper coverage was the state reform school for boys, established in 1857 some six miles south of Lancaster. At first known as the State Farm, the name was changed in 1885 to the Boys' Industrial School (or BIS, as most people called it), and much later to the Fairfield School for Boys (or FSB).[74] For over a century this institution would provide jobs for local residents and remain a familiar topic of conversation and speculation, especially when there were warnings of State Farm/BIS boys who had run

Tree-lined walkway and cottages at the Boys' Industrial School (BIS). Photo c. 1930. Tobias Studio Collection, FCDL.

away and might be lurking about Lancaster, or when parents and teachers warned darkly that certain boys in town might end up at the reform school if they did not settle down and behave themselves.

The State Farm also provided entertainment for townsfolk when the boys came up to Lancaster to put on programs of various sorts. As early as September 1866, for example, the boys gave a series of presentations in the old city hall, typically consisting of "singing, recitations, declamations, [and] dialogues," with admission charges going to raise money for books, band instruments, and other equipment.[75]

If young Lancaster boys were sometimes frightened at the thought of ever landing in the nearby reform school, adults were horrified at the prospect that they might end up at the county infirmary, also known in common parlance as the "poorhouse," a term that lasted well into the twentieth century. The first infirmary, consisting of modest wooden build-

Fairfield County Infirmary. Photo c. 1930. Tobias Studio Collection, FCDL.

ings, was erected north of Lancaster in 1828 on the present State Route 37. These buildings gave way to a two-and-a-half-story brick structure in 1840, which was enlarged through subsequent additions. Surrounding the infirmary was a working farm, where more able-bodied residents helped to provide food for the institution.[76]

Besides caring for the old and infirm, the community acted in 1882 to create a beautiful site for the final resting place of its citizens, a new cemetery that became one of the most enduring improvements of the age.[77] Discussions about a new town cemetery had surfaced as early as 1875, doubtless in response to the recent growth in population. City council considered several sites before settling on what became the Forest Rose Cemetery, in the far north end of Lancaster.[78]

Although the older Elmwood Cemetery in the South End would continue to be used for burials, the new Forest Rose Cemetery, named after the local frontier heroine of the same name, was much larger and far more dramatic in layout. In fact, the creation of Lancaster's Forest Rose Cemetery as a beautifully landscaped park for the dead was part of a larger cemetery movement in the United States, which originated in such spectacular creations as Mount Auburn in Boston (1831), Laurel Hill in Philadelphia (1836), and Spring Grove in Cincinnati (1845). Such cemeteries were a

Forest Rose Cemetery. Photo by author, 1997.

new phenomenon in the United States, and in the western world, arising from romantic conceptions of a connection between earthly beauty and the divine.

Beautifully landscaped cemeteries, with elaborately carved monuments and mausoleums, also permitted the families of departed loved ones to demonstrate their continued devotion to deceased members, who remained as part of the family in a "family lot" that survivors could tend and embellish as an extension of their own homes. These new attitudes reflected not only the continuing romanticism of the Victorian age but also the growing material wealth of late-nineteenth-century Americans and a sentimental emphasis upon family life. Wealthier and more prominent families could even proclaim their importance with large monuments or mausoleums in the local cemetery, at the same time that they demonstrated their loyalty and devotion to departed members by making frequent visits to the burial ground. Often, such visits took the form of a Sunday afternoon stroll to the family plot, with additional stops at the graves of other families and friends. Though such attitudes toward death and burial have been widely accepted for over a century, earlier Americans would have viewed a beautifully landscaped cemetery with elaborate monuments as wasteful, vain, and indicative of a lack of faith in eternal life.[79]

Forest Rose Cemetery, Lancaster's contribution to the romantic cemetery movement, had originally been a burial ground for the German Lutheran and English Lutheran Churches, which had separate but nearly adjoining grounds on the future Forest Rose site. In 1882 the two churches donated their graveyards to the city of Lancaster, which appointed a board of trustees to acquire additional land and to oversee the design of Forest Rose Cemetery.

The cemetery's location at what was then the far north end of town, at the point where Columbus Street curved around a steep hillside, was an excellent choice for the new burial ground. At the top of the hill were steep sandstone cliffs, already known to residents as Flat Rocks. From various parts of the cemetery one could gaze down upon Lancaster, or across to the hills and dramatic rock formations that framed the town. In picturesque prose that typified the Victorian era, a writer for the *Gazette* described the vista from Forest Rose Cemetery on a sunny afternoon in September of 1882, the year that the expanded grounds opened as a public facility:

> From no point around this beautiful [town] is a more captivating, a broader, fuller, sweeter scene presented than from the main drive over the face of this hill in Forest Rose Cemetery.... It was a ravishing picture, one sufficient to elicit expressions of surprise and rapture.... To the southeast the grim old brow of Mt. Pleasant showed itself above the acclivity at our left, a glistening mass of yellow rock.... Spread out like the huts of some gigantic aviary, lay the [town], which can be seen in almost its entirety, and on beyond, in the blue distance, like a dark belt of beautiful embroidery, sweep around the Hocking Hills.[80]

Still other public improvements of the era emphasized the health and safety of Lancaster residents. Of great importance among these was a municipal waterworks. During the early decades, residents had obtained their water from abundant springs in the area or from private cisterns and wells. In 1877 the council established the first municipal waterworks, which seemed to mean little more than pumping water out of the old canal through mains along the principal streets of town. This water apparently was not filtered, and certainly was not chlorinated, and it is unclear whether the supply was used for drinking purposes. A stand pipe, or water

Engine House 1, erected in 1899. Photo 1910. Tobias Studio Collection, FCDL.

tower, was erected at the southeast corner of Chestnut and High Streets (one of the highest points in Lancaster) to provide sufficient pressure. Perhaps because of pollution, the Lancaster waterworks abandoned the canal as a source in 1881 and began drilling wells into a large underground aquifer between the canal bed and the Hocking River just west of the intersection of Wheeling Street and Memorial Drive, a well site that remains active at the time of this writing. Filtration of water also began in 1881, and in 1898 the water department built a large reservoir on a hill north of town, known thereafter as Waterworks Hill.[81]

With a modern waterworks that could supply abundant pressure for the entire town, Lancaster organized its first professional fire department in 1893. Six years later, in 1899, it erected a new engine house, located just beyond High Street on the south side of Chestnut Street. Constructed of red brick, its most notable feature was an attractive Romanesque bell tower. Like so many other structures built during Lancaster's Victorian age, this engine house has continued to serve residents throughout the twentieth century.[82]

Besides pointing with pride to their public buildings, Lancastrians in the latter third of the nineteenth century liked to emphasize the growing

St. Peter's Lutheran Church, built 1875–1882. Photo c. 1920s. Tobias Studio Collection, FCDL.

A summer religious service at the Methodist campground, early twentieth century. Tobias Studio Collection, Cartoon Research Library, OSU.

number of handsome churches that punctuated the skyline near the center of town. By the end of the Victorian period, these were First Presbyterian, St. John's Episcopal, St. Mary Roman Catholic, First Methodist, African Methodist Episcopal, St. Peter's Lutheran, English Lutheran, Emanuel Lutheran, Trinity Evangelical, Grace Reformed, United Brethren, and First Church of Christ Scientist. The most impressive of these were the new Gothic-style edifices put up by St. Mary Catholic in 1864, St. Peter's Lutheran in 1882, and First Presbyterian (actually Gothic-Romanesque) in 1892. The new St. Peter's resembled a small cathedral, with life-sized wooden statues of Christ and the four evangelists in the chancel.[83] These ecclesiastical structures were part of a continuing nineteenth-century revival of Gothic forms, which many saw as the truest architectural associations with Christianity. Such churches, with their stained-glass windows and soaring towers, were calculated to symbolize the triumph of Christian faith at the same time that they were intended to reflect the given denomination's prosperity and to attract additional members—yet another example of the Victorians' unabashed mixture of sentiment and materialism.[84]

Revivalism continued to be an important part of religious life in Lancaster during the Victorian age, a time when emotional approaches to religious subjects were very much in vogue throughout the western world. Camp meetings, which combined fiery warnings about the dangers of hell with the transcendental appeal of worshiping in a natural setting, were annual summer events in Lancaster and Fairfield County and received generous coverage in the press.[85] Local churches, and especially the Methodists, also held indoor revivals during the winter months. In March 1882, for instance, the *Gazette* commented on the series of meetings at the Methodist Church, where "nightly is the altar filled with penitents who seek the pardon of sin, and a savior's love."[86]

The Methodists established a campground in 1877 on West Fair Avenue. On the grounds were a hotel, auditorium, and individual cottages. A number of famous speakers would appear at the Lancaster campground over the decades, including William Jennings Bryan and Billy Sunday. Besides preaching the gospel, speakers at the campground often denounced the evils of alcohol and urged the faithful to "take the pledge" of total abstinence.[87]

Back in Lancaster, some of the religious-minded also attacked "Demon Rum." Alcoholic beverages had been consumed in Lancaster and Fairfield County from the first days of settlement in the form of whiskey, beer, and wine.[88] Indeed, the brewing of beer was a major enterprise in Lancaster as early as the 1840s, initially led by Younghans and Sons and later by the Becker Brewery. Several individuals, including John S. Snider from the 1860s through the 1880s, were successful in growing grapes and making wine for a small commercial market.[89]

Although most residents then and now used these products responsibly, abuse of alcohol had plagued the town from the start. As early as 1801, anyone found in a state of public intoxication was ordered, under a resolution made by a group of prominent citizens, to dig a stump from the main street or, upon refusal to do so, suffer a whipping.[90] According to Lancaster's first historian, George Sanderson, this vigilante action was effective, at least for the time being.[91] The ease with which residents could purchase and consume alcohol was also a problem during the early decades of the nineteenth century, because anyone could sell alcohol from his place of business. To regulate this practice the village council passed, in

1834, an ordinance that required the purveyors of alcohol to purchase a license for the then substantial sum of $25. The ordinance subjected sellers of alcoholic beverages to fines up to $100 if they allowed gambling or drunken and disorderly conduct on their premises.[92] In 1865 the city council required all drinking establishments to close at 11:00 P.M., and in 1874 the council forbade the serving of alcohol in pool halls and billiard rooms.[93] Though regulation and licensing may have helped somewhat to mitigate the problem, public drunkenness remained serious enough that a council ordinance in 1861 established a chain gang as a punishment for drunk and disorderly offenders.[94]

Organized temperance groups appeared in response to the problem of alcohol abuse as early as 1842, when a group of local men led by Dr. M. Z. Kreider and banker John M. Creed organized what would become a chapter of the Washington Temperance Society. In the summer of 1853, Lancaster hosted a mass temperance meeting that drew delegates from the other thirty-one states then in the union, with numerous speeches and processions.[95] Like other efforts to curb alcohol abuse in town, this early temperance movement had little long-term effect, for in 1874, at a time when Lancaster counted about 6,000 inhabitants, there were some thirty-three establishments selling alcoholic beverages—from saloons and billiard halls to hotels and grocery stores.[96]

Inspired by the foundation of the Women's Christian Temperance Union (WCTU) in Hillsboro, Ohio, in early 1874, churchgoing women in Lancaster set out to attack alcohol through an onslaught against the purveyors of drink. On March 9, 1874, a group of these women gathered at the First Presbyterian Church on North Broad Street. While several dozen remained at the church to pray, a line of forty to fifty women marched down Broad Street to Main and began entering hotels and saloons, where they sang and prayed and asked proprietors to sign pledges to close down their establishments, continuing their action for several days. Some proprietors refused to admit the women and in some places they received rude treatment from the patrons. Fearing for their livelihoods, the saloon keepers and other purveyors assembled after the first day of protests and promised to impose certain restrictions on themselves, such as closing at 11:00 each evening, agreeing to remain closed all day Sunday, and refusing to sell alcohol to minors. While causing a local sensation, the ladies' crusade did little to rid Lancaster of drunkenness and alcoholism, and in retrospect their efforts seem quite naive. Yet their crusade was sincerely

Interior of Lancaster's Masonic Temple, 1908. Tobias Studio Collection, Cartoon Research Library, OSU.

motivated by the belief that drink was sinful and that their own moral witness could make a difference, attitudes that were integral to the Victorian belief in the possibilities of moral improvement and the middle-class emphasis on hard work, sobriety, and self-restraint.[97] Far more sensible to later generations was the establishment in 1891 of a "sanitarium" to treat alcoholics, located at the corner of East Chestnut and Maple Streets, and under the direction of Dr. George M. Boerstler.[98]

Although some residents found the ladies' crusade against alcohol unseemly and even "unladylike," such moral campaigns on the part of women were increasingly acceptable as Victorian Americans looked upon "the fairer sex" as the most important moral influence in the home. For in towns and cities, where men were going out of the house to work each day (as opposed to farm families, where men and women were likely to work in close proximity to each other), women were increasingly in charge of the household, and especially the nurturing and disciplining of

Farmers exhibiting prize cattle at the Fairfield County Fair, early twentieth century. Tobias Studio Collection, Cartoon Research Library, OSU.

children. If alcohol threatened the home—and the welfare of children—a women's crusade against drink could be justified as an extension of Christian motherhood.[99]

In line with this kind of thinking about gender roles, Lancaster women began to engage in a variety of organized charitable activities during the Victorian period. These included the Ladies' Benevolent Society, which in January 1876 put on a benefit concert in the public auditorium, with the proceeds going to "poor relief," and the somewhat similar Women's Relief Corps in the mid-1890s.[100] There was also a Social Reading Club in the 1870s, made up of more well-to-do women who came together to discuss books and to present literary insights, and a kindred group during the 1890s known simply as the Lancaster Literary.[101]

It is no coincidence that middle-class Victorian men created a vigorous life of all-male lodges and clubs at a time when women were increasingly the center of family life, and when the interests and inclinations of the two

Fairgoers admire apples and other fruits on display, early twentieth century. Tobias Studio Collection, Cartoon Research Library, OSU.

sexes were thought to be very different.[102] Such clubs also provided important contacts for businessmen and professionals, who could use lodge connections to economic advantage. By 1900 Lancaster men supported a host of lodges, including the Masons, the International Order of Odd Fellows, the Knights of Pythias, and the Ben Butterfield post of the Grand Army of the Republic (GAR).[103] Beyond the lodges themselves, more educated sets of local men established a series of literary clubs during the latter decades of the nineteenth century that were much like earlier efforts along these same lines.[104] For men of military inclinations, there was a local militia company known as the Sherman Light Guards, later the Mount Pleasant Guards.[105] And for those who enjoyed owning and shooting firearms, there was the Lancaster Gun Club, which sponsored an annual shooting contest. The winner of the eighteenth such event, held in July 1892, was Edson B. Olds Smith.[106]

Beyond the organizations and clubs themselves, Lancastrians could enjoy an almost constant round of entertainments during the Victorian age. There were public lectures, debates, band concerts, choirs, Swiss bell ringers, Indians in native costume, jugglers, ventriloquists, magicians, and numerous theater performances, both amateur and professional. Most of these took place in the public auditorium (both the old and the new), or in the Opera House on Chestnut Street.[107] Circuses continued to come to town, as on June 27, 1872, when P. T. Barnum's "Greatest Show on Earth" arrived to thrill residents of all ages.[108] In October 1866 a large crowd gathered to see a man walk a tightrope stretched between two buildings across Main Street, pushing a wheelbarrow before him while blindfolded and with his feet tied in a cloth sack.[109] There were also a number of hot-air balloon ascents, the earliest of them in June of 1852. In the late 1890s there were several parachute jumps from balloons. One "aeronaut," who ascended from the center of the fairground's racetrack, barely escaped serious injury when his "chute" came down in a treetop on the west slope of Mount Pleasant.[110]

Every October there was the Fairfield County Fair. In 1870 the Fairfield County Agricultural Society purchased an additional 6.5 acres on the north side of the fairgrounds for a new half-mile racetrack. Four years later the society erected a large exhibition hall for horticultural displays as well as for handcrafts and the finer arts.[111] There were night horse races by gaslight in 1889 and 1890, and in 1883 the fair managers erected an amphitheater for women only, who could sit and watch the races without fear of being exposed to cigar smoke, profanity, or other crude habits of men folk.[112]

Besides annual events such as the fair, individuals and small groups enjoyed fishing in the old reservoir, as well as in the Hocking River and various creeks. And for some, rat hunts were a sport as well as an attack on a real menace to local health. There was also a roller skating rink in town as early as 1871, the location of which is uncertain, where skating contests provided another form of entertainment for participants and spectators alike. At the end of the century, camping out in tents, at various points in the countryside around Lancaster, became all the rage.[113] A nationwide bicycle craze swept Lancaster in the 1890s, made possible in part by the modern-style vehicle with a low frame, pneumatic tires, and front and back wheels of equal size. Cycling groups pedaled their way down streets and over country roads in weekend rallies. In August 1898 several hundred cyclists put on a colorful parade through downtown Lancaster.[114] For the less genteel, there were bare-knuckled prize fights, such as the one that

The Hillside Hotel, early twentieth century. Tobias Studio Collection, Cartoon Research Library, OSU.

took place in a Main Street saloon in 1887. There was no referee, and the men fought until one of them gave up.[115]

There is no record of just who participated in such entertainments and events, but a number of them were clearly limited to middle- and upper-class audiences. Poorer residents could not afford the cost of a bicycle or the price of admission to the circus or various entertainments at the Opera House. Rat hunting, fishing, or swimming in rivers and creeks were free and presumably open to all, regardless of wealth or social standing.

The Smith family at Christmas Rocks, south of Lancaster. Photo by Edson B. Olds Smith, 1880s. Author's collection.

Once electric trolleys arrived, undoubtedly the most exciting improvement of the era, imaginative residents used them for a variety of entertainments. In order to celebrate their twenty-ninth wedding anniversary, William Goetz and Caroline Bauman Goetz (the German-born owners of the Hillside Hotel on Main Hill and known to everyone as Billy and Callie) loaded four cars with their friends and treated them to a "trolley concert," with a chorus and musicians seated in one of the cars.[116] On another occa-

The soda fountain at Reed and Walters Drug Store, early twentieth century. Tobias Studio Collection, Cartoon Research Library, OSU.

sion the very popular Goetzes served a progressive dinner on the trolleys to some sixty guests, with a subsequent course brought out from the Hillside Hotel with every round trip.[117]

The Hillside Hotel (demolished in 1959) was located about halfway up Main Hill on the south side of the street and was itself a favorite center of entertainment. Besides being a residential hotel with a capacity for forty boarders, the establishment became a popular site for wedding receptions and a variety of social entertainments. The Goetzes themselves provided music for these events, with Billy playing a "midget piano" and Callie singing. It was doubtless this small instrument, with Billy at the keyboard, that went into one of the cars for the trolley serenade. Billy also happily hoisted the piano into a wagon and carted it off to some rural grove—often Jacob's Ladder, south of town—where he played for picnickers.[118]

For the less strenuous, there might be a stroll downtown to an ice cream parlor or soda fountain, or to an appointment to have one's picture

A tough-looking baseball team in motley outfits, c. 1890s. Tobias Studio Collection, FCDL.

taken on Main Street at a succession of studios that appeared just after the Civil War—again, for those who could afford it.[119] And like men and women throughout the country, residents read and gossiped about the latest incidents of vice and crime as revealed in the local newspapers—of theft, poultry raids, infanticide, suicide, murder, illegal prize fighting, cock fights, street brawls, and public drunkenness, however infrequent they were by big-city standards.[120]

The most sensational crime of the period was a fatal shooting on Main Street in November 1881. Herman Peter, the owner of a gun shop, fired three shots into Philip Betz as Betz passed by his establishment and allegedly called Peter's wife and daughter insulting names. The shooting was the culmination of several years of quarreling between the two men, who had once been friends.[121]

Nor were the corridors of local government immune from crime. In 1889 two clerks at city hall were charged with embezzling $4,200. After being indicted by a county grand jury, they confessed to the wrongdoing and agreed to repay the money, leading the prosecutor to drop the charges against them.[122]

Far less serious were complaints brought before city council in 1884 against a police officer, Gotlieb Jurgensmier, for frequenting saloons while "on the beat."[123] "Jergy," as everyone knew the officer, was apparently forgiven, since he remained on the force for many years thereafter. Jergy had the reputation as a tough cop, and all anyone had to do was yell "Here comes Jergy" in order to disperse a group of roughneck boys.[124] Likewise on the mild side—but certainly scandalous—was a newspaper report in 1895 that a dozen or so high school girls, many of them from the best families in Lancaster, were caught smoking cigarettes on the school grounds.[125]

Numerous social activities reflected the Victorian era's increase in leisure time and disposable income, but none so much as "baseball fever," which gripped Lancaster as early as May 30, 1867, when the *Gazette* began to carry the weekly scores of local teams.[126] That same year the *Gazette* informed readers that they could purchase the latest equipment—"balls, bats, and all the paraphernalia of the great national game"—at the Sifford and Son Drug Store.[127] The 1890s even saw the establishment in Lancaster of a "female baseball club" that, according to press reports, played before large crowds. Notions about proper activities for women were beginning to change at century's end.[128]

Social events in the lives of prominent Lancastrians often received extensive coverage in the local newspapers. One colorful example was an account of the wedding, on July 26, 1876, of Mary Eleanor Ewing to Edward Marion Brown. Mary Eleanor was the granddaughter of the late Thomas Ewing and the daughter of Mr. and Mrs. Philemon B. Ewing. The *Gazette* described the wedding at St. Mary Roman Catholic Church and the reception that followed in great detail:

> The bride wore a white satin dress, enframed with laced corsage and tulle. . . . The afternoon was taken up with the reception at the residence of the bride's parents, on the corner of High and Wheeling streets [known to later generations as the 1834 Stanbery-Rising House], whose commodious apartments . . . were filled with richly and elegantly attired ladies and gentlemen. . . . Throughout the house there was one continued buzz of delighted and happy voices, drowned only in bursts of laughter or music and song from the parlors.[129]

The article went on to list the most impressive wedding gifts and the names of their donors. Among the gifts mentioned in the *Gazette* were a set of diamond earrings, silver creamer and sugar bowls, a silver fruit dish, a frosted silver coffee urn, one dozen gold spoons, a Japanese writing desk inlaid with mother of pearl, an oil painting, a silver fruit basket, and a bronze clock.[130] Though such a public accounting of gifts might appear unseemly and even crass to later generations, it was quite acceptable among Victorians, who put much store in recording the various physical manifestations of their good fortune.

The funerals of well-to-do or famous residents of Lancaster also received extensive newspaper coverage, as was the case upon the death of Thomas Ewing, who died on October 26, 1871, some five years before his granddaughter's elaborate wedding. In honor of Ewing, the city council asked that all businesses in town close between 11:00 A.M. and 1:00 P.M. on the day of the funeral.[131]

The obituary in the *Gazette* began with a reference to the dreadful suffering Ewing had endured "with heroic fortitude" during the last days of his life, attended by his daughter, Ellen (Mrs. William Tecumseh Sherman). The article went on to describe the "sitting room" in the Ewing residence, at the northwest corner of Main and High Streets, where Ewing lay for viewing by family and friends, ending with a description of the body itself: "Lying in cold embrace of death, the once commanding countenance and the towering form still indicated the physical greatness of the man. The features wore a solemn, dignified and calm expression; the noble brow and massive 'dome of thought' . . . gave the imagination scope for endowing the clay with all the grand intellectual attributes that inspire respect and excite the admiration."[132] Though probably offensive to most late-twentieth-century sensibilities, this description of Ewing's remains reflects the Victorian era's fascination with the drama of death combined with a greater acceptance of its reality than in later generations. The passing of other well-known Lancastrians attracted similar attention. William Medill, a former governor of Ohio, died in 1865. Seven years later, residents learned of the death of Hocking H. Hunter, a prominent member of the local bar and the first "white child" born within the boundaries of Lancaster. The town's most famous son, General William T. Sherman, succumbed to the "great leveler" in 1891, followed by his brother, John Sherman, in 1900.[133]

Although both the Sherman brothers had left Lancaster long before their deaths, the family was represented in town for many years by their sister, Mary Elizabeth Sherman, who married lawyer and merchant William J. Reese. In the decades just after the Civil War, the Reeses were part of an inner circle of what might be called Lancaster's upper class. Of like standing were members of the Maccracken, Effinger, and Ewing families.[134]

Successful men who had come to Lancaster more recently were in the process of founding their own prominent families. Besides Theodore Mithoff, Ernest Becker, Albert Getz, and Andy Bauman, already mentioned or discussed, the most important of these were merchant and banker Philip Rising (of what would later be called the Fairfield National Bank), Henry B. Peters (an officer of the same bank, who married Rising's daughter, Emma Idelle) and newspaper publisher Thomas Wetzler (of the *Eagle*). Only Wetzler and Peters were native-born citizens, the other five being German immigrants.[135]

German birth was clearly no obstacle to social and economic mobility, even though such men might be subjected to a degree of good-natured kidding about their accents. This lack of prejudice was understandable, given the substantial numbers of German-speaking residents in town since the very beginning. In the U.S. Census for 1860, 430 residents, or 10 percent of Lancaster's total population, gave one of the German states as their place of birth.[136] Twenty years later, in 1880, 440 Lancaster residents, 6.5 percent of the total, were listed in the census as being from Germany. Census returns for both 1860 and 1880 show that those of German birth lived in all areas of town and that there was no discernable "German" neighborhood.

Second among the foreign born were the Irish, who amounted to 4.5 percent of Lancaster's population in 1860 and just 2 percent in 1880. Next were residents from England, Scotland, or Wales (1.7 percent in 1860 and .7 percent in 1880), followed by those from France (1 percent in 1860 and .4 percent in 1880) and Canada (.4 percent in 1860 and .2 percent in 1880).[137] The total foreign-born population in Lancaster was 17.5 percent in 1860, and 10 percent in 1880. As with the Germans, other foreign-born residents did not live in any discernable ethnic enclaves, and could be found in various parts of town.[138]

For Lancaster's foreign-born, virtually all of whom were from northern and western Europe, ethnic background did not translate into residential segregation, nor was it a bar to social and economic mobility. This was

Lancaster's African Methodist Episcopal Church, with the tower of Engine House 1 in background to the right. Photo mid-twentieth century, FCDL.

not the case for Lancaster's African American population. In 1880 there were 211 blacks residing in Lancaster, representing 3.1 percent of the total population. In absolute numbers, the black population had increased by 70 persons since 1860, but as a percentage of the 6,803 people who lived in Lancaster at the time of the 1880 census, the local African American community had declined slightly from its level of 3.3 percent in 1860. Of the 94 blacks who listed employment (virtually all of the adult males as well as many of the adult women), the largest number (20) were domestic servants. Next came laborers (12) and after them, barbers (11). Nine could be classified as skilled workers, represented by 5 carpenters, 2 plasterers, 1 blacksmith, and 1 shoemaker. If occupational rankings were significant, these 9 men in skilled or semiskilled trades formed the upper end of the socioeconomic ladder among Lancaster's African Americans.[139]

Despite the hard work and economic contributions of these men and women, it is clear that racial segregation, by custom rather than by law as in the South itself, existed in Lancaster during the post–Civil War period. Census returns from both 1860 and 1880 reveal that blacks lived primarily in two areas. One was in the South End along the 200 blocks of East Walnut and East Locust Streets, both of which were close to the African Methodist Episcopal Church. The other concentration of African Americans was in the 400 block of East Mulberry and East Wheeling Streets. This area was also within easy walking distance of the church. But it may have emerged as a black enclave because it was just at the bottom of the "Hill," where Lancaster's large antebellum houses stood and where many blacks worked as domestic servants.[140]

Racial segregation prevailed in Lancaster's public schools, at least on the elementary level, until the mid-1880s.[141] And blacks attended their own church.[142] Accounts in the *Gazette* of "colored" band concerts, "colored" picnics, "colored" cakewalks, "colored" religious revivals, and "colored" dramatic performances provide additional evidence that racial segregation prevailed in virtually all social activities.[143]

Though subject to customary segregation, Lancaster's African American population created a community for themselves that offered spiritual and emotional support as well as enjoyable leisure activities. In January 1870, for example, Lancaster's African Americans celebrated the ratification of the Fifteenth Amendment to the U.S. Constitution (which, in theory anyway, guaranteed the right to vote for all citizens regardless of race) by putting on what the *Gazette* called a "band serenade."[144] The year before, Lancaster's blacks had held a debate in the public auditorium on the question of female suffrage, with four participants taking the affirmative and four the negative. Among the affirmative arguments was the contention that women needed to have the vote in order to demand equal pay and to do their part, as the more moral of the two sexes, in ridding the country of political corruption.[145] Whether or not the white population attended such activities, or how they might have interpreted them, is unclear.

The comparatively late establishment of a local GAR post, which came only in 1882, and the failure of Union war veterans to provide Lancaster with a permanent Civil War monument suggests, perhaps, that there was less enthusiasm locally about the outcome of the Civil War, including the emancipation and enfranchisement of former slaves, than in certain other northern towns. A temporary wooden obelisk, which was supposed to be replaced by a permanent stone version, was erected in the southwest section of the town square in 1881. It was then transferred to the northeast side of the square (near the later bandstand) when the fountain occupied the southwest site in 1890. Over the years termites attacked the monument and began eating away at the wood, and in 1905 the crumbling shaft went off to the town dump without so much as a mild protest from anyone.[146]

Although there was no permanent monument to the Civil War, politics in Lancaster and Fairfield County continued to be affected by the conflict, as Democrats and Republicans—locally and nationally—used memories of the war to condemn the opposition party.[147] Southerners remembered that their homeland had been invaded and, in some cases, destroyed by the "Yankee Republicans." In the North, Republicans branded Democrats as the party of treason and rebellion, and urged veterans to "vote the way you shot"—a tactic then known as "waving the bloody shirt." There were echoes of these tactics in Lancaster, but they were not so intense or so long-lived as elsewhere in the United States, perhaps in an effort to heal local divisions and "to put the war behind them." The Republican *Gazette* continued to regale voters with accounts of Dr. Olds's "treasonable activities," even as the old Copperhead won reelection to the state legislature, and to ridicule the *Eagle* for its opposition to the newly formed GAR (nationally rather than locally).[148]

After 1868 or so, the tactic of criticizing the opposition party on the basis of its position in the Civil War began to fade from the local scene. It would have done little good in any case, since the Democratic Party remained entrenched in both Lancaster and Fairfield County. In every presidential election from 1868 through 1896, the Democratic candidate carried the town and surrounding county, while the Democrats maintained a stranglehold on local contests. Even the great Civil War hero, Ulysses S. Grant, lost badly in Lancaster to the Democrat Horatio Seymour in the presidential election of 1868, and failed by equally wide margins in his contest for reelection against Democrat Horace Greeley four years later.[149] Nor did being an Ohioan do any good for Republicans Rutherford B. Hayes in 1876 or James A. Garfield in 1880, who, like their Republican predecessors, went down to defeat in Lancaster and Fairfield County.[150]

Even the close personal connections to Lancaster of 1884 Republican presidential candidate James G. Blaine failed to make a significant difference in the local election. As a first cousin to Maria Boyle (Mrs. Thomas) Ewing, an eleven-year-old Blaine had come to Lancaster in 1841 to prepare for college at the local Howe's Academy and had boarded with the Ewings during his year at the school. Blaine returned to Lancaster during the campaign of 1884 and was feted with an elaborate torchlight parade. But neither the parade nor his reminiscences that night of his school days in Lancaster were enough to sway local voters, among whom he lost to Democrat Grover Cleveland by a vote of 837 to 724, or 54 percent to 46 percent.[151]

The other presidential candidate to visit Lancaster during the Victorian period was Democrat William Jennings Bryan, who had set his party on fire with the stirring "Cross of Gold Speech" at their convention in 1896. Bryan arrived in Lancaster by train at 10:00 in the evening on October 19, 1896, just weeks before the November election. From the depot Bryan and his wife proceeded up Broad Street in a carriage pulled by four white horses. Upon reaching the square, Bryan spoke from a platform lighted by four electric spotlights. Standing before a huge crowd, he began with attacks on leading Republicans, including Lancaster's native son John Sherman, and ended with a predictable peroration for the "free and unlimited coinage of silver." The latter was a plan that Bryan and the Democrats believed would create rising prices and help debtor farmers during the lingering economic depression that had begun three years earlier.[152]

Although Bryan lost the national election to Ohio's William McKinley, he carried Lancaster in November. But Bryan won in Lancaster by a smaller margin than any Democratic contender for the presidency since the end of the Civil War, with 1,006 votes to McKinley's 950, or 51.4 percent to 48.6 percent.[153] A large majority of Lancaster's voters were indeed Democrats, but they were largely conservative Democrats, who had long been attracted to the party's devotion to states' rights, small central government, and noninterference with the economy. Bryan's fiery oratory and his inflationary plan based on free silver doubtless struck some local Democrats as too radical, resulting in a smaller vote for Bryan than for the more conservative Democrat, Grover Cleveland, who in 1892 had won by over 55 percent of the local vote, and in 1888 by over 58 percent of the vote.[154] Even though it would take two more generations for the Democratic party to emerge as the nation's liberal party, the process of making Lancaster into a Republican stronghold, unforeseen in 1896, had perhaps begun in a modest way during the McKinley-Bryan contest.

In addition to presidential campaigns, with exciting visits from major candidates, Lancaster observed other national and world events during its

Victorian age. During the Franco-Prussian War of 1870–71, the local German population made no secret of its support for Prussia, then in the process of creating a united Germany. The *Gazette* even published an English translation of the new German national hymn, "Die Wacht Am Rein," on the front page of its edition for August 25, 1870. In April 1871 the same newspaper announced a German Peace Jubilee (celebrating the end of the Franco-Prussian War) to be held in Columbus on May 1, adding, "We consider ourselves *Deutsche* enough to go along and rejoice with the crowd that will represent Lancaster on the occasion."[155] In its issue for May 4, the *Gazette* gave a long and stirring account of the jubilee. Three to four hundred Lancastrians had boarded a special train for Columbus early in the morning, accompanied by the Lancaster Military Band, "in full force, which gave two or three stirring pieces of music on the starting of the train."[156] Arriving in the state capital, the local contingent found the place seemingly "converted into an absolute German city. . . . Every where the American and German colors were displayed together. . . ." There was also, according to the *Gazette*, "an immense revolving banner of black, red and orange, hung with the portraits of the German Emperor, Princes, and prominent generals of the late war. . . ." Framed by such festive decorations, the Lancaster group marched proudly down Columbus's High Street, to the cadence of their military band.[157]

The next big event was the celebration of the nation's centennial of independence on July 4, 1876. Residents from all over Lancaster and Fairfield County converged on the downtown that morning, where they beheld a Main Street festooned with flags, banners, and evergreen branches. There was a large parade, featuring a number of horse-drawn floats, through downtown and adjoining streets. Several of the floats carried little girls dressed in white with "Martha Washington caps." The "colored citizens" had their own wagon with a decorated arch in front that proclaimed "1776, Slavery—1876 Freedom." In the afternoon there were speeches at the fairgrounds, with a large replica of the Liberty Bell hanging over the speakers' stand. The afternoon program included a reading of the Declaration of Independence and music from a hundred-member "Centennial Chorus." In the evening there was a huge fireworks display in the downtown square. Again and again, in speeches, mottos, and floats, residents proclaimed their faith in improvement, assured that their country was far better off in 1876 than a hundred years earlier.[158]

The return of Lancaster's volunteers at the end of the Spanish-American War of 1898 resulted in another great outpouring of patriotic emotion. The men marched through a flag-bedecked town to the sound of booming canons, screaming factory whistles, the clanging of bells, and the cheers of spectators.[159]

Throughout this brief conflict, the Lancaster newspapers had offered stirring accounts of Lancaster's Mount Pleasant Guards (Company I), which had served as occupation troops in Puerto Rico.[160] And unlike some of the large cities of the East Coast, where certain intellectual and political figures opposed their country's decision to annex the Philippines, there was not a murmur of recorded protest in Lancaster or Fairfield County against the birth of America's overseas empire.

At the end of the Spanish-American War, as throughout its Victorian age, most Lancastrians, like Americans as a whole, remained confident about their town and its prospects for the future. Although Lancaster's days as a frontier town were well in the past, it did continue to perform many of the functions for the surrounding area that it had done from the earliest days: it remained a market or point of transshipment for agricultural goods; it provided retail shopping, banking, legal, and governmental services; and it offered an array of entertainments, as well as a focus for civic celebration and community consciousness. Lancaster's many new churches, public buildings, and cultural organizations also testified to its belief in physical, social, and moral improvement.

FOUR

# Boom Town
## Industrial Lancaster

THERE IS EVERY REASON to believe that most residents of Lancaster greeted the twentieth century with optimism. The nation's economy was expanding after the severe economic depression of the mid-1890s, and the United States had recently conquered an overseas empire from Spain at very little cost in blood or treasure. In Lancaster the gas boom of the late 1880s was finally beginning to pay off, as the return to national prosperity and the availability of cheap gas touched off extensive industrialization in town. And at the turn of the century a new form of transportation made its appearance in Lancaster—namely, the automobile—that would eventually lead to decentralization of the population and allow for the possibility of an edge city on the outskirts of town by century's end (a result that no one could foresee at the time). Responding to rapid growth, Lancaster created parks, built new schools, paved streets, and undertook other improvements.

Residents of Lancaster ushered in 1900 with a thirty-minute blast from the deep-toned steam whistle of the Becker Brewery and by a peal of bells from the city hall tower.[1] The new year not only marked the beginning of a new century in most citizens' minds (with purists arguing that 1901 was actually the first year of the twentieth century), but it was also the centennial anniversary of Lancaster's founding back in 1800.[2] For reasons that are now unclear, the town did little to observe this anniversary. The Ohio Archaeological and Historical Society had offered its assistance in staging a commemoration but the offer was, inexplicably, turned down at a public meeting.[3] Then in June of 1900 a group of business and civic leaders belatedly met and planned a celebration for mid-September, but there are no newspaper reports, or any other indications (including minutes of the city

## CHAPTER FOUR

One of the many successful oil wells at Bremen. Leonard Hajost Collection.

council), that the September celebration took place.[4] The board of trade and city council did manage to publish, in 1901, a book about Lancaster's past and present.[5]

There was far more excitement over the discovery of oil some ten miles east of Lancaster, in the Fairfield County village of Bremen, than there was over reaching the community's century mark. The discovery of gas in Lancaster had prompted the search for oil in Bremen, since oil and gas were often found in the same vicinity. Leading the enterprise just north and east of Bremen was J. E. Purvis, who formed his first company and drilled his first well in 1896. This undertaking, along with other early wells in the area, produced very little result. Then, in July 1907 Purvis struck oil in the so-called Bremen pool, and by 1909 a total of twenty-eight wells in the area were pumping some seven hundred barrels a day. The oil bonanza received coverage in newspapers throughout the nation and attracted "wildcatters" from far and wide. A number of Bremen residents even sank wells in their backyards, and for a while the village was a forest of wooden derricks. Several residents of Lancaster invested in Purvis's ventures, including banker Henry B. Peters.[6] In Bremen itself, the oil boom spawned the village's first real industry, the Westerman Boiler and Tank Works. Founded in 1909 (and still in business at the end of the twentieth century), Westerman specialized in oil equipment and storage devices.[7]

Although full-blown industrialization came later to the Lancaster area than to many other communities in the United States, it was nevertheless part of a vast economic revolution in the western world. There were three main aspects to this revolution: the replacement of animal power and human labor by machinery and new forms of energy (on the farm as well as in factories and mills), more rapid and dependable modes of transportation, and the growth of towns and cities. All three aspects were interrelated and all three led to a vast increase in the production of goods and services, generally of higher quality and at lower prices than ever before, and a loss of independence by workers.

In addition to the cheap fuel available in Lancaster, the creation of a board of trade in 1897, which changed its name to the Lancaster Chamber of Commerce in 1913, helped to attract new industries by publicizing the advantages of coming to town.[8] But even as the board of trade was organizing itself, Lancaster could boast of several industrial enterprises, including the manufacture of bridges (Hocking Valley Bridge Works), the making of farm implements (Hocking Valley Manufacturing), flour milling (the Mokena and Deeds Mills), stone quarrying (the Allegheny and Sharp Quarries), paper box fabrication (the Frankenberg Brothers), brewing (Ernest Becker), and the making of shoes and glass.[9] Of these, the shoe and glass industries were by far the most important during the first three decades of the twentieth century, in providing many more jobs and far greater total income than the other enterprises combined.

In addition to the shoe firm that had been established in Lancaster by Colonel Albert Getz back in 1889, there were three more shoe factories in town by the turn of the century: the Lancaster Shoe Factory, the Fairfield Shoe Factory, and the Ohio Shoe Factory, all owned by the Henry C. Godman Company of Columbus. Godman had also bought controlling interest in the Getz firm at the end of 1890, and over the next decade had opened the other three factories in town. The largest of these facilities stood on the southwest corner of Columbus and Mulberry Streets (later the RBM Building), which opened in 1900.[10] As the century began, the four Godman installations were turning out some 8,000 pairs of shoes each day and had an annual payroll of $200,000.[11]

In 1900 yet another new industry came to town, drawn by the cheap gas. This was the Consumer's Carbon Company, which produced some 150,000 elements for electric lightbulbs each day, reportedly one-fifth of those being consumed in the world at that time.[12]

Also of growing importance in Lancaster at the turn of the century was its glass industry, attracted to town by cheap gas with which to fire its furnaces. The earliest of the local glass firms was Ohio Flint Glass, which came to Lancaster in 1899. At the time it specialized in globes for kerosene lamps and in patterned tableware. The firm failed in 1905, but in failing it paved the way for Lancaster's most important twentieth-century industry.[13] This was Hocking Glass, which would merge with Anchor Cap in 1937 to become the Anchor Hocking Glass Company. More than any other enterprise, Hocking (and then Anchor Hocking) would leave its imprint on almost every aspect of local life, especially after the decline of Lancaster's shoe industry in the mid-1930s.[14]

Hocking Glass was the creation of Isaac J. Collins (1874–1975). Born in Salisbury, Maryland, Collins left school at age fourteen with an eighth-grade education, and several years later turned up in western Pennsylvania, where he became associated with the Phoenix Glass Company. In 1903 Collins settled in Lancaster as head of the decorating department of Ohio Flint Glass. When Ohio Flint failed two years later, Collins managed to raise some $8,000 from Lancaster associates and another $25,000 from a businessman and friend in Pittsburgh named Edward B. Good, with which he purchased the defunct company and started Hocking Glass. Beginning in 1905 Collins built his business slowly but steadily by producing a cheap line of tableware that sold mainly in five-and-ten-cent stores. Contributing further to Collins's success, first as president and then as chairman of the board, was his ability to attract a number of loyal and capable lieutenants.

Collins married in 1912, but was separated (though apparently not divorced) from his wife, Lillian, who lived for decades in Columbus. Childless, Collins's main interest aside from the glass company was the breeding and racing of fine horses. He also spent a good deal of time in New York pursuing business matters and, it was thought, one or more "romantic interests" over the years. Although he soon became the wealthiest and most influential man in Lancaster, he was not an especially active participant in its social life. Indeed, the person in Lancaster with whom he may have felt most comfortable was bar and restaurant owner Jerry Maher, whose establishment Collins had patronized when he first came to town

Isaac J. Collins, founder of Hocking Glass, shown as an older man pursuing his favorite avocation, horse racing. FCDL.

and who shared Collins's fascination with race horses and the track.[15] Nor would anyone describe Collins's Colonial Revival house at the top of Mulberry Hill, where he lived alone with a few servants, as the kind of mansion that many successful industrialists built during the early years of the twentieth century. Jealous of his privacy, Collins seldom volunteered any information about himself, preferring to listen rather than to speak, and would even decline to submit any material for his entry in *Who's Who in America*. In 1947, *Forbes* magazine would write, "Few people know where Ike Collins came from, how old he is, what religion he follows, what he thinks, or what he does. Even fewer of his friends, if they think they know the answers, are willing to break his silence for him without his nod—which he virtually never gives."[16]

Besides Hocking Glass, another mainstay of local industry was the Lancaster Lens (later renamed Lancaster Glass), established in 1911 by

Edmund Dickey. Realizing the need for lenses and reflectors in both the automobile and movie industry, Dickey decided to take advantage of an emerging market and of Lancaster's cheap supply of gas.[17] Rounding out the list of new twentieth-century industrial enterprises was the Fairfield Paper and Container Company in the village of Baltimore, about eight miles north of Lancaster. Established in 1907, the company specialized in the manufacture of corrugated boxes.[18]

With so many new industries, it is not surprising that Lancaster's population rose from 8,991 in 1900 to 13,093 in 1910, for a decennial increase of 46 percent. By 1930, the year that the Great Depression began to set in, the town's population reached 18,716, representing a thirty-year increase of 108 percent. Fairfield County as a whole grew more slowly than Lancaster, advancing from 34,259 in 1900 to 44,010 in 1930, for an increase of just 22 percent—or only one-fifth of the percentage growth sustained by Lancaster during the same period. However, subtracting the numbers for Lancaster from the county totals reveals that the county outside Lancaster itself added only 26 persons between 1900 and 1930, for a minuscule rise of less than 1 percent.[19] It would appear that many individuals and families were leaving their farms and villages during the first three decades of the twentieth century, many of them for jobs in Lancaster.

Serving this increase in population, along with the various local industries, was an augmented transportation system. The two already-established railroad lines carried raw materials into the area and finished goods out. Laborers who could not or who did not wish to walk to work could use Lancaster's electric trolley system, which purchased several new cars in 1915.[20]

In addition to trains and trolleys, residents could take advantage of a new passenger transport provided by the Scioto Valley Traction (or interurban) line. The interurban began service between Lancaster and Columbus in July 1904, powered by an electrified "third rail" that ran immediately parallel to one side of the tracks. (Another traction route ran south of Lancaster to the Boys' Industrial School.) Riders could board the interurban car for Columbus at a small station on the north side of Main Street, now number 219, situated between Columbus Street and Memorial Drive. From there, they traveled out North Columbus Street along the regular trolley tracks, during which time the car obtained its power from the overhead trolley wires. While making its way up Columbus Street, the car took on passengers at each corner, much as the trolleys did, before turning

One of the interurban cars, after completing its "last run" in 1930. Tobias Studio Collection, FCDL.

west at Edgewood Avenue, where it switched to the third rail for power. En route to Columbus it stopped at the Methodist campground, as well as at Hooker, Carroll, and Canal Winchester, all in Fairfield County. The interurban offered service every hour in both directions and was more convenient than the train, which ran at longer intervals. Interurbans were also cheaper to operate than trains, making the service from Lancaster to Columbus more affordable than the railroad.[21]

The third rail posed a danger to anyone who touched it, with the possibility of serious electric shock or even death as a consequence. Parents in the town's North End lectured their children repeatedly "not to touch the third rail." Such warnings sometimes went unheeded, as when one of this author's aunts touched the rail on a dare and was hurled several feet through the air. She got up dazed but otherwise unhurt.[22]

By 1904, the same year that the interurban line began service, an even more novel form of transportation—the automobile—was appearing on Lancaster streets that would eventually put the interurban line out of business. The first motorcar to appear on Lancaster streets may have been a

The V. C. Wolfe family, proud owners of a new automobile, in front of their home at 324 East Sixth Avenue, c. 1910. Tobias Studio Collection, FCDL.

new "locomobile," driven to town from Columbus on September 25, 1900, with the distance covered in two hours.[23] Just five years later, on the night of June 30, 1905, a Lancaster attorney who went rushing to Columbus to be with his dying father managed to beat the interurban car there, making the thirty-mile trip in just an hour and fifteen minutes.[24]

Meanwhile, the Lancaster City Council had begun to pass ordinances to regulate these new and often dangerous contraptions. In June 1903, at a time when there were about two dozen automobiles owned by local residents, council passed the first speed-restriction law: "Be it ordained . . . that it shall be unlawful for any person or persons to propel or cause to be propelled any automobile, locomobile, or like vehicle upon any of the public highways of . . . Lancaster, Ohio[,] at a greater rate of speed than ten miles an hour."[25] Six years later, in 1909, council restricted the speed of automobiles to eight miles per hour in the downtown and to fifteen miles per hour in residential districts.[26] This legislation also required auto drivers to stop and let horses pass. Such laws appeared to do little good, for the local newspapers were full of complaints about speeding autos, often seen careening up North Broad Street in the evenings at twenty-five or thirty miles an hour. In 1907 council banned cars from Lancaster's cemeteries, claiming that their noise and speed were a "defamation of the dead," though the ban went largely unenforced.[27] Five years later, in 1912, council prohibited the use of loud horns on automobiles.[28] Outraged citizens shouted, shook their fists, and complained to town fathers about the automobile menace. But motor cars were too quick, too convenient, too profitable, too fascinating, and too clean (at least when compared to having horse manure all over the streets) for them to disappear.[29]

Bad roads were soon a common complaint among residents throughout Lancaster and Fairfield County (as they were nationwide). In March 1917, at a time when there were nearly 4,000 automobiles registered in Fairfield County, the *Gazette* urged its readers to support the building of what was being called the Sherman-Sheridan Highway, which would place "Lancaster on a good through pike from Cincinnati to Wheeling." This route closely paralleled or passed over the old Zane's Trace and would later be known as U.S. Route 22.[30] Highway improvement and the relocation of highway routes would become a constant source of local discussion—and often of heated contention—in the years ahead. So too would the placement of traffic signals, the first electric traffic lights being installed in 1920 at the intersections of Broad and Main and of Columbus and Main.[31]

By the early 1920s there were enough good roads to lure local motorists on ambitious auto vacations, such as the cross-country trip undertaken in the summer of 1923 by Dr. Henson M. Hazelton, his wife, Lillian, and their son, Perrin (well known in later years by his nickname, Pel). Upon their return from Los Angeles, where Dr. Hazelton attended the annual meeting of the American Medical Association, the doctor published a lengthy, serialized account of their adventure in *The Fairfield Motorist*, a monthly periodical put out by the Fairfield County Automobile Club. In their 1922 Hudson Coach, which they called "Nancy" (doubtless a continuation of the old habit of naming the family horse), the Hazeltons encountered some wonderfully paved roads as well as some truly horrible ones, such as "the Kansas Gumbo" or the dusty, deeply rutted, and stony trails of New Mexico. Then, while homeward bound, another car struck "Nancy" some two dozen miles east of Grinell, Iowa. Although the car was wrecked beyond repair, the Hazeltons were only shaken up a bit and traveled the rest of the way home by train.[32]

If the Hazeltons were fortunate to escape unhurt from their acci-

The south side of Main Street between Center Alley and Columbus Street, early twentieth century. Hickle's department store is clearly visible. (Most of these buildings are still standing a century later.) Tobias Studio Collection, Cartoon Research Library, OSU.

dent, too many others from Lancaster and Fairfield County would not be so lucky, as reports in the newspapers of death and serious injury from automobiles were making clear. Eventually the automobile would transform nearly every aspect of national and local life. One of the early economic casualties of the automobile was the interurban line to Columbus, which ceased operation in the fall of 1930, after a flood of affordable cars in the 1920s had deprived it of numerous passengers.[33] A generation later, the automobile would even threaten Lancaster's downtown with extinction, though no one appeared to realize this possibility from the vantage of the 1920s.

For the time being, anyway, the downtown was safe as a merchandising center, as a symbol of civic pride, and as a stage for civic celebrations and commemorations—a role that it had played since Lancaster's days as a frontier town. In addition to the older commercial buildings in the Federal, Italianate, and Mansard styles, two of the banks, the Hocking Valley and the Fairfield National, erected massive facades during this period in a

The Effinger House and row of shops to the rear. The Sherman Armory is visible on the right. Photo 1920s. Tobias Studio Collection, FCDL.

Roman Imperial style to suggest both wealth and security to their customers. These older financial establishments had to compete with two newer banks—the Farmers and Citizens, which opened in 1892, and the Lancaster National Bank, founded in 1909.

The downtown skyline was also punctuated by the cone-shaped tower of the Columbian Building on the south side of Main Street, halfway between Broad and Columbus. Shoppers could stop at the Tobias Studio, established back in 1889 and located during this period in the Hotel Martens building, and have their portrait taken by old J. H. Tobias or one of his sons, Roy and Lloyd, the three of them being known as the town's premier photographers. And in 1906, shoppers could take advantage of a new market house, located on the southeast corner of Wheeling Street and Front Street, later called Memorial Drive.[34]

The town square, with its fountain, benches, and trees—often known as Fountain Square during the first half of the century—formed an oasis on hot summer afternoons. The north end of the square was still framed by the 1823 Effinger House, with its elegant, fan-lighted doorway and matching window above, and extending from the rear of the house, a

Colonial Revival houses of the 1920s, 500 block of East Fifth Avenue. Photo by author, 1998.

pretty row of red-brick shops with bay windows for displaying merchandise.[35] Across the street from the Effinger House, on the northeast corner of the square, was the new home of the Lancaster Athletic Club, erected about 1900 and featuring two-story white columns across a wooden Colonial Revival structure that was also painted white.[36] In 1926 the American Legion would place a 105-mm captured German howitzer cannon in the square, just across Broad Street from the athletic club.[37]

Many of the new houses going up all over town during these first three decades of the twentieth century were also in the Colonial Revival mode, a building style that was sweeping the United States as many Americans turned against complex Victorian motifs and looked back to the Colonial period somewhat nostalgically—and often mistakenly—as a better and simpler time, before the upheavals of industrialization and rapid urban growth. At first, these Colonial Revival houses were boxy wooden affairs, with a few rounded posts across a rectangular front porch and perhaps a crude Palladian window cut into a triangular roof gable. Such houses began to appear a half mile or so north of downtown, especially along Fair Avenue, Reber Avenue, and Park Street; and for several blocks east of High Street—along Mulberry and King Streets in particular. In the 1920s the Colonial-style houses became less boxy, with more external details such as small-paned sashes, dormer windows, L-shaped floor plans, and attractive brick chimneys, with many of the yards surrounded by white picket fences. Such houses were particularly noticeable on the 200 and 300 blocks of East Allen Street and East Fifth Avenue, both of which were tree-lined.[38]

It was also during the first three decades of the twentieth century that four major residential districts would emerge in Lancaster and define the life of the town in many ways, at least until post–World War II housing developments greatly altered the residential picture. With the same prosaic and predictable names that were common in many other towns throughout the Midwest, these were the North, South, and East Ends, and the West Side. Although these areas were and are difficult to delineate with any great precision, it is probably safe to say that the North End began around Allen Street and continued along the Columbus and Broad Street corridors as far as the fairgrounds (in the case of Broad Street) and Forest Rose Cemetery (in the case of Columbus Street). In the 1920s, the North End started to turn west along the Old Columbus Road into what was called the Avondale development.

The East End commenced somewhere east of North High Street, and by the late 1920s it had reached as far as Cherry Street. To the north, this section was bounded by Fair Avenue, where Mount Pleasant and the fairgrounds precluded any immediate building, and to the south by Mulberry Street.

The South End lay just below Chestnut Street and included two very different kinds of neighborhoods. To the southeast, where the land rose toward the hill on which Lancaster's most prominent families continued to reside, there were spacious and generally attractive houses. To the southwest, however, where the land was flatter and bordered the railroad tracks, the old canal bed, and a number of mills, warehouses, and freight yards, the houses were smaller, cheaper, and far less attractive. When Lancastrians spoke of the South End as an undesirable place in which to live, it was this area, near the convergence of South Columbus and South Broad Streets—the old Carpenter Addition—that they usually had in mind.

The West Side was almost any place west of the Hocking River. Because it was a low-lying area, much of it resting on a floodplain, very little building took place in the area until the location there of Ohio Flint Glass and then of the Hocking Glass factory in the early twentieth century. The houses that arose on the West Side were generally small or modest-sized and of frame construction. Although most of them were built for factory workers at the glass factory (but not by the glass factory itself),

Harrison Avenue houses on the West Side, built in the early twentieth century and typical of houses owned by workers at Hocking Glass (and then Anchor Hocking Glass). Photo by author, 1998.

nearly all were single-dwelling houses, especially in the so-called Pioneer Addition around West School, with the exception of a few twins and some two-story wooden rows. A small shopping district soon grew up along Harrison Avenue, where residents could purchase groceries, dry goods, furniture, clothing, medicines, and many other items. For seventy years, beginning in 1902, the Thomas grocery at 324 Garfield Avenue was a West Side institution where neighbors came to shop and talk.[39] The West Side also had its own elementary school, a Methodist church, and in later years, a branch of the Fairfield County Library. Such services gave the West Side certain semblances of a separate town, a status that was reinforced by its being on flat land opposite the more elevated portions of central Lancaster, as well as by the Hocking River, which could only be crossed by the bridges at Fair and Sixth Avenues or at Wheeling Street.[40] The Wheeling Street Bridge carried trolley cars to and from the West Side, a service that began about 1906.[41]

Because the West Side was home to numerous laborers at the Hocking Glass factory, many middle-class families shunned it as a respectable address, and even in the late twentieth century some local realtors continue to steer newcomers away from West Side properties. West Side children came to have a reputation, often unfairly, for being "tough kids," an allegation that many West Siders wore as a badge of pride, with the often-heard boast of "West Side against the world!"

Not included in any of these residential areas, as alluded to earlier, was what might be called the central district, which included the beautiful Federal and Greek Revival–style houses on Wheeling and Main Hills (and beginning in the early twentieth century along the parallel Mulberry Hill, just one block north of Wheeling Street). These continued to be owned by the town's old elite, along with the more successful new residents, such as I. J. Collins and the other top executives at Hocking Glass. With what might be called Lancaster's upper class residing "on the hill," middle-class families tended to live in the North End and increasingly, by the 1920s, in the East End, leaving the South End and the West Side for blue-collar workers. But there were many exceptions to this rule of thumb, since it was not unusual to find a mixture of occupations and incomes on a given street. For example, a medical doctor, furniture-store proprietor, hatchery owner, tinsmith, factory worker, wholesale fruit dealer, high school teacher, and delivery man might all live on the same block in the North or East Ends—in contrast to large cities, where residential areas were likely to be much more segregated by income, occupation, or social class.[42]

Yet another factor mitigating against extreme social divisions was the absence of private schools in the early twentieth century (unless one counts the small Catholic school system), with the consequence that nearly everyone in town attended the one public high school. And because of a growing population, school enrollment expanded greatly during the first three decades of the century. In September 1900, for example, the Lancaster Board of Education announced that there were 1,309 children in the system, the largest in its history up to that point.[43] The arrival of new industries only added to the school population. Thus, in 1904 the school board erected the Utica School, which served students living south of the Hocking River. In 1913 came the Cedar Heights School, located several blocks south of the West Side plant of Hocking Glass. The board also erected new structures for several already established elementary schools: North in 1917, South in 1931, and East in 1939.[44]

But the most impressive growth in the local schools came at the secondary level, as modern business and industry increasingly demanded

Lancaster High School, showing original 1906 building on left, the 1917 addition in middle, and the 1932 auditorium addition on right. Photo early 1930s. Tobias Studio Collection, FCDL.

high school educations for their employees. The passage of a state law in 1921, which required school attendance in Ohio from the age of six to eighteen (unless released to work at sixteen), was an official recognition of this need.[45] By the early 1920s, a high school education was a standard expectation for local youngsters.

The Lancaster Board of Education moved to meet growing enrollments by erecting a new Lancaster High School at the northeast corner of Mulberry Street and Pearl Avenue, a space later occupied by the west wing of Stanbery School. This red-brick structure, executed in the Colonial Revival style, opened in January 1906 and expanded with a nearly identical wing in 1917.[46] In less than a decade these facilities were overcrowded and inadequate for the educational needs of the local economy. Thus, the school board proposed in 1924 to build a new and larger Lancaster High School, with the old building serving as a junior high, which in turn would alleviate much of the overcrowding in the elementary schools.[47]

According to the school superintendent, J. J. Phillips, high school enrollments in Lancaster were increasing by some 50 students each year, with the total number going from 250 in 1906, when the Mulberry Street facility first opened, to 700 in 1924, for an increase of 280 percent in just eighteen years. As a result, many classrooms had ten or more students beyond their intended capacities, while the lack of study-hall space required some students to do their lessons in the back of the classroom while students in the rest of the room recited or listened to teachers' lectures. There were also insufficient spaces and equipment for the many vocational programs that the high school offered or wished to offer.[48]

Plans for the new high school were indeed impressive and would have made both the building and the educational program among the most progressive in the state. The home economics department, for instance, would include a suite of "practice rooms," including a dining room, bedroom, bath, and fitting rooms, a facility that was similar in concept to the "practice houses" being constructed for home economics majors on many college campuses at the time. In this way students would learn how to manage a household through textbooks as well as through hands-on experience, a central concept in progressive education. In addition, there would be shops for wood and metal working, drafting, electronics, auto mechanics, pattern making, and printing, along with music rooms and well-equipped laboratories for physics and chemistry. There would also be an auditorium with seating for 1,400, a spacious gymnasium, a new library, and enough classrooms to anticipate immediate future needs. The plans called for a $450,000 bond issue.[49]

In order to galvanize support for the issue, which would be submitted for a public referendum on November 4, 1924, school authorities staged an hour-long parade the day before the election that included all 3,000 children then in the public system. The children marched down Main Hill and up Broad Street, both decorated with American flags. Accompanying each school was a drum corps, the children carrying banners with statements calling for the new high school.[50] Despite the march, the endorsement of both newspapers, and the support of numerous civic groups, the bond issue went down to defeat, losing by nearly 900 votes out of the approximately 6,000 that were cast. The negative vote was especially high on the West Side, where a majority of residents were factory workers at Hocking Glass.[51]

Given the clear need for a new high school, the obvious benefits it would bring to the entire community, and the small increase in property taxes ($5.25 per year for the average homeowner, or just $131.25 over the twenty-five-year period until the schools bonds were paid off), it is hard to understand why the issue went down to defeat. While there are no surviving explanations, it is probable that numbers of voters, many of whom had grown up in small villages and rural areas where they had completed eight years of education or less in one- and two-room schoolhouses, simply could not understand the need for a more modern educational system. The statement "If it was good enough for us, it's good enough for them" would unfortunately be heard for years to come and continue to hold back progress in local education. The legal requirement in Ohio that all school bond issues (and operating levies) be submitted for approval by the general electorate had also proved—and would continue to prove—a handicap to the public schools. (By contrast, many other states allowed elected school boards themselves to authorize new taxation.)

Three years later, in the fall of 1927, the board approached voters again with a bond issue to build a new high school. There was another parade of school children and endorsements from both the *Eagle* and the *Gazette*, but the issue met defeat once more, this time by 1,200 votes. The board tried again in 1929, but for an addition to the old high school rather than for an entirely new building. This time the issue passed by a slim margin, and the Mulberry Street school received a new auditorium, gymnasium, and library, a number of classrooms, and various shops, which were completed by the opening of classes in 1931. Because of inflation during the five years since the bond issue had first been proposed, the extensions to the high school amounted to as much ($450,000) as an entirely new facility would have cost back in 1924.[52] It would take more than three decades and many hard-fought battles before Lancaster could build a completely new high school.

Lancaster's Catholic school system also underwent expansion during the first three decades of the century. In 1907 St. Mary parish erected a new elementary school at Chestnut Street and Pearl Avenue, with an addition in 1918. During 1929–30 the parish built a new high school adjacent to the elementary facility.[53]

The emergence of high school as a universal experience had a major impact on local youth and would remain an important touchstone in the lives of many residents for the rest of their lives. What amounted to compulsory high school attendance extended the time of preparation for life,

The St. Mary elementary school and high school. Photo 1930s. Tobias Studio Collection, FCDL.

as opposed to earlier decades when youths in their early teens often went to work or became occupied full-time on the family farm. Teenagers, a new name for the high school group, now spent more time with their peers than they did with their parents and were as likely to be influenced by the views of their classmates as by their elders—often to the alarm of the older generation.

In the years after graduation, the high school took on a nostalgic glow for many, and especially for those who did not go on to college. Asking about—or volunteering—the year of one's graduation also became a way of identifying with others. The year that some absent third party might have graduated was a favorite topic of discussion, as friends or family members speculated endlessly about whether "Bill graduated in my class—or in your sister Jane's." Associating someone with an earlier class might even give mild offense, since the person was, in effect, accused of being several years older than he or she really was. Then there were the equally endless debates about who had married whom in which graduating class, who had had children or gotten divorced, what various classmates did for a living, whether the persons in question had remained in town or served in the military, and so forth. Many graduates kept careful track of such information by making notations in pen or pencil beside each senior picture in the yearbook (known as the *Mirage* at Lancaster High since its appearance in 1910). Identification with one's graduating class was further strengthened by reunions every five years or so, with some classes in the late twentieth century managing to celebrate sixty-fifth or even seventieth reunions.

With a growing recognition of childhood and youth as separate developmental stages—if only in a somewhat hazy and informal way by local parents—it is not surprising that organized activities emerged for local youngsters during the first part of the twentieth century. By 1912 a Boy Scout troop had been established in Lancaster, with some 40 members, who spent two weeks camping in tents near Sugar Grove (about five miles south of town). In 1928 the Rotary and Kiwanis service clubs collaborated with the Young Men's Christian Association (founded locally in 1927) to build a youth camp, known as Camp Ki-Y-Ro, southwest of Lancaster on the Hamburg Pike. The local Young Women's Christian Association had been established in 1913.[54]

Despite such organizations, most youngsters continued to arrange their own entertainment during the first years of the twentieth century. Attorney Charles Drinkle (1891–1991) remembered several swimming holes along Hunter's Run and the Hocking River. In the fall he joined other boys in "nutting" expeditions, which meant collecting walnuts, butternuts, hickory nuts, and chestnuts in the abundant woods on the edge of town. In winter, Drinkle and his chums went coasting and ice skating. When the Hocking River overflowed and then froze, he recalled, they skated over the low-lying "prairies" on the West Side.[55]

Not all the news about young people was positive, as an editorial in the *Gazette* in late October of 1924 indicated. Here the writer complained of the weeklong vandalism that typically accompanied Halloween, as boys went on a rampage "upsetting lawn swings and porch furniture or removing small outbuildings [that is, outhouses] and the like." Apparently innocent of modern child psychology, the editorialist suggested that a few strokes with Dad's razor strap was the best cure for such mischief.[56]

For adults, new recreational and social activities coexisted with certain patterns from the past. Men's lodges, for example, continued to flourish, with the Elks (1900), the Moose (1912), and the Eagles (1930) joining the list of older lodges in Lancaster.[57] The GAR remained active until age and death made the veterans' organization moribund by the 1930s. A high point in the history of the local Ben Butterfield Post was its hosting of the Ohio GAR Encampment in Lancaster during May 1902. Metal arches, illuminated with hundreds of electric lightbulbs, framed all four sides of the intersections of Main and Broad Streets. Arising from the center of these arches was a metal tower bedecked with banners and flags. Atop the tower stood the statue of a Civil War soldier and on the sides were oval portraits of presidents Abraham Lincoln and William McKinley (assassinated just a year before).[58] As the GAR began to dwindle in membership, its presence as a veterans' group was assumed by the American Legion, a nationwide organization first established for men who had served during World War I. Lancaster's American Legion post was founded during the summer of 1919, but unlike the GAR, whose members thought their experiences too unique to include the veterans of subsequent wars, the American Legion would assure its survival by opening itself to veterans of subsequent generations.[59] Rounding out the list of men's lodges and organizations were the two service clubs founded in Lancaster during the early twentieth century, Rotary (1918) and Kiwanis (1919).[60]

As Lancaster prospered and more well-to-do members of the community wished to display new signs of social distinction, several select clubs emerged in town. The earliest of these was the Lancaster Athletic Club (LAC), launched in 1893. Among the founders and early members were Edson B. Olds Smith, Dr. Michael Effinger, Henry B. Peters, W. B. Maccracken, H. H. Giesy, and George P. Rising—all successful businessmen, professionals, or members of old Lancaster families. The white-columned clubhouse that the members erected in 1900 on the northeast corner of the town square contained the latest indoor exercise equipment, including a bowling alley and swimming pool (the first such indoor facility for Lancaster), and a gymnasium with running track, basketball court, parallel bars, climbing rope, and exercise horse. There were also a lounge and several meeting rooms. Membership was limited to four hundred men. The club was later dissolved in 1958, and for a while the building functioned as a recreational facility open to the general public, appropriately renamed the White Columns. The building was demolished in 1962 to make way for a new Fairfield Federal Savings and Loan building.[61]

The Lancaster Country Club, established in 1909, also attracted well-to-do residents interested in exercise and sports (especially in golf), and in the long run may have been partly responsible for the demise of the athletic club downtown.[62] The moving force behind the club was banker

The Lancaster Athletic Club. Photo c. 1930. Tobias Studio Collection, FCDL.

Henry B. Peters. Other charter members were C. B. Whiley, W. H. House, W. H Stuckey, Philip R. Peters (son of Henry Peters), McClelland Martens, Von S. Goetz, George M. Hickle, Edward Delancy, P. L. Clark, and J. L. Denny, all successful businessmen or professionals.[63] The country club's rural setting just south of Lancaster was attractive to members, as similar surroundings were to those who joined other country clubs throughout the United States and who associated their clubs with country estates and the sort of wealth that allowed large pieces of land to be set aside for purely recreational uses.[64] Since the Lancaster Country Club grounds paralleled the interurban route to the BIS, members could take the traction car "out to the club," although this means of transport was short-lived, as most members acquired automobiles by the 1920s.[65] The existence of a local country club did not produce deep social rifts in town, though some members did view their membership as a badge of social distinction. Certain non–club members, on the other hand, would complain over the years about "country-club snobs" or make snide remarks about members who allegedly did not have enough money to pay their initiation fee and had to borrow it from one of the banks.

Yet another elite organization in town was the Elizabeth Sherman Reese Chapter of the Daughters of the American Revolution (DAR), established locally in 1900 and named in honor of General Sherman's sister, Elizabeth.[66] The National DAR, which had been founded in 1890, was one of a number of national lineage societies that emerged around the turn of the century and that had certain connections to the larger Colonial Revival in the United States. In addition to asserting that the Colonial days had some valuable lessons for latter-day Americans, membership in the DAR and other lineage societies was a way of proclaiming that one belonged to an "old family" whose roots in America went back to at least the mid-eighteenth century, an important factor, at the time, in being able to claim upper-class status. In the case of the DAR, those applying for membership had to prove that at least one ancestor had served in the American Revolution. This meant that an individual who had recently immigrated to the United States or whose family had not been in the country since before the Revolution (thereby excluding nearly anyone whose ancestors were not from the British Isles, Germany, or somewhere else in northern and western Europe) could not join the DAR. Such exclusivity, of course, by no means detracted from the fact that Lancaster's DAR has contributed to the success of a number of civic and charitable causes in the century since its founding.[67]

A truly classless society had never existed in Lancaster, but the emergence of what might be called exclusive clubs probably did weaken community solidarity.[68] Yet despite such restrictive organizations, most social and leisure activities in Lancaster could still be experienced and enjoyed by many people in town, and especially by the middle class. They could attend, for example, numerous theatrical performances, musical entertainments, and lectures. In October 1908, there was "Robinson's Talking Passion Play," about Christ's crucifixion, presented at the Opera House on Chestnut Street).[69] In November 1902 audiences packed the public auditorium to see a series of tableaux about the history and accomplishments of the American Red Cross.[70] It was also in this auditorium that residents could hear, in October 1908, a stirring lecture on the "Fine Art of Detection" given by Lloyd C. Douglas (1877–1951), then pastor of Lancaster's English Lutheran Church.[71] Douglas would go on to become one of the most famous religious writers in the nation's history, best known for *The*

Hippodrome movie theater, north side of Main Street, near intersection with Columbus Street. Photo c. 1915. Leonard Hajost Collection.

*Robe* (1942) and *The Big Fisherman* (1948), both made into highly successful movies.[72] Yet another notable speaker of the period was General Sherman's son, Thomas, a Jesuit priest, who made a presentation on the subject of socialism at the auditorium in December 1903.[73] (Just what the younger Sherman had to say about the subject was, unfortunately, not recorded.) More exciting for most of Lancaster's male population were the frequent wrestling matches staged at both the Opera House and the public auditorium.[74]

Although live presentations of all sorts would not die out completely, the appearance of moving pictures seriously undermined their popularity.[75] The first "experimental" showing of moving pictures in Lancaster seems to have been at the county fair in 1897, where visitors could view one of Thomas Edison's early kinetoscopes.[76] Commercial movies made their Lancaster debut in 1904, when a theater called the Dreamland opened on Main Street. Several other movie houses came in rapid succession: the Hippodrome (later known as the Liberty) in 1906, the Princess in 1907, the Majestic in 1908, the Lyric in 1913, the Palace in 1929, and the Broad in 1938. (Of the earliest movie houses, only the Lyric and the Liberty would make the transition to talking pictures and survive—along with the later Palace and Broad Theaters—into the post–World War II period.) The most sumptuous of these establishments was the 1,000-seat Palace, a gaudy, gilded house of entertainment, complete with a pipe organ, that was intended to make viewers feel that they were palace royalty, if only for a few hours.[77] In the late 1920s the Fairfield County Ministerial Association threatened to sue the theater owners to stop the showing of films on Sundays, charging that they were desecrating the Sabbath, but they withdrew their suit upon learning of the legal fees that they were likely to incur in a court fight.[78]

What was playing at the various movie houses and what one thought of certain movies now became a staple item of conversation that strengthened a sense of common experience in Lancaster. The movie schedules even had a predictable impact on traffic patterns, as the trolleys and later the buses became jammed just before and after the shows. When automobiles became the preferred mode of transportation, people living along Broad, Columbus, or Main Streets could almost set their clocks in the evening by the increased flow of cars around 7:00, 9:00, and 11:00 P.M.

As in the past, various kinds of athletic contests provided diversion and predictable subjects for conversation. Besides the wrestling matches, baseball mania continued into the new century, with all sorts of interesting contests, as when the town's doctors and lawyers faced off against each other in 1904. The lawyers won 16–11 with considerable assistance from Judge Thurman T. Courtright, who "hiked the score" by hitting a home run with two men on base.[79]

But in the early twentieth century, football began to eclipse baseball in popularity, partly because high school students and alumni could identify so strongly with their teams (and with a sport that took place completely within the school year). Lancaster High School fielded its first football team in 1901, and soon the local newspapers were carrying accounts of the local eleven.[80] During the early 1930s, at a time before Lancaster had its own radio station, fans unable to attend out-of-town games could call Jerry Maher's restaurant and bar at 151 West Main Street to get the final score, which would have been telephoned long-distance from the host

Air show, Fairfield County Fairgrounds, August 22, 1912, FCDL.

town.[81] Since games were invariably played in the afternoon at a time when high school football fields were without lights, fans could safely telephone Maher's place anytime after 5:00 P.M. for the game results. Throughout the first decades of the century (and for many years thereafter) Lancaster's greatest football rivals were Newark and Zanesville, both somewhat larger than Lancaster at the time, but similar towns in many ways. Beginning in October 1925, all home games took place at the new North Field, built behind the North Elementary School at Broad and Allen Streets, with seating for 2,000 fans.[82] Before that, the games appear to have been played at Eagle Park in the south end of town.[83]

Some entertainments introduced residents to the latest in technological marvels, such as in August 1912, when the local Elks Club sponsored an air show at the fairgrounds. Two aviators in a Curtis biplane thrilled a packed grandstand, as well as many atop Mount Pleasant. After taking off, the aviators circled the downtown and landed back at the fairgrounds with a low swoop over the racetrack. One of the planes nearly crashed when it hit a fence, snapped a guy wire, and broke one of its wheels. Fortunately, neither the aviator nor anyone in the crowd sustained injury.[84] By the 1920s flights over Lancaster had become commonplace, and the first of several private "airfields" had opened on the outskirts of town. Lancastrians obtained access to practical, long-distance air travel in 1929 with the opening of Port Columbus, though few, because of the cost and the novelty of air travel, would take advantage of it for another generation.[85]

Other entertainments, like the comic strips in the newspapers, were far less spectacular but far more dependable. One of the most popular comic characters of the era, Buster Brown, was the creation of Lancaster native Richard Fenton Outcault (1863–1928). Outcault had grown up in his parents' home at 120 West Allen Street, and had first learned to paint from Dr. Gabriel Miesse, a well-known Lancaster physician, artist, and musician. After working as a graphic artist in Cincinnati and taking further training in Paris, Outcault went to work for Joseph Pulitzer's *New York World*, where he came up with a comic strip known as *Hogan's Alley*. Later, after Outcault began working for William Randolph Hearst's *New York Journal*, he began a cartoon series called *The Yellow Kid*, which featured a yellow background. This use of yellow in the comic strip, along with the newspaper wars between Hearst and Pulitzer, led critics of sensational journalism to coin the phrase "yellow journalism" to describe the tactics of publishers like Hearst and Pulitzer.

In 1902 Outcault introduced his *Buster Brown* comic strip, with Buster's dog Tige and his sister Mary Jane (the name of Outcault's Lancaster-born wife, Mary Jane Martin, as well as their daughter, Mary Jane). The strip was a huge hit and appeared in newspapers all over the United States. Outcault took advantage of this by licensing about two hundred products to use both the name and image of his cartoon characters, including Buster Brown and Mary Jane shoes. In the 1940s, some two decades after the cartoonist's death, there was also a *Buster Brown* radio program.[86] Buster Brown and his prosperous, middle-class family were doubtless more congenial to Lancaster residents than Outcault's Yellow Kid, for the Yellow Kid had depicted life in a tough urban neighborhood that was far removed from the everyday scenes of Lancaster, Ohio.

Equally far removed from the world of the Yellow Kid was Buckeye Lake, a dozen or so miles north and slightly east of Lancaster at the very edge of Fairfield County. Created when canal builders had enlarged the old Buffalo Swamp into the Licking Reservoir, the lake had ceased to func-

Postcard of Buckeye Lake Park, c. 1920s. Courtesy Mrs. Harold Reed.

tion as a link in the Ohio canal system in the 1890s, when canals around and through the lake area were abandoned altogether by barge traffic. Thus, in 1894 the Ohio legislature made the old reservoir into a state park under the new name of Buckeye Lake.[87]

Over the next several decades the lake emerged as a major resort and recreation spot. In 1904 the state began removing many of the old stumps and tree trunks that had remained in the lake from when the reservoir had first filled, and which were proving a great hazard for boaters.[88] The lake had been accessible by railroad as early as the 1870s, but it was the completion of the Columbus, Buckeye Lake, and Newark Traction (that is, interurban) line in 1903 that opened the lake to a wider public.[89] A typical destination for "day trippers" was Buckeye Lake Park, which opened at about the same time as the interurban line and which was owned and operated for many years by the traction company itself.[90] Such trolley or traction car parks, as they were often called, were being built all over the United States at the time as a way of attracting additional riders during the warmer months.[91]

Located on the north side of the lake in Licking County, Buckeye Lake Park reached its peak in the 1920s and 1930s. There were rides, game booths, boat excursions, a large roller-skating rink, the Lake Breeze Hotel,

Picnic Point, Crystal Pool (so sparkling clean that its proprietors invited visitors to come and experience the healthful pleasure of swimming in "purified drinking water"), and the Crystal Ball Room, overlooking the pool and lake, where all the big bands of the era came to play. (Such bands often consisted of three to five trumpets, an equal number of trombones, five saxophones, a piano, drums, and bass.) There were several other ballrooms at the park, including the Pier Ballroom, but the Crystal was the longest lasting and the most memorable.[92] Just west of the park was the Buckeye Lake Yacht Club, founded by sailing aficionados in 1906, with its clubhouse on an island just a few yards beyond the shoreline.[93]

Yet another point of interest was Summerland Beach at the western end of the lake, so named by a group of spiritualists who lived in the area and who, according to local lore, named the place after their word for heaven—that is, "Summerland."[94] During the 1930s, after the spiritualists had departed, there was a hotel, dance pavilion, and swimming area on the site. (Still later, Summerland Beach was purchased by the Apostolic Church, which has continued to hold summer revivals there as the twentieth century comes to an end.) Not far from Summerland Beach stood the Weldon ice cream factory, which the same family has owned since the 1920s, with its two-story wooden front porch and cream-colored wooden booths inside. At the opposite end of the lake, a short-lived polo club was organized in 1929 at Harbor Hills by a group of businessmen who had witnessed the sport on the East Coast.[95]

More prosperous families from Lancaster, Columbus, and Newark (the county seat of Licking County, in which the northeast section of the lake lay) began to erect summer cottages around the lake, and by the end of the 1920s, when automobiles made the entire area more accessible, the shores were lined with summer homes. Lancaster families liked to build on the Fairfield County portion of the lake, often called the "Lancaster side," while those from Newark seemed to prefer the Licking County portion, or the "Newark side." (Columbus residents also tended to locate on the Newark side, since it paralleled the interurban line and later the main highway from Columbus to Newark.) Rivals in sports as well as commerce, Lancaster and Newark residents occupied separate sides of the lake, though residents came together at Buckeye Lake Park, where Lancaster girls danced with Newark boys and where summer romances resulted in not a few Lancaster-Newark weddings.

Whether on the Lancaster or the Newark side, the majority of Buckeye Lake cottages were primitive by later standards. Most were small frame structures without insulation or any sort of heating; and in an age before air conditioning, second-story lofts, which often housed sleeping quarters, could feel like ovens at the end of a hot summer day. Few of the cottages had inside toilets, and owners had to obtain their drinking water from hand-pumped wells, with the water so high in iron content that drinking glasses quickly turned orange. And compared to the scenic lakes in Minnesota, upper New York state, and elsewhere—not to mention the beaches along the Atlantic coast—Buckeye Lake would not have ranked high on any national list of resort communities: the lake was barely five miles long and less than a mile wide at any point. Its waters were often muddy and could become very low during summer droughts. But compared to the monotony of intersecting streets back in Lancaster or the gently rolling farmland of northern Fairfield County, Buckeye Lake took on a slightly exotic and even romantic aura in the minds of visitors and summer residents alike. To see a sailboat drifting across the lake or to listen to the waves lapping against the shoreline was to be transported to another world.

Owning a cottage "at the lake" was also another small badge of social distinction for Lancaster families fortunate enough to afford such a luxury, however modest. Summers at the lake provided yet another source of conversation over the years, as well as a bond among those middle-class Lancastrians who had grown up with the Buckeye Lake experience.[96] This author's mother and aunts often laughed about how, as young children, they had mistaken the blue herons of Buckeye Lake for storks and had warned their mother to hide whenever one of these long-legged birds appeared, fearing that another brother or sister was about to drop from the sky. Other memories focused on the grocery boat from Millersport, which showed up daily at their dock, announcing itself with a bell and later a horn. Children who had been "good that day" could usually count on some sort of sugary treat.[97]

Besides getaways to Buckeye Lake, Lancastrians continued to enjoy the many scenic points south and west of town. In addition to the sites in adjacent Hocking County, there were several favorite places for hiking and picnicking in Fairfield County, including Jacob's Ladder, Riven Rock, and Christmas Rocks (all near the BIS), Beck's Knob west of town, and Flat Rocks, overlooking the Forest Rose Cemetery.[98]

Residents could read about such outings in the two Lancaster newspapers, most commonly on the society pages. These pages also listed wedding engagements and anniversaries, with fiftieth anniversaries becoming increasingly common as longevity increased. In addition, readers learned about bridge luncheons, teas, picnics, birthday parties, masquerades, sewing circles, dinner parties, club meetings, dances, family and school reunions, out-of-town guests, tips on the latest fashions, and family vacations. A section on vital statistics listed births and deaths, along with the most recent hospital admissions and discharges. Weddings in particular occupied a good portion of the society pages, as did vivid descriptions of social functions at the Lancaster Country Club. Typical of these was an item that appeared in the *Gazette* for July 23, 1932: "[A] Friday party at the Country Club, a dinner-dance, arranged by a group of junior members, provided not only a delightful event but a huge success.... Colorful flowers from the garden were used for the tables, with dinner served at seven-thirty o'clock.... Covers were laid for a company of fifty.... High Hatters orchestra played for dancing from nine until twelve o'clock with a group of members joining the guests for the dance."

In contrast, the local news contained numerous stories about crimes, trials, and civil suits that their editors knew would provide "entertaining reading" and, hopefully, increased circulation. Accounts of burglaries and runaways from the BIS were the most common fare in the crime category, with a "sensational" case popping up every once in a while, such as the armed robbery of the Palace movie theater in June 1932. After holding up the cashier at gun point and absconding with ten dollars in cash, the robber fled on foot up North Broad Street, where a police officer shot him in hot pursuit. Stunned by a scalp wound, from which he swiftly recovered, the robber was tried and sentenced to ten to twenty-five years in the Ohio Penitentiary.[99] A generation earlier, newspaper readers learned that a West Side stone mason had shot his estranged wife, then turned the revolver on himself and "blew his brains out."[100]

Amusing to later generations are the accounts of lawsuits over foul language in the early years of the century. One such incident that came before the court in June 1904 involved a Lancaster man who began cursing a neighbor, within earshot of the neighbor's wife, because he had been asked to remove his cow from that neighbor's property. The accused pleaded guilty of using obscene language "in front of a lady" and was fined nine dollars by the municipal judge.[101] More titillating was the account in 1907 of a police raid on a "hoochy-coochy" act in a "seedy" establishment along the alley between Main and Wheeling Streets in the downtown district. The dancing girls were arrested and, dressed in tights, were brought before Mayor L. H. Purcell, who fined them each five dollars for participating in a show that was "not fit to be presented anywhere."[102]

One of the most widely followed judicial proceedings of the early twentieth century was undoubtedly the trial for assault and battery in 1917 against public school superintendent S. H. Layton, charges that were brought against him by the Lancaster High School principal, Dean Hickson. According to newspaper reports, Hickson went into Layton's office on the morning of May 2 to complain about what he considered to be the superintendent's undue interference with his work. A shouting match ensued, during which Layton slammed Hickson against the wall and began choking him. Two passing students who saw the melee burst into the office and rescued Hickson. Layton was tried and found guilty, but his conviction was reversed on appeal because of allegedly improper jury instructions by the judge. Nevertheless, Layton lost his job as superintendent of the Lancaster schools.[103]

In addition to newspaper stories about crime or improper activities, the city council responded to what appeared to be an increase in antisocial behavior with a barrage of new legislation: In 1906 it required all establishments selling alcohol to close between 11:30 P.M. and 5:00 A.M.[104] Three years later, in 1909, council forbade gambling in Lancaster and authorized stiff fines ranging from $100 to $500 for anyone violating the ordinance, and that same year it imposed a $200 penalty for carrying a concealed weapon (including a pistol, bowie knife, or dirk).[105] In 1912 council imposed a curfew of 9:30 in the summer months and 8:30 during the winter for all minors under sixteen.[106] Those who refused to pay municipal fines could be sentenced to "hard labor" anywhere within the corporation limits of Lancaster.[107] Other legislation was for reasons of safety: In 1912 council prohibited the sale of fireworks in Lancaster, and that same year it forbade the construction of wooden buildings in the downtown district as a precaution against fire.[108]

Despite such local legislation, Lancaster did not face either the scope or the intensity of the problems, including festering slums, endemic violence, and corrupt political machines, that plagued the country's largest cities. Yet many towns like Lancaster believed that they had to imitate many of the improvements undertaken by large urban areas in order to show that they were up-to-date and to attract new business and industry.[109] In addition, an increasing population and familiarity with certain public amenities elsewhere led to calls for such improvements.

Trolleys, gas lights, and a telephone system (first established locally in 1882) all allowed Lancastrians to claim that they could enjoy the same conveniences as the big cities but without most of their problems.[110] So did the paving of streets, a process that had begun in the 1890s and that continued into the early decades of the century. As might be expected, the Main Street shopping area, from Broad Street to Columbus Street, was the first to be paved, in this case with brick. This occurred in 1890. Eight years later, in 1898, the brick paving was extended east on Main Street, from Broad Street to Maple Street.[111] During the next four decades, other streets received a covering in brick, with those thoroughfares closest to the downtown being treated before those further out. By the late 1920s, nearly every built-up street in town had a facing of dark red bricks, with those on the very edge of town having a surface of gravel.[112] And with paving usually came the construction of storm sewers. Indeed, anyone reading through the city council records of the early twentieth century will find that the local legislators spent much of their time over petitions from property owners asking to have their street paved or drainage improved.

The building of brick or flagstone sidewalks often accompanied the street paving, though not always. City council required uniform sidewalks on Main Street for the first time in 1886, but it was not until 1912 that it directed all property owners to construct sidewalks along their property lines.[113] Yet another mandate was the numbering, beginning in 1908, of each and every building and residence in town.[114]

Lancaster streets received their first electrical lighting in 1886, made possible by the establishment of the Lancaster Electric Light Company two years before. The first three electric street lights appeared at the intersections of High and Main, Broad and Main, and Columbus and Main, all in 1886.[115] The coming of electricity also allowed Lancaster to install, in 1899, the first electrically powered police call boxes in the state, which were placed at strategic points throughout town, at a time when most residents still did not have telephones.[116]

While such police call boxes reflected the faith of most Americans in the benefits of science and technology, many citizens, locally and in the nation at large, could also look back and conclude that certain positive aspects of the past were being lost in the process of modernization. One way to recapture this past, they believed, was through the preservation of

Mount Pleasant and a portion of Rising Park, with the Fairfield County Fairgrounds in forefront of picture. Photo c. 1930. Tobias Studio Collection, FCDL.

the natural landscape by setting aside certain lands as public parks. The creation of playgrounds and recreational areas in portions of such parks—or in separate locations—was also a favorite project of many social reformers in the early twentieth century, who worried that the urban landscape was stultifying for children both physically and emotionally, and that sedentary occupations for middle-class adults were robbing them of the outdoor exercise essential for good health.[117] The establishment of Lancaster's Rising Park in 1909, which included historic Mount Pleasant, was part of this wider park movement.

Mount Pleasant—or Standing Stone, as the Wyandot Indians had called it—already loomed large in local affections and imagination. It had been the site of the romantic Forest Rose saga and thus seemed a genuine connection to an earlier time. The property had passed through a number of hands over the years, and at the turn of the century it belonged to a man named Frederick Buschmeyer. Buschmeyer had made elaborate plans to build a resort hotel at the summit, to be reached by a small incline railroad running up the north side. He went so far as to sink casings at the summit for a water well, the remains of which can be seen at the time of this writing, and to prepare a roadbed up the slope (which would later become the main approach to the "mountain," known as the Tarhe Trail). But he failed to interest sufficient investors, and the development came to a halt before

The stone shelter house at Rising Park, begun in 1939 as a project of the Works Progress Administration (WPA) and completed by the Lancaster Park Board about 1940. Photo 1940s. Tobias Studio Collection, FCDL.

very much damage could be done to the site. The frustrated Buschmeyer then erected a high board fence around the base of Mount Pleasant and attempted to charge a fee of ten cents to anyone who wished to enter.[118]

Since Lancastrians had always taken it for granted that Mount Pleasant was open to the public, more than a few residents were outraged by the fence and entrance fee. Among them was Philip Rising. Rising (1824–1909) was one of Lancaster's wealthiest and most respected businessmen of the day, whose life seemed to personify the American dream. A German immigrant who had come to Fairfield County with his parents at age fourteen, Rising started his business career in Lancaster as a grocery clerk, later becoming a bookkeeper, the proprietor of a clothing store, and then a founder and president of what became the Fairfield National Bank. Befitting his great success, Rising lived in the large brick residence on Main Hill that was built by William J. Reese in 1834.[119]

On December 8, 1908, Rising purchased the seventy-three acre Mount Pleasant property from Buschmeyer at the then impressive price of $16,000, and on December 15 he presented it as a Christmas gift to Lancaster. Rising made only two stipulations: (1) that the property be called Rising Park, and (2) that it be "a free public park for park purposes only," thereby prohibiting restaurants or concessions of any sort on the premises. Unfortunately, Rising did not live to see the formal dedication on July 5, 1909, having died several months before.[120]

Thirteen years later, in 1922, Lancaster received another public park with the donation of 23.8 acres of land at the intersection of West Sixth Avenue and what is now North Memorial Drive. The parcel, known ever since as Miller Park, was a gift of Charles and Julia Hutchinson in the memory of Frederick Miller (whose identity has become uncertain in the decades since).[121] The Lancaster Park Commission extended the park in 1936 when it purchased 9 contiguous acres from William G. Brenner, who had operated a rug factory on the site.[122] (Lying between the old canal bed and the Hocking River, all this property making up Miller Park had once been a marsh and subject to frequent flooding until the river was "channeled" in 1912.) The park commission constructed baseball diamonds in Miller Park, where the high school team as well as many industrial and civic leagues played ball for several decades.

The acquisition of Miller Park also offered a solution to the festering question of where to locate a municipal swimming pool. A public pool campaign had begun as early as 1915, when Lancaster's Boy Scouts launched a drive to collect funds for such a facility, with the idea that it would be built somewhere in Rising Park. Other organizations like the Rotary Club, the senior class of Lancaster High School, and a number of private individuals contributed to the fund. But the park board adamantly refused to allow a swimming pool there, insisting that such a "concession" violated the deed of gift from Philip Rising. Even the collection of 7,000 signatures on a petition, a resolution from the city council urging the park board to reconsider, and editorials in the local newspapers supporting the Rising Park site failed to reverse the decision. The acquisition of Miller Park and the opening of a pool there in 1923 effectively defused the issue and provided the town with its first public swimming facility (one that remains in operation—with several renovations—as the twentieth century comes to a close).[123]

Another local outgrowth of the movement for parks and the "out-of-doors experience" was Lancaster's Fresh Air Camp on Kinkead Hill in the town's North End. The camp was opened sometime after 1914 by Lancaster's first public health nurses, Flora and Fannie Howe, unmarried sisters and Boston natives who spent their lives assisting low-income residents in town. The camp, which was just behind the Howes' bungalow, was for what were then called underprivileged youth, who came each summer for a week in the woods.[124] Both the camp and the Howes' nursing activities were local echoes of programs that had originated among settlement house workers in large cities such as Chicago, New York, and Boston.[125]

Another reform movement that was echoed in Lancaster was the drive to prohibit alcohol. Although the anti-alcohol cause had roots stretching well back into the previous century, locally as well as nationally, the movement received a tremendous boost from the general atmosphere of reform during the early twentieth century. The result was a nationwide ban, through the Eighteenth Amendment to the United States Constitution (ratified in 1919), on the manufacture, sale, and transportation of alcoholic beverages.

Some residents of Lancaster had assisted in this crusade against alcohol through such activities as temperance rallies in Columbus or through the local unit of the Women's Christian Temperance Union.[126] In November 1908 the famous saloon-smasher Carry Nation gave a fiery talk to a packed house in Lancaster's public auditorium, after which her audience could buy miniature pearl hatchets, symbolic of the real hatchets that Nation had used in her saloon-smashing escapades.[127] The *Eagle*, in its coverage of the lecture, surmised that many who had gone that night were attracted by Nation's celebrity status rather than because they supported a legal ban on alcohol.[128]

Those who opposed Prohibition in Lancaster pointed out that the town's thirty-one saloons did a half-million dollars worth of business each year and argued that Prohibition would be ruinous to the local economy. The anti-alcohol forces replied that the saloons themselves produced nothing and that therefore the huge sums of money squandered in the saloons could be better spent on a multitude of more constructive items, such as supplies for men to paint their houses "instead of their noses."[129]

Evidence suggests that Lancastrians were more or less equally divided over the question of banning alcohol. In a statewide referendum held in 1915 to determine whether Ohio would go dry, the vote in Lancaster was

Anti-Prohibition cartoon, *Eagle*, October 13, 1928.

1,423 for the ban and 1,528 against, or 47 percent in favor and 53 percent opposed. In another referendum two years later, 51 percent favored statewide Prohibition and 49 percent opposed it.[130] It was also in 1917 that the East End of Lancaster, defined as that portion of town east of Maple Street, voted to go dry under provisions of Ohio's local option laws that allowed individual communities, including municipal wards, to ban alcohol within their boundaries. Because of this local option initiative, the Last Chance Saloon, which had operated for years at the corner of Main and Cherry Streets, was forced to close.[131] In both 1915 and 1917 the Prohibitionists lost the statewide vote, but finally succeeded, albeit narrowly, in 1918. The results in Lancaster in 1918 were 52 percent in favor, and 48 percent against.[132]

The *Eagle*, which remained the voice of the town's majority Democrats, was openly critical of the Prohibition movement, as Democrats tended to be throughout the country. In October 1908, for instance, it ran a long article quoting a number of prominent clergymen in the United States who opposed banning alcohol, thereby trying to undercut the assertion by temperance groups that banishing drink was a Christian duty.[133] And from the stories that still circulated in this author's childhood about the large number of Lancastrians who made "home brew" once Prohibition went into effect, it would seem safe to conjecture that many residents continued to oppose the measure until it was finally repealed in 1933.

The contention that Prohibition was unpopular among many local inhabitants after it went into effect is also reinforced by stories in the local press about law enforcement officers smashing illegal stills and seizing whiskey that had been smuggled into Lancaster in trucks, automobiles, and railroad cars.[134] Accounts of local citizens who had been poisoned or even killed by drinking denatured alcohol further undermined support for "the noble experiment."[135] The *Eagle*, which had opposed Prohibition from the beginning, reacted to such deaths with a cartoon in October 1928 depicting a row of gravestones in a cemetery, with one of them reading "Poison Booze Victims." Above the cartoon was the caption "Life of the Party."[136] The Republican-oriented *Gazette*, on the other hand, seems to have been more positive about Prohibition, as was the Republican Party as a whole.[137]

The speed with which the Lancaster Brewery, the successor to the old Becker establishment, began producing beer under its new Forest Rose label in the summer of 1934, just after repeal, shows that there was a public ready and willing to consume it. It is also significant that Fairfield County voters overwhelmingly approved the repeal of Prohibition on both the state and national level in a referendum held as a part of the general election in November 1933.[138]

The drive for women's suffrage (that is, the right to vote by women), another large reform movement of the early twentieth century, appeared to have had only a handful of vocal advocates in conservative Lancaster. A few local women attended suffrage rallies in Columbus, but there did not seem to have been any demonstrations in Lancaster in favor of the women's vote.[139]

The fact that Lancaster was not home to a large and vocal suffrage organization does not mean that the Lancaster women were inactive. Many of them contributed to causes that improved local life. One of these was the Froebel Study Club, founded in 1899 by a group of Lancaster women who named their organization after Friedrich Froebel, the German educator and founder of the kindergarten movement. The club devoted itself to children's causes and, fittingly, sponsored the first kindergarten in Lancaster, the precise date and location of which are now unknown.[140]

Women had also organized a number of literary clubs, and in 1902 these groups came together to form the City Federation of Women's Lit-

The Park Street Hospital, opened in 1907. Photo c. 1910. Tobias Studio Collection, Cartoon Research Library, OSU.

erary Clubs. Representing a combined membership of some six hundred women, the federation bought books for the public library, planted trees at Rising Park, purchased a public drinking fountain, and supported the establishment of a local hospital.[141] Typical of these groups was Lancaster's American Literary Club, organized in 1929. Each member had to give an oral book review at least once a year, and the club used money raised from dues to benefit a number of charities.[142]

The Fairfield Garden Club, another organization of great interest to local women, likewise emerged during this period. Founded in 1924 as the Dahlia Club, the organization soon moved away from its exclusive focus on dahlias and changed its name to the Fairfield Garden Club in 1930 to reflect that shift. In the years ahead, the club would hold numerous flower shows, share gardening information and skills, and promote civic beautifi-

Lancaster's first public hospital, opened in 1915 on Ewing Street near the intersection with East Sixth Avenue. Photo c. 1930. Tobias Studio Collection, FCDL.

cation. Among the club's best-known projects have been the planting of flowering crab apple trees around the Rising Park Pond and recurrent projects to plant trees, shrubs, and flowers on the public square downtown, and particularly in the area around the fountain.[143]

Led by the DAR, various women's groups were instrumental in securing Lancaster's first public hospital, a necessary adjustment to the town's growing population. There had been several private hospitals in town since the early twentieth century, most notably the one at 224 Park Street (opened in 1907), which was actually a large two-story frame house. The operating room was on the first floor and the bedrooms on the second, with the doctors themselves often carrying their patients upstairs following surgery. Before that, doctors typically operated on patients in their own homes, with the most serious surgeries being performed in one of the Columbus hospitals. After much debate about a suitable site, the city purchased a ten-acre tract between Ewing Street and Baldwin Run and there erected a three-story brick hospital that opened in 1915.[144]

By the time the new hospital became a reality, the European powers had plunged themselves into the most catastrophic war in history. Just two years later the United States would join the war, and Lancastrians, as they had in former wars, would rally to the colors. What they could not know was that this war would mark the start of an unsettling period in their town, as it did in many other communities throughout the nation.

FIVE

# Turmoil, Depression, and War
## The Town Endures

During the nearly three decades between the American entry in World War I and the end of World War II, national events had less of an impact upon Lancaster than they did in many other parts of the United States. In addition to the two world wars, these events included the Great Depression of the 1930s. Though these events affected residents somewhat less than in other communities around the country, they nevertheless left a mark on the local scene. Like other periods in the town's history, this time of depression and world wars offers distinct examples, on a small scale, of how larger forces affected real communities. This time of turmoil, like the Civil War period a half century before, also revealed that social and cultural divisions continued to exist in Lancaster, though in more muted form than in larger towns and cities.

In agreement with the great majority of Americans, most residents of Lancaster were horrified by the outbreak of war in Europe in the summer of 1914. On July 30, just as war was being declared, the *Gazette* lamented that civilization had made no moral progress at all in the past three thousand years, adding, in reference to the supposed Christianity of the warring nations, "A Christianity that is only in name and theory won't get a nation anywhere." Meanwhile, the *Eagle* found it hard to believe that "the nations of Europe will permit assassins to involve them in a war that would endanger her very civilization."[1] Over the next two and a half years, readers of Lancaster's two newspapers followed accounts of the carnage across the Atlantic as the death toll began to mount into the millions, and as German submarine warfare brought the United States ever closer to hostilities.

Despite their initial horror over the war in Europe, and despite the mounting cost of this most hideous of conflicts, Lancastrians showed enthusiastic support for an American declaration of war in April 1917. On

April 2, the day that Congress convened to consider President Woodrow Wilson's war message, all 2,500 students in the Lancaster schools held patriotic "demonstrations" at their individual buildings, under a directive handed down from the superintendent. At East School, for example, the children assembled in the first-floor hall, where they sang "America the Beautiful," "Hail Columbia," "Old Glory," and "The Star-Spangled Banner." As they sang, the children faced a large American flag draped across the hallway. At Lancaster High the students sang patriotic tunes to the accompaniment of the school orchestra, after which the minister of the First Presbyterian Church, the Reverend Irvine L. Dungan, gave an account of relations between the United States and Germany since the beginning of the conflict in Europe, predicting that Congress would quickly declare war.[2] That same day members of the Lancaster DAR, who had assembled for their regular meeting, sang patriotic songs and pledged their full support to the nation.[3] Then on the evening of April 6, the day that Congress formally declared hostilities against Germany, Lancaster's four Boy Scout troops marched from the Sherman Armory to city hall, where they volunteered their services to Mayor H. L. Repass.[4]

If anyone in Lancaster opposed the declaration of war—and there was considerable opposition among various groups and individuals in the nation at the time—they apparently kept quiet about it. Nor were there any recorded verbal or physical attacks against residents of German ancestry in Lancaster or Fairfield County, as there were in places like Columbus and Cincinnati.[5] This is understandable given the considerable size of the local German American community and the large numbers of business and civic leaders of German ancestry who were widely respected at the time. And in a town the size of Lancaster, where almost any family was known to many other individuals and families, attacks on German American residents were unlikely.

Approximately 2,000 men from Lancaster and Fairfield County went off to war. The first group to report was Lancaster's "Company L" of the Ohio National Guard, who reported to the Sherman Armory on July 15, 1917. Joining with national guard units from all over the United States, Company L became part of the famous Rainbow Division, so-called because of its diverse geographical origins and officially known as the 166th Infantry, Forty-second Division. The Rainbow Division was one of the first to join the American Expeditionary Force in France and saw action at Chateau Thierry, St. Mihiel, and Meuse-Argonne.

Eighty of those who joined the armed forces from Lancaster and Fairfield County lost their lives during the war, 43 of them from wounds or disease while overseas and another 37 from disease in military camps before they could leave the States. Some of them died at Camp Sherman, just outside Chillicothe, Ohio, which had the highest death rate from influenza in Ohio during the late summer and early fall of 1918. The folks back home read with horror about this plague that carried off 178 young men at Camp Sherman in a matter of weeks.[6]

The flu also claimed a number of victims in Lancaster. Although there are no precise mortality figures for the disease, the *Gazette* reported that there had been sixty-seven funerals in Lancaster during October 1918 (the peak month of the epidemic) as opposed to only twenty-four funerals in October of 1917. The newspaper believed that most of these forty-three additional deaths could be attributed to the flu.[7]

Already well organized for civic and charitable activities before the American declaration of war, the women of Lancaster and Fairfield County mobilized for the emergency. The Women's Liberty Loan Committee of Fairfield County sold a total of $628,300 in war bonds. Women of the local Council of National Defense gave canning demonstrations and donated jellies and fruits to the hospital in Lancaster. They also galvanized women throughout the county to knit socks, scarves, sweaters, and other garments for the men in service. Women were likewise in the forefront of Red Cross work.[8]

In reaction to the news, false as it turned out, that the Germans had agreed to an armistice on November 7, 1918, thousands of people poured into downtown Lancaster for an impromptu parade.[9] When a real armistice came on November 11 the town was better prepared and held an even more massive parade that evening, beginning at 7:30 P.M. The parade began with the fire department, including their new motorized truck, followed by the police, the Grand Army of the Republic (that is, Civil War veterans), the Spanish War veterans, the chamber of commerce, the Red Cross, the Navy League, the Boy Scouts, workers from the various industries, and students from the local schools. The shoe workers carried lighted Japanese lanterns, and the railroad workers, illuminated kerosene lanterns. There were several dummy Kaisers carried through the streets in coffins and at least one Kaiser hanging in effigy from a mock gallows.[10]

A second celebratory parade greeted the return of Company L to Lancaster on May 17, 1919. The company commander, Captain William

Captain William Belhorn, Company L, Rainbow Division, United States Army, carrying flowers given to him by a grateful town during the World War I victory parade, May 17, 1919. Tobias Studio Collection, Cartoon Research Library, OSU.

Belhorn, received a bouquet of carnations from the "shoe factory girls," and from the Red Cross, a bunch of fleur-de-lis tied with Rainbow colors—both of which he carried in the parade down a Main Hill thronged with spectators.[11] (Belhorn would be elected Fairfield County sheriff in the 1930s, mayor of Lancaster during World War II, and, for many years, would be the proprietor of a popular news and sporting goods store called The City News.)

Doubtless no one in the parade, or in the crowd that May afternoon, realized that the fear and uncertainties that had been unleashed by the war would soon inspire a wave of hatred and repression throughout the United States. One manifestation of that troubled atmosphere in Lancaster and Fairfield County was the Ku Klux Klan. The Klan had been founded in the South just after the Civil War as a white supremacist organization that terrorized the recently emancipated slaves and, in particular, tried to keep them from voting. This first Klan was destroyed for the most part by occupying Union armies, but it was revived in Atlanta, Georgia, in 1915. In addition to prejudice against African Americans, the renewed Klan castigated

Jews, Catholics, and "foreigners." After World War I, which did much to stir up fear in the United States, the Klan began recruiting in the North, led by two unscrupulous publicity agents, Edward Young Clarke and Elizabeth Tyler, who made large sums of money by retaining a percentage of each initiation fee.[12]

The Klan was especially strong in the lower half of Ohio, where white Southerners had settled since the early nineteenth century and continued to settle after World War I in search of jobs. Although Klansmen in southern Ohio did sometimes vent their anger against blacks and other minorities, their main target was Roman Catholics, whose numbers were growing and who appeared to undermine conservative Protestant beliefs. Those attracted to the Klan also feared that Catholics posed a grave threat to American democracy, charging that Catholics owed absolute obedience to a foreign power, that is, the Pope in Rome. In addition, many conservative Protestants, often called fundamentalists at that time as well as later, became alarmed at what they saw as challenges to a literal reading of the Bible by liberal clergy and theologians. Such cultural conservatives were also concerned at the growth of what they viewed as immoral behavior during the so-called revolution in manners and morals in the 1920s. However, many Protestants belonging to more liberal denominations were appalled by the Klan and sometimes criticized it openly.[13]

Residents of Lancaster probably became Klan members, as they did in other communities in Ohio and elsewhere, for a variety of reasons. Some joined out of genuine hate and intolerance, some for the political and economic opportunities that membership might offer, some because it was simply "the thing to do," and others because they sincerely believed that the Klan was a force for reform that would rescue the nation from modern immoralities and dangerous foreign influences. A researcher during the mid-1920s, when the Klan had reached its peak, believed that only a small minority, perhaps 5 percent of Klan members, were genuine haters and that the vast majority had joined the Klan for the other reasons listed above.[14]

Although Klansmen burned crosses and held marches in Lancaster, and engaged in verbal smears against Catholics and the Protestants who defended them, there were no reports of Klan violence in town. Local Klansmen did take part in two massive rallies at Buckeye Lake, one in 1923 and the other in 1925, that were attended by the heads of the Klan organization in the United States, including the Imperial Wizard, Hiram Evans.

Organizing these events was David C. Stevenson, leader of the Klan in the Midwest, who had a summer home at Buckeye Lake.[15]

On October 25, 1924, Klansmen from throughout central Ohio held a large "konklave and barbecue" in Lancaster, with a torchlight parade through downtown and assorted activities at the fairgrounds. Tellingly, neither of Lancaster's newspapers lifted a voice in protest over the event, though the *Eagle*, perhaps reflecting the Democratic Party's continuing appeal to Catholics nationally as well as regionally, carried only a small notice about the "konklave" in Lancaster.[16] The Republican *Gazette*, on the other hand, printed a description of the festivities that was particularly colorful and positive in tone:

> An orderly crowd numbering thousands lined the streets downtown where the parade was viewed to good advantage. The impression was especially beautiful as the robed figures turned the corner of High and Main streets and marched down Main Hill in the glare of hundreds of red light torches carried by klansmen. . . . After reaching the fairgrounds the marchers circled the race track which was illuminated with red and green lights. . . . A crowd of spectators estimated between 15,000 and 20,000 witnessed the event. . . . Three large crosses were burned and several bombs were exploded as part of the demonstration. An airplane bearing an electrically lighted cross gave spectators a thrill as it circled the field and then flew over the city.[17]

Because of the opprobrium in which the Klan would later be held, local Klan members were not forthcoming about their activities in later years. However, an interview in 1981 with Hubert Eyman Sr., a longtime dentist, member of the board of education, and a strong opponent of the Klan, gave some indication of the pressure that the Klan could put on individuals to join. Often when Eyman stepped out of his office into the hall, a neighboring optometrist would badger him to join the Klan. After consistently refusing, the Klan put Eyman on its "Catholic blacklist," even though he was a lifelong Protestant. His practice suffered for several months as a result, until a number of Catholic families discovered what the Klan had done to him and became some of his most loyal patients.

Eyman also remembered that Klan support had contributed significantly to the election of Bert Alspach, as mayor of Lancaster in 1923, and of Roy McNaughton, as sheriff of Fairfield County in 1924, a remembrance that is confirmed by the local newspapers of the time.[18] Getting its members elected to public office was a tactic that the Klan used throughout the country in order to extend its influence into government itself.[19] Under the circumstances, any complaints to local law enforcement agents about Klan activities would have been futile.

After reaching a peak membership nationwide in 1924, the Klan began to decline, and by the end of the decade it had all but disappeared. Several factors led to its demise, including internal squabbles, revelations of financial corruption, and resentment in the North over attempts by Southerners to keep control of the organization. But the most important factor leading to the downfall of the Klan was the murder conviction of David C. Stevenson, the head of the Midwest Klan. Stevenson and another Klansman had abducted, assaulted, and raped a young Indianapolis woman who, in her shame and humiliation, poisoned herself. After these revelations it was difficult to claim that the Klan was a moral organization that wanted only to uphold Christian teachings or to save the United States from a variety of modern evils.[20] No doubt the advancing prosperity of the second half of the 1920s also undercut the Klan's popularity, feeding as it did on economic uncertainties during the years just after World War I.

It is ironic that the Klan should have made a strong showing in Lancaster at a time when both its foreign-born and African American populations were lower, as a percentage of the whole, than at any time in at least six decades. What this suggests is that the Klan's attraction locally had less to do with hatred of particular groups than it did with vague fears during a time of rapid changes in American life as a whole.

Whatever the case, the foreign-born population of Lancaster in 1920 was just 1.8 percent—with Germans, at .7 percent of the town's inhabitants, continuing to lead the list of those born outside the United States. This foreign-born population in 1920 had declined from 4.3 percent in 1900, from 10 percent in 1880, and from 17.5 percent in 1860. Lancaster's African American residents were only 1 percent of the total in 1920, as compared to 2.1 percent in 1900, 3.1 percent in 1880, and 3.3 percent in 1860.[21] The sharp decline of German immigration to the United States, which had been large in Midwestern towns and rural areas during the nineteenth century, was probably the main reason that the foreign-born population of Lancaster had grown smaller. The falling off of its black community probably had to do with the lack of jobs beyond domestic service and unskilled labor for most blacks, with the consequence that many young blacks moved away in search of better opportunities. This at least was the explanation given by Holly Saunders, an African American resident whose family has lived in Lancaster for several generations. In a 1997 interview Saunders, who has written and spoken widely about the history of the local black community, explained, "Lancaster [back then] was considered a really prejudiced town. If you were from Lancaster, you were considered a bonded slave."[22]

Roman Catholics, around whom most Klan opposition centered, were also a relatively small minority, though their ranks were certainly larger than local African Americans. There are no overall figures for the religious affiliations of Lancastrians at any period. But even if one assumes that all inhabitants of Irish ancestry and a quarter to a third of those with German roots (not including the Pennsylvania "Dutch") were Catholic, one would have to conclude that Catholics did not represent more than 10 or 15 percent of residents who identified themselves with a particular church.

Beyond any consideration of the Klan itself, Lancaster's African Americans continued to face various forms of segregation and discrimination. Most of them still resided in the South End or in the East Wheeling/East Mulberry Street neighborhood. The schools were now integrated, but most restaurants did not serve blacks, and several eateries had signs outside that read "We cater to the Caucasian Race Only," notices that remained into the middle 1940s. The local movie houses required blacks to sit in the last two or three rows and to give up their places if white patrons could not find seats, a custom that lasted until the World War II period. Blacks could swim at the Miller Park pool only on Fridays, since the pool was cleaned on Friday night.[23]

Kenneth Saunders, the father of Holly Saunders and an African American who has lived in Lancaster all his life, confirmed a long-held oral tradition that Lancaster's African American community itself acted to limit the number of black newcomers to town through a so-called "screening committee," which determined whether or not a would-be resident could rent or buy property in the black neighborhoods. Saunders believed that the screening committee, which operated into the 1950s, enjoyed support and encouragement from the city government itself (though, understandably, there has been no documented evidence of such official support).[24] The decreasing population of this African American community, its willingness to limit its own size, and its acquiescence in Lancaster's unwritten rules on race relations were probably among the reasons there were few if any outward acts of violence against local blacks. Reflecting this attitude was the oft-heard comment, even in this author's childhood and youth: "Oh, we have a nice class of colored people here in Lancaster. They never cause any trouble and know how to stay in their place."[25]

Experiencing less discrimination but still feeling the sting of prejudice from time to time was Lancaster's small Italian population. There had been a handful of residents of Italian background in the vicinity since as early as the 1840s, but Italian immigration to Lancaster did not become significant until the first decades of the twentieth century, as was the case with Italian immigration throughout the United States as a whole. Many of Lancaster's Italians were drawn to town by jobs at Hocking Glass and settled on the West Side near the plant. According to genealogist Agnes Moio, Lancaster's Little Italy, long gone by the late twentieth century, "included O'Gara Avenue, Baker Street, Miller Avenue, and West Mulberry Street between Busby and Sylvan avenues."[26]

Paul Pulsinelli recalled that the families on these streets spoke Italian among themselves and often went on outings together. Many of the older women, he added, never learned to speak English and only left the neighborhood to attend mass at St. Mary Church. Yet because the Italian community remained small, there was no question of establishing a separate Italian parish, and thus Lancaster's Roman Catholics were spared the sorts of divisions that came with ethnic parishes in many large cities in the United States. Pulsinelli also remembered that some non-Italian parents warned their children to stay away from Italian kids, warning, "They might knife you."[27] Descendants of many early-twentieth-century Italian families remain in Lancaster, including such well-recognized names as Agosta, Cenci, Dandrea, Eramo, Grilli, Macioci, Perigo, Pulsinelli, Probasco, Trego, and Ventresca.

Lancaster also had a small Jewish community during the first decades of the twentieth century.[28] The first Jewish resident appears to have settled in Lancaster about 1907, and by the 1930s there were several dozen Jewish families in town. According to the 1920 federal census schedules, some twenty adults in Lancaster listed their "mother tongue" as Yiddish, a language spoken by Jews in central and eastern Europe. Because the census did not record information about religion, this is the only official indication of Jewish residents at the time in Lancaster. Twelve of the twenty gave Russia as their place of birth, four as Austria, three as Poland, and one

Women chatting on a summer afternoon in the 1930s in front of Epstein's Shoes on Main Street, owned and operated by one of Lancaster's many successful Jewish families. Cover page of *FHQ*, Spring 1986.

as Hungary.[29] Thus, the majority of Lancaster's Jews, in 1920 at least, appeared to be from eastern Europe, the most recent and the most numerous group of Jews coming to the United States at the time.

Although Jews tended to live in the North and East Ends, there was no distinctly Jewish neighborhood. In 1925 Lancaster's Jews purchased the former Emanuel Lutheran Church on East Chestnut Street and established the B'nai Israel Synagogue. Most of these Jewish families made a living through retail businesses, the names and proprietors of which were well known in Lancaster over several decades. These included Henry Morris's Syndicate dry goods store, Epstein Shoes, the Lancaster Fruit Company (of Jacob Mellman, Morris Yabrove, Albert Long, and Jacob Bogroff), Albert Schatz's Lancaster Auto Parts, Harry Abrams's Fashion Ladies Ready-to-Wear, Leo Kessel's Palace Theater, and Sam Silver's fruit and vegetable stall at the Wheeling Street Market House. These men, as well as the other Jewish residents of Lancaster, were successful businessmen who were well respected by the non-Jewish population. Because of this, both Jews and gentiles agree that there was very little anti-Semitism in Lancaster, though some anti-Jewish sentiment undoubtedly came up in private conversations and Jews were not admitted to certain clubs in town.[30]

Yet the prosperity in which Lancaster's Jews participated with the rest of the town appeared to be threatened for a few frightening weeks in the late winter of 1924. For on the night of March 6–7, a massive fire totally destroyed the Hocking Glass Plant on the West Side. The night sky was filled with an orange-red glow that could be seen for miles around, as fire equipment rushed to the disaster from as far away as Columbus. Assisted and encouraged by a subscription of funds from local residents, the company decided to rebuild on the same site and, taking advantage of the total destruction, to erect an entirely new plant with the latest and most productive equipment, which allowed Hocking Glass to emerge even stronger than before the fire.[31]

Five years later a genuine economic disaster, known as the Great Depression, began to grip the nation and much of the world. In Germany the Depression helped bring Adolf Hitler to power and thus contributed to launching World War II. Throughout the industrialized world, millions of men and women lost their jobs, while central governments grew stronger in an attempt to cope with the ravages of mass unemployment and economic dislocation. In the United States the Depression ended twelve years of Republican rule and led to the election of Franklin D. Roosevelt and his controversial New Deal. In contrast to such momentous events, there were not as many dramatic changes in Lancaster.

As it did elsewhere, the Depression reached a peak in the local area during the early 1930s. It is not surprising, then, that the first organized efforts to deal with the Depression locally did not come until December 1930, when a Central Welfare Association opened in downtown Lancaster on West Main Street. The task of this agency was to coordinate private relief, but it later distributed public foodstuffs, such as the two "car loads of government flour" that arrived in July 1932.[32] Also responding to the crisis was Lancaster's Salvation Army, which had been established in 1900.[33] By the early months of 1933, the worst period of the entire Depression, some 3,471 persons in Fairfield County were on state relief rolls.[34] These persons represented slightly under 8 percent of a total county population of 44,010 in 1930.[35] Although these numbers represented a significant amount of suffering, they were modest in comparison to the situation in Ohio cities such as Cleveland, Akron, and Youngstown, where more than half of all industrial workers were unemployed at the height of the Depression.[36]

In contrast to many other communities, none of Lancaster's four banks went out of business during the Depression. When President Roosevelt did close the banks for four days (March 5–8, 1933), Lancaster managed to pay its public employees in cash, leaving the treasurer's office so short of coinage that it had to call on two local Sunday schools to change some of its paper currency.[37]

Perhaps because of their historic devotion to the Democratic Party, residents of Lancaster and Fairfield County were among the earliest beneficiaries of funds from the New Deal's Public Works Administration (PWA), established in June 1933 and used largely for building and maintaining roads.[38] After its establishment in April 1935, the Works Progress Administration (WPA) provided jobs for a wider variety of the unemployed. Lancaster's WPA was administered by A. M. Judson, whose staff included Ruth B. Fuller, later a well-known local newspaper columnist. Under grants from the WPA, Lancaster repaved a number of streets.[39] The WPA also operated several nursery schools in town, funded a canning "factory" on Lincoln Avenue just west of the present Memorial Drive, where women canned locally grown fruits and vegetables that were distributed to the needy, and helped to finance Lancaster's first sewage disposal plant, a venture that had been discussed for nearly twenty years.[40] Then there was the Civilian Conservation Corps (CCC), which had a local headquarters on Camp Ground Road west of Lancaster. The unmarried young men employed by the CCC planted trees on Lancaster's Sheridan Drive and undertook reforestation projects in the Hocking Hills south of town, including those at Rock House and Ash Cave. These men, who were housed, fed, and clothed by the CCC, received thirty dollars a month for their work, twenty-five of which went home to their families.[41]

Farmers in the county were, if anything, harder hit by the Depression than workers in Lancaster, for agricultural prices, already in a slump during the 1920s, fell even further during the Depression. Hot, dry summers and a local dust storm in 1934 only made matters worse.[42] Funds from the federal government paid to local farmers to reduce corn and hog production in 1934 assisted a number of farmers, as would similar federal subsidies in the future. The coming of the Rural Electrification Administration, created by an executive order from President Roosevelt in 1935, made life easier for area farmers, who could now illuminate their homes, barns, and outbuildings with electricity and take advantage of various implements and appliances, such as refrigerators and mechanical milkers.[43]

Doubtless because of the disastrous drop in farm income, the county school system, which was then and still remains separate from the Lancaster system, found itself in serious difficulty. In March of 1932, for instance, teachers at Bremen, Carroll, Berne Union, Rushville, and Stoutsville had their salaries reduced by an average of 12 percent. By contrast, the Lancaster schools did not have to resort to salary reductions and met their payrolls and other obligations without difficulty throughout the Depression.[44]

According to the board of education itself, the relative financial health of the Lancaster schools owed to the fact that local industry, for the most part, was not badly affected by the Depression. Hocking Glass, for example, continued to produce several low-cost lines of tableware (including so-called Depression glass) and did not have to lay off any of its employees, though there were times during the worst months of the Depression when some did not enjoy a full week's work.[45] Employment at the Godman shoe factories in Lancaster was far less steady. According to Foster Williamson (later the proprietor of an auto repair shop on the West Side and an amateur magician), he had only two months of full-time work at Godman during 1931 and 1932, and then received eight dollars a week for his efforts.[46]

In the face of low wages and uncertain hours, Godman employees formed a union, Local 214 of the Boot and Shoeworkers, and sought recognition from Godman. This union recruitment at the local shoe factories took place in late 1933 and early 1934 amidst a nationwide organizational effort that was encouraged by the National Industrial Recovery Act (NIRA), passed by Congress in June 1933. The act urged industries to draw up codes of fair practice that included minimum wage and maximum hour regulations and asserted the rights of employees to join unions and bargain collectively.

In Fairfield County this wave of unionization led to the tremendous growth of the Central Labor Union, established in 1932 as an affiliation of various unions in the county that belonged to the American Federation of Labor.[47] The Central Union held a mass meeting on the afternoon of March 11, 1934 (a Sunday), at the public auditorium, where the principal speakers were C. H. Griffey, superintendent of the Lancaster schools, and Thomas "Tom" Joyce, president of the Central Labor group. According to Joyce, the purpose of the meeting was "to organize every worker in Fairfield County."[48] As Joyce spoke, the nation's auto workers were threatening a massive strike and in the weeks ahead, while the working men and women of Lancaster and Fairfield County were organizing unions and seeking recognition, the newspapers were filled with stories about strikes, lockouts, and negotiations in one industry after another throughout the United States.

Under President Charles Eck, the union at Godman Shoes protested to management about a new wage plan, implemented in March 1934, that figured wages solely on piecework rather than on a combination of piecework and hourly wages that had prevailed up to that time. Although there was talk of a walkout, the union took no action against Godman until a strike by workers at the Godman shoe plants in Columbus broke out later that year on August 24.[49]

The leaders of the Boot and Shoeworkers in Lancaster, now headed by acting president Charles Shaner, denied that their walkout had anything to do with the strike in Columbus, citing company violations of seniority rights and the dismissal of some union workers as the reasons for their action. However, the timing of the union walkout in Lancaster, which began on September 2, would appear to be more than coincidental.[50] Violence soon erupted as striking employees attacked those who were continuing to work. The worst incidents occurred on September 5 at the factory on the southwest corner of Columbus and Mulberry Streets (a building later used by RBM and still later by Fairfield Industries). There, strikers attacked several groups of women who had not joined the walkout. Their clothes were torn and several sustained minor injuries. Strikers also accosted the driver of a car who had come to pick up several women after work. They smashed one of the car windows, hit the driver in the mouth and eye and one of the female passengers in the lip. Lancaster police fired tear gas into the crowd to stop further violence.[51] Then, on September 14, a Godman truck driver from Lancaster named George Hansel was assaulted by six Lancaster men, assisted by another from Columbus, who threw a four-pound rock through his windshield. Hansel lay in a Logan hospital for several days near death but eventually recovered.[52]

Godman president Fred Miller responded to the strikes in both Columbus and Lancaster by announcing on September 6 that the shoe factories in both places would be closed until October 1. Citing concern for the safety of workers as his reason for doing so, this action was known in labor circles of the day as a "lockout," a tactic being used by many owners to defeat strikers by engendering support from employees who wanted to

One of Lancaster's four Godman shoe factories, located on the southwest corner of Columbus and Mulberry Streets and the scene of the worst violence during the shoe strike of August–October 1934.

continue working and from the larger community, which stood to lose a good deal of money during the strike. By this time the Lancaster union was insisting on recognition from Godman, the marking of each shoe to state that it was made by union labor, and the establishment of a closed shop—that is, Godman would agree to hire only union members in the future. Despite the efforts of a federal mediator, Godman refused to give in to union demands; and shoe workers went back to reopened factories in mid-October with little to show for their efforts.[53] By then Godman itself had been crippled by lost sales and lost markets. Four years later, in 1938, all its Lancaster factories closed for good, though the Columbus operation would continue until 1957.[54]

Throughout the strike, Lancaster police made it clear that they would not tolerate violence at the shoe factories. On the morning of September 7, Police Chief Gail Sesler assured a reporter for the *Gazette* that the department was well equipped "to stop all disturbances at the start of trouble and will not hesitate to use them when [the] occasion [arose]." Two weeks later, on September 21, Mayor Charles E. Moore issued a proclamation stating that anyone caught disturbing the peace or defacing and destroying property would be "dealt with in the most severe manner permitted by law." In order to back up the mayor's proclamation, eighteen "special police," who may have been hired from a private agency, augmented the regular force.[55] Then, as if to show that the order was serious, police arrested an out-of-town man whom they accused of being a Communist agent sent for the purpose of agitating the Godman strikers, though there was apparently not enough evidence to bring charges against him.[56]

Although some local businesses sympathized enough with the strikers to send food to those walking the picket lines, the business community as a whole was unsympathetic. As a sign of their displeasure, a large group of business and professional men, calling themselves a citizens committee, met on the evening of September 19 at the Lancaster Chamber of Commerce, where some sixty-one merchants signed an agreement not to extend credit to any strikers, adding that the strike had been engineered by "a small group of individuals who, through devious means, have affected a majority of . . . wage earners who really want to stay on their jobs."[57] The next morning, representatives of this group fanned out all over town to sign up merchants who had not attended the meeting the previous evening. On October 3 all four banks in Lancaster joined the credit boycott.[58] Clark Beach, editor of the Republican-oriented *Gazette*, sided with the business community in a number of editorials, including one that appeared on the front page on September 18:

> There is a grave danger of Lancaster going hungry. We do not mean just those out of work but nearly everyone. . . . Lancaster gets its money to buy food from just two places, Godman and Hocking Glass. . . . Godman is not working. . . .
>
> Your home is here, your children go to school here, your friends live here, your father or mother live here and you have loved ones buried here. . . . [But] here we are fighting among ourselves, losing wages, losing business and generally making a fool of ourselves while in neighboring towns they are working and eating and watching the scrap without paying any admission.[59]

The *Eagle*, which continued to orient itself toward the Democratic Party, condemned that "small minority group within the ranks of local Union Labor" who had behaved irresponsibly, but not the strike itself.[60]

Over at the *Gazette*, publisher Beach refused to let up on the union even after the strike was over, and in another front-page piece, which

Thomas "Tom" Joyce and grandson Jimmy. Joyce headed the local Flint Glassworker's Union during the unionization of Lancaster's glass factories in the mid-1930s and remained an important labor leader in town for many years thereafter. *Forbes*, November 15, 1947, p. 60.

appeared on October 9, he proclaimed that the six-week work stoppage had cost the town exactly $135,770.35 in wages—not including the money lost to merchants, landlords, and many others in town. Such suffering had been visited on Lancaster, according to Beach, because a group of "radicals" had insisted on a closed shop.[61]

Meanwhile, union efforts at Hocking Glass were meeting with more success. Recognition of Local 519 of the American Flint Glassworker's Union proceeded relatively smoothly, in part because the union, led by Tom Joyce (who also headed the Central Labor group), asked for a union shop as opposed to a closed shop. That is, the company would be free to hire whomever it wished, whether or not they belonged to the union. However, within thirty days of being hired, workers would have to become members of the Flint Glassworkers. Joyce, who was actually an employee of the Lancaster Lens, negotiated a similar agreement with the Lens Company.[62]

Joyce's own moderate stance toward unions was doubtless another reason that Lancaster's glass industry escaped the sort of ugliness that accompanied the failed attempts of local shoeworkers to gain recognition from Godman. In an interview that he gave in 1947, Joyce explained his mild view of labor-management relations:

> *A man should be able to run his business with a minimum of interference.* When any of my union boys come up with grievances which seem to me to be interfering with company rights, I tell them to lay off. . . . And here's another thing: *I don't believe in strikes.* They cost too much money—workers' money. The easiest thing in the world for a union official is to call a strike. It's dramatic, it makes headlines, but too often the worker comes out second best. It's much harder but more effective to sit things out over a conference table [emphasis in the original].[63]

For its part Hocking Glass, which was represented in the negotiations by Vice President and General Manager William V. Fisher, agreed to comply with the glass industry code under the National Recovery Administration (NRA), which recognized the right of glassworkers to form unions. Indeed, Fisher and union leader Joyce were both members of Fairfield County's "compliance board," a group that had been established by the NRA to oversee local cooperation with the recovery legislation passed by Congress.[64] Although unionization at Hocking Glass occurred without a strike, union leaders did threaten to take such action if the union were not recognized. Coming during the same year as the Godman troubles, such a threat frightened many in town who envisioned a complete paralysis of the local economy.

In order to encourage labor peace and a positive attitude toward the company by employees, Hocking Glass began to sponsor a Labor Day picnic and celebration in 1936 (a tactic that had been used by many industries throughout the country to maintain labor peace).[65] Another more specific motive was doubtless to undercut any Labor Day programs sponsored by the union itself, as had occurred in September 1934, when the American Flint Glassworkers staged a large rally at the fairgrounds.[66] Pulling out all stops for the 1936 picnic, the glass company staged a daylong series of Labor Day events in Miller Park. There were pony rides, a circus aerial act, and merry-go-round; free ice cream, lemonade, and soda pop; and swimming at the Miller Park pool, with admissions paid by the company. Two large tents provided shade. The day ended with a fireworks display, again courtesy of Hocking Glass.[67]

Music for the 1936 Labor Day gala came courtesy of the Glassco Band and Glassco Glee Club, both made up of employees. These musical groups were just two of the recreational and social activities organized by Hocking Glass in another bid to bring about harmony and good will toward the company (again, fairly common practices among large American industries). There were also bowling, baseball, basketball, and volleyball teams. Some years later the company offered a glowing description of such activities to the newspaper public: "Men and women from the shops, warehouses, lehrs, furnaces, offices—from every plant, in every department and division . . . combine their interests and skills in a voluntary association known as 'Glassco,' an employees' club fostering a widely diversified program of Athletics, Entertainment, and Welfare."[68]

To insure themselves a continuing good press, Hocking Glass purchased the *Gazette,* Lancaster's traditionally Republican newspaper, for an undisclosed price from owner and editor Clark Beach, in October 1934. Among the new directors of the *Gazette* was I. J. Collins himself, founder and president of Hocking Glass.[69]

The *Eagle* also ceased to be a potential worry to the glass company in early 1936 when the two newspapers, long political rivals, merged to become the *Lancaster Eagle-Gazette,* with the first combined issue appearing on March 11 of that year.[70] The merger was part of a national trend, as newspapers—once instruments of the political parties—turned increasingly to advertising for their incomes and became business enterprises in their own right rather than mouthpieces for sponsoring parties. With an emphasis upon advertising dollars, newspapers could ill afford to alienate potential customers through partisan appeals. And because their own prosperity depended upon the well-being of the entire community, such independent newspapers became unabashed boosters of the town, with virtually no criticism of local business and industry.

The *Eagle-Gazette* merger came about through the initiative of Charles Sawyer (1887–1979) of Cincinnati, principal owner of Ohio News, Inc., which at the time controlled some twenty-nine newspapers in the state. Sawyer bought a controlling interest in the *Eagle* from the Wetzel family, which had long been the main owners of the paper. Sawyer then sent R. Kenneth Kerr to Lancaster as the *Eagle*'s publisher in late 1935 to manage the details of the merger and then to become publisher of the combined newspapers. Hocking Glass remained a major stockholder after the merger, reflected by the fact that William V. Fisher, vice president of

R. Kenneth Kerr, publisher of the *Lancaster Eagle-Gazette* and the town's most enthusiastic booster from the late 1930s to the early 1950s. *Forbes*, November 15, 1947, p. 118.

Hocking Glass, sat on the *Eagle-Gazette* Board of Directors.[71] Although principal owner Charles Sawyer was a prominent Democrat, he belonged to the conservative wing of the party, was outspokenly pro-business, and was unlikely to be partial to labor unions or to be critical of business practices. Sawyer would go on to become U.S. Ambassador to Belgium and Minister to Luxembourg (1944–45), and later President Harry S. Truman's secretary of commerce (1948–53). As commerce secretary, Sawyer would gain much publicity when he reluctantly seized, on Truman's orders, the nation's steel mills because of a crippling strike during the Korean War. (The United States Supreme Court invalidated this seizure in a landmark case known as *Youngstown Sheet and Tube Co. v. Sawyer*, 1952.)[72]

*Eagle-Gazette* publisher Kenneth Kerr (1898–1953), a native of Washington Court House, Ohio, now became Lancaster's principal booster.[73] Under his direction the newspaper steered clear of controversial issues and became a cheerful booster of any project that promised to engender civic pride, bring about harmony and cooperation, or promote business and industry. "If it's for Lancaster, the *Eagle-Gazette* is for it" became the editorial motto that appeared in every issue of the paper.[74] And in order to recognize men and women in Lancaster who had contributed to community well-being, Kerr instituted, in 1938, the awarding of an orchid each week to some outstanding individual. Every Saturday afternoon until the early 1970s, when the prize was discontinued, the recipient's name appeared in a box in the right-hand corner of the masthead, along with a brief listing of the activities and personal qualities that had merited the award.[75] Anyone who received the orchid could bask in the glow of weeklong congratulations from family, neighbors, and friends: "Guess who received the orchid this week?" or "Did you see who got the orchid?" became a predictable source of conversation that ranged from pleasure, surprise, and sometimes doubt as to whether the recipient truly deserved the distinction. Talking about "the orchid," like discussing high school graduating classes or what was playing at the movie theaters, emerged as a recurrent topic that provided a reassuring sense of community and comradeship for many that transcended both social class and personal interests.

When it came to the subject of Hocking Glass itself, or to any of its officers, Kerr and the *Eagle-Gazette* were careful to say little or nothing, either positive or negative, about the glass company. However, the newspaper did run frequent, full-page broadsides that looked as if they might have been supplied by the National Association of Manufacturers—or by some other pro-industry organization. These broadsides praised labor for its essential contribution to the nation's prosperity at the same time that they played down the advisability of labor-management conflict, called upon workers to cooperate with management, and held out the possibility that workers themselves might rise into the ranks of wealthy industrialists.

The broadside that ran in the *Eagle-Gazette* on October 31, 1936, was typical. Depicting a contented laborer looking down from a scaffold onto an executive arriving in an expensive car, the worker says to himself, "I knew him when he pushed a wheelbarrow." Reinforcing the idea that most anyone could ascend to the highest ranks, the accompanying text asserts, "A big percentage of the 'higher-ups' in American industry started at the bottom of the ladder," a statement that is not supported by studies of social mobility in the first half of the twentieth century.[76] That same month another such broadside depicted a bronzed and muscular young worker standing upright, arms folded, with an appeal in bold letters beside him that reads "Help Protect the name of Labor!" The message that followed was calculated to leave no doubt in readers' minds that the way for workers to keep their good names was to cooperate with their employers: "Honest, loyal workmen are determined to continue this [American economic] progress and uphold the good name and good faith of labor as a whole. Willingness to co-operate with industry is the keynote of past success. It holds the only sure hope for the future."[77] Beneath each broadside was the credit line "Published in the Interest of a Better Lancaster by the *Lancaster Eagle-Gazette*." Although the editors obviously wanted readers to see these messages as neutral on the question of labor and industry, it is clear that they were pro-industry and against any sort of group consciousness on the part of working men—or the idea that labor unions should question the wisdom of management decisions.

In reality the *Eagle-Gazette*, as well as local industry as a whole, had few worries when it came to labor-management relations in the late 1930s, or of industrial prosperity in the area. Although the closing of the Godman shoe factories in 1938 was undoubtedly a hardship for some, the merger of Hocking Glass with Anchor Cap Company in 1937 more than made up for the loss. In that year the Anchor Cap Company, which manufactured a variety of closures for bottles and jars, along with sealing machinery, "acquired all properties, assets, and business" of Hocking Glass in exchange for 60 percent of its capital stock. The deal was arranged so that Hocking Glass interests—namely, I. J. Collins, president; William V. Fisher, vice president; and Thomas C. Fulton, treasurer—remained in control of the new Anchor Hocking Corporation. As a consequence of the merger, Anchor Hocking became one of the largest producers of glass tableware and closures in the world, with offices and plants throughout the United States. Shortly after the merger, in 1938, Anchor Hocking established its corporate headquarters in downtown Lancaster, in a red-brick office building overlooking the northwest corner of the town square. The structure, with a series of bay windows along its second and third stories, had a vague Colonial Revival look about it that complemented neighboring buildings. Although visitors as well as residents often remarked at such humble headquarters for one of the nation's largest industries, this understated building echoed the low profile that Anchor Hocking Glass, and Collins in particular, wished to maintain in the public eye.[78]

Although 1938 was a difficult year for much of the country, as the United States slipped into what has been dubbed the Roosevelt Recession (due to cutbacks in government spending), Lancaster and Fairfield County felt few effects of the slowdown, according to the *Eagle-Gazette*.[79] In addi-

This attractive but unimposing building on the northwest corner of Main and Broad Streets housed the Anchor Hocking corporate headquarters for half a century, from 1938 to 1988. Photo by author, 1997.

tion to the Anchor Hocking merger, the establishment or expansion of other industries were doubtless responsible for this happy state of affairs. In late 1938, for example, the Ray-O-Vac Battery plant in Lancaster added five hundred more workers to its force.[80] In 1939 the Irving Drew Shoe Company moved to Lancaster from Portsmouth, Ohio, and began manufacturing special-order shoes in the former Godman (and before that, Getz) Shoe Factory on the northwest corner of Forest Rose Avenue and Mulberry Street.[81] That same year the Hermann Manufacturing Company, a maker of machine tools that had first come to Lancaster in 1923, took over part of another Godman building near the southwest corner of Columbus and Mulberry Streets.[82] In 1940 the Big Bear supermarket chain of Columbus opened a store in still another former Godman factory on the southeast corner of the same intersection.[83] Other positive indicators of economic health included an announcement in 1938 by Lancaster's banks that the value of their check clearings now equaled a pre-Depression high of $2 million. That same year enrollment in the Lancaster schools reached the then record high of 3,852 students. In addition, some

Crowds line downtown streets, shown here at the corner of Main and Broad Streets, for the "last roundup" of Lancaster's trolleys in October 1937. Tobias Studio Collection, FCDL.

fifty new houses were going up in various parts of town during the spring and summer of 1938.[84]

Another sign of progress to many was the replacement in 1937 of Lancaster's trolleys with brand-new General Motors buses. These arrived from the GM plant in Pontiac, Michigan, in mid-October, replacing the old trolleys on the 30th of that month. Thousands of residents lined the streets to witness the nostalgic "last roundup," as the trolleys made their final run to the barns at Fair Avenue and Broad Street and as the new buses rolled out to take their places, with nearly identical routes.[85] Whether this switch to gasoline-powered buses, rather than to new trolley cars, was part of what some urban historians have characterized as a well-organized conspiracy by GM to destroy "light-rail" transit is impossible to know.[86]

But the most important indication of progress and economic health, at least symbolically, was the opening of a new hotel in 1940 known as the Hotel Lancaster. The hotel represented, in fact, a subsidy that the community was required to pay for having Anchor Hocking agree to locate its

Lancaster's new General Motors buses parade down Main Hill, led by one of the oldest trolleys, which had been converted from an even earlier horsecar, October 1937. Courtesy Mrs. Perrin Hazelton.

general offices in town, for president I. J. Collins threatened to locate them elsewhere unless Lancaster took immediate steps to erect a first-class, modern hotel. A committee under the chamber of commerce, headed by *Eagle-Gazette* publisher Kenneth Kerr, raised the necessary $227,000 by selling $100 shares in the enterprise to area businesses and individuals.[87]

The site chosen for the hotel was on North Broad Street, directly across the alley from the Anchor Hocking headquarters. The property had once been occupied by the elegant 1823 Effinger House, which Collins himself had purchased and demolished back in 1929 with the idea of erecting a hotel on the site a year or so later. Doubtless because of economic uncertainties during the Depression, Collins decided to postpone the plan until the merger of Hocking Glass with Anchor Cap in 1937 made the construction of a new hotel an urgent priority for the company.[88] In any case, the makeup of the hotel's board of directors, which included William V.

The newly completed Hotel Lancaster, photographed May 14, 1940. Tobias Studio Collection, FCDL.

Fisher, vice president and general manager of Anchor Hocking, and Cyrus L. Fulton, assistant treasurer of the glass company, ensured that the establishment would be run in the best interests of Anchor Hocking. Another of the directors, the ever-present Kenneth Kerr, could also be counted on to support the glass interest.[89]

The new, red-brick Hotel Lancaster, designed in a simplified Colonial Revival mode, was attractive and blended well with the overall "Colonial" atmosphere of the adjacent square. Besides meeting the hospitality needs of Anchor Hocking, the hotel coffee shop and bar became immediate attractions for local citizens.[90]

In order to mark the hotel's opening and to showcase Lancaster's progress, the town held a weeklong celebration during the first week of June 1940, called the Parade of Progress, that in many ways resembled a miniature world's fair. (It was perhaps no coincidence that the New York World's Fair had just opened for its second season.) The celebratory week in Lancaster began with a huge parade, featuring fifty floats and nine marching bands. Downtown there was a street carnival with rides, games, and sideshows. The Sherman Armory served as an exhibit hall where some thirty local firms showed off their products. Friday of Progress Week was Etta Kett Day, so named for the popular comic strip by Paul Robinson, when members of Lancaster's Quota Club, a service organization of business and professional women founded locally in 1923, took over all public offices for the day.[91] The *Eagle-Gazette* did its part by publishing a special edition on June 3 that ran to 120 pages and that featured the hotel completion along with all the other marks of progress in town.[92] Many of these ideas and events would be used ten years later as part of Lancaster's sesquicentennial celebration.

Perhaps the final indication of Lancaster's and Fairfield County's relatively good fortune during the Great Depression was a respectable growth in population in the decade between 1930 and 1940. During this period Fairfield County went from 44,010 to 48,490, for an increase of 4,480 inhabitants—or 10.2 percent. This was greater than the increases in any of the surrounding counties: Franklin, with 7.1 percent; Pickaway, with 6.3 percent; Hocking, with 5.3 percent; Licking, with 3.9 percent; and Perry, with -1 percent.[93] Lancaster's growth was even more impressive than that of Fairfield County as a whole, going from 18,716 in 1930 to 21,940 in 1940, for an increase of 17.2 percent. If one figures the county growth without Lancaster's population included, then Fairfield County by itself increased by just under 5 percent.

Lancaster's growth was also much larger than any of its traditional rivals in south-central Ohio. The closest was Chillicothe with an increase of 9.8, followed by Circleville with 8.3 percent, Newark with 2.9 percent, and Zanesville with 2.9 percent. Even Ohio's three largest cities failed to grow as much, in percentage terms, as Lancaster during the Depression decade: Columbus experienced a rise of 5.3 percent and Cincinnati of just 1 percent, while Cleveland lost 2.4 percent of its inhabitants.[94] Although Lancaster's growth in the 1930s did not equal the pace of the 1920s (27.3 percent), or of the first decade of the twentieth century (45.6 percent), it was actually higher than the 12.3 percent registered during the ten years between 1910 and 1920.[95] Thus, the economic boom that had begun in Lancaster at the beginning of the twentieth century had carried the community through the Great Depression in much better condition than most other cities and towns in the United States.

Such prosperity, combined with a continuing bent toward conservative politics, led local voters to begin abandoning their historic allegiance to the Democratic Party. The first genuine crack in the solid Democratic wall occurred in 1899 when Henry Clay Drinkle (father of the twentieth-century attorney Charles Drinkle) was elected a Common Pleas Court judge.[96] This was such a novelty that the *Eagle* described Drinkle as a "Curiosity in the Court House."[97] It was not until the 1920s, however, that any real trend away from Democratic dominance was apparent. From 1900 through 1916, for example, Democratic presidential contenders won every election in Fairfield County, despite an exciting campaign visit in 1912 by Theodore Roosevelt, who gave a brief but rousing speech downtown. However, the Democratic vote in Lancaster had already begun to decline in comparison to the county, and in 1904 the Republican Roosevelt had actually carried Lancaster while losing the county as a whole. In 1920 Warren G. Harding, an Ohio son, became the first presidential contender to carry Fairfield County.[98]

The first big break for local Republican hopefuls came in 1924, when Republican Calvin Coolidge swept both Lancaster and Fairfield County and the Republicans captured the majority of county offices for the first time in history. (One of the few Democratic survivors in 1924 was this author's great-grandfather, Absalom Hartman, who won a second term as county commissioner.)[99] Two reasons would seem to account for the Republican success that year: One was national prosperity, which suggested to most voters that they should keep the Republicans in power. The other was the strong local support that the Ku Klux Klan gave to Republican candidates at a time when the Republican Party was sponsoring severe immigration-restriction laws in Congress. And as Lancaster came to depend more and more upon industry for its economic well-being, the Republicans' pro-business stance, through advocating high tariffs, sound money, and low internal taxes, may have appealed to more and more local residents.

These same platforms, along with continuing prosperity on both the local and national scene, helped to produce huge victories for Republican Herbert Hoover in both Lancaster and Fairfield County in 1928.[100] The fact that Democrat Al Smith was a Roman Catholic from New York City, who spoke with a strong urban accent, was doubtless another important factor in Hoover's local victory. Some Lancastrians received their first news of this election while in the movie theater when results appeared on the screen as soon as they came in from the Associated Press, courtesy of the *Eagle*.[101]

Had the Great Depression not occurred, the local shift toward the Republican Party might well have continued into the 1930s. Instead, the Depression caused Fairfield County to choose Franklin Roosevelt in 1932, though only by some 2,000 votes out of the roughly 18,000 ballots that were cast.[102] And it appears that Hoover may have won Lancaster itself. Unfortunately, the newspapers did not break down the results by wards and precincts in 1932, but a straw vote among students at Lancaster High School produced a two-to-one victory in favor of Hoover, a result that doubtless reflected the political preferences of many parents—and doubtless the incumbent Hoover's name recognition among the students.[103]

The presidential campaign in 1932 touched off some particularly sharp sparring between the *Eagle* and the *Gazette* during this last presidential election before their merger. On November 4, just four days before the election, the Republican *Gazette* published a half-page appeal from the glass industry—and from I. J. Collins in particular—that warned readers against voting for Roosevelt and the Democrats because of their advocacy of lower tariffs. Only the high tariff policies of Hoover and the Republicans, the appeal went on to say, would protect the American glass industry and thereby jobs in Lancaster and Fairfield County from foreign competition.[104] The following day an editorial in the *Gazette* praised this glass industry statement and urged voters to follow its advice at the polls.[105] The *Eagle* branded such talk as desperate scare tactics by the Republicans and accused Republican industrialists of trying to intimidate workers into voting for the GOP. In the words of the *Eagle*'s editorialist, "Every employer of labor who attempts to intimidate or coerce his workmen [into voting Republican], should be pilloried by the public scorn and indignation of those who are free from duress to exercise the privileges of American citizenship, and particularly should such conduct be resented at the ballot box as a lasting warning that such methods are execrated in a land where the citizen is still a sovereign, at least, on election day."[106]

By 1936 the two papers had combined to form the *Lancaster-Eagle Gazette*, and as an "independent" newspaper it took no stand on the election. In any case Roosevelt, whose New Deal policies had helped many in Lancaster and Fairfield County, swept both town and county in 1936. Roosevelt captured just under 61 percent of the countywide vote, which was almost exactly the same as his majority in the nation as a whole.[107] In 1940, however, Roosevelt barely carried Fairfield County, racking up a majority of only 481 votes, while his rival, Republican Wendell Willkie, actually won Lancaster by 130 votes.[108] Four years later, in 1944, Roosevelt lost both Lancaster and Fairfield County to Republican Thomas E. Dewey by 2,595 votes countywide—giving Dewey a majority of 57 percent.

In local contests, the balance was also tilting once again toward the Republicans. In Lancaster the Democrats held onto city hall throughout the 1920s but lost it in 1933, when the Republicans began a sweep that would last, with few exceptions, for several decades.[109] In the county, the Democrats dominated the Courthouse until 1924, when the Republicans won a majority of offices for the first time since the county was founded nearly a century and a quarter before. The Republicans maintained their hold on the county in 1928, but lost it in 1932, 1936, and 1940. Because the county elections were held at the same time as presidential elections (and city offices in the off years), courthouse elections were more likely to be affected by the presidential results, a factor that would help to account for the Republican victories in 1924 and 1928 and the Democratic success from 1932 through 1940. Then, in 1944, with Roosevelt receiving the smallest majorities nationwide of his four runs for president, the county Republicans won a sweeping victory that they would continue to hold, for the most part, for the rest of the century.[110]

The reasons for this movement away from a strong traditional allegiance to the Democratic Party to an equally strong preference for the Republicans by the early 1940s are not difficult to understand. For while local voters remained basically conservative and skeptical about the need for strong central government, the Democratic Party, which had historically espoused such views, became the party of big government under Roosevelt and his Democratic successors (at least, until the early 1990s). When the Republican Party—partly from a need to distinguish itself from the Democrats and later through its influence from conservative members —became the principal critic of strong central government and the champion of states' rights and local government (while continuing to maintain a pro-business stance), voters in Lancaster and Fairfield County gradually switched their allegiance to the GOP.

It was not that local voters had changed, but that the parties themselves had undergone a realignment. As late as October 11, 1928, for example, an editorial in the *Eagle* could describe the Republicans as the party of big government and the Democrats as devotees of states' rights and local control.¹¹¹ Another factor in the realignment probably stemmed from the increasing connection in local voters' minds between middle-class status and the Republicans' pro-business orientation. Thus many men and women in Lancaster and Fairfield County came to associate being a Republican with middle-class respectability and even with upper-class aspirations.

By the time this political realignment was falling into place in the early and mid-1940s, the United States found itself once more at war. As in 1914, most Lancastrians were horrified by the outbreak of World War II in early September of 1939. And even more than in 1914, they seemed determined to stay out of the conflict, as were most other Americans. Yet they grew ever more alarmed as Hitler conquered much of Europe and threatened the British Isles, while Japan went on a rampage through East Asia.¹¹²

In contrast to the outpouring of patriotic excitement that had greeted the American declaration of war against Germany in 1917, Lancastrians were far more subdued—again like most other Americans—following the Japanese bombing of Pearl Harbor on December 7, 1941, and the subsequent declarations of war against Japan, Germany, and the other Axis powers. They had learned from World War I how deadly and inglorious war could be, and thus faced a second world conflict with a sense of realism and grim determination to do what had to be done. Such were the sentiments of the *Eagle-Gazette*'s editorial page, just three days after Pearl Harbor, on December 10: "We cannot fail to win in the long run, though the run may be longer than we can see at the moment. . . . Our standing before the world; and especially our status as the principal protector of the western hemisphere, demand complete and final victory—nothing less. We are going to see this through to the bitter end, knowing full well that the cost will be heavy, the burden great, and the losses grievous."¹¹³

This somber determination stood out in stark contrast to the way local residents had greeted their country's declaration of war back in 1917, with patriotic outpourings in the schools. There were no such demonstrations in 1941. And only five days after Pearl Harbor, residents read in their newspapers that a young Lancaster man, a Naval gunner named Eugene Oscar Roe, was among the dead in Hawaii.¹¹⁴ Before the war ended it would claim the lives of 156 men from Lancaster and Fairfield County.¹¹⁵

The folks back home kept track of their friends and neighbors in the military through a regular column in the *Eagle-Gazette* called "Our Men in the Service," compiled and written by then city editor Perrin "Pel" Hazelton, who kept close track of every local person in the ranks. By war's end Hazelton had assembled a file of more than five thousand names of local servicemen and servicewomen, along with information on their activities and whereabouts.[116] The newspaper was also filled with photographs of local couples who had married far from home—near bases and training camps where they had been stationed.

The impact of war on life in Lancaster and Fairfield County was not all that noticeable until 1943, when the nation began to approach full-scale mobilization of its resources. Ration books appeared for the first time on February 24 of that year. In April the Fairfield County public schools, as distinct from the Lancaster public schools, announced that its rural and village schools would open somewhat later in the fall than usual so that farm children could be home to help with wartime harvests. In Lancaster a proposal by council in May to tear down the fountain on the town square and donate it to the local scrap drive raised the ire of the Fairfield Garden Club and was consequently withdrawn, thus saving one of the town's principal landmarks from becoming a victim of the war. In September Lancaster launched its third war-bond drive, in October daylight savings time went into effect, and in December the local draft board began calling "pre–Pearl Harbor fathers," that is, men who had been exempted so far from military service because of their status as parents before the United States had entered the war in December 1941.[117] And throughout the war there were calls to donate blood to the Red Cross, almost continuous bond sales and scrap drives, civil defense meetings, air raid drills in the schools, and trial blackouts, in case of a highly unlikely bombing attack from the enemy.[118] The overall economy had improved so much by late 1943 that the city council abolished the office of relief director, which had been created during the Depression.[119]

Lancaster's movie theaters offered a full bill of wartime pictures, such as *Days of Glory* starring Gregory Peck, which was showing at the Palace Theater in August 1944.[120] Two months later, in October, the theme of the Fairfield County Fair was "Food For Freedom," with "A Concrete Demonstration of the Methods by Which Patriotic Fairfield Farmers are Producing."[121] Local churches held special services throughout the war to pray for the men and women in the military, as they did on D-Day, June 6, 1944, when American and British forces stormed the beaches of Normandy to begin the liberation of Europe.[122]

However, unlike communities with military bases or major war indus-

From left to right: the author's father, Miles R. Contosta; mother, Betty J. Mowry Contosta; aunt, Ruth Contosta Rinehart; and uncle, Forest Rinehart. Both Contosta and Rinehart were pilots in the Army Air Corps in World War II, seen here during leave in Lancaster.

tries, Lancaster was not inundated with new workers or military personnel. Local business and industries generally prospered during the wartime boom, but there was no massive retooling as in the auto industry, which went from making automobiles and trucks to turning out tanks and airplanes. Nor were new industries set up to churn out war goods, despite attempts in Lancaster to obtain a war industry for the empty Godman Shoe Factory on the southwest corner of Columbus and Mulberry Streets.[123] In this sense, those who lived and worked in the area were insulated in many ways from the war's effects on the home front. As an illustration, this author's father often remembered that when he was home on leave, but still wearing his Army Air Corps uniform with his "wings" pinned prominently above his pocket, it was not unusual for him to walk through downtown Lancaster and have a friend or acquaintance stop and say, "Now *what's* your branch of the service?" In the war, as in the Depression, Lancaster was much less affected by outside forces than other American communities.

Local residents greeted President Truman's announcement of the

Japanese surrender on August 14, 1945, by pouring into the streets of downtown Lancaster. There were no parades and floats, as there had been at the end of World War I—just a wild, impromptu honking of horns, ringing of bells, blasting of sirens, dumping of torn paper from office windows, and the setting off of firecrackers and small fireworks all over town. Most evident were the streams of cars that clogged downtown as they made their way up and down Main Street, anticipating their postwar release from gasoline rationing.[124]

No one knew quite what to expect that delirious late summer evening of victory and relief. Most, no doubt, hoped for a return to more normal times after a decade and a half of crisis and emergency, beginning with the Depression and extending through World War II. For those who had lost close friends and loved ones, of course, life would never be the same. What no one in Lancaster could know was that their town was about to embark upon a period that many would come to see as a golden age.

SIX

# The Town at High Noon
## Postwar Lancaster

FOR MANY RESIDENTS OF Lancaster, the two decades after World War II have come to represent a golden age, a high noon for their Midwestern town.¹ World War II and the Great Depression were now behind them, however mild their effects had been locally compared to many other communities in the United States. New industries moved into the area as many older ones continued to prosper, and the population rose at a moderate but healthy pace. Big-city problems continued to seem far away, and downtown Lancaster remained a symbol as well as a center of civic pride and community identification. While a proliferation of new automobiles and new highway construction were paving the way for great demographic shifts, these changes were not immediately apparent to most residents during the decade or so after the war.²

The years just after World War II were an especially heady time. Hollywood came to town, Lancaster and Fairfield County celebrated the sesquicentennial of their founding, and *Forbes*, a business magazine with a national readership, featured Lancaster as a model American community.

Hollywood came in the form of Twentieth Century Fox, which descended on Lancaster in June 1947 to film the last segment of a movie entitled *Green Grass of Wyoming*. The movie was based on a novel by Mary O'Hara, the third of her Flicka series, that had been preceded by *My Friend Flicka* and *Thunderhead*, both already made into successful films. As with so many important local events, it was *Eagle-Gazette* publisher Kenneth Kerr who had used his contacts, in this case with a theatrical agent, to bring the moviemakers to Lancaster.

Predictably, residents of Lancaster and Fairfield County brimmed over with excitement. The stars flew into Columbus and then were escorted to

Members of the cast and director of *Green Grass of Wyoming* are greeted on the sidewalk outside the Hotel Lancaster by local dignitaries, June 1947. Left to right in semicircle: Mayor Fred Von Stein; Louis King, the director for Twentieth Century Fox; *Eagle-Gazette* publisher R. Kenneth Kerr; Linda Fulton, daughter of Anchor Hocking executive Cyrus Fulton (handing the bouquet of flowers); actress Peggy Cummins; and actor Burl Ives. Courtesy Mrs. Perrin Hazelton.

Lancaster by a fleet of police motorcycles with sirens blasting as they drove down North Columbus Street, turned east on Main Street through downtown, and then proceeded up Broad Street, where a greeting party awaited them at the Hotel Lancaster. Waiting outside the hotel were Mayor Fred Von Stein, Police Chief Sam Husler, Kenneth Kerr, and other dignitaries. The visiting movie cast included veteran performers Lloyd Nolan, Burl Ives, Charles Coburn, and Geraldine Wall. The younger cast members were Bob Arthur and the Irish-born Peggy Cummins, who had come to the United States only two years before.[3]

Much of the wild excitement that gripped movie fans as the stars arrived, at a time before television had robbed the movies of some of their glamour and importance and when filming on location was not as common as it would be later, can still be imagined from an editorial that appeared in the *Eagle-Gazette* on June 2, 1947:

> What is so rare as a movie company in June in a mid-Ohio town thousands of miles away from Hollywood? So if the public excitement should at times verge slightly on hysteria, consider that suddenly finding movie production going on right in your own backyard is a community thrill we can't react to with nonchalance. To us *[Green Grass of Wyoming]* will be the ten best pictures of the year rolled in one, and every performance . . . an Academy Award Winner.

Each day while the filming went on, from June 4 through June 22, thousands of men, women, and children from Lancaster, Fairfield County, and all over central Ohio descended on the fairgrounds to catch a glimpse of the stars, to see—firsthand—how a movie was made, obtain autographs, take snapshots, or simply bask in the glory of it all. Admission to the fairgrounds was free and Twentieth Century Fox awarded fifty silver dollars every hour to the holders of lucky numbers in order to assure the large crowds needed to simulate the atmosphere of an important horse race.[4] During the second week of filming, amusement rides, games, and concession stands appeared on the grounds, giving the whole place a carnival flavor. One afternoon Burl Ives, a well-known folksinger of the day, entertained crowds in the grandstand by singing "Blue Tail Fly," with several of the other cast members forming an impromptu chorus.[5] Counting on huge Sunday crowds, which reportedly reached 40,000 or more on each of the three weekends of filming, the racing scenes—including one of a horse and his sulky driver crashing into a specially made balsa wood replacement of one set of rails—took place on successive Sunday afternoons. Because of cloudy weather on the first two weekends in particular, the filming demanded more time than anticipated, much to the delight of local folks.[6]

During the two and a half weeks of shooting, Twentieth Century Fox virtually took over the Hotel Lancaster. Local residents often milled around outside to catch a glimpse of the Hollywood celebrities as they came in and out, and some—largely members of the press—were lucky

# CHAPTER SIX

Filming the last scene of *Green Grass of Wyoming* on the racetrack at the Fairfield County Fairgrounds in June 1947. Actor Charles Coburn is the sulky driver. Next to him, with back to camera, is actress Peggy Cummins. *Eagle-Gazette* publisher R. Kenneth Kerr, who is partly visible behind the horse, played a small "walk-on" part as the governor of Ohio. Courtesy Mrs. Perrin Hazelton.

enough to chat with the actors at the hotel bar. Ives was particularly open to such casual conversation and kept in touch for many years with several people he met in Lancaster.[7]

Just as exciting as the filming of *Green Grass of Wyoming* was its world premier nearly a year later, held in Lancaster at both the Palace and Broad Theaters on Tuesday, May 25, 1948. Festivities began on Saturday the 22nd with a Soap Box Derby on Main Hill in the afternoon. That evening the Lancaster High School band played a concert at the fairgrounds, where movie-premiere queen Virginia Jessup and her attendants were presented to the crowd, followed by a fireworks display. On Monday at 6:30, Twentieth Century Fox hosted a cocktail party at the hotel for invited guests. Later that evening there was a World Premier Grand Ball in the gymnasium of Lancaster High School, with the film stars making a brief appearance about ten o'clock. On Tuesday there was a two-mile-long parade with marching bands and elaborate floats, after which Kenneth Kerr hosted a cocktail party at his home in Rosebank for the cast, local dignitaries, and special guests. That night those lucky enough to obtain one of the 1,500 combined seats of the Palace and Broad Theaters sat down to see the world premier of *Green Grass of Wyoming*.

Actually, the Palace was the center of the opening-night showing, where the film began at 8:00, while viewers at the Broad had to wait until 8:30. The stars arrived outside the Palace in big, expensive cars, much as they might have back in California, while onlookers had one last thrill of glimpsing Hollywood in Lancaster.[8] In the intersection of Broad and Main Streets the words GREEN GRASS OF WYOMING had been painted in huge green letters. Kenneth Kerr, Lancaster's principal cheerleader, who had played a small part at the end of the movie, was of course delighted.[9] Both the filming and the premier had given Lancaster press coverage throughout Ohio, while viewers across the nation would see beautiful scenes of Lancaster, which was mentioned by name in the movie.

The film itself was not a box-office hit, as the two earlier Flicka movies had been, but that made little difference to the many men, women, and children of Lancaster and Fairfield County, who had experienced more Hollywood glamour in a few weeks than they ever imagined possible. The making of *Green Grass of Wyoming* in Lancaster was also another of those events that helped to knit the community together by providing endless hours of conversation, a conversation that continues more than a half century later among those who remember that special time, and even among those of younger generations who have only heard about it from parents or grandparents. (In June of 1998 the community celebrated the fiftieth anniversary of the film's debut with a parade and screening of the movie at the fairgrounds amphitheater, attended by a retired Peggy Cummins.)[10]

Residents had hardly recovered from the world premier when they began preparing to celebrate their sesquicentennial in 1950. Festivities unfolded between Sunday, June 4, and Sunday, June 11.[11] The week opened with an interdenominational vesper service at the fairgrounds amphitheater.[12] On Monday, "Kiddies' Day," there was a pet parade in the afternoon, followed by a bubble-gum blowing contest. On Monday evening the sesquicentennial queen, Marilyn Neff, received her crown out at the fairgrounds, followed by the first of five presentations of a pageant called "The Epic of Standing Stone."[13] Tuesday was "Homecoming Day," with historical tours and a barbecue at Rising Park for former residents of Lan-

"Etta Kett Day," June 8, 1950, during Lancaster's weeklong sesquicentennial celebration. The two "jail birds" who have been arrested by the ladies, armed with squirt guns, are Perrin "Pel" Hazelton (left) and Jim Wagonseller (right). This stockade stood beside the city hall on Broad Street. Visible in the background are (right to left) the Trout Building, the Broad movie theater, and the Hotel Martens. Courtesy Mrs. Perrin Hazelton,

caster and Fairfield County, as well as local men and women who belonged to the Old-timers Club.[14] Also opening on Tuesday were rides and carnival concessions, known collectively as the "Mardi Gras event," in the middle of Main Street from Broad Street to Memorial Drive.[15] One of Lancaster's old trolleys, in storage since 1937, had been hauled downtown to serve as an on-site headquarters for the sesquicentennial.[16] And at the Sherman Armory, there was another exhibit of local industries, as there had been ten years earlier for the Parade of Progress.

On Wednesday there were band concerts, square dancing, and a milking contest downtown. "Etta Kett Day" claimed most of Thursday, when women "took over" all government offices and public services, as they had ten years before during the Parade of Progress. Although it was all good-humored, the antics connected with this event might strike many women

Perrin "Pel" Hazelton and Virginia Mowry Hazelton at the Sesquicentennial Ball, American Legion, June 9, 1950. Courtesy Mrs. Perrin Hazelton.

a half century later as demeaning or even insulting, as women "policemen" arrested men for loitering on the streets, raced around to put out a rubbish fire set by the fire department, and swept Main Street with brooms and dustpans as a lesson to the real streets department as to how they should keep Lancaster's thoroughfares neat and clean.[17]

The highlight of Friday was the Sesquicentennial Ball, held that evening at the American Legion Hall on Main Hill. Those attending had to wear historical costumes, for which there were prizes in several categories.[18] The huge sesquicentennial parade came on Saturday afternoon. The line of marchers was over three-and-a-half-miles long with some three hundred units, including thirty floats and twenty-five marching bands, that wended their way through the streets of Lancaster.[19] The final event was a horse show and rodeo at the fairgrounds on Sunday night.[20]

There was also a beard-growing contest that week. Among the winners were seventy-three-year-old Charles Griggs, former owner of the Princess movie theater, for the whitest beard; Carl Boeger for the blackest beard; and Fred Hatcher for the best wax mustache.[21] And throughout the week, celebrants of all ages could be seen wearing felt caps with feathers

A portion of the sesquicentennial parade, June 10, 1950, as it passes through the intersection of Broad and Allen Streets. North School is in the background and a brick pavement (still typical of many Lancaster streets in 1950) is evident in the foreground. Courtesy Mrs. Perrin Hazelton.

sticking out of one side, which made them look more like members of Robin Hood's merry band than early-nineteenth-century pioneers.

Attempts to present the 150-year history of Lancaster and Fairfield County took several forms. One was a display of antiques and other "historical items" in store windows downtown. These attracted much attention, but there does not seem to have been any attempt at historical interpretations of the displays, either individually or as a whole.[22] Then there was the pageant at the fairgrounds, "The Epic of Standing Stone," staged each evening from Monday through Friday. Although it was produced and directed by a commercial enterprise that specialized in pageants, all the talent was local, including the choruses, narrators, players, and musicians. Herbert Turner, a Lancaster feed-mill owner and longtime collector of historical sources and artifacts, assembled the historical material for the script.[23]

Town pageants had become popular in the early twentieth century and were frequently used to show connections between past and present, and particularly to demonstrate the progress that had occurred over the decades. By and large the "Epic of Standing Stone" did not move along these lines, but concentrated instead on early events in Lancaster and Fairfield County. Of the twenty scenes in this production of one hour and forty-five minutes, only two were set in the twentieth century. Ten of them, including three on the Forest Rose legend, dealt with the period even before settlement and eight more focused on the nineteenth century, with a decided emphasis upon the earlier decades of the 1800s. As might be expected in the hometown of General Sherman, one whole scene dealt with Sherman's brief visit to Lancaster after the Civil War, with no mention of Copperhead Edson B. Olds or even a hint at the intense local opposition to the war by many residents. The two twentieth-century scenes involved a 1906 automobile and a WPA work site. The latter showed a group of men "just idling" while a sign read "Men Working," a backhanded comment about the New Deal that typified local sentiment about the welfare state.[24] Of course, there was nothing about the Godman Shoe strike or the period of union organization in the middle 1930s.

The several thousand persons who saw the pageant doubtless went away with vaguely nostalgic feelings about a heroic past, but without any understanding of what had made their community successful despite conflicting interests, difficult times, and shifting forces on the local, national, and international stage. No pageant can treat such subtleties in any depth, of course, but such themes might have been introduced to some degree during the evening.

Far more helpful than either the pageant or the historical window displays in presenting the local past was the massive sesquicentennial edition put out by the *Eagle-Gazette* on Saturday, June 3, 1950. Running 400 pages, the largest newspaper issued in Ohio up to that time, it was publisher Kenneth Kerr's and his staff's contribution to the 150th anniversary party. The front page carried the facsimile of a congratulatory letter from President Harry S. Truman to Kerr, which was doubtless arranged by Truman's then secretary of commerce and principal stockholder in the *Eagle-Gazette*, Charles Sawyer. With 700 advertisements, 147 of them full-page, the sesquicentennial edition was no doubt a great financial success for the newspaper as well as a tremendous public relations coup.[25]

The sesquicentennial edition brimmed with historical accounts of various persons, institutions, businesses, industries, and events in Lancaster and Fairfield County. Much of this material came from back issues of the

*Eagle-Gazette* and from its predecessors, the *Eagle* and the *Gazette*. A good deal of this information had been culled by Myron T. Seifert, a former resident of Bremen then teaching at West High School in Columbus, who was described as a historian and "newspaper researcher." Another major contributor of material was Lewis Cook of Basil, an authority on Fairfield County folklore. Perrin "Pel" Hazelton, then associate editor at the *Eagle-Gazette*, had the job of compiling, editing, and writing up this mass of data, a task that he accomplished during a single five-month period.[26]

In his front-page "Greeting," publisher Kerr announced that the theme of this mammoth edition was progress—past and future. Although the theme of progress occurred frequently throughout the four hundred pages, and especially in the advertisements, readers would have had a difficult time understanding just how and why such progress had taken place. Nor was there a basic chronological unfolding of local history in the sesquicentennial edition. The ten sections of forty pages each were vaguely thematic and some of the historical articles in each related to the section's overall theme, though many of the shorter pieces seemed to have been inserted simply because they fit into various spaces on the page. The first section, for example, was of an introductory nature, with historical pieces that ranged all over the board. The next two sections dealt largely with local businesses, with a fourth devoted entirely to Anchor Hocking. The next segment featured other local industries, followed by sections on churches and schools, another on culture and leisure activities, and then a section on the villages and townships in Fairfield County. The final two sections had no discernable focus and are best labeled miscellaneous.

It would have taken a very knowledgeable and careful reader to go through the numerous but widely scattered historical pieces and come away with any sense of precisely how local history had emerged over the past 150 years. Even so, the sesquicentennial edition became an important keepsake, and especially to those 4,000 or so individuals who purchased the unfolded "flat editions" that were bound in leather and stamped in gold lettering with their names. These became a mental reference point for remembering the sesquicentennial, in addition to becoming an important research tool for future historians.

Though not as widely distributed locally as the sesquicentennial edition of the *Eagle-Gazette*, a 1947 feature article about Lancaster in *Forbes* magazine generated a great sense of pride and well-being during the early postwar period. The *Forbes* feature was the idea of magazine editor Malcolm Forbes himself, who had spent a year in Lancaster following his graduation from Princeton in 1941. Remembering that Ohio and Virginia had produced the largest number of U.S. presidents, Forbes's father had suggested the move to Lancaster, where Malcolm, in theory at least, could put together a chain of weekly newspapers and use them as a platform for launching a political career. (This is precisely what Charles Sawyer had done, but it is doubtful that Forbes had this particular example in mind.) With money provided by his father's friends, Malcolm purchased two weeklies known as the *Fairfield Times* and the *Lancaster Tribune*. The venture failed, in part because Forbes ran up against wartime shortages of newsprint and machine parts. His romance with a Lancaster girl from a well-to-do family "on the hill" also fell apart. Forbes joined the army and closed the two papers down at the end of 1942, but he maintained fond memories of Lancaster for the rest of his life and even kept in touch with several friends from town.[27]

Occupying almost the entire *Forbes* issue for November 15, 1947, the Lancaster story was highlighted on the front cover by a color photograph of Main Street at night, with a full moon shining down from the west. The overall title of what was actually a collection of articles and vignettes was "Free Enterprise—in Terms of a Town," with an introduction by Malcolm Forbes. The object of these pieces, according to Forbes, was "to show how our economy works in terms of *real people* in a real town [emphasis added]."[28] Forbes considered Lancaster to be an "ideal community" for such a demonstration, since all three basic elements of the nation's economy could be found there, "Functioning side by side, day after day": "Big Business," "Main Street," and "Rural America."[29]

In order to show how real people functioned in these three areas, the magazine offered profiles of twelve men and women. In industry, these were "tycoon" I. J. Collins (founder of Anchor Hocking Glass and then chairman of the board), labor leader Tom Joyce, glass worker Jack Fisher, and foreman Ralph Beck. *Forbes*'s Main Street personalities were banker Philip Rising Peters (president of the Fairfield National Bank), department store owner Thomas Wiseman, publisher Kenneth Kerr, salesgirl Marilyn Miller, and grocer Merrit H. Brown (manager of a Kroger's food market). In the rural sector there were Agricultural Adjustment administrator Ellwood Butler, Fairfield County Fair manager Russell Alt, and farmer Wendell George.

The magazine seemingly could not say enough about Lancaster's

Downtown Lancaster: Main Street, looking west from the intersection at Broad Street, early 1950s. Tobias Studio Collection, FCDL.

small-town beauty, charm, and sense of peace: there were so many trees along the streets, according to *Forbes*, that it was "difficult to know where business ends and homes begin. . . . Not only is everything clean and attractive, but the stores, factories, and offices are comfortably thriving, and retailers, manufacturers, and workers are getting along nicely."[30]

The article went on to present an overall picture of the local economy that would make any chamber of commerce proud. Readers learned that Lancaster was then a town of about 24,000 people, the great majority of them native born. There were only two small apartment buildings and some 6,500 houses, 85 percent of them owned by their occupants. These dwellings were almost uniformly well kept, and "nowhere was there anything approaching a slum."[31] This feat of domesticity had been accomplished even though wages in the glass factories were somewhat low according to national standards, averaging about 97 cents an hour, or $40.00 per week. But the steadiness of the work, season after season, compensated for the lower wage scale and made Lancaster's industrial workers good credit risks who could borrow money at modest rates for houses and other large purchases. And supplementing employment at Anchor Hocking were numerous jobs in some ten smaller but significant industries, listed by *Forbes* as Lancaster Lens (lenses and reflectors), Alten's Foundry (metal castings), Hermann Manufacturing (machine tools), Irving Drew (shoes), Lancaster Mould Company, Stuck Mould Works, Ray-O-Vac (flashlights and batteries), Hocking Manufacturing (metal castings), and the Loroco Industries (paper specialties).[32]

*Forbes* counted more than 400 retail establishments, concentrated in the downtown but also in other locations around Lancaster, that served the town's 24,000 residents as well as many of the 26,000 additional inhabitants of Fairfield County. Worth repeating is the magazine's description of the downtown as it looked on a summer day just after the war:

> The intersection of Main and Broad streets, dominated by the [town] hall, is the heart of the trading and business area. Standing here, one can look up and down the streets to see most of the bigger stores, banks, hotels, moving picture houses, and offices. The outlook is typically Midwestern. The architecture is varied, the streets wide and clean. Two small parks, both crowded with trees and shrubbery and one with a large fountain, add a green and restful touch.[33]

The only mild criticisms of Lancaster were for the *Eagle-Gazette* and Anchor Hocking Glass, undoubtedly the two most powerful influences in town at that point. The newspaper, *Forbes* pointed out, lacked the fervor of a crusading press, adding that many residents missed the era of two daily newspapers and the editorial combat that had flared from time to time.[34] Labor leaders, the magazine went on to say, were especially critical of the way the one hometown newspaper generally ignored union activities. In part, such criticism may have been Malcolm Forbes's own mild revenge at failing to crack the *Eagle-Gazette*'s monopoly during his brief fling at journalism in Lancaster.

The *Forbes* piece on Anchor Hocking was even more critical, though politely phrased. The company, it was alleged, had encouraged its employees to buy housing in the countryside outside Lancaster (though how this was accomplished was not explained) as a way of breaking down labor solidarity. Along these same lines, the magazine accused Anchor Hocking of using the Lancaster police to keep a labor organizer from the Congress of Industrial Organizations (CIO) from entering town. Since Anchor Hocking wanted to keep Lancaster a "large country town" that it could control,

*Forbes* went on to say, it had made little effort to attract new companies to the area that might add to the population or exert an upward pressure on wages.[35] (In fact, for many decades thereafter, there was an oft-repeated oral tradition in Lancaster that Anchor Hocking even took active steps to discourage new industries from entering the community, though there was never any concrete proof that this was happening.) In any case, such criticism from a pro-business magazine was significant indeed.

The *Forbes* feature concluded that Lancaster could look forward to a promising future, and during the two decades or so after World War II that prediction certainly came true.[36] On the industrial front several new firms moved into the area, presumably without the encouragement of Anchor Hocking. The first of these was the RBM Division of Essex Wire, which manufactured a variety of electrical switches for automobiles. Originally established in Logansport, Indiana, it took its name from the initials of the men who had founded it: Ivan R. Reddinger, William Ball, and Wallace Morris. Some time later this company was acquired by Essex Wire. The RBM, as nearly everyone called it, opened its Lancaster plant in the fall of 1947 in the old Godman Shoe Factory building on the southwest corner of Columbus and Mulberry Streets, where the worst turmoil had erupted during the shoe factory strike back in 1934. By 1950 the RBM employed some 600 workers with an annual payroll of $1.25 million.[37]

Coming to Lancaster two years later, in 1949, was the Diamond Power Specialty Corporation, which manufactured a variety of accessories for boilers and power plants. Like the RBM, Diamond had been founded elsewhere, in this case Detroit, Michigan, back in 1903. By the early 1940s it had several plants scattered around the Detroit area and began looking for a site where all its operations could take place under one roof. Diamond selected Lancaster because it was large enough to supply the required labor force, but small enough so that the company could afford to buy the amount of land that it needed. Railroad facilities for shipping and receiving were yet another attraction. By the early 1950s, Diamond Power employed about five hundred workers, and in 1957 the company broke ground for a large addition to the plant.[38]

Several smaller industries also located in Lancaster during the early postwar period. Among these were Lancaster Electro-Plating in 1947 and the Gay-Fad Studios, which in 1946 began producing decorated glassware with multicolored designs fired permanently into the glass.[39] Yet another glassmaking enterprise, though tiny and very different from the mass-produced products of Lancaster's glass industry as a whole, was the glass-blowing studio of Carl and Steve Erickson in Bremen. The Swedish-born Ericksons started the operation in 1946 and spent several years training local men in the fine art of glassblowing. Ericksonware went mostly to department stores and upscale gift shops all over the country until the shop closed in 1960.[40]

Several older industries in the area underwent expansion during this period. In 1955 the Lancaster Lens opened a TV-bulb finishing plant. Two years later the Lens acquired controlling interests in Indiana Glass and officially changed its name to Lancaster Glass. Up in the village of Baltimore, the Fairfield Paper and Container Company was acquired by Gaylord Container in 1955. And in the village of Millersport, the Midland Screw Corporation erected a new plant, with financial assistance from the Millersport Community Development Association.[41]

As industries thrived and expanded, Lancaster's downtown remained a busy and prosperous place and was the scene of many civic events during the postwar years. The best-known and most-frequented establishments were Lancaster's two department stores, Hickle's and Wiseman's. Situated on the south side of Main Street, and slightly more than halfway between Broad and Columbus Streets, Hickle's, opened in 1900, presented a more old-fashioned look than Wiseman's. It had several large ceiling fans that pushed hot air around the store on summer afternoons, as little change boxes clattered and banged their way from the sales clerks to the central cashier upstairs—and back again—pulled along by a continuously moving cord inside a narrow, caged causeway.[42]

Wiseman's was diagonally across Main Street from Hickle's, on the north side of the commercial thoroughfare. It claimed to be the lineal successor of several stores dating all the way back to 1834, becoming the Charles P. Wiseman Company in 1916. Charles's son, Thomas Wiseman, had taken over in the early 1930s and remained a familiar sight around the store throughout the 1950s, where he was known to nearly all his customers as "Tom." In 1946 Wiseman began an extensive remodeling of the store, on the advice of a New York designer, that included recessed ceiling lights and a simplified art deco look to the counters, interior walls, and street facade. Unlike Hickle's, Wiseman's had air-conditioning, and its nearly silent pneumatic tubes swished customers' money from sales counters to the cashier's booth on the mezzanine level. Wiseman's was thought to have a higher quality of merchandise than Hickle's, in addition to car-

Salesgirl Marilyn Miller, an employee of Harrison's women's apparel shop. *Forbes*, November 15, 1947, p. 77.

rying more up-to-date fashions. When an interviewer from *Forbes* magazine asked Wiseman if he worried about competition from the big department stores in Columbus, he answered that local residents would continue to prefer the convenience of shopping in their own hometown where they could expect friendly, efficient service from his clerks.[43] (What Wiseman could not envision, just ahead, was the age of shopping malls and the near collapse of Lancaster's downtown.)

Indeed, sales clerk Eva Friesner, who worked at Hickle's rather than Wiseman's, remembered in a 1981 interview that all the "salesgirls" had their regular customers, who would often wait until their own "girl" was free rather than go to another clerk. Friesner knew her customers by name and served some of them for decades. Working hours for Friesner and other female department-store clerks were long: from 8:00 to 5:30 P.M. Monday through Friday and from 8:00 to 9:00 P.M. on Saturdays.[44] And the pay was low: Marilyn Miller, a clerk at Harrison's, a women's apparel shop, told *Forbes* magazine in 1947 that she earned just $35.00 a week, despite ten years of experience in various secretarial, clerical, and sales positions.[45]

But for a young, middle-class woman like Miller, at age 28 and without a college education, there were few other opportunities for employment in Lancaster at the time.

Tired shoppers could always refresh themselves at one of the drugstore soda fountains downtown, such as Beiter and Flege's or Gallagher's (which had comfortable wicker-back chairs at the counter). Equally popular was Pritchard's soda fountain and restaurant, which, like the others, was an after-school hangout for both Lancaster High and St. Mary students.[46] For those who wanted something stronger, Jerry Maher's bar, opened in 1904, was still a fixture on Main Street and would remain so until Maher's widow closed the establishment in 1970.[47] The most popular eating place in the early postwar period was Cy Albert's Clock Restaurant, located since 1937 on Main Hill just above city hall.[48] Simply sauntering along downtown streets was another common activity for adults and teenagers alike, who knew that they were bound to bump into several friends or acquaintances.[49]

In addition to the old and familiar storefronts, there were several changes downtown during the late 1940s and 1950s. Wiseman's makeover just after the war, as already mentioned, was the most ambitious. Hickle's renovated its first-floor front in 1957, while S. S. Kresge expanded by demolishing the old Kirn Hotel building next door. Two years earlier, in 1955, Sears and Roebuck opened its first retail store in Lancaster on the northeast corner of Main and Columbus Streets. Beginning in May 1956, the downtown stores shifted from staying open until 9:00 on Saturday nights to having nine-o'clock hours on Friday night, a reflection of the fact that Friday was now the last day of the workweek for most, making Saturday evening more a time for socializing than for shopping. The change may have also stemmed from the fact that the town was continuing to grow faster than the county, with the consequence that Saturday, once a big day for rural shoppers, was less important than in the past.[50]

With continuing prosperity, it is not surprising that Lancaster experienced a steady growth in its population. Between 1940 and 1950 the town went from 21,940 to 24,180 people, and then to 29,916 in 1960. This made for a growth rate of 10.2 percent in the 1940s and 23.7 percent in the 1950s.[51] In Fairfield County the numbers increased from 48,490 in 1940 to 52,130 in 1950, and then to 63,912 in 1960, for a growth rate of 7.5 percent in the 1940s and 22.6 percent in the 1950s.[52]

Most Lancastrians viewed the growth in population and real estate as positive. This attitude came through in an *Eagle-Gazette* editorial in June 1950 complaining that the official U.S. census count for Lancaster of just over 24,000 was a gross understatement of the town's real population:

> No one had expected less than 25,000 and many ventured an estimate as high as 30,000. "It's unbelievable," was the almost universal comment from [public] officials and the man in the street. . . . Look at all the new homes, people said, pointing to the post-war additions and large new real estate developments. Look at the growth of local industries; the new factory [Diamond Power]. . . . Look at the increase in school enrollments; the greater number of water meters in the [town]; the continued demand for dwellings despite new construction.[53]

Meanwhile, the expanding local economy and a dramatic increase in birth rates, a nationwide phenomenon known as the baby boom, placed a severe strain on the schools. The Lancaster schools, as well as many districts throughout the United States, had to resort to "half-day" sessions in which classrooms served two separate sets of students, one that came about seven in the morning and stayed until noon, and another that arrived shortly after noon and remained until five in the afternoon or so. In order to do away with this half-day arrangement, which parents as well as educators agreed was unsatisfactory in the long run, there was no choice but to erect new schools.

As in the past, the board of education faced a struggle to convince voters to pass the necessary bond levies. For unlike the new suburban school districts outside Cleveland, Cincinnati, Dayton, or Columbus, where the vast majority of adults were young married couples with children and where most had middle-class jobs, Lancaster authorities had to appeal to elderly adults on fixed incomes whose children were long out of school, in addition to many unskilled workers who did not always appreciate the need for better facilities. This is not to say, of course, that all factory workers and retired persons voted against school bond issues and operating levies.

In any case, by 1954, after several classes of baby-boom children had entered school, it was clear to educators that a number of facilities had to be built. Under the leadership of a new superintendent, J. E. "Jack" Brown, who would serve in that capacity from 1954 to 1968, the Lancaster schools embarked upon an ambitious building program, though the first of the necessary bond issues had succeeded under Brown's immediate predecessor, Superintendent Paul Wenger.[54] The initial attempt at convincing voters failed at a special election in March 1953. Although the issue won just over 50 percent of the vote, it fell short of the 60 percent then required by state law for such school issues. Just over a year later at the 1954 May primary, the bond issue passed, after intensive lobbying that involved door-to-door solicitation, by a resounding 69 percent of the ballots cast.[55]

The bond issue provided $2.1 million, with funds for a new elementary school and the town's first junior high schools. The elementary building, opened in 1956, became the Tallmadge School, named for one of Lancaster's great nineteenth-century businessmen and entrepreneurs, Darius Tallmadge. Located on Lewis Avenue, Tallmadge School served new housing in this area. In 1957 the district opened its first junior high schools, General Sherman on the West Side (just beyond the Hocking River between Union Street and Fifth Avenue) and Thomas Ewing in the East End (on Fair Avenue between Madison Avenue and Boyd Street). Like Tallmadge, the two junior highs carried the names of famous nineteenth-century residents.

The dividing line between the two junior high districts created much unhappiness among some parents from the North End who objected to their children going across the Hocking River to school and being thrown together with "tough West Side kids." But mostly everyone adjusted to the situation within a few months and the students from the North End and the West Side got along well, with very few incidents. The two junior highs did, however, give some false ammunition to those who were looking to accuse the school board of wasting taxpayers' money. Some of these naysayers immediately complained about a few tropical plants in certain glass-enclosed spaces, or insisted that the brass-plated railings at General Sherman were made of solid gold.[56]

Meanwhile, the public schools of Fairfield County underwent another round of consolidations and building construction. During the late 1950s and early 1960s, there were consolidations of the Amanda and Stoutsville schools, the Carroll and Bloom Townships schools, the Thurston and Liberty Township schools, and the Bremen and Rushville area schools, the last under the name of Fairfield Union.[57]

Despite the growth in schools, housing, business, and industry, there were many areas of continuity with the prewar period. Lancaster High

## CHAPTER SIX

A Friday night football game under the lights at North Field, c. 1950s. Curriculum Resource Center, Lancaster City Schools.

School continued to play its football games at North Field, behind the North Elementary School, which were invariably played on Friday nights now that the field had lights. On game nights the high school band marched from the old Mulberry Street school, south on High Street for two blocks, and then down Main Hill before turning up Broad Street for a dramatic arrival at North Field. At Homecoming, there was a huge bonfire in the fairgrounds on the Thursday night before the big game, where a player from the enemy team was burned in effigy. There was also a Homecoming parade through downtown Lancaster with floats designed and built by each class, and a Homecoming dance in the high school gym after the game, where the Homecoming queen and her court received their crowns. All this excitement took place within the space of six or seven square blocks in or near the center of town, providing a unifying spectacle that thousands of residents could see and talk about during the fall season, and especially when Lancaster High won the Central Ohio League championship, as it did several times during the postwar period.

Dependably, the second week in October brought the century-old Fairfield County Fair, usually a time of bright blue skies, crisp autumn air, and trees that were just beginning to take on their brilliant autumn colors.

A familiar scene at the Fairfield County Fair, 1965. Fairfield County Agricultural Society.

Folks from Lancaster and surrounding farms and villages poured into the fairgrounds, which had been prepared weeks ahead with newly painted barns and carefully trimmed ancient sycamores that stood like tall, mottled columns against a blue-domed sky. The throngs of visitors looked over the livestock, examined the prize vegetables and baked goods in the Art Hall, met old friends, ate greasy French fries and sticky cotton candy, thrilled to the amusement rides, tried—usually in vain—to win a teddy bear, or just escaped for a few hours into the exotic flavor of sideshows and carnival music. One of the highlights each year was the school band concert on the racetrack, always on a Wednesday in those days. This show concluded with a performance of "massed bands," made up of some six or seven hundred youngsters playing together—all standing proudly in front of the grandstand with their bright uniforms in the different school colors, which band mothers and booster clubs had purchased with the proceeds from endless raffles and bake sales.[58] The fair closed on Saturday night with a rodeo, at least into the mid-1950s, and later in the decade with an auto daredevil act where cars leapt off ramps, drove through lakes of fire, and smashed into each other.

Although the fair remained the most important local event throughout the postwar period, voters failed in November 1956 to approve a county bond issue for $900,000 that would have funded a large exhibition hall and auditorium at the fairgrounds. To be called the Coliseum, an often-used name at that time for such facilities, the building would have been located just inside the fairgrounds on the northwest corner of Fair Avenue and Broad Street, then and later the site of the county highway garages (which would have been relocated). For reasons that are unclear four decades later, the bond issue failed miserably, garnering only 36 percent of the vote.[59]

Though there was no Coliseum to greet fairgoers, October remained a favorite time for driving down through the Hocking Hills, for taking a hike "up on Mount Pleasant," or for exploring the wooded hills that ringed Lancaster. Many parents allowed boys to go off for most of the day, with a peanut butter sandwich and an army-surplus canteen full of water, to race up and down the hills in hot pursuit of imaginary Indians. There was always the possibility that someone would get hurt by falling over one of the steep cliffs that jutted from the surrounding hillsides. This fear was realized every year or so in newspaper reports, like the one in August 1962 that told of an eight-year-old boy who died after falling seventy-five feet from the top of Mount Pleasant.[60]

For those lucky enough to have cottages at Buckeye Lake, there were summers of swimming, boating, and fishing. And whether or not the family had a place at the lake, Buckeye Lake Park continued to draw large crowds for at least a decade after the war.[61] The lake, too, could be dangerous, with predictable accounts in the newspapers each summer about boat accidents and drownings. In 1955 there were at least two accidental deaths at the lake, one of a thirteen-year-old boy who rode his bicycle over the spillway on the North Bank, the other of a drowning victim who was recovered from the muddy lake bottom after five days of rescuers' dragging the lake with grappling hooks.[62]

Back in Lancaster, new activities for youth emerged during the postwar period. Beginning in 1956 there was an annual Soap Box Derby, where homemade cars coasted down Main Hill, which was lined with spectators, between High and Broad Streets. Because of the unevenness of the pavement and the disadvantages to contestants, the derby moved in 1960 to a specially constructed site on the BIS Road.[63]

In 1958 Lancaster opened a new YMCA/YWCA facility, later called the Family Y, on West Sixth Avenue after years of planning and fund-raising.

Ladies gather for a luncheon at the First Presbyterian Church of Lancaster, 1950s. Courtesy Mrs. Perrin Hazelton.

Although it was especially beneficial to local youth, residents of all ages used its indoor swimming pool, gymnasium, exercise rooms, and meeting spaces.[64]

Despite such new activities Lancaster continued to offer a pedestrian-friendly atmosphere, a remnant of the pre-automobile age that remained largely intact during the postwar period. Children could walk to the movies or the library, go to stores, and visit friends and relatives on their own, giving them an independence that suburban children could never know. Many adults enjoyed this same walking world, especially those who did not own cars or who preferred not to drive everywhere.[65]

In most ways adult socializing continued along familiar lines. An *Eagle-Gazette* column called "News Taken For Grant-Ed," written by society editor Juanita Grant, allowed residents to read about the latest birthday parties, wedding anniversaries, bridge parties, club luncheons, style shows, and country club dances, though the descriptions were not as full and glowing as they had been a generation earlier.[66] As late as 1959, residents of Lancaster could also see minstrel shows put on by the Burnt Corkers (established in 1941), in black face, as the name of the group suggested.[67]

That this might be offensive to the town's small African American community apparently bothered no one in the white community. Throughout the 1950s the social highlight each winter was the Candlelight Ball, held at the Elks Lodge and sponsored by two hospital auxiliaries (known as "Twigs"), with all proceeds benefiting the local hospital.[68]

Newspaper readers could also learn in late 1959 of a new restaurant and bar called Old Bill Bailey's, located at 200 Harrison Avenue on the West Side. For the next twenty-five years owner Ben Smith, a Navy veteran of World War II and a former brick layer, entertained customers nightly on the piano, invariably opening with the tune "Won't You Come Home Bill Bailey," after which the establishment had been named. Family and friends often joined Smith at the piano, playing their own instruments or offering vocal solos, while customers sang along.[69]

In addition to the newspaper, residents of Lancaster and vicinity could receive news over their own radio station, WHOK, which began broadcasting in 1948. In addition to news, sports, weather, and conversations with local personalities, WHOK specialized in country and western music for many years.[70]

Of course, not all the news was good. Although the crime rate in Lancaster was low in comparison to big cities, crime was not absent from the scene. Most crimes involved petty burglaries and thefts, though there were several violent and sensational crimes during Lancaster's high noon. In December 1956, for example, a man shot himself in his car before his estranged wife's house, and a month later, in January 1957, a man stabbed his brother-in-law to death. In March 1959 a local man went berserk, murdering his wife and eleven-year-old daughter in their beds with a hammer and then killing himself and four other children by carbon monoxide poisoning in the family car. In November 1954, residents read with horror about a nurse who confessed to dumping her premature twins into a trash can on the West Side and burning their bodies. But the most gripping case involved accusations against a Lancaster physician, Dr. Joseph Geer, after his wife, Constance, died of what the Fairfield County coroner ruled was "drug intoxication." Coming just after the sensational trial of Dr. Samuel Sheppard, who had been found guilty of killing his wife in the Cleveland suburb of Bay Village, the Geer case attracted national headlines. Geer later confessed to falsifying narcotics prescriptions, was sentenced to two years of probation, and was stripped of his license to practice medicine.[71]

Yet none of these crimes, however terrible, represented the sorts of random violence that afflicted big cities or that stemmed from widespread social and economic depravation. Rather, they appeared to be crimes of passion committed by individuals whose behavior did not stem from widespread poverty or social decay.

Nevertheless, big-city crime, at least big-city juvenile crime, did have an indirect impact on Lancaster and Fairfield County through the Boys' Industrial School, or BIS, as everyone continued to call this institution located some five miles south of town. With a rise in "juvenile delinquency" during the postwar years, enrollment at the BIS swelled to over 1,000 by the spring of 1957. It was relatively easy for boys to escape from the premises, where there were no walls or fences to keep them in, and hardly a month went by without a story in the *Eagle-Gazette* about runaways stealing cars or breaking into houses and stores in search of money.[72] Though these accounts were alarming, no one in the local community seems to have been hurt by an escapee. What is more, the institution was a source of employment for scores of residents. For boys growing up in Lancaster, the BIS was a tangible and frightening reminder of how fortunate they were, a thought sometimes drummed into them by parents who held up the reform school as the ultimate sanction for bad boys.

A more pleasant topic of conversation during these years was the antics of Lancaster's most famous character, Henry Weaver Davidson (c. 1895–1957). Earlier generations had undoubtedly witnessed their own town characters, but none has been so well documented as Davidson, whose death in August 1957 merited a full-scale obituary with photograph in the *Eagle-Gazette*. The son of a successful Lancaster attorney, Davidson lived on a modest inheritance from his family and from the proceeds on several patented inventions, none of which was especially successful. Standing six feet two inches tall and weighing about 250 pounds in his prime, Davidson sported a full beard and long, unkempt hair. His mind was full of inventive ideas, such as a flying motorcycle that would allow its driver to swoop over vehicles in a traffic jam, steered only by its rider's movements in the seat. Among Davidson's real inventions, for which he actually secured a patent, was a motor-driven wheelbarrow, which he exhibited in numerous parades.

Whenever there was a crowd or pubic event, Davidson found his way there—and not only in Lancaster. He traveled across the country several times in an old hearse, and would show up, seemingly out of nowhere, in crowd scenes that appeared on the front pages or in the Sunday magazine sections of major metropolitan newspapers. The hearse that Davidson drove invariably carried signs and sayings. One of these read "All the nuts in this car are tight, except the one behind the wheel."[73] Another advised, "Gossip runs down more people than automobiles."[74] Davidson was also a constant walker, who delighted in treating those he met on the street to a sample of his homespun philosophy. In his will, Davidson left the bulk of his estate to the Junior Chamber of Commerce, or Jaycees, who used the money to put up a headquarters building on South Broad Street.[75] While some residents were repelled by the man's wild hair and beard, most looked upon "Old Henry" as a lovable eccentric who added warmth and spice to the town.

Although Henry Weaver Davidson may have found gossip more dangerous than automobiles, cars were killing more and more local residents in this age before mandatory seat belts and other safety features. In the four years from 1957 through 1960, approximately seventy persons died in motor vehicle accidents in Lancaster and Fairfield County, nearly half the number from the area who had lost their lives in all of World War II. Among those killed were eighty-two-year-old Charles Griggs, former owner of the Princess Theater and a much beloved figure in town, and twenty-three-year-old Donald Hutsler, the son of Lancaster police chief Sam Hutsler.[76]

There were no public memorials to these victims of American motor technology, but every year, as they had for decades, Lancastrians remembered those who had died in the nation's wars. Memorial Day, earlier known as Decoration Day, took on special significance during the years just after World War II. Every May 30, at nine in the morning, the Memorial Day parade assembled at Main and High Streets. The various veterans' units, supplemented by contingents of Cub Scouts, Brownies, Boy Scouts, Girl Scouts, Blue Birds, Camp Fire Girls, and several marching bands, proceeded down Main Hill to Columbus Street, where they turned north to Forest Rose Cemetery. A half block or so from the cemetery gates, the units slowed to the half-step cadence used in a funeral march as one of the bands played appropriate music. There was then a brief ceremony at a memorial made of white wooden crosses representing the local men killed in two world wars, followed by taps that echoed over the hillsides above.[77] There were no longer any Civil War veterans to march or ride in the parade or take part in the ceremonies. The last Lancaster survivor, probably Albert Getz, founder of the town's first shoe factory, had died back in

1935. The last Fairfield County survivor, Lewis N. Heiston, had died in 1946.[78] But there were still aging Spanish-American War vets to participate and many vibrant World War I survivors, who joined the far larger ranks of World War II men—and later those who fought in the Korean War.[79]

The Korean conflict broke out in June 1950, just two weeks after Lancaster had wrapped up its sesquicentennial celebrations. Before it was over, thirty-seven men from the area had lost their lives in Korea.[80] For those who fought in the war, as well as for those who stayed home, the Korean War marked an increased consciousness about the threat of Communism. The war ended in July of 1953, but the simmering contention between the United States and the Soviet Union and the fear of an all-out confrontation between the Communist World and the Free World, a phenomenon known as the Cold War, unsettled local residents as it did the entire nation. Thus, during Lancaster's high noon there was always a black cloud on the horizon that threatened to destroy everything in a nuclear holocaust.

Lancaster residents experienced the Cold War in many ways. Air raid drills sent students scrambling for cover under their desks, while civil defense tests halted traffic for up to twenty minutes on Lancaster streets, with all traffic lights on red. As the *Eagle-Gazette* described one such test, "Ambulances, police, sheriff's cars and fire department vehicles, with sirens screaming, drove over pre-assigned routes . . . to warn the public of the red test alert."[81] During the Korean War there was also a unit of the ground observer corps in Lancaster, established to scan the skies for enemy planes. Operating from an old shack on Shimp's Hill just north of town, the volunteer spotters called in a description of each aircraft seen overhead to a center in Columbus, which could then alert fighters at Lockbourne Air Force Base to attack and bring down enemy planes.[82] The likelihood of an air attack from the Soviet Union, even if launched over the North Pole, was, of course, extremely unlikely at the time, a point that many clear-thinking Lancastrians pointed out, sometimes as a gentle chiding to the men and women who volunteered at the ground observer station. In fact, the only damage done to local property by aircraft during the Cold War in Lancaster was inflicted by U.S. Air Force jets from the Lockbourne base, which set off loud sonic booms as they crashed through the sound barrier while flying over town. The worst of these episodes occurred in March 1954 when a sonic boom damaged a nursing home and shattered the glass in several downtown store windows.[83]

It is difficult to know how much the Cold War dampened spirits locally. Perhaps most affected were the children whose air raid drills at school led some to have recurring nightmares of nuclear annihilation. Then there were a few hysterical teachers who went overboard on visions of a Russian invasion of the United States, with hordes of brutal Red soldiers marching down Lancaster's streets and hauling kids off to slavery in Siberia. Many more teachers took advantage of the Sputnik scare in 1957—when the Soviets beat the United States by putting an artificial satellite into orbit around the earth—to lecture students on how it was their patriotic duty to study their math and physics in order to defeat the Communists on the frontiers of science and technology. Fortunately, there were no charges of Communist subversion in Lancaster and no witch hunts against teachers in the public schools. Such events were unlikely in a town where anyone so accused was bound to be a well-known or well-respected citizen, friend, and neighbor.

The only real disasters to afflict residents during the years after World War II were of the natural variety, such as floods, high winds, and snowstorms. One of the worst thunder- and windstorms of the period swooped down on Buckeye Lake in July 1954 following record-breaking heat of 104 degrees.[84] But by far the worst natural disaster of the period was the flood that hit the West Side of Lancaster in the summer of 1948. The deluge came at 11 P.M. on July 21, with more than three inches of rain pounding the area in just an hour. Within twenty minutes after the downpour, the Hocking River went over its banks and dumped flood waters eight and ten feet deep into low-lying West-Side homes. Many residents were asleep and literally fled for their lives, some having to be evacuated from housetops or rescued from tree branches. Over five hundred houses sustained damage, and dozens of roads throughout the area became impassable. Kenneth Kerr, as chairman of the local Red Cross disaster committee, coordinated these rescue efforts. In an interview for the *Eagle-Gazette* Kerr said he was most impressed by the way neighbor had helped neighbor in an outpouring of community spirit: "It was absolutely miraculous, . . . this solicitous spirit of West Side residents and other Lancastrians. . . . People pitched in and helped one another in many ways. . . . When disaster committee members inquired about this or that family, thought to be marooned in their home, neighbors would say, 'we've brought them out,—they're all right and in a safe place.'"[85] Besides prompting demonstrations of neighborly support and community spirit, the 1948 flood, coming only a decade after serious floods in 1935 and 1937, led to the building of a number of flood-control dams along the principal tributaries of the Hocking River, which have prevented such flashflooding in the years since. (There had been other damaging floods in Lancaster during 1873, 1907, and 1913.)[86]

Another emergency provided by mother nature, but which brought more inconvenience than extensive property damage, was the "big snow" of 1950. This freak snowstorm, coming as it did in late autumn, began on Thursday, November 23, and lasted on and off throughout the weekend, with the worst coming on Saturday afternoon and evening. Total accumulation in Lancaster was 25.5 inches. Making matters worse were low temperatures that hovered just above zero and gale-force winds that whipped the snow into drifts 8 and 10 feet high. A number of Lancaster fans were trapped in Columbus, where they had gone to see the annual grudge match between the Ohio State Buckeyes and the Michigan Wolverines. Once again neighbors helped neighbors, as well as total strangers. Some fifty people had to spend Saturday night at the Palace Theater, while a group of farmers near the village of Baltimore waded through drifts to rescue fifteen passengers stranded in a Greyhound bus. Four buses and approximately thirty automobiles also became snowbound on Saturday night a mile or so from the Lancaster corporation limits, and about forty individuals took refuge in the nearest building, which was radio station WHOK. The next morning neighbors in the area brought soup, sandwiches, and hot coffee to the station. Most factories and businesses had to close down, and the schools in Lancaster and Fairfield County did not open again until December 4. Lancaster lacked snow-plowing equipment at the time, and on Sunday the mayor asked residents to shovel out their streets by hand. All day Sunday, neighborhood men worked shoulder to shoulder digging through the drifts in a spirit of good-natured cooperation that many never forgot. During the following week, late Indian-summer temperatures as high as 60 degrees made deep dents in the snow, and by Christmas it looked as if nothing had ever happened.[87]

Perhaps because it affected so many more people than the flood of 1948 and did less damage, residents remembered the big snow for decades to come as a special time of coziness and sharing. Such memories would help to sustain their town after its high noon—during uncertain times to come.

SEVEN

# Suburban Lancaster
## Toward the Edge City

During the four decades after 1960, Lancastrians began to feel the effects of a number of forces that took their town in new directions. Some of these forces, such as the automobile, had been present for many years but had not greatly affected the physical fabric of the town until the emergence of new highways and the advent of Lancaster's first shopping centers as the 1960s began. These highways gave rise to new patterns of retail and residential development, as townspeople followed residents of many other communities throughout the nation in moving to the suburbs. Meanwhile, many long-established retail businesses abandoned the downtown for the shopping centers or closed their doors for good. Other downtown businesses, in a panic to provide convenient parking, demolished numerous historic buildings. Even Lancaster High and the local Catholic high school abandoned their sites near downtown and headed for the suburbs. By the early 1980s downtown Lancaster had ceased to be a major commercial center and source of communal identity, a role that it had played since the founding of the frontier town nearly two centuries before.

At the same time, Lancaster was feeling the effects of global competition. Some of its industries went out of business completely, while Anchor Hocking Glass, long the dominant player in the local economy, was sold to outside interests who almost immediately closed the company's central offices in Lancaster. In response, many Lancastrians found jobs in Columbus, thirty miles northwest of town. At the same time, increasing numbers of Columbus residents, looking for more affordable housing and seeking to escape from what they saw as "urban problems," moved into the northern parts of Fairfield County and into Lancaster itself. In the process Lancaster became enmeshed in a large metropolitan region centering around

Columbus. There was no longer one commercial and civic center, but many centers, within Lancaster—and within the region as a whole. Thus, by the end of the twentieth century Lancaster could be defined as several demographic clusters, at least one of them approaching Joel Garreau's definition of an edge city. This emerging edge city, along with the other clusters of life and work, exists within a larger swirl of residential and economic activity within the central Ohio region. In this sense, Lancaster has joined many other American towns in becoming part of a vast demographic shift.

Most Lancastrians entered the 1960s with little idea of what lay ahead. "A City of Progress" was how Mayor Clarence E. Miller described Lancaster at the end of 1965, and there were many accomplishments to which he and others could point during the middle 1960s.[1] For example, Anchor Hocking announced in July 1964 that it would undertake a half-million-dollar expansion of its West Side installation (also known as Plant 1). The following year, in March 1965, the Lancaster City Council purchased 340 acres of land along Route 22 East for an industrial park. Within two weeks of the announcement, Irving Drew Shoes revealed that it would construct a storage complex at the park, and in April General Mills proposed to build a food-processing plant there, which opened in November 1966. It was also in March 1965 that Lancaster Glass said it would double the size of its electronics division. A year later Lancaster Electro-Plating unveiled plans for expansion.[2]

Another indication of progress for most residents of Lancaster, and of surrounding Fairfield County, was the extensive highway construction completed in the early 1960s. This process had actually begun back in 1954 when city council had appropriated $5,000 for a study of "arterial highways" in and around the town. The resulting projections called for improving U.S. Route 33, which joined Lancaster to Columbus and areas further north and west, and to Athens and other points south and east. According to the plan there would also be a bypass around Lancaster for U.S. Route 22, instead of its running through the downtown along Main Street. The Route 33 "expressway," as this double-lane divided highway was called at the time, opened in August 1960, but the Route 22 bypass, which was projected to go just north of Lancaster, was stalled and then abandoned because of intense opposition by several property owners along the proposed route, an opposition that city council heeded when it tabled the necessary legislation in June 1962.[3]

As all over the nation, highway improvements encouraged the purchase and use of more automobiles in the region at the same time that they opened up more possibilities for suburban housing developments and outlying businesses.[4] The 1954 federal tax code, which allowed for the accelerated depreciation of new commercial development, was also a powerful stimulus to the building of shopping centers and shopping malls all over the United States. Because there was little available land in downtowns, there were few benefits to spending on commercial improvements in these older areas. The result was a flurry of shopping center construction all over the United States, beginning in the middle and late 1950s. As with residential real estate, the federal government was playing a powerful role in the suburbanization of America.[5]

Significantly, Lancaster received its first real shopping center in the aftermath of this new tax provision and in the very same year, 1960, that the Route 33 improvement was completed. Named the Plaza Shopping Center, it was located along Route 33 itself, or Memorial Drive (in honor of World War II veterans), as Lancastrians had called the highway through town since 1948.[6] The shopping center occupied part of the old canal reservoir site, along with a steep rise in the landscape to the west of the former reservoir basin known as Cold Spring Hill, which was leveled for the construction. Spearheading the center's construction were two local developers, Gail Wacker and Kelly Hannan.[7] With approximately twenty-five stores, the Plaza held its grand opening on May 18, 1960. A number of these businesses, such as Gray's Drugs, were new to the area, but in most cases the plaza outlets, J. C. Penney included, had relocated from downtown or elsewhere in Lancaster.[8]

In addition to the Plaza Shopping Center itself, other stores or clusters of stores increased in number along the two major roads out of town, namely Route 22 and Route 33. On East Main Street, as Route 22 was known in the area, a small shopping center featuring a Kroger's supermarket, opened at about the same time as the Plaza Center. But it was the Route 33 corridor (North Memorial Drive) that became the more powerful commercial magnet. By the mid-1960s it was lined with gas stations, appliance stores, car dealerships, grocery stores, and fast food restaurants of all kinds, with the usual jumble of signs that fought for drivers' attentions and looked almost exactly like their counterparts all over the United States.

Another cluster of businesses grew up along Sheridan Drive in the northeast section of Lancaster, at the instigation of Gail Wacker. This

One of many strip shopping centers along the Route 33 corridor in Lancaster. Photo by author, 1998.

complex started in 1959 with the Tiki Swim Club, taking its name from the nationwide Polynesian craze, a fad originating in the immensely popular Broadway musical and movie *South Pacific,* and also from the spectacular postwar voyage by Thor Heyerdahl across the Pacific in a reed boat called the Kon-Tiki.[9] Three years later, in 1962, Wacker and other investors built the Tiki Bowling Lanes next to the pool. In the early 1970s a movie theater, retail shops, and several sets of townhouses would complete the Tiki complex.[10]

Although most of these locations were technically inside the Lancaster corporation limits, they were just as suburban in character as similar developments outside larger towns and cities across the country: that is, they were in outlying areas of Lancaster, and they catered to customers with automobiles by placing themselves along major thoroughfares and providing free parking in lots surrounding their businesses. Thus, even as a modest-sized town, Lancaster felt the increasing effects of suburbanization.

It was not long until Lancaster's churches began to follow businesses into the suburbs. For instance, St. Mary Roman Catholic erected two new parishes in the early 1960s: St. Mark in the vicinity of new housing on the

West Side, and St. Bernadette in the eastern suburbs. Several Protestant denominations, including Grace Reformed (United Church of Christ), also moved to the outskirts.[11]

Even Lancaster High School, which for decades had sat firmly in the center of town, moved to the suburbs in 1963. This new building represented the fulfillment of a dream that the school board had first proposed forty years earlier in the mid-1920s, but had abandoned for lack of voter support in favor of expanding the original Mulberry Street buildings. But Lancaster's growth, exacerbated by the postwar baby boom, threatened to overwhelm the high school in the early 1960s. And because the high school stood in a well-kept residential area, acquiring land for a new school near the old site would have meant purchasing and demolishing numerous houses, an expensive as well as a controversial proposition. In addition, the original wings of the high school building, put up in 1906 and 1917, were in very poor condition and would have had to come down in any case.

After a $4.1 million bond issue for a new high school suffered a defeat in November 1958, voters passed the measure in May 1959. Although the Mulberry Street location was not feasible for the new building, the school board did prefer a somewhat central location for the facility and conceived of a plan to erect a high school in the northwest corner of the Fairfield County Fairgrounds, which was used only during the busiest days of the fair for parking. However, the fair board refused at least four requests to allow the high school to occupy its property, and school authorities even considered suing to obtain the land. In the end, the school system purchased land behind the Thomas Ewing Junior High, part of which faced State Route 37 as it made its way north out of town.[12] At the time, many residents considered this site to be "out in the country," about as far removed from the center of Lancaster as one could imagine, and there was much criticism about the decision.

The new high school opened in the fall of 1963, complete with cafeteria, gymnasium, auditorium, library, vocational shops, and classrooms. The school also boasted a planetarium, a gift of Dorothy Bell Whiley (Mrs. Philip Rising) Peters. She dedicated it to the youth and citizens of Lancaster "for the fostering of scientific knowledge" in memory of her husband, Philip Rising Peters, and her son, Henry Charles Peters. A new outdoor athletic facility, Fulton Field, was made possible, in part, by a gift from Anchor Hocking executive Cyrus L. Fulton in memory of his parents.[13]

In 1971 Lancaster's Catholic high school also moved out along Route

Suburban campus of the "new" Lancaster High School on Route 37 North, surrounded by acres of lawn on one side and acres of asphalt parking lots on the other, with few architectural clues that it might be a school rather than an office building or manufacturing facility. Photo by author, 1998.

The "old" Lancaster High School at Mulberry Street and Pearl Avenue, whose architecture clearly designates it as a school. Parallel to Mulberry Street, with a retaining wall and sidewalk and facing a row of trees and residences across the street (not depicted here), this was a sheltered setting on a warm human scale. Photo 1950s. Curriculum Resource Center, Lancaster Public Schools.

37, just a mile or so north of the recently built Lancaster High School. Formerly known as St. Mary High School, and from 1961 to 1972 as Bishop Fenwick High School, the new facility was called the William V. Fisher Catholic High School. Following the death of William V. Fisher, for many years vice president and general manager of Anchor Hocking, his Catholic widow had donated the funds to erect the school as a memorial to her husband (who himself was Protestant).[14]

Whereas many if not most students could walk to the old high schools, public and Catholic, the vast majority now had to take school buses, have parents drop them off at school, or drive their own cars. Consequently, parking lots surrounded the schools, and especially Lancaster High, catering to the car in the same way as any shopping center. And when the new Lancaster High opened in the fall of 1963, the soda fountains downtown seemed nearly deserted after school for the first time in anyone's memory.[15] Nor would downtown streets echo with the Lancaster High fight song as the band marched down Main Hill on its way out to North Field.

Following both high schools to the Route 37 corridor was Lancaster's branch of Ohio University, the main campus of which was in Athens, some forty-five miles southeast of Lancaster. The "branch," as nearly everyone called it, had been established in 1956 as an evening program that operated out of the old Lancaster High School on Mulberry Street. When the high school relocated on Route 37 the branch went with it. Then in 1968 Ohio University, with financial assistance from a community fund drive, opened its own new building just north of the high school. Ohio University–Lancaster (or OU–L) offered day as well as evening classes and soon became the largest of Ohio University's branch campuses.[16]

By the time the Ohio University campus and the two high schools relocated on the fringes of town, many residents had made the move to suburbia, even though most of the new developments took place within the corporation limits or were soon annexed by Lancaster. The reasons for "moving out" were similar to those in most communities across the nation. In Lancaster as elsewhere, many young families concluded that new housing was, by definition, better than older models. Low interest rates during the two decades after World War II, and even lower rates through the Veterans Administration (VA) or Federal Housing Administration (FHA), placed new construction within the reach of many residents. Guidelines drawn up by both the VA and FHA encouraged lending

A portion of the Ohio University Campus at Lancaster, completed 1968. Photo by author, 1998.

institutions to prefer the financing of new housing over the purchase of older homes whose values, government officials believed, might not hold up as well as the newer construction.[17] One factor that did not figure in Lancaster's suburbanization was "white flight," for the African American population remained minuscule and continued to decline in the decades after World War II. In 1990 African Americans made up only .5 percent of the total population, or approximately one-sixth the percentage of African Americans in 1860, and one-half of that in 1920. Other "minorities" were also minuscule in 1990, with Hispanics at .5 percent of the total, Asians at .4 percent, and "others" at .2 percent.[18]

This lack of racial motives in the suburbanization of Lancaster suggests that suburban movement would have taken place on a large scale throughout the nation even if race were not a factor. Although racial prejudice was undoubtedly one factor in suburbanization during the postwar period, it is probable that the automobile, highway construction, postwar prosperity, and lending guidelines had more to do with this vast demographic movement than race itself, a hypothesis that may deserve further investigation.

CHAPTER SEVEN

238

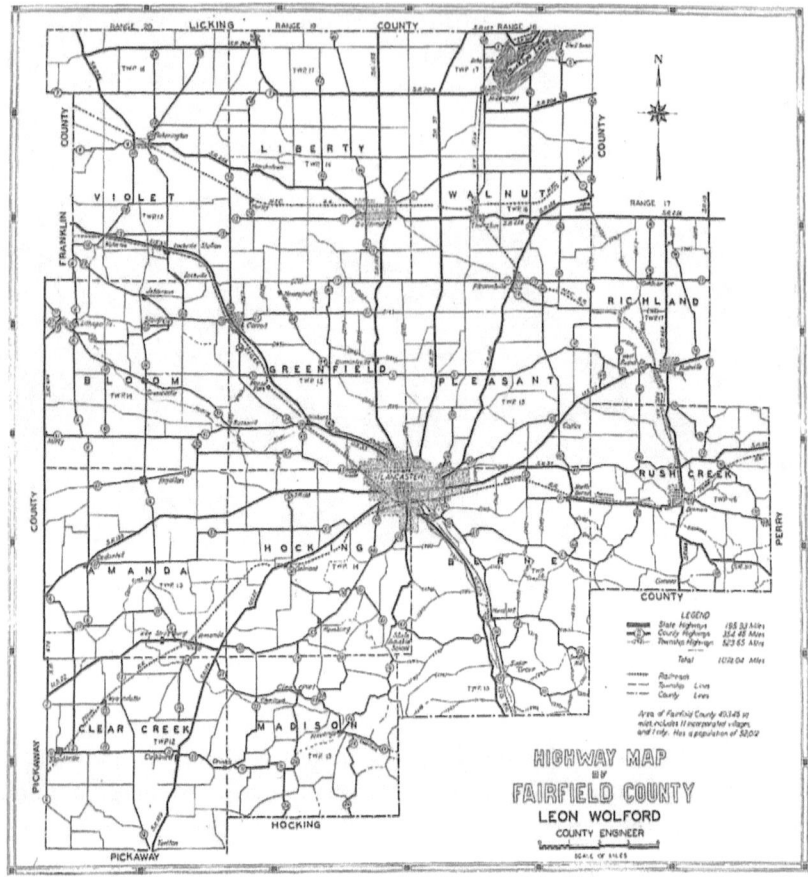

Highway map of Fairfield County, c. 1950. Tobias Studio Collection, FCDL.

In Lancaster one of the earliest and most successful suburban developers was Frank Gorsuch, who came to town in 1942 as an insurance agent and then became a real estate broker just in time for the postwar building boom. Gorsuch bought prefabricated houses from National Homes of Lafayette, Indiana, and between 1947 and 1950 he erected approximately one hundred houses southwest of town in a development that he called Rosedale. Gorsuch later named his firm Fairfield Homes, and it remains a major developer as the twentieth century comes to an end.[19] Another large-scale suburban developer was L. C. Durdin, whose 98-acre undertak-

Map of Lancaster, c. 1950. Tobias Studio Collection, FCDL.

ing, known as the Huffer-Durdin Addition, went up on the far east end of Lancaster during the mid-1950s.[20]

This Huffer-Durdin Addition, like virtually all the subdivisions at that time (and later), was annexed by Lancaster, a necessary step for the developers who depended upon the town to extend water, gas, and sewage, as well as police and fire protection. Because of these more or less assured annexations and because there were no other incorporated villages or towns in close proximity, Lancaster did not become surrounded and ultimately strangled by politically independent suburbs, unlike many large cities (especially on the East Coast).[21]

Yet life in Lancaster's suburbs was not unlike what one might find elsewhere. In order to keep down expenses at a time when a good 40 percent of building costs went into such things as wiring, plumbing, and the latest kitchen and bathroom fixtures, the new suburban homes did not come with front porches. Zoning requirements, first enacted in Lancaster in 1939, also required that new houses be set back far enough (at least sixty feet from the center of the street), so porches, from which residents could see or be seen, would have made little sense in any case.[22] Instead of sitting on the porch in the evening where they could greet or talk with passing neighbors, Lancaster's suburbanites, like their counterparts all over the country, spent much of their outdoor time in the backyard or stayed indoors with air conditioners running full blast in houses that had been built on cornfields, with not a native tree in sight.[23] Since zoning requirements also forbade commercial establishments in what were designated, after 1939, as residential areas, Lancaster's suburban dwellers had to do virtually all their shopping by car.[24] Although zoning had protected new residential neighborhoods from the noise and pollution of industries and even small manufacturing establishments, the zoning laws had also deprived them of many of the conveniences, such as corner drugstores and grocery stores, that had been common in older neighborhoods.

And even in Lancaster, nearly all the new houses were beyond the reach of local bus routes, and thus the subdivisions had to cater to the automobile with driveways and built-in garages or car ports. The car culture was now supreme, a fact that was reflected in the demise of the local bus service at the end of March 1969. Unlike the retirement of Lancaster's trolleys thirty-two years before, when thousands lined the streets to wave farewell, few noticed or lamented the passing of the town's public transportation.[25] (Passenger trains had discontinued service to Lancaster at the end of 1949, though there was still bus service to Columbus and several other towns and cities in the region.[26]

Other indications of the automobile culture were the appearance of two drive-in movie theaters: the Skyview Cruise-In Theater on East Main Street, which opened in 1948, and the City Drive-In on West Fair Avenue, which opened slightly later.[27] Just as popular—and accessible all year round—were the drive-in restaurants. Although there were several in Lancaster, the most famous was Jimmy's, home of the "Jaw Breaker," a double-decked hamburger with a secret sauce concocted by owner Jimmy Mast. Jimmy's opened in 1953 on East Main Street, and in 1955 Mast established a second Jimmy's on North Memorial Drive.[28] For a high school kid with a car, Jimmy's was prime cruising turf, just as the drive-in movies (also known as the "passion pits") were favorite destinations for a summer date, or even a carful of teenage friends.

The drive-ins, the new highways, and an ever increasing flood of cars posed a great threat to Lancaster's downtown. Indeed, downtowns all over the country were suffering in much the same way, because virtually all of them had been conceived and built in a pre-automobile age, and on a pedestrian scale that could not easily provide sufficient parking spaces for a generation on wheels.[29] In Lancaster, almost anyone in a car found that it was more convenient to patronize the Plaza Shopping Center or other outlying retail establishments than to look for a parking space downtown. The opening in 1968 of the large Eastland Shopping Mall in the southeast section of Columbus, only twenty miles or so from Lancaster and even closer to farms and villages in the northern part of Fairfield County, took still more business from downtown Lancaster.[30]

The first and most natural instinct of Lancaster's downtown merchants was to fight back by trying to imitate certain features of the shopping centers and malls. Anticipating competition from the Plaza Shopping Center, for instance, a number of merchants formed the Progressive Businessmen's Association in the fall of 1959. Its president was Thomas "Tom" Alfred, then owner of the Lyric movie theater and a grandson of the nineteenth-century entrepreneur Theodore Mithoff.[31] That same fall the Progressive Businessmen inaugurated an off-street parking system by convincing several owners to pool their lots. The first two hours of parking would be free, after which customers would have to pay twenty-five cents for each additional hour, with lot owners to be reimbursed on a monthly basis. The businessmen also discussed the idea of a pedestrian shopping mall on Main Street, with the street closed to all vehicular traffic. The key to making this happen, they believed, was a Route 22 bypass that would take "through traffic" out of the center of town.[32] In October 1960 the businessmen decided to stay open until 9:00 in the evening on both Monday and Friday in an attempt to compete, to a limited extent, with shopping center hours.[33]

Not included in the merchants' plans was a recognition that the preservation of historic buildings in the downtown could play a significant role in its revitalization. On the contrary, a number of businesses began demolishing old, physically sound, and architecturally attractive structures in order to put up new buildings or, in most cases, to obtain more parking

242

Part of the desert of asphalt created on West Wheeling Street, between Broad Street and Center Alley, when buildings were demolished in the post-1960 period to provide parking for downtown businesses. Evident is the "snaggle-tooth" effect made by the back ends of various Main Street structures and by the side of the telephone building (on right). Photo by author, 1998.

space for their customers. Unfortunately, the message that rehabilitating older structures is often cheaper in the long run than new construction was not yet widely understood. Nor was there a widespread realization at the time that a restored downtown could attract shoppers throughout the area, although it was becoming clear that Disneyland's "Main Street" had already tapped into a growing nostalgia for the old downtowns.[34]

Consequently, a number of downtown businesses in Lancaster, and especially its banks and thrift institutions, began to demolish one structure after another, some of them dating to the earliest days of the town. Besides losing a significant part of its physical past, entire street perspectives were obliterated. This was especially true of the north side of West Chestnut Street and the south side of West Wheeling Street, both of which backed up against the Main Street stores. By pulling down numerous buildings along Chestnut and Wheeling Streets, the downtown merchants created a desert of asphalt, interrupted here and there by a structure that had somehow escaped demolition, offering what one might call a snaggle-toothed view into the dingy and often rundown back ends of Main Street establishments. Buildings that were not pulled down, such as the post–Civil War Trout Building just south of the fountain, was renovated beyond recognition. There, the building's handsome Italianate roof brackets disappeared, as did its red-brick facade and Italianate fenestration, behind a veneer of simulated marble.[35] In fairness, it should be said that many of the demolished properties had been or were about to be vacated, but taking them down meant that they would not be there at a later time, when there might be greater interest in restoration and rehabilitation.

Among the other casualties downtown was the old Hillside Hotel, once the site of so many convivial dinners and musical evenings, which fell to the wreckers in 1959. The Chestnut Street Opera House, long occupied by A. B. Vlerebome wholesale grocers, went down in 1962. That same year the Lancaster Athletic Club on the northeast corner of the town square disappeared, as did an exceedingly attractive 1806 Federal-style house, long adapted as a shop, that had stood for nearly sixteen decades just around the corner from the athletic club on Main Street.[36] The once elegant, Mansard-roofed Hotel Martens on the northwest corner of Broad and Chestnut fell in 1971. Two years later, another fine Mansard commercial building came down on the opposite side of Broad Street to make way for a new police station.[37] By the mid-1970s so many buildings had been demolished that someone returning to Lancaster from a fifteen- or twenty-year absence would hardly have recognized the downtown.

Partly in response to the destruction of one historic building after another, downtown as well as in some of the older residential districts, a group of local women embarked upon a series of informal discussions in the summer of 1962 that led, a year later, to establishing the Fairfield Heritage Association.[38] The initiative came from Ruth Wolfley Drinkle (1903–93), who invited five other women to her home to discuss ways of saving and preserving Lancaster's historic architecture.[39] Drinkle had just returned from a trip to Williamsburg and various historical sites in Philadelphia and southern Pennsylvania, including Gettysburg. This experience had caused her to conclude that many homes and buildings in Lancaster and Fairfield County were just as attractive and just as architecturally significant as those she had seen in the East. To her daughter, Mary Alice Kuhn, who had accompanied her on the trip, she declared, "Lancaster has

Ruth Wolfley Drinkle, principal founder of the Fairfield Heritage Association, and her husband, Charles Drinkle, longtime Lancaster attorney and civic leader, stand before their own historic house on West Mulberry Street, c. 1978. Courtesy Mary Alice Drinkle Kuhn.

many homes just as historic as these—for our part of the country. We mustn't lose them!"[40] Also enthusiastic about the idea of preservation was Ruth's husband, Charles Drinkle, a longtime Lancaster attorney whose great-grandfather, Isaiah Vorys Sr., had designed and built a number of Lancaster's fine early-nineteenth-century dwellings, including the 1824 Garaghty-Mumaugh House.[41]

The five women who joined Drinkle in launching the Heritage Association were all from influential Lancaster families. These were Caroline Peters Rockwood, a granddaughter of Henry B. Peters and daughter of Philip Rising Peters, both presidents of the Fairfield National Bank; Mary Peters "Petie" Smith, the wife of funeral director Irvine Smith, and a cousin of Caroline Rockwood; Emilie Martin, whose attorney husband, George Martin, came from a long line of distinguished lawyers and judges; Marian Furniss, daughter of a prominent Lancaster physician and wife of John F. Furniss, the owner of a successful insurance agency; and Mary Kathryn Vlerebome, whose husband, Arthur Vlerebome, had just retired from his family's wholesale grocery business. Caroline Rockwood's mother, Dorothy (Mrs. Philip) Peters, became honorary chairman of the group and assisted "by entertaining visiting professionals and speakers in her home [on Wheeling Hill]."[42]

Having such women take the lead in founding and sustaining historical and preservation societies had become quite common throughout the United States. These women possessed the time, the knowledge, the financial resources, and the social and professional connections to conceive of such plans and to make them a reality. Ruth Drinkle and Emilie Martin, for example, could call upon the legal skills of their lawyer husbands, who had been law partners for many years. Their friendships with the Rockwood, Smith, Peters, and Vlerebome families gained the support of many others in Lancaster.

From the beginning, the six women and their small cadre of initial supporters sought the advice of professionals in historic preservation. Among them was Professor Milton Osborne, an architect who had recently retired from the faculty of Penn State University and whose wife, Lillie Bookwalter Osborne, had grown up in Lancaster. Osborne had renovated and restored President Dwight D. Eisenhower's Gettysburg farmhouse and had advised a number of Pennsylvania towns, including Gettysburg, Hollidaysburg, and Carlisle, on planning and preservation issues. The group also turned to several local individuals who were well versed in the architecture and history of Lancaster and Fairfield County.[43] Among these was Charles Goslin (1904–90), then manager of the Mattox clothing store and a well-respected naturalist and raconteur who had published, since 1953, a Saturday column in the *Eagle-Gazette* called "Nature Notes."[44] Another early consultant was Herbert Turner (1905–86), who had provided historical material for the sesquicentennial pageant in 1950 and who was a well-known collector of local artifacts from the period of early settlement and the restorer of a historic home known as Spook Hollow (c. 1820).[45]

Besides drawing upon the knowledge and expertise of residents like Turner and Goslin, Ruth Drinkle and her group took advantage of an already widespread if unfocused consciousness about the architectural heritage of Lancaster and Fairfield County. As early as 1901, for example, the centennial history of the community, put out by the Lancaster Board of Trade and the city council, showcased the town's historic houses in a number of half-page photographs.[46] There had also been occasional articles in the local newspapers about places of historic interest, including a suggested historical tour for fair visitors that appeared in the *Eagle-Gazette* during October 1936.[47] A long, front-page article about Lancaster's past had also appeared in the *Eagle*, October 22, 1929. In the mid-1950s the Fairfield County Commissioners published a small guide to historical and scenic places in the county.[48] And in 1945 Dorothy Ent Coleman, who later became an art teacher at Lancaster High School, wrote a master's thesis at Ohio State University on Lancaster's early-nineteenth-century architecture.[49]

Sixteen years earlier, in 1929, Lancaster had received one of the town's earliest and most attractive homes, the 1824 Garaghty-Mumaugh House, willed to the citizens of Lancaster as a museum by Mary Francis "Fannie" Mumaugh, whose father, John Mumaugh, had purchased it from its original owner, Michael Garaghty.[50] Though the Mumaugh House had been saved, the destruction (also in 1929) of the century-old Effinger House by Anchor Hocking's I. J. Collins had angered a number of historically minded individuals, though no one had wanted to challenge the powerful Collins, who himself had little or no regard for the local past.[51]

Thus, in early 1963, with such a background of interest in local history and architecture and with the advice and assistance of a number of individuals, the six Lancaster women and a growing number of supporters secured a nonprofit charter of incorporation for the Fairfield Heritage Association. At the first annual meeting in November of that year, the association elected an initial slate of officers, with Ruth Drinkle as first president. Drinkle would continue to be a mainstay of the association for over two decades and in 1978 would publish, with the support of the association, a well-illustrated book entitled *Heritage of Architecture and Arts in Fairfield County, Ohio*. In addition to highlighting the most important examples of local architecture, Drinkle gave considerable space to specimens of early furniture and decorative objects made in Lancaster and Fairfield County. The purpose of this book was to call attention to historic architecture and arts in the local area and to assist in saving and preserving them for future generations.[52]

Long before Drinkle published her book, however, the Heritage Association sponsored a multitude of lectures and exhibits to encourage historic preservation and to attract members. The most successful of these events has been the annual historic house tour, first organized by Fran Utley, whose husband, George Utley, was president of Drew Shoes. This highly successful event, known as the Pilgrimage Tour, was held during the first week of May each year and attracted thousands of persons from all over the region and beyond. Likewise successful in raising consciousness about local history and preservation issues was the *Fairfield Heritage Quarterly*, begun in 1979 and sponsored by the Heritage Association. Two other publications of the association also drew attention to local history. The first was *Crossroads and Fence Corners* (1976, 1980), a two-volume collection of naturalist Charles Goslin's newspaper columns. The second was *Campfire to Courthouse* (1981), by elementary school teacher Laura Kerr (no relation to former *Eagle-Gazette* publisher R. Kenneth Kerr).[53] This was written to accompany an annual tour and local history program for elementary school children that was coordinated by teacher Betty Arnsbarger, who also provided illustrations for the Kerr book.[54] It was in 1981, too, that the association launched an oral history project, which eventually resulted in three large volumes of transcribed interviews.[55]

In addition to publishing books, conducting tours, and sponsoring lectures, the Fairfield Heritage Association purchased in 1973 and subsequently restored The Georgian, one of Lancaster's most important historic houses and whose deterioration was a main reason that the six

Restored entrance to The Georgian, originally built in 1832 by Samuel F. Maccracken. Photo by author, 1997.

women founders had come together eleven years before. Named "The Georgian" by the proprietors of a tea room and gift shop that operated there during the 1930s and 1940s, the house, built by Samuel F. Maccracken, was more accurately described as a cross between late Federal and Greek Revival styles.[56] The large red-brick house, located on the northeast corner of Broad and Wheeling Streets, had been completed in 1833. Since its restoration, The Georgian has functioned as a headquarters for the Heritage Association, as well as a historic house museum with a number of furnishings either belonging to the original owners (the Maccrackens) or that had been crafted by Lancaster and Fairfield County artisans during the first half of the nineteenth century.[57] In 1982 the Heritage Association took title to a second museum property, the birthplace of General William T. Sherman and Senator John Sherman, known as The Sherman House. The house, on Main Hill, had been acquired by the city in 1947, was deeded over to the state in late 1949, and had been operated by the Ohio Historical Society since 1951.[58]

From time to time during these years there was a degree of dissatisfaction among some local preservationists over the Heritage Association's emphasis upon fine architecture and furniture. Among the dissatisfied was Herbert Turner, who in the late 1940s had revived a moribund Fairfield County Historical Society (originally founded in 1915). In 1953, in observance of Ohio's sesquicentennial of statehood, Turner had been largely responsible for obtaining, equipping, and then moving an authentic log cabin to the Fairfield County Fairgrounds, where it has been opened to the public at fair time ever since. Following upon this effort, the fair board itself secured about a dozen nineteenth- and early-twentieth-century buildings from various points of the county, including a one-room schoolhouse, country church, train station, rural doctor's office, general store, and early gas station, each with period furnishings. None of these structures would qualify as fine architecture and, in contrast to Lancaster's beautiful nineteenth-century homes, they are the types of buildings that men and women of humbler backgrounds would have used. In 1986 Turner donated his own collection of Fairfield County pioneer artifacts to the Ohio University campus in Lancaster, where it is on display in that institution's library.[59]

Differing views over what was worthy of preservation were fortunately mild and never became a subject of heated public debate.[60] By the time Lancastrians joined in celebrating the bicentennial of American Independence in 1976, interest in local history was greater than ever and appeared unaffected by conflicting interpretations of the past. Among the events during Independence week that year was the dedication of the "restored Georgian" after nearly four years of work. Another highlight

The bandstand on Zane Square, erected 1976. Photo by author, 1997.

was the dedication, on July 3, of a new bandstand on the northeast corner of the town square, a project of the Diamond Unity Management Club, an organization of managers from the Diamond Power firm. (In 1965 this area had been renamed Zane Square in honor of Lancaster's founder, Ebenezer Zane.)[61] There was also a huge parade on July 3, and various downtown merchants put up historical displays in their windows, much as they had for Lancaster's sesquicentennial twenty-six years before, though not on so lavish a scale. Out at the fairgrounds there were rides and concessions, and on the evening of the 4th a giant fireworks display.[62]

To protect Lancaster's many historic homes from future destruction, the Heritage Association, with support from Mayor Edward Rutherford and council member Charles Lantz, obtained a historic district ordinance from city council in 1977.[63] At the core of the Historic Lancaster District was "Square 13" of the original town grid, an area between High and Broad Streets that was bounded by Wheeling Street on the north and Main Street on the south.[64] The historic district itself was larger than Square 13, since it extended as far east as Pearl Avenue and to certain portions of Memorial Drive on the west. Its northern boundary corresponded roughly to the alley just beyond Union and King Streets, with its southern edge alternating between Chestnut and Walnut Streets.[65]

The 1977 ordinance also established the Historic Lancaster Commission, made up of five members whose charge was to "maintain and enhance the distinctive character" of the district, with a focus on the streetscape and neighborhood character. Upon receiving approval for restorations or renovations from the committee, property owners within the historical district qualified for exemptions from local property taxes ranging from ten to twelve years. Property owners who wished to demolish a structure—or any exterior architectural feature on a "listed building"—in the historic district had to apply for a permit from the commission. In cases where the commission denied such permits, the property owner had to wait six months, during which time an alternative use for the property would be explored. If after this period no other use had been found, the owner could go ahead with demolition. Fines ranging from $100 to $5,000 could be levied against anyone who failed to follow this procedure.[66] Critics have charged that this historic district was not large enough and that the six-month waiting period, while alternative uses were sought, was inadequate to safeguard Lancaster's architectural heritage.

Fortunately, the Historic Lancaster District did include the downtown, though it was twenty years too late to save more than a dozen significant buildings in the commercial area. However, anticipating the historic district, and to some degree serving as a catalyst for it, was a historic preservation and urban design study of Main Street, the traditional center of downtown. This study was commissioned by the Fairfield Heritage Association in conjunction with the Downtown Business Association and was undertaken by a firm called Townscape, whose offices were in Medina, Ohio. In a report dated June 30, 1975, Townscape made a number of recommendations. It also provided guidelines for preservation and renovation along with some rough sketches for individual facade treatments.[67]

Overall, Townscape urged preservation of the nineteenth-century character of Main Street between Broad and Columbus Streets. Central to accomplishing this, the report went on to say, was the need to disabuse downtown property owners and the public alike of the widely held notion that "anything old must be . . . inferior or at least non-functional." Often just the opposite was true, for much of what was "already built [was] superior in material, craftsmanship and esthetic form" to what was being constructed in the mid-1970s. At the same time, the report warned those commissioning new buildings to reject slavish imitations of earlier styles and instead to concentrate on designs that were compatible in "shape, color, mass, detail and functions [with the older built environment]."[68] The report went on to observe that many of the first-floor facades on Main Street had been repeatedly renovated to reflect the latest design fads, while the second and third stories had remained much the same as when originally constructed. The solution was to peel away these ground-floor facades to reveal original entrances and fenestrations (at least where they had not been destroyed altogether), which would once more match the upper stories and go a long way toward authentic restoration and preservation.[69]

As politely as it could, the report pointed out that too many "acres of asphalt" had already been provided for downtown parking and recommended that parking spaces be consolidated into "decks and covered garages," which would open up space for attractive new retail shops in place of ugly expanses of blacktop. Above all, no more of Main Street's old and solidly constructed buildings should be sacrificed for additional parking spaces.[70] The report ended by reiterating the great potential for Lancaster's downtown, but warned that immediate steps had to be taken in order to realize these possibilities: "All these advantages will fail in the long run if [Lancaster's] elected officials, commercial leaders and civic institutions do not strengthen the existing architectural environment, add complementary new structures, enhance parking arrangements and create a *pedestrian world* which is exciting to experience [emphasis added]."[71]

Pursuant to the Townscape Report and the 1977 ordinance creating a Historic Lancaster District, merchants collaborated with the Heritage Association to found the Downtown Area Rehabilitation Effort (DARE) in 1978. This group engaged the services of city planner Joseph C. Madonna, who urged the city government to purchase land downtown by issuing bonds and later selling this property to a developer or developers who would put up new office buildings, shops, and an attractively landscaped parking garage, in addition to restoring and rehabilitating many older buildings.[72] In a related initiative, DARE urged downtown property owners to take advantage of facade easements, that is, signing over the right to alter restored facades in exchange for tax benefits or matching funds from the Ohio Historic Preservation office.[73] By the end of 1979 a number of downtown property owners had completed or at least begun facade restorations, including Reed's Total Discount, the Harmony House gift shop, Hammonds men's clothing store, the Lancaster Book and Office Supply, and the general offices of Anchor Hocking.[74]

Despite the various efforts over two decades to revitalize downtown Lancaster, the trend in this central shopping district continued generally downward. In 1960, Wiseman's department store, a mainstay of the downtown business district for decades, closed, though this event probably had as much to do with owner Tom Wiseman's ill health as with the business climate itself. Leo Baughman and Avery Harrison, who both had run clothing shops on Main Street, collaborated to establish a new clothing store in the old Wiseman building. They called it Manson's, but it was unsuccessful and closed after only a brief run in 1960 and 1961.[75] Hickle's department store took over the Wiseman's building in 1965, while continuing to operate its "old" store across the street, but in 1984 Hickle's itself succumbed after eighty-four years of business.[76] Just a year before, in 1983, three longtime businesses also closed their doors for good: S. S. Kresge's, after sixty-seven years on the southwest corner of Main and Broad Streets; The City News (newspapers, magazines, and sporting goods), after forty-seven years in business; and Harraway's Children Center, after many years on Main Street. Reed's Total Discount Drug Store, which could trace itself back to Reed and Walters Drugs, established in 1906, ceased operation in 1981, along with Harmony House gift shop, another old and familiar establishment. These closings occurred just a year after "the last picture show" downtown, when the Lyric Theater folded after sixty-seven years.[77]

As another sign of the times, all four of Lancaster's longtime banks had been acquired by larger, out-of-town financial institutions, and at decade's end only two of these merged banks still had offices downtown. The old Equitable Federal Savings and Loan, which became a branch of Bank One of Columbus, also remained downtown, as did the Fairfield Federal Savings and Loan, which continued under local ownership.[78] However, a new, locally owned financial institution, The Standing Stone Bank, opened in May 1989.[79] On the negative side of the ledger, a devastating fire in November 1989 destroyed a commercial building at 128–130 West Main Street that dated to the 1880s. What was left of the structure had to be demolished, leaving yet another vacant lot.[80]

Unfortunately, the fire and multiple business closings downtown were only part of a series of alarming events that had beset Lancaster and much of the rest of the United States over those two decades. Among these forces were the Watergate scandal and the nation's retreat from Vietnam in the early 1970s, followed swiftly by an energy crisis, soaring inflation, high unemployment, and increases in foreign competition.

The great majority of Lancastrians supported the Vietnam War, as they had the nation's other foreign wars over the years. Some 4,500 residents of Lancaster and Fairfield County served in the military during the Vietnam era, defined as the years 1961 to 1975, though not all of them in Southeast Asia itself.[81] There would not appear to have been any organized protests locally against the war until President Richard Nixon ordered American forces into Cambodia in April of 1970. This "Cambodian incursion," which was widely interpreted as a widening of the war, caused college campuses across the nation to explode with demonstrations. In contrast, students from the Ohio University campus in Lancaster staged a peaceful memorial service at the large shelter house in Rising Park on May 8 for the four students shot and killed at Kent State University on May 4. The students quietly called for an end to the war and prayed for those who had fallen.[82]

Almost as unsettling as the escalating death toll in Vietnam was the frustration that many Americans felt about being trapped in a seemingly endless war that the country could not win. This sense of vulnerability was only reinforced by the Arab oil boycott during the winter of 1973–74. Lancaster residents had to contend with closed service stations, long lines at the pump, higher prices, and "odd-even" rationing that permitted motorists to purchase gasoline on odd or even days, depending upon whether their license plates ended in odd or even numbers. But the local area, which generally drew its fuel from domestic supplies, fared better than the Atlantic Seaboard states, which imported most of their oil from abroad.[83] Also unsettling were record-cold winters during the late 1970s, including a severe blizzard on January 26–30, 1978.[84] Unlike the "big snow" of November 1950, which was quickly followed by warm temperatures, the cold weather hung on after the blizzard of 1978 and was aggravated by low energy supplies, leaving none of the snug memories of the 1950 snow.

At the same time, many parts of the Midwest were suffering from economic woes, as industries that had once seemed invincible were scaling back production or shutting down altogether. The causes were multiple, but they included increased foreign competition, aging and inefficient plants, and the shift to a postindustrial age, where automation and the movement to a service-oriented economy led to the elimination of many factory jobs. For a time it looked as if Lancaster might be immune from

Anchor Hocking's Plant 1 on the West Side of Lancaster, surrounded by workers' houses. Photo c. 1960s. Courtesy Anchor Hocking Glass Company.

this process. In 1972 Lancaster did experience a significant closing, when the General Mills facility, which had opened in 1966, shut its plant. Fortunately, Ralston Purina took over this plant in 1973.[85] A half dozen years later, in 1979, the Boys Industrial School south of town, known since 1963 as the Fairfield School for Boys (FSB), closed as a youth facility, but reopened a year later as a correctional institution for adult offenders; it was eventually renamed the Southeastern Ohio Correctional Institution. Although it was a different sort of place than in the past, the facility continued to provide jobs for area residents.[86]

So far luck was holding, but in the mid-1980s even Lancaster experienced a number of plant shutdowns or reductions in force. In July 1983, Alten's Foundry, established nearly a century before, ceased operation, and in October of the same year Stuck Mould closed its Lancaster plant.[87] The following year Anchor Hocking let go some 270 office employees in a massive restructuring, and in May 1985 the company closed its Plant 2 (in the southeast part of Lancaster), with a loss of some 500 factory jobs.[88] Then in July 1987, Anchor Hocking shareholders approved an acquisition by the Newell Company of Freeport, Illinois. Within a week of the takeover, Newell announced the elimination of 110 managerial positions at the Lancaster headquarters, and in 1988 Newell closed the corporate offices in downtown Lancaster altogether and eliminated several hundred jobs at the one remaining production facility (Plant 1) in town.[89] For the first time in fifty years, Lancaster could no longer boast that it was the site of one of the nation's largest corporations. Nor would the local population be leavened by the arrival of managers and executives who had grown up in other parts of the United States, and who had often brought new vision and new energy to Lancaster's civic and cultural life.

By the time of the takeover, Anchor Hocking's founder, I. J. Collins, had been in his grave for a dozen years, having died at age 100 in 1975. Enigmatic to the end, Collins had rejected repeated advice from his attorney to set up some kind of trust or foundation in order to avoid heavy death taxes. Out of an estate of approximately $15 million, more than $8 million went to pay taxes. Most of the remainder was divided equally among his three nieces as well as a fourth woman who was apparently not related to Collins. In addition, he left small sums to several personal employees, to the Lancaster YMCA, and to St. John's Episcopal Church (where he was a member). Why Collins preferred to allow the government to take more than half his estate, rather than to leave some sort of permanent endowment for the benefit of the town that had helped to make his fortune, remains a mystery. Unlike the Ball family of Muncie, Indiana—manufacturers of glass canning jars who endowed a local teachers college that eventually became Ball State University—Collins did not attach his name to any local institution, enterprise, or civic space.[90] Ironically, Fairfield County used its share of the taxes from Collins's estate to assist in building a new public library at Broad and Mulberry Streets, an institution that he had not supported in life.[91] By the time of this writing, at the end of the twentieth century, Collins's name is fading from public consciousness, a consequence that this very private man might well have wished.[92]

Despite the economic difficulties of the 1980s, the majority of Lancaster residents have remained politically conservative. Clarence E. Miller, who served as a city councilman (1957–63), then as mayor (1964–65), and finally as a U.S. congressman for thirteen successive terms (1967–93), describes himself as a moderate conservative and lifelong member of the Republican Party. The conservatism that he shares with most inhabitants of the area stems from a belief that people can and should take care of themselves and not rely upon the government to solve their problems.[93]

The AEP clock tower, completed 1991, on the northwest corner of Main Street and Memorial Drive, offers a visual anchor to the west end of downtown. Photo by author, 1998.

This widespread view has not precluded conservative Democrats from winning local office. Such was the case with former mayor Edward Rutherford, a lifelong Democrat who viewed himself as a conservative and who believed that one of the biggest problems with government, at all levels, is bloated bureaucracy and too many regulations.[94]

In any case, Lancastrians were fortunate that private enterprise was sufficient to carry them through the Anchor Hocking buyout and to lay the ground for better times. In fact, several new economic enterprises had come to town during the decade or so before the Anchor Hocking acquisition and the scaling back of its operations in Lancaster. Among the most significant of these was a division of American Electric Power (AEP), which managed coal-mining and electrical-generating operations in Ohio and West Virginia. AEP first came to Lancaster in 1976, and in 1990–91 it erected an attractive red-brick building with a large clock tower on the northeast corner of Main Street and Memorial Drive, where the Alten's Foundry had once stood. By the time it occupied this facility, AEP had approximately 250 employees in Lancaster.[95]

Giving an additional boost to local employment was a second industrial site, known as the Rock Mill Industrial Park, opened in 1987 on West Fair Avenue. By the mid-1990s, ten enterprises had located there, including several industries that were wholly new to the area.[96] Anchor Hocking remained the largest single employer in town, but its 1,500 employees were only about half the number who had worked for the company a generation earlier.[97]

Also assisting the local economy, though it was far more controversial, was the River Valley Mall, which opened in 1987.[98] Located on the northwest edge of town between Route 33 (Memorial Drive) and the Hocking River, this first enclosed mall in Lancaster, developed by David Glimcher of Columbus, included a branch of the Columbus-based Lazarus department store in addition to about fifty other retail businesses. Critics contended that the mall would further undermine the downtown, create massive traffic jams on Route 33, and even threaten the town's water supply. Bowing to this criticism, a bare majority of city council repealed its earlier authorization of some $2 million for extending utilities to the mall site. Glimcher threatened to sue for breach of contract, and Lancaster mayor Edward Rutherford, who had been a strong advocate for the mall and the leading public figure in bringing it to Lancaster, vetoed the council's repeal.[99] The council then followed through with the necessary legislation and appropriations.[100]

A decade after the opening of the River Valley Mall, Lancaster mayor Art Wallace, who once was a member of the Anchor Hocking management team, believes that the mall helped to cushion the effect of the Anchor Hocking buyout. The mall not only provided jobs for local residents, he asserts, but it drew shoppers from a much wider area than ever before—especially from Hocking and Perry Counties to the south.[101] Furthermore, former mayor Rutherford believed that the mall kept many local residents from continuing to do a good deal of their shopping on the

Part of Lancaster's edge city, the River Valley Mall on Route 33 (North Memorial Drive), is surrounded by acres and acres of parking lots and lacks the sheltering scale of the old Main Street shopping corridor. Photo by author, 1998.

outskirts of Columbus and even attracted shoppers from the area directly south of Columbus itself.[102]

Because of its size and location on the major north-south highway (Route 33), the mall quickly became a new focal point for Lancaster. In addition to the stores themselves, developers put up apartments, restaurants, supermarkets, and even a motel on the fringes of the mall. And just east of the mall, the Borror Company of Columbus began, in 1996, the first of 700 new single-dwelling houses in a development known as River Valley Highlands. When finished, this residential development promises to add some 2,000 residents to Lancaster, about half of whom are projected to move in from the Columbus area, with plans to commute back and forth from their jobs in the capital city.[103]

The area around the River Valley Mall is thus coming to resemble what journalist Joel Garreau has called an *edge city*. Garreau uses this term to describe the emergence of new office and merchandising centers on the edges of towns and cities and along major highways, far from the old downtowns, generally in places where there had been only farms and fields a generation before. According to Garreau, the edge city has five major characteristics: it offers at least 5 million square feet of office space;

A massive housing development, known as River Valley Highlands, adjoins the edge city just east of the mall. Photo by author, 1998.

it has 600,000 or more square feet of retail space; it is a major source of jobs; it is seen by the population as one location; and, in its spread out form along the highway, it is very different from the old compact downtowns of earlier decades.[104] Although Lancaster's River Valley Mall and the development immediately around it does not qualify as one of Garreau's edge cities in terms of its total office and retail space, it does qualify in all other respects, and in time there is a real possibility that it might reach the square footages set forth by Garreau. Though not meeting the space requirements, the mall area is a major source of jobs, is seen as one location by residents and visitors alike, and is very different in organization and looks from the old downtown.

At the same time that the mall area is emerging an edge city for Lancaster, the northwest edge of Lancaster, where the mall is located, is becoming something of an edge city for Columbus, thirty miles to the northwest. Although Lancaster is not, at the end of the twentieth century, a large city, with a population approaching 40,000, the "edge city" phenomenon is nevertheless real.[105] That this phenomenon has appeared in a community the size of Lancaster only gives weight to the argument that much of the United States is undergoing a demographic transformation that increasingly blurs the old definitions of suburb, village, town, and city.

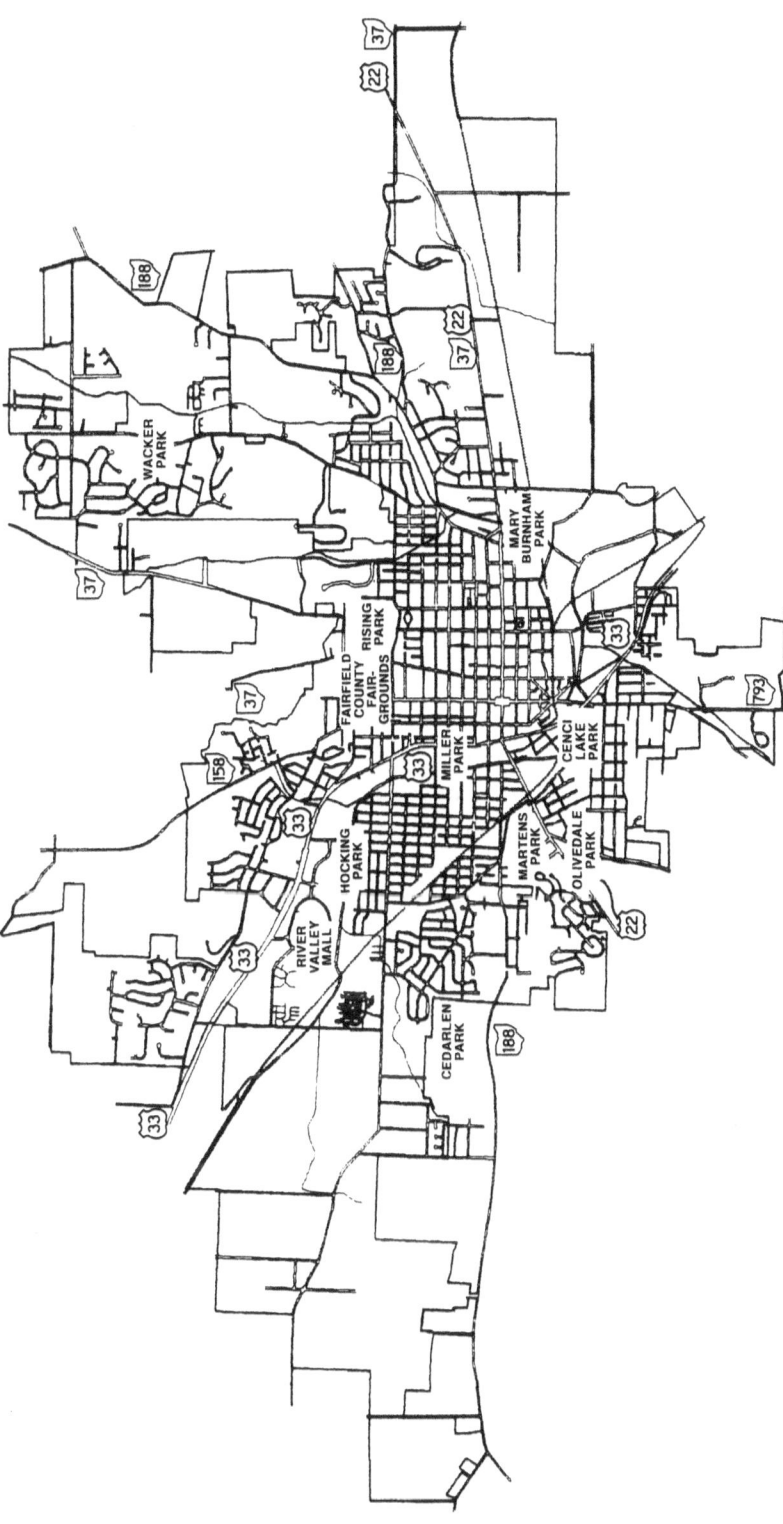

Map of Lancaster, 1998. Courtesy Department of Engineering, City of Lancaster.

The edge city around the River Valley Mall is clearly dependent upon the automobile and itself generates increased traffic, estimated to have risen by about 2 percent annually since the opening of the mall.[106] By 1997, between 36,000 and 40,000 vehicles were passing the mall along Route 33 every day—Monday through Thursday—with up to 50,000 on Fridays and days before certain holidays. The latter figure is approximately five times as large as the vehicle count in the early 1960s and twice as great as the number in 1986, just before the opening of the River Valley Mall.[107] Traffic backups and long delays are virtually guaranteed each morning and afternoon, giving rise to renewed pressure for a "33 bypass." By the mid-1990s, the Ohio Department of Transportation had put the bypass on a list of priorities, and it looks as if the bypass will become a reality during the first decade of the twenty-first century.[108] But it is unclear just how this new highway will affect businesses that have grown up along "33"—and just what sort of development will be stimulated by the bypass itself.[109]

Not in doubt is that the bypass will eliminate more open land, as the existing Route 33 has done and is continuing to do. At the time of this writing, there are only twelve miles along Route 33 of what could be called open country in the entire thirty miles separating downtown Lancaster from downtown Columbus. Specifically, there is an eight-mile stretch of relatively open land between Coonpath Road on the outskirts of Lancaster and the community of Canal Winchester, just across the Fairfield-Franklin county line. There is then a two-mile commercial strip as the highway passes through Canal Winchester, and only four more miles of somewhat undeveloped land from the edge of Canal Winchester to the southern reaches of Columbus at Hamilton Road.

Also feeling the effects of this metropolitan sprawl is the old Fairfield County community of Pickerington. Located in Violet Township, directly abutting Franklin County and the southernmost portions of Columbus, Pickerington has experienced explosive growth during the last three decades of the twentieth century and had enough inhabitants in 1991 to be certified as a city by the state of Ohio. At century's end, Pickerington's population is approaching 8,000, in startling contrast to the several hundred persons who lived in the village before World War II. Equally telling, enrollment in the Pickerington public school district increased from about 1,300 students in 1970 to over 4,000 in 1990.[110] In 1974 Columbus itself annexed a small tract in the Pickerington vicinity, and thus inside Fairfield County, and has attempted several other annexations in the area, which have been blocked by the Fairfield County commissioners.[111] State Route 256, which connects Pickerington to Interstate 70 and thus to the southeastern suburbs of Columbus, is also emerging at the end of the twentieth century as another potential edge city in Fairfield County, with its shopping centers, office buildings, movie theaters, and other enterprises.[112]

Such development in the Pickerington area, as well as in Lancaster and at various other points in the county, has resulted in the continuing loss of farmland. In the twenty-year period between 1973 and 1992, for instance, the number of farms in Fairfield County declined from 1,750 to 1,200.[113] In area, some 36,000 acres of farmland were lost in Fairfield County to development between 1970 and 1995, and there seems no end in sight. This disappearance of tillable soil is, in fact, a statewide problem, prompting the Ohio legislature to begin exploring ways to deal with the crisis. The main cause throughout the state, most experts agree, is suburban sprawl.[114]

In economic terms, however, Lancaster and Fairfield County have recovered fully from their slumps in the 1970s and 1980s and are experiencing considerable growth as the century comes to an end. Indeed, by the mid-1990s, Fairfield County had one of the highest population increases of any county in the entire state. While population in Ohio grew by just 2.8 percent between 1980 and 1994, the number of residents in Fairfield County rose by 22 percent during the same period, from 93,678 to an estimated 114,738.[115]

In Lancaster itself, the figures are also impressive. Assuming that the official estimate of 39,500 holds for the year 2000, Lancaster will have experienced a growth rate of 14 percent over its 34,500 inhabitants in 1990.[116] This contrasts with the period 1980–90, when Lancaster's population actually declined for the first time in any 10-year census period of its entire 200-year history, falling from 34,953 to 34,507, for a loss of 1.3 percent. In fact, Lancaster's projected rate of increase for the 1990s promises to be larger than for any other 10-year period since the end of World War II—with the exception of the period 1950–60, when the population rose from 25,180 to 29,926 (or 24 percent). For the decade 1960–70, the figures were 29,916 to 32,911 (or 10 percent); and for 1970–80, they were 32,911 to 34,953 (or 6.2 percent).[117]

However prosperous Lancaster might be, not everyone in town is benefiting from the growth in the local economy and population. The area just south and west of downtown—the old South End—which comprises federal census tract 319, had a poverty rate in 1990 of just over 35 percent.

Other areas just north and west of downtown, lying in tracts 316 and 323, also had high rates of poverty in 1990. (In all, nearly 5,000 residents, or 13.9 percent of the total population of Lancaster, lived in poverty, as defined by the federal government.) As might be expected, the wealthiest sections of Lancaster are on the northern and eastern edges of town, in tracts 314 and 315 respectively. An exception to this is the hillside of still coveted pre- Civil War homes on Wheeling and Mulberry Streets.[118]

However uneven Lancaster's prosperity might be, its population growth during the 1990s, combined with anticipated growth into the next century, has led the school system to project an enrollment increase of 1,000 students in the five years between 1998 and 2003, necessitating the construction of new schools.[119] Other school systems in Fairfield County are feeling similar strains, as the county population rose from 103,472 in 1990 to an estimated 121,457 in 1997, for an increase of 17.4 percent in just seven years. This represented a higher rate of growth than for any of the five surrounding counties. In descending order the other county percentages were as follows: Hocking (Logan area), 12.6; Pickaway (Circleville area), 10.3; Licking (Newark area), 8.7; Perry (New Lexington area), 8.2; and Franklin (Columbus area), 5.8.[120]

At a time that both Lancaster and Fairfield County are experiencing renewed growth, and as the town approaches its bicentennial year, there are signs that the downtown is struggling back to life. A number of building facades have been restored over the past twenty years or so, and new shops have been attracted to the old Main Street, often because of the low rents. Among the new businesses downtown are antique shops, restaurants, art galleries, and for the first time in many years, a well-stocked independent bookstore. Several banks remain downtown, while some of the larger buildings house law offices, the local chamber of commerce, and the central offices for both the Lancaster and Fairfield County schools. Meanwhile, an expanding population in both Lancaster and Fairfield County has forced local government authorities to erect new facilities in the downtown area or to put offices in former commercial properties. In addition, both the mayor and council have committed themselves in the late 1990s to repair and upgrade the infrastructure of downtown, with new curbs and sidewalks, storm sewers, street trees, benches, trash receptacles, and attractive street lights much like the "boulevard lamps" that were taken down three decades ago. Most of the money for this work is coming from loans and grants by the federal government. Indeed, at the

Restored shop fronts, more than a century old, provide a pleasant walkway on a human scale on the south side of Main Street between Center Alley and Columbus Street. Photo by author, 1998.

end of the 1990s, nearly all available space downtown is being utilized in some way, with approximately 3,000 employees finding jobs in the greater downtown area.[121]

Even if the downtown revival were to continue and the old district would become once again an important destination for shopping and socializing, it would be only one of many such places, in contrast to the monopoly status that it enjoyed before 1960. In the wider region, it would be but a single point within what the U.S. Census Bureau has defined as a metropolitan district, with its center in Columbus and extending for some fifty miles around the state capital. Included in the metropolitan district are all the other old towns in the central Ohio region against which Lancaster has so often measured itself: Chillicothe, Circleville, Zanesville, and Newark.

Although the term *edge city* helps to define the cluster of business and commercial activities around Lancaster's River Valley Mall (as well as Lancaster's relationship to Columbus itself), the term *galactic metropolis*, coined by urban geographer Pierce Lewis, seems a fitting description of the wider region in which Lancaster finds itself as the twentieth century comes to an end.[122] In this galactic metropolis, downtown Lancaster and the River Valley Mall are just two of many stars in the swirl of shopping districts, office complexes, and neighborhoods that now characterize central Ohio.

As just one constellation within a larger metropolitan galaxy, Lancaster must face the possibility of losing its sense of identity and communal pride. Consciously or unconsciously, one way that Lancastrians have sought to maintain deep roots in the past is through festivals and historic commemorations.[123] One of these is the Zane Square Festival, held annually since 1975 during a weekend in mid-August. Actually the festival is a craft show on the downtown square, where exhibitors and various concessionaires offer their wares from canvas-covered booths. There is also live music from the bandstand.[124] This event attracts thousands of people, and for several days it transforms the old downtown once again into "the place to be." Several villages in Fairfield County have likewise established annual festivals that draw large crowds. These include the Millersport Sweet Corn Festival in late August, and the Oktoberfest in Bremen.[125] October continues to bring the Fairfield County Fair, as it has for a century and a half. In the late 1990s, well over 100,000 people were attending this event, now extended from the traditional four to six full days.[126]

Also impressive is the Lancaster Festival. Established in 1985, this series of musical performances during the last two weeks of July attracts thousands of visitors to Lancaster to hear both classical and popular music, much of it performed by nationally and even internationally renowned artists. Presentations take place in schools, churches, the downtown bandstand, and in a specially erected shell on the campus of Ohio University–Lancaster. Other activities accompany the music festival, including an "Art Walk" where artists exhibit their works in stores along Main Street.[127] The festival has become a great source of pride to many citizens, who can bask in their town's growing reputation for music and the arts.

Far more important in maintaining a sense of uniqueness and continuity with the past is the ongoing historic preservation movement in Lancaster and the staging of historic events. The donation to Fairfield County in 1995, by the Peters family, of the 1834 Reese-Peters House for use as a

The 1834 Reese-Peters House, donated to Fairfield County as a museum for the decorative arts. Photo by author, 1998.

decorative arts museum was perhaps the most significant accomplishment for historical preservation since the restoration of The Georgian two decades ago.[128] But the Sherman House and events surrounding the life of General William Tecumseh Sherman remain the centerpiece of Lancaster's historical consciousness. Each year, on or around February 8, the Fairfield Heritage Association sponsors a dinner in honor of Sherman's birthday, usually with someone dressed, in military garb, as Sherman.[129] On other occasions the entire Sherman family are impersonated in period dress, most frequently at the Sherman House itself. And to honor Sherman during Lancaster's bicentennial, the community has erected a seven-foot-high bronze statue of this favorite son on Zane Square, financed by individual contributions.[130]

No one has yet proposed to dress up as Dr. Edson B. Olds, Lancaster's Civil War Copperhead who, in his day, had a local following every bit as large as General Sherman's. Nor would anyone expect Olds to be the center of historical attention. Yet Lancastrians would do well to remember that their forbearers were deeply divided over the Civil War, as were many other communities throughout the nation. If nothing else, the town's ability to put such divisions behind it and to move on could serve as a note of encouragement in times of disagreement and distress. Most of all, the growing fascination with Sherman suggests that Lancastrians are longing to identify with what they see as a heroic past in the age of the edge city. The frontier town of 1800 is far away indeed.

# Conclusion
## Into the Future

THROUGHOUT ITS TWO-HUNDRED-year history, Lancaster has been shaped by change. Despite wars, depressions, and economic booms, the effects of these changes have been, by and large, gradual ones. And until the early 1960s, most of these changes had the effect of strengthening the town's identity and reinforcing the community's civic, commercial, and social center in the downtown. At the same time, Lancaster's residential expansion had also proceeded along predictable lines—moving from the center, with each new neighborhood growing out from the one below.

During the past four decades, new highways and more and more motor vehicles led to an increasing decentralization of living and working patterns. As a consequence, hundreds of acres of rich and irreplaceable farmland were paved over or built upon, workers faced longer and more expensive commutes, and the air became more polluted by automobile exhaust.

Just as important was an erosion of community identity, as residents went off to work and shop in every direction and as the downtown lost its role as a center of local life. Also in decline was a human scale to the built environment. Instead of feeling sheltered or even embraced by small stores and shops that came directly out to the sidewalk, shoppers confronted acres of dreary asphalt surrounding a mall, or a series of smaller commercial boxes along highway strips with approaches invariably blocked by a row or two of parked cars. Vanishing, too, were the experiences of being able to stroll past a neighbor's front porch, to converse across a small front yard, or to walk to a nearby market. Lack of sidewalks in the new subdivisions, the disappearance of the front porch, the impossibility of building neighborhood stores because zoning ordinances did not allow them in a world designed to accommodate automobiles rather than pedestrians—all were responsible for such conditions.

Contrary to the notion that history repeats itself, the past would not return—either in Lancaster or anywhere else. For the personalities, technologies, and events of one era never reappear in exactly the same way. Yet human beings can learn from the past, and indeed, our only way of understanding the present or speculating about the future is based upon past experience and past knowledge. As Lancastrians move into their third century, they can look back at the more positive aspects of their community that are vanishing and take steps to combine the best of the past with the best of what might lie ahead. Many residents and community leaders are doing just that at the end of the twentieth century, as are urban historians and planners in the nation at large. In this context, several observations seem in order:

## Managing Growth

Lancaster and vicinity are growing in both population and economic opportunity at the end of the twentieth century. As an attractive town with few "urban problems" that is accessible by motor highways, railroads, and air transportation, this growth is likely to continue for the near future. Mayor Art Wallace has expressed a hope that Lancaster will not grow much beyond a population of 50,000. Whether or not its growth can be halted at this level is unknown, but Lancaster can take steps to limit development by creating "growth boundaries" around the town. These have been tried with some success by a number of communities, including Lexington, Kentucky, Portland, Oregon, and Lancaster, Pennsylvania (the historic namesake of Lancaster, Ohio, and the origin of many of its early settlers). By projecting desirable growth some twenty years into the future, such a boundary could define where development might take place.[1] Land outside the limits could be reserved for agriculture or forestry. In order to be effective, of course, growth boundaries would have to be coordinated on the county and even regional level. Such boundaries would not only help to limit growth, but they would go a long way toward halting the destruction of farmland and the wasteful dispersion of residents over wider and wider areas.[2] With Lancastrians' historic distaste for government regulation, any proposal of growth boundaries would likely provoke much opposition, but the concept could be approached through an ongoing program of education and discussion.

**Studying the Impact of Projected Highways**

After decades of proposals for a Route 33 bypass, this new highway is projected for the first decade of the twenty-first century. Informed and continuous investigations about the impact of this new road, including serious public discussion, might avoid some of the more negative aspects of the bypass, especially by limiting the character and scope of development along this route west and south of Lancaster.[3]

**Considering Public Transportation**

There has been a revival of interest in public transportation in many urban and suburban areas throughout the United States as an alternative or supplement to building new highways. A light rail line (an updated version of the old interurban system) could alleviate much of the congestion along the Route 33 corridor from Lancaster to Columbus. This line might parallel the tracks of the old Hocking Valley Railroad or the highway itself. Such a line would have to be built with public funds and operated by a regional transit authority.[4]

**Cooperating in Regional Planning**

As an emerging edge city that is tied to the fate of the entire region, Lancaster cannot afford to face the future alone. Managing growth, preserving open land, solving transportation problems, and protecting the environment will require cooperation and planning throughout the central Ohio region—and beyond.

**Extending Parks and Street Trees**

Lancaster has a superb system of parks that many wish to see preserved and augmented. Extending a parklike atmosphere along residential streets through the planting and preservation of street trees is already a priority in Lancaster. Trees are helping to absorb the major greenhouse gases created by automobiles, namely carbon dioxide. They also soften the visual land-

Attractive houses on relatively small lots in the 400 block of East Allen Street. Photo by author, 1998.

scape, cool homes in summer, create a sense of outdoor corridors and rooms, and like properly scaled buildings, give residents a feeling of being enclosed and protected.[5]

**Making Lancaster Pedestrian Friendly**

Zoning laws might be changed to allow appropriate commercial facilities in residential neighborhoods so that inhabitants do not have to use their cars for every shopping trip. Pedestrian crossings could be made safer and more attractive. Such measures would be of special benefit to the young, the elderly, and others who do not have easy access to an automobile. Zoning changes that allow for small building lots in the older parts of Lancaster, such as those that prevailed before Lancaster's first zoning code in 1939, could encourage the construction of attractive new housing close to the center of town and could contribute further to making Lancaster hospitable to pedestrians, at the same time promoting economy in the use of land.[6]

## Restoring and Reviving the Downtown

Proposals in place to make downtown Lancaster once more an attractive and economically viable destination will further encourage a pedestrian scale. A revitalized downtown will also bring real dollars into Lancaster by keeping retail business at home and by attracting shoppers from other communities. Further, restoring and reviving downtown will give residents the renewed experience of having a special and emotional center for the community.[7]

## Encouraging Historic Preservation

Lancaster's historic preservation movement has led to the saving and restoration of many attractive and historically important structures. Local preservation efforts have also contributed greatly to Lancaster's reputation for the beauty of its built environment. At the same time, a lively sense of the past has helped residents to connect themselves with a community over time and to feel a sense of shared pride and shared struggle. Strengthening historic preservation will be crucial for maintaining this link between past and present.[8]

## Maintaining Lancaster's Town Character

Above all, Lancaster will have to work hard to maintain its character as a town. Its town atmosphere has attracted people in the past and continues to keep many residents in Lancaster as it celebrates its two-hundredth year. Because increasing numbers of Americans are leaving cities and suburbs for places like Lancaster, it will be a challenge to maintain this town atmosphere. Hard work, dedication, and careful planning could continue to make Lancaster a successful town, even as it enters the age of the edge city.[9]

No one can predict what the future will bring for Lancaster. An understanding of the past, and the forces that have shaped the town over two centuries, offer the only indications of where it might be headed.

# Notes

## Introduction

1. *Statistical Abstract of the United States, 1996*, p. 43.

2. Taking note of this increase, which had combined with a growing migration of Americans from cities and metropolitan suburbs into smaller communities, *Time* magazine published a cover story on December 8, 1997 (pp. 52–65), on the revival of what it called America's "Small Towns."

3. For a discussion of the small town in American literature, see Walter Holbling, "From Main Street to Lake Wobegon and Half-Way Back: The Mid-West Small Town as a Literary Place in 20th Century U.S. Literature," in Hans Bertens and Theo D'haen, eds., *The Small Town in America* (Amsterdam, 1995), pp. 97–108. See also Ima Herron, *The Small Town in American Literature* (Durham, N.C., 1939); David Plowden, *Small Town America* (New York, 1994); and Page Smith, *As a City on a Hill: The Town in American History* (New York, 1966).

4. For example, Harriet Beecher Stowe, *Oldtown Folks* (Boston, 1869).

5. On Lewis's *Main Street*, see Mark Schorer, *Sinclair Lewis: An American Life* (New York, 1961), especially pp. 267–97. See also Sherwood Anderson, *Home Town* (New York, 1940).

6. On this topic, see Dwight W. Hoover, "Social Science Looks at the Small American Town," in Bertens and D'haen, eds., *Small Town in America*, pp. 19–29.

7. Robert S. Lynd and Helen Merrill Lynd, *Middletown: A Study in Modern American Culture* (New York, 1929; reprint, 1956), pp. 112–15, 221–22. See also Arthur J. Vidich and Joseph Bensman, *Reflections on Community Studies* (New York, 1964).

8. For example, see Mitchell Gordon, *Sick Cities: Psychology and Pathology of American Urban Life* (Baltimore, 1966); Jane Jacobs, *The Death and Life of Great American Cities* (New York, 1961); and John H. Mollenkopf, *The Congested City* (Princeton, 1983).

9. For a superb bibliographic discussion of suburban studies, see Margaret Marsh, "Reconsidering Suburbs," *Pennsylvania Magazine of History and Biography*, October 1988, pp. 576–605.

10. Garrison Keillor, *Lake Wobegon Days* (New York, 1985).

11. For an excellent account of historical writing on villages and towns since the 1960s, see Robert R. Dykstra and William Silag, "Doing Local History: Monographic Approaches to the Smaller Community," in Howard Gillette Jr. and Zane Miller, eds., *American Urbanism: A Historiographical Review* (New York, 1987).

12. See Paul Boyer and Stephen Nissenbaum, *Salem Possessed: The Social Origins of Witchcraft* (Cambridge, Mass., 1974); Stanley Buder, *Pullman: An Experiment in Industrial Order and Community* (New York, 1967); and Carol O'Connor, *A Sort of Utopia: Scarsdale, 1891–1981* (Albany, N.Y., 1984).

13. For example, Anthony C. F. Wallace, *Rockdale: The Growth of an American Village in the Early Industrial Revolution* (New York, 1978), or Michael Birkner, *A Country Place No More: The Transformation of Bergenfield, New Jersey, 1894–1994* (Rutherford, N.J., 1994).

14. Richard C. Wade, *The Urban Frontier: The Rise of Western Cities, 1790–1930*, with introduction by Zane L. Miller (1959; reprint, Urbana, Ill., 1996).

15. This point of view is tellingly and eloquently presented by Gregor Dallas, *The Final Act: The Roads to Waterloo* (New York, 1996), p. vii.

16. Joel Garreau, *Edge City: Life on the New Frontier* (New York, 1991). For Garreau's definition of the edge city, see in particular pp. 4–9, 425–26.

17. For a good case study of such a declining community in Ohio, see Richard O. Davies, *Main Street Blues: The Decline of Small-Town America* (Columbus, 1998).

## Chapter One

1. Wade, *Urban Frontier*, p. 30.

2. See Edward W. Wolfe et al., *Geology of Fairfield County* (Columbus, Ohio, 1962).

3. *Lancaster Eagle-Gazette*, Sesquicentennial Edition, June 3, 1950 [hereafter *E-G Sesqui*], B-7, G-16, 18. This sesquicentennial edition was not a superficial newspaper sketch of local history but a massive, 400-page history of Lancaster and Fairfield County published in a newspaper format and offered in bound, "flat" copies. It contains much information that cannot be found elsewhere.

4. On Native Americans in Ohio, see Byron Walker, *Indian Cultures of Ohio* (Columbus, 1973), and Erminie Wheeler-Voegelin and Helen Hornbeck Tanner, *Indians of Ohio and Indiana Prior to 1795*, 2 vols. (New York, 1974).

5. George Sanderson, *A Brief History of the Early Settlement of Fairfield County* (Lancaster, Ohio, 1851), pp. 7–8; Charles R. Goslin, *Crossroads and Fence Corners: Historical Lore of Fairfield County* (Lancaster, Ohio, 1976), 1:21–23.

6. *E-G Sesqui*, G-18.

7. Ibid., H-22.

8. A condensed though equally romantic account of the rescue of Forest Rose was given by Sanderson in his *Brief History*, pp. 8–14.

9. On Zane and the Zane family, see Charles R. Goslin, "Zane Family," in Goslin Notebooks, vol. 6, Fairfield County District Library [hereafter FCDL]. See also Norris F. Schneider and Clair C. Stebbins, *Zane's Trace* (Zanesville, Ohio, 1973).

10. Sanderson, *Brief History*, p. 14; Goslin, *Crossroads and Fence Corners*, 1:44–55.

11. For context on this phenomenon, see Wade, *Urban Frontier*, pp. 1–35.

12. Ibid., p. 30.

13. For a good discussion of Southern and New England influences in the area, see Richard Lyle Power, *Planting Corn Belt Culture: The Impress of the Upland Southerner and Yankee in the Old Northwest* (Indianapolis, 1953). On patterns of settlement in Ohio and surrounding states of the Old Northwest, see Andrew R. L. Cayton and Peter S. Onuf, *The Midwest and the Nation: Rethinking the History of an American Region* (Bloomington, Ind., 1990), pp. 25–42.

14. C. M. L. Wiseman, *Centennial History of Lancaster, Ohio, and Lancaster People* (Lancaster, Ohio, 1898).

15. Patsy Kishler, "Who, What, When and How of Immigration to Fairfield County, Ohio." This typescript work may be found in the genealogy room of the Fairfield County District Library in Lancaster. Although undated, the Kishler study appears to have been done in the 1980s.

16. In order not to have figures that were skewed by the listing of children for some male migrants into Fairfield County, I did not include such offspring in my count of Kishler's names.

17. Sanderson, *Brief History*, p. 19; Goslin, *Crossroads and Fence Corners*, 1:57.

18. Kishler, "Immigration to Fairfield County."

19. His Highness, Bernhard Duke of Saxe-Weimar Eisenbach, quoted in *E-G Sesqui*, H-28; Wiseman, *Centennial History*, p. 69.

20. Hollie Ann Saunders, "Black Citizens Trace Long, Local Heritage," *E-G*, February 2, 1983; Hervey Scott, *A Complete History of Fairfield County, Ohio* (Columbus, 1877), p. 281.

21. "History of Negro . . . in This County," *E-G*, July 3, 1976.

22. Ibid.

23. Wiseman, *Centennial History*, p. 62.

24. See Donald A. Hutslar, "The Log Architecture of Ohio," *Ohio History*, Summer–Autumn 1971, pp. 172–269.

25. Sanderson, *Brief History*, p. 18. For context on Lancaster's earliest years, see Randolph C. Downes, *Frontier Ohio, 1788–1803* (Columbus, Ohio, 1935).

26. See Leslie Robert Jones, *History of Agriculture in Ohio to 1880* (Kent, Ohio, 1983).

27. Goslin Notebooks, vol. 6, FCDL.

28. *E-G Sesqui*, G-38; Herbert M. Turner, *A History to Remember: The Story of Settlement in the Upper Hocking Valley* (Lancaster, Ohio, 1976).

29. On this matter elsewhere in the early Midwest, see Wade, *Urban Frontier*, pp. 39–71.

30. Ibid., p. 34.

31. The 1810 estimate appeared in Joseph Scott, *A Geographical Dictionary of the United States* (1810). The figure for 1815 was given by Dr. John Cotton, who took an extensive tour of Ohio in that year. Cotton's account was reported in Wiseman, *Centennial History*, p. 53. The Joseph Scott estimate was found in Jo Libert, "You Can't Get There from Here," *Fairfield Heritage Quarterly* [hereafter *FHQ*], Winter 1985, p. 6.

32. John L. Andriot, ed., *Population Abstract of the United States* (1983) 1:620.

33. Quoted in Libert, "You Can't Get There from Here," p. 3.

34. Ibid.

35. John Melish, quoted in *E-G Sesqui*, H-28.

36. Andriot, *Population Abstract*, 1:618–23.

37. *E-G Sesqui*, A-21.

38. *Eagle*, April 26, 1817.

39. Ibid., September 5, 1816.

40. *E-G Sesqui*, C-2.

41. Ibid., I-8.

42. *Eagle*, April 3, 1817.

43. Ibid., September 11, 1817.

44. Ibid., October 23, 1817.

45. Ibid., March 19, 1818.

46. Ibid., April 23, 1818; Catherine McQuaid Steiner and Bruce E. Steiner, *High Style and Vernacular: Ohio Furniture, Decorative Arts, and Craftsmen, 1800–1850* (n.p., 1988), p. 72.

47. Ruth W. Drinkle, "Tall Case Cocks of Fairfield County," *FHQ*, Summer 1980, pp. 4–5; See also Ruth W. Drinkle, *Heritage of Architecture and Arts in Fairfield County, Ohio*, 2d ed. (Lancaster, Ohio, 1994), pp. 26, 27, 64, 86. Wiseman, in his *Centennial History*, states that Timothy Sturgeon came to Lancaster in 1802, while Drinkle gives the date 1800. Wiseman's book contains short biographies of both Sturgeon and Woltz (pp. 35–36, 331). See also Steiner and Steiner, *High Style and Vernacular*, p. 70.

48. Wiseman, *Centennial History*, pp. 340–41.

49. *E-G Sesqui*, C-11.

50. Steiner and Steiner, *High Style and Vernacular*, pp. 7–11.

51. The City Council Minutes of November 26, 1883, describe the market

house as having "a brick substructure and a frame superstructure." It was at the November 26 meeting that council ordered demolition of the market house.

52. Virginia Fetters, "To Market To Market," *FHQ*, Summer 1985, p. 2. A drawing of the market house may be found in Drinkle, *Heritage of Architecture and Arts*, p. 21. A photograph of the market house is also reproduced in Edward S. Ebbert, *Lancaster and Fairfield County Ohio* (Lancaster, Ohio, 1901), p. 30.

53. Goslin Notebooks, vol. 8, FCDL.

54. Frank J. Roos Jr., "An Investigation of the Sources of Early Architectural Design in Ohio" (Ph.D. diss., Ohio State University, 1937), pp. 44–45; Richard V. Francaviglia, *Main Street Revisited: Time, Space, and Image Building in Small-Town America* (Iowa City, 1996), pp. 86–89, 93–94.

55. Fourth Street was the last of these numbered streets to disappear as a name, becoming High Street in 1868. See Council Minutes, February 21, 1868.

56. Wiseman, *Centennial History*, pp. 60–62.

57. Goslin, "Original Town of Lancaster," Goslin Notebooks, vol. 8, FCDL.

58. Goslin, *E-G*, April 3, 1982.

59. Wade, *Urban Frontier*, p. 28. See also John W. Reps, *Town Planning in Frontier America* (Columbia, Mo., 1980).

60. Wiseman, *Centennial History*, p. 62.

61. A drawing of the plan for Carpenter's Addition was found by the author in Goslin Notebooks, vol. 8, FCDL. See also Michael Southworth and Eran Ben-Joseph, *Streets and the Shaping of Towns and Cities* (New York, 1997), pp. 20–27.

62. On this point, see Grady Clay, *Close-Up: How to Read the American City* (Chicago, 1980), p. 49.

63. This discussion of architecture is based on David R. Contosta, "Origins of Early Domestic Architecture in Lancaster, Ohio," *The Old Northwest*, Fall 1981, pp. 201–16. An oral presentation of this same material was presented by the author at a meeting of the Middle States American Studies Association, University of Delaware, April 7, 1979, and at a meeting of the Great Lakes American Studies Association, Miami University, April 8, 1983.

64. On the origins and early development of Chillicothe, see Robert B. Casari et al., eds., *Chillicothe, Ohio, 1796–1996: Ohio's First Capital* (Chillicothe, 1995), pp. 1–22.

65. Richard V. Campen, *Ohio: An Architectural Portrait* (Chagrin Falls, Ohio, 1973), p. 24.

66. Wiseman, *Centennial History*, p. 347; Drinkle, *Architecture and Arts*, p. 19.

67. Drinkle, *Architecture and Arts*, pp. 46, 47.

68. This was a type that also prevailed throughout western Pennsylvania at the time. See Charles Morse Stoltz, *The Early Architecture of Western Pennsylvania* (Pittsburgh, 1936; reprint, 1996), p. 43.

NOTES TO PAGES 26–32

69. Rexford Newcomb, *Architecture in the Old Northwest* (Chicago, 1950), p. 66; Drinkle, *Architecture and Arts*, pp. 56–57; Wiseman, *Centennial History*, p. 27; Steiner and Steiner, *High Style and Vernacular*, p. 70.

70. Wiseman, *Centennial History*, pp. 95–96, 245–46; Drinkle, *Architecture and Arts*, pp. 53–55.

71. On the characteristics of New England–style houses in Ohio, see I. T. Frary, *Early Homes of Ohio* (New York, 1970), p. 127.

72. Wiseman, *Centennial History*, pp. 53–57.

73. Ibid., p. 374; Drinkle, *Architecture and Arts*, p. 79.

74. See Whitleny B. Tussing, "Early Housing in Lancaster, Ohio, 1800–1845" (master's thesis, Miami University, 1986).

75. See Wade, *Urban Frontier*, pp. 101–28.

76. Stoltz, *Early Architecture of Western Pennsylvania*, p. 16.

77. Goslin Notebooks, vol. 7, FCDL.

78. For comparisons with other early towns and cities in the Midwest, see Wade, *Urban Frontier*, pp. 129–57. See also Cayton and Onuf, *Midwest and the Nation*, pp. 43–64.

79. Wiseman, *Centennial History*, pp. 14–15.

80. Sanderson, *Brief History*, p. 19.

81. *Eagle*, February 16, 1833.

82. Wade, *Urban Frontier*, p. 132.

83. Ebbert, *Lancaster and Fairfield County*, pp. 15–16.

84. *Eagle*, July 25, 1816.

85. Ibid., December 31, 1820.

86. On the role of Masonry and militia units in other frontier towns and cities, see Wade, *Urban Frontier*, p. 130.

87. *Eagle*, February 11, 1819; Wiseman, *Centennial History*, p. 132.

88. Wiseman, *Centennial History*, pp. 132–38.

89. For example, *Eagle*, August 1, 1816.

90. Ibid.

91. Ibid., September 28, 1833.

92. Such social problems occurred early in other Midwest communities. See Wade, *Urban Frontier*, pp. 72–100.

93. Scott, *History of Fairfield County*, p. 3; Goslin, "Fairfield County," Goslin Notebooks, vol. 3, FCDL; Lawrence J. Marzulli et al., *The Development of Ohio's Counties and Their Historic Courthouses* (Columbus, Ohio, n.d.), p. 110.

94. Scott, *History of Fairfield County*, pp. 144–48.

95. Ibid, p. 21.

96. Richard Lingerman, *Small-Town America: A Narrative History, 1620–Present* (Boston, 1980), p. 118; Wade, *Urban Frontier*, p. 12. For example, in Lancaster an

unofficial council passed an ordinance in May 1827 that attempted to regulate the weight of butter sold in Lancaster's market house. See *E-G Sesqui*, H-12, 13.

97. Wiseman, *Centennial History*, p. 190. The city council minutes of September 9, 1870, specifically refer to the market house as Lancaster's "Old City Hall."

98. Wiseman, *Centennial History*, p. 184.

## Chapter Two

1. On the history of American canals in general, see Carter Goodrich et al., *Canals and American Economic Development* (New York, 1961), and Ronald E. Shaw, *Canals for a Nation: The Canal Era in the United States, 1790–1860* (Lexington, Ky., 1990). See also George R. Taylor, *The Transportation Revolution, 1815–1860* (New York, 1968).

2. See Carl Abbott, *Boosters and Businessmen: Popular Economic Thought and Urban Growth in the Antebellum Middle West* (Westport, Conn., 1981).

3. On the Ohio canals, see Harry N. Scheiber, *Ohio Canal Era: A Case Study of Government and the Economy, 1820–1861* (Athens, Ohio, 1969).

4. Kyle W. Armstrong, *An Appreciation of Buckeye Lake* (Coshocton, Ohio, 1952), pp. 32–33; Donna Fisher Braig, *My Buckeye Lake Story: A Memorable History of "The Playground of Ohio"* (Millersport, Ohio, 1997), pp. 17–21.

5. Armstrong, *Buckeye Lake*, pp. 31–35.

6. Scott, *History of Fairfield County*, p. 150; Wiseman, *Centennial History*, pp. 30, 35, 57–60, 94, 96, 302; Goslin Notebooks, vol. 6, FCDL.

7. *Gazette*, May 3, 1831.

8. Scheiber, *Ohio Canal Era*, p. 101. For a good description of the remains of the Lancaster Lateral Canal (at least as they existed in the early 1960s), see Goslin, *Crossroads and Fence Corners*, 1:38–40.

9. Wiseman, *Centennial History*, p. 191.

10. B. W. Carlisle, quoted in Scott, *Fairfield County*, p. 150.

11. Ibid., p. 151; *Eagle*, July 9, 1836; Goslin Notebooks, vol. 6, FCDL; Shaw, *Canals for a Nation*, pp. 130–31.

12. Andriot, *Population Abstract*, 1:621.

13. Ibid., p. 621.

14. Ibid., p. 618.

15. Ibid.

16. Goslin Notebooks, vol. 7, FCDL.

17. *E-G Sesqui*, G-16; Marc E. Miller, interview by author, August 13, 1997.

18. *E-G Sesqui*, B-19.

19. Goslin Notebooks, vol. 3, FCDL.

20. One of the best works on romanticism remains Jacques Barzun, *Classic, Romantic, and Modern* (Chicago, 1961).

21. Scheiber, *Ohio Canal Era*, p. 37.

22. Wiseman, *Centennial History*, pp. 57–60; *Eagle,* February 20, 1830.

23. Wiseman, *Centennial History*, pp. 269–70; Jo Voss, "A Walk through Lancaster's Square 13" (Lancaster, Ohio, 1992), p. 11.

24. Voss, "A Walk through Lancaster's Square 13," p. 18.

25. For photographs of these houses, many of them in color, as well as brief historical sketches, see Drinkle, *Architecture and Arts.*

26. Goslin Notebooks, vol. 8, FCDL.

27. *Eagle,* May 4 and 25, 1833.

28. Wiseman, *Centennial History*, pp. 154–56.

29. Harold Reeves, interview by Harry Kilbarger, n.d., in Oral History Project, Fairfield Heritage Association [hereafter FHA], vol. 1, FCDL.

30. *E-G Sesqui,* C-29.

31. Goslin, *Crossroads and Fence Corners,* 1:69.

32. *Eagle,* June 25 and July 9, 1836.

33. Goslin Notebooks, vol. 3, FCDL.

34. *E-G Sesqui,* H-24.

35. Quoted in "Early Fairfield County Lawyers," pamphlet published by the Fairfield County Bar Association, 1990, p. 2.

36. By 1838 the Chillicothe Turnpike was known as the Zanesville and Maysville Turnpike. Both of these were successors to Zane's Trace. See *Gazette,* February 22, 1838.

37. Oscar and Lilian Handlin, *Abraham Lincoln and the Union* (Boston, 1980), pp. 33–57.

38. Wiseman, *Centennial History,* pp. 25–26.

39. Ibid., pp. 75–82.

40. George D. Martin, "Early Lancaster Lawyers," *FHQ,* Summer 1987, pp. 4–6; Wiseman, *Centennial History,* pp. 105–6.

41. Martin, "Early Lancaster Lawyers"; Wiseman, *Centennial History,* pp. 106–8, 253–55; Lorle Porter, "A Test of Lofty Ideals," *FHQ,* Winter 1996, pp. 2–4; *Dictionary of American Biography* [hereafter *DAB*], 6:238–39.

42. *E-G Sesqui,* C-8.

43. Wiseman, *Centennial History,* pp. 190–91.

44. *Gazette,* March 22, 1844; Wiseman, *Centennial History,* pp. 14–15.

45. Sanderson's lecture was first published in the *Gazette* on March 22, 1844. It was reprinted as a pamphlet in 1851 by Thomas Wetzler of Lancaster. See also Scott, *History of Fairfield County,* p. 99.

46. *Eagle,* March 16, 1833.

47. *E-G Sesqui,* B-39. A still useful work on this phenomenon of a national upper class is E. Digby Baltzell, *The Protestant Establishment: Aristocracy and Caste in America* (New York, 1964).

48. Wiseman, *Centennial History*, pp. 83–84; Scott, *History of Fairfield County*, pp. 282–83.

49. Andriot, *Population Abstract*, 1:620.

50. The numerical increases for these towns are as follows: Newark, 2,705 to 3,659; Circleville, 2,329 to 3,411; Chillicothe, 3,977 to 7,100; Zanesville, 4,766 to 7,929; and Columbus, 6,071 to 17,034. See Andriot, *Population Abstract*, 1:618, 619, 621, 623.

51. Shaw, *Canals for a Nation*, p. 204.

52. Wiseman, *Centennial History*, pp. 83–87; *Gazette*, February 16, 1844.

53. *E-G Sesqui*, B-27.

54. Ibid., B-2.

55. Wiseman, *Centennial History*, p. 118; Scott, *History of Fairfield County*, p. 286; Ivan M. Tribe, "Dream and Reality in Southern Ohio: The Development of the Columbus and Hocking Valley Railroad," *The Old Northwest*, Winter 1978, p. 338.

56. Scott, *History of Fairfield County*, pp. 285–86; Jo Libert, "Fairfield County's Case of Railroad Fever," *FHQ*, Summer 1984, p. 3.

57. *E-G Sesqui*, G-11.

58. Andriot, *Population Abstract*, 1:620.

59. The numerical increases of these towns between 1850 and 1860 were as follows: Zanesville, 7,929 to 9,229; Chillicothe, 7,100 to 7,626; Newark, 3,659 to 4,675; and Circleville, 3,411 to 4,383. See Andriot, *Population Abstract*, 1:618, 621, 623.

60. Council Minutes, April 21, 1859.

61. Ebbert, *Lancaster and Fairfield County*, p. 45.

62. Virginia Fetters, "Heigh-Ho Come to the Fair," *FHQ*, Fall 1979, p. 2; Scott, *History of Fairfield County*, pp. 96–97.

63. *Gazette*, July 26, 1860.

64. See Lee Benson, "Ethnocultural Groups and Political Parties," in Felice A. Bodadio, ed., *Political Parties in American History, 1828–1890* (New York, 1974), pp. 585–605, and Cayton and Onuf, *Midwest and the Nation*, pp. 65–83.

65. Kishler, "Immigration to Fairfield County."

66. The author derived these percentages from a microfilm of the manuscript schedule of the Eighth Census of the United States, 1860, made available by the U.S. Bureau of the Census.

67. Scott, *History of Fairfield County*, pp. 57–58.

68. See Bernard Bailyn, *The Origins of American Politics* (New York, 1967); Daniel Walker Howe, *The Political Culture of the American Whigs* (Chicago, 1979); and Cayton and Onuf, *Midwest and the Nation*, pp. 84–92.

69. For wider context on this issue, see Donald J. Ratcliffe, "Politics in Jacksonian Ohio," *Ohio History*, Winter 1979, pp. 5–36.

70. *Eagle*, June 2, 1832.

71. Ibid., October 12, 1833.

72. *Gazette*, June 23, 1840.

73. Ibid., August 14, 1844.
74. Ibid., December 20, 1844.
75. Benson, "Ethnocultural Groups and Political Parties," pp. 586–90, 601.
76. Scott, *History of Fairfield County*, p. 58; *Gazette*, July 5, 1855; John B. Weaver, "Ohio Republican Attitudes towards Nativism, 1854–1855," *The Old Northwest*, Fall 1983, pp. 289–306; Cayton and Onuf, *Midwest and the Nation*, pp. 87–90.
77. *Gazette*, September 20, 1855.
78. Ibid.
79. Scott, *History of Fairfield County*, p. 58.
80. *Gazette*, February 9, 1860.
81. Eighth Census of the United States, 1860.
82. "History of Negro," *E-G*, July 3, 1976.
83. Ibid. That many underground railroad sites are more imagined than real is skillfully demonstrated in Byron Fruehling and Robert H. Smith, "Subterranean Highways of the Underground Railroad in Ohio: An Architectural, Archaeological, and Historical Critique of Local Traditions," *Ohio History*, Summer–Autumn 1993, pp. 98–117.
84. Ibid.; Wilbur Henry Siebert, *The Mysteries of Ohio's Underground Railroads* (Columbus, Ohio, 1951), pp. 188–91; Jeanne Innis, "Underground Railroad," *Zane Monthly*, April 1983, 18–19; *E-G*, January 23, 1988.
85. *Gazette*, November 8, 1860; *Eagle*, December 6, 1860.
86. *Gazette*, April 18, 1861; Terry Cochran and Bob Matters, "Fairfield County in the Civil War: A Different View," *FHQ*, Summer 1986, p. 1.
87. Council Minutes, April 20, 1861.
88. Ibid., April 23, 1861.
89. *Gazette*, April 18, 1861.
90. Cochran and Matters, "Fairfield County in the Civil War," p. 1.
91. *Gazette*, May 23, June 20, June 27, 1861.
92. James A. Rawley, *Turning Points of the Civil War* (Lincoln, Neb., 1989), pp. 24–25.
93. Wiseman, *Centennial History*, p. 360; *Gazette*, July 25, 1861.
94. *Gazette*, August 8, 1861.
95. Cochran and Matters, "Fairfield County in the Civil War," p. 2; *E-G Sesqui*, C-34, 35.
96. *Gazette*, February 20, April 17, 1862.
97. Ibid., July 9, 1863.
98. Council Minutes, July 22, 1863.
99. *Gazette*, November 26, 1863.
100. Michael Fellman, *Citizen Sherman: A Life of William Tecumseh Sherman* (New York, 1995), pp. 3–7; Stanley P. Hirschson, *The White Tecumseh: A Biography of William T. Sherman* (New York, 1997), pp. 5–9.

101. According to Sherman's brother, John, Cump had already been baptized in the Presbyterian Church at Lancaster. If true, this double baptism was in clear violation of the Nicean Creed and general Christian teaching, which allows for only one baptism. See Hirshson, *White Tecumseh*, p. 7.

102. Fellman, *Citizen Sherman*, p. 6.

103. See Jack Detzler, "The Religion of General William Tecumseh Sherman," *Ohio History*, Winter 1966, pp. 26–34, and Hirshson, *White Tecumseh*, pp. 22, 46, 364–68.

104. *Gazette*, December 31, 1863.

105. Ibid., September 8, 1864.

106. Ibid., June 2, 1864.

107. E. T. Hooker to Mrs. Webb, January 13, 1863. This letter was shared with the author by its owner, John "Jack" Furniss Jr., who is a descendent of Nimrod Webb.

108. *Gazette*, May 23, 1863.

109. Ibid., May 22, 1862.

110. *Eagle*, June 13, 1861.

111. Ibid., April 11, 1861, May 23, 1861, August 3, 1861, November 10, 1864.

112. Ibid., September 25, 1862, October 2, 1862, January 8, 1863.

113. Ibid., July 16, 1863.

114. *Gazette*, May 2, 1861.

115. Ibid., June 11, 1863.

116. Ibid., June 4, 1863.

117. *Eagle*, June 11, 1963.

118. Ibid., February 4 and 11, 1864.

119. On the Copperhead movement, see Grady Wood, *The Hidden Civil War: The Story of the Copperheads* (1942; reprint, New York, 1964), and Frank L. Klement, *The Copperheads of the Middle West* (Chicago, 1960). Both books mention Olds and his activities.

120. Jo Libert, "Dr. Edson Baldwin Olds, Fairfield County's Notorious Civil War 'Traitor,'" *FHQ*, Spring 1989, pp. 6–8.

121. *E-G Sesqui*, C-14.

122. *Eagle*, August 14, 1862.

123. Ibid., December 11, 1862.

124. Ibid., December 18 and 25, 1862.

125. *Gazette*, November 10, 1864; *Eagle*, November 10, 1864.

126. Rawley, *Turning Points of the Civil War*, pp. 171–204.

127. Ibid., p. 165.

128. In an interview with the *E-G* that appeared on May 18, 1953, Smith spoke of his grandfather Olds only as a Lancaster businessman and elected office holder.

129. For further reading on this concept, see Richard D. Brown, *Modernization:*

*The Transformation of American Life* (Prospect Heights, Ill., 1988), especially pp. 108, 123, 162, 164, 170, 174–75; Cayton and Onuf, *Midwest and the Nation*, pp. 90–92.

130. *Gazette*, April 13, 1865.

131. Ibid., April 20, 1865.

## Chapter Three

1. On the Victorian age in the United States, see Daniel Walker Howe, ed., *Victorian America* (Philadelphia, 1976), and Thomas J. Schlereth, *Victorian America: Transformations in Everyday Life* (New York, 1991).

2. Tribe, "Dream and Reality," pp. 337–57.

3. Jo Libert, "Fairfield County's Case of Railroad Fever," *FHQ*, Summer 1984, p. 3.

4. Council Minutes, September 2, 1867.

5. Tribe, "Dream and Reality," p. 343.

6. *Ohio State Journal*, June 15, 1869; *Gazette*, June 21, 1869; Council Minutes, January 7, 1869.

7. Tribe, "Dream and Reality," p. 342.

8. *Gazette*, June 30, 1870.

9. Ibid., July 29, 1869.

10. *Eagle*, August 2, 1898; Ebbert, *Lancaster and Fairfield County*, p. 25.

11. Quoted in *Eagle*, July 29, 1869.

12. Council Minutes, May 3, 1867, January 22, 1869.

13. Ibid., July 21, 1869.

14. Tribe, "Dream and Reality," p. 346.

15. Ibid., p. 343.

16. *Gazette*, March 13, 1873.

17. Ibid., November 21, 1867.

18. Ibid., February 13, 1873, March 13, 1873, April 10, 1873, September 7, 1882.

19. Goslin Notebooks, vol. 6, FCDL.

20. "Lancaster Municipal Gas Company, 1888–1988," pamphlet, published 1988 by the Lancaster Municipal Gas Company, FCDL, pp. 3–4; Goslin, "Nature Notes," *E-G*, February 13, 1965; *Gazette*, March 6, 1928; *E-G*, October 31, 1975.

21. Wiseman, *Centennial History*, pp. 290–91.

22. *Eagle*, July 12, 1929; Ebbert, *Lancaster and Fairfield County*, p. 179.

23. "Lancaster Municipal Gas Company," p. 5; *Eagle*, July 12, 1929.

24. *E-G Sesqui*, C-10, 18.

25. On Smith, see the article by Perrin Hazelton in *E-G*, May 18, 1953.

26. Goslin, *Crossroads and Fence Corners*, 1:68–72; *Gazette*, August 4, 1888; Ebbert, *Lancaster and Fairfield County*, pp. 50–53.

27. Virginia Fetters, "Coping with the Cold," *FHQ*, Winter 1979, p. 3; "Lan-

caster Municipal Gas Works," p. 5. The city council authorized free gas to new manufacturing establishments on March 25, 1889.

28. Goslin Notebooks, vol. 7, FCDL; "Lancaster Municipal Gas Company," p. 11.

29. *E-G*, June 5, 1964, September 6, 1989.

30. *Eagle*, June 21, 1892; Dwight Barnes, "Grand Army of the Republic Dies Out," *E-G*, August 27, 1997; Ebbert, *Lancaster and Fairfield County*, p. 120.

31. Jo Libert, "Home Brew: The Story of Bismark Beer," *FHQ*, Winter 1990, pp. 2–4; Wiseman, *Centennial History*, pp. 292–93.

32. Andriot, *Population Abstract*, 1:618–23.

33. Ibid.

34. *Gazette*, March 9, 1871.

35. Goslin, *Crossroads and Fence Corners*, 1:91.

36. Ibid.

37. Ibid.

38. *E-G Sesqui*, C-3.

39. Council Minutes, June 15, 1888.

40. *E-G Sesqui*, C-11.

41. Ibid., G-2, 33.

42. Drinkle, *Architecture and Arts*, pp. 128–38.

43. Ibid, pp. 128–29.

44. *E-G Sesqui*, H-2.

45. A copy of this map appears on the end sheets of Drinkle, *Architecture and Arts*.

46. *E-G Sesqui*, G-26.

47. The best historical account of the 1871 Fairfield County Courthouse is Charles R. Goslin, "The Fairfield County Courthouse Story," a pamphlet published by the County Commissioners of Fairfield County in 1986. See also *Gazette*, March 28, 1967, and February 22, 1972.

48. For an obituary of Orman, see *Gazette*, August 3, 1900.

49. Ebbert, *Lancaster and Fairfield County*, p. 105; Wiseman, *Centennial History*, pp. 212–13.

50. Goslin, "Fairfield County Courthouse"; *Gazette*, March 28, 1867, February 22, 1872.

51. Clair C. Stebbins, *Ohio's Court Houses* (Columbus, Ohio, 1980), p. 29. See also Lawrence J. Marzulli et al., *The Development of Ohio's Counties and Their Historical Courthouses* (Columbus, Ohio, n.d.).

52. *Gazette*, September 17, 1874.

53. According to the Council Minutes of June 14, 1886, Bauman's first name was Andrea, a name that he apparently did not like to use, preferring the initial "A." for business purposes and the name Andy among friends.

54. Virginia Fetters, "A. Bauman, 1840–1919: A Man for All Seasons," *FHQ*, Fall 1992, pp. 2–6.

55. Council Minutes, November 28, 1881, November 26, 1883, December 10, 1883, April 27, 1885.

56. Jo Libert, "The Fountain," *FHQ*, Summer 1980, p. 6. The city council authorized the fountain on March 3, 1890.

57. Ebbert, *Lancaster and Fairfield County*, pp. 47–49; Voss, "Lancaster's Square 13," p. 5. For a good color photograph of the 1898 city hall, see Drinkle, *Architecture and Arts*, p. 179. The public library had also been located in the previous city hall, beginning in 1889. See Council Minutes, February 11, 1889.

58. For more on the small-town opera house phenomenon, see Helen Hooven Santmyer, *Ohio Town* (Columbus, Ohio, 1962; reprint, 1998), pp. 213–29.

59. *E-G*, June 7, 1962.

60. Dwight Barnes, "Lancaster's Hotel Martens," *E-G*, June 15, 1994.

61. Council Minutes, June 2, 1889, May 28 and June 9, 1890.

62. Dianne and Rod Jedlicka, *FHQ*, Summer 1981, pp. 2–3, 6; *E-G*, October 14, 1941, September 6, 1962.

63. *Gazette*, July 6, 1900.

64. *E-G*, October 27, 1973; Ebbert, *Lancaster and Fairfield County*, pp. 44–45.

65. *E-G Sesqui*, I-28, 29.

66. Ibid.; *E-G*, September 10, 1963.

67. *Gazette*, April 4, 1867.

68. Ibid., June 15, 1892.

69. Ibid., August 1, 1878. It would appear that the 1851 North School building was not taken down for some five years after the 1873 structure was erected on the same grounds.

70. *E-G*, September 12, 1963, June 20, 1968.

71. Knepper, *Ohio and Its People*, p. 188. This law may not have applied, at least technically, to the high school, since the 1848 law had only required communities of twenty or more African Americans of school age to provide a separate facility.

72. *E-G Sesqui*, I-26.

73. *Gazette*, April 27, 1882; Goslin notebooks, vol. 7, FCDL.

74. Ebbert, *Lancaster and Fairfield County*, pp. 63–72. A good contemporary description of "The State Farm" appears in *Gazette*, January 30, 1868.

75. *Gazette*, March 29, 1866, September 2, 1869.

76. Ebbert, *Lancaster and Fairfield County*, p. 61; *Gazette*, January 19, 1871; Goslin Notebooks, vol. 6, FCDL.

77. On Forest Rose Cemetery, see Ebbert, *Lancaster and Fairfield County*, pp. 56–58, and Charles Goslin, "The Cemeteries of the City of Lancaster, Ohio," pp. 6–7, FCDL.

78. Council Minutes, April 8, 1875, April 9 and September 17, 1877, January 23 and March 20, 1882.

79. On the phenomenon of the romantic cemetery movement, see Colleen McDannell, *Material Christianity: Religion and Popular Culture in America* (New Haven, Conn., 1995), pp. 103–31, and Schlereth, *Victorian America*, pp. 290–93. For a personal discussion of the place of such cemeteries in communities like Lancaster, see Santmyer, *Ohio Town*, pp. 111–24.

80. *Gazette*, September 28, 1882.

81. Ebbert, *Lancaster and Fairfield County*, pp. 53–55; *Gazette*, January 3, 1873, November 5, 1874; Council Minutes, November 12, 1874, December 10, 1878.

82. Ebbert, *Lancaster and Fairfield County*, p. 55; *E-G*, September 19, 1972, October 31, 1974.

83. Ebbert, *Lancaster and Fairfield County*, pp. 75–87; *E-G Sesqui*, E-26, F-5, 22, 39, I-26, 32, K-4, 8, 12, 16, 22, 26.

84. On the Gothic revival, see Calder Loth and Julius Trousdale Sadler Jr., *The Only Proper Style: Gothic Architecture in America* (Boston, 1975).

85. *Gazette*, September 2, 1869, July 20, 1876, August 8, 1878.

86. Ibid., March 2, 1882.

87. Ibid., August 1, 1904, July 29, 1932; *E-G*, June 10, 1950, July 31, 1988, July 9, 1990; Joe Ionne, "On the Old Campground," *Columbus Dispatch Sunday Magazine*, June 11, 1972; William L. Graybill, "Camp Meetings and Lancaster Camp Ground," *FHQ*, Summer 1998, pp. 2–3, 6.

88. On the reality of widespread and often heavy drinking in nineteenth-century America, see W. J. Rorabaugh, *The Alcoholic Republic: An American Tradition* (New York, 1979).

89. *E-G Sesqui*, B-13, 31, C-39.

90. This case offers yet another example of an unofficial local government well before Lancaster's incorporation as a village in 1831.

91. Sanderson, *Brief History*, p. 20.

92. *E-G Sesqui*, C-17.

93. Council Minutes, June 5, 1865, March 5, 1874.

94. *E-G Sesqui*, B-31.

95. Ibid.

96. Jo Libert, "Demon Rum and the Ladies Crusade of 1874," *FHQ*, Winter 1984, pp. 2–3, 5, 6; Wiseman, *Centennial History*, pp. 187–90.

97. Contemporary coverage of the 1874 women's crusade against alcohol appeared in the *Gazette* for February 12, March 5, and March 12, 1874. On Victorian middle-class attitudes toward alcohol in other places like Lancaster, see Cayton and Onuf, *Midwest and the Nation*, pp. 87–88.

98. *E-G Sesqui*, G-4.

99. There is abundant literature on the topic of women's reform activities as an extension of motherhood. Particularly helpful is Colleen McDannell, *The Christian Home in Victorian America, 1840–1900* (Bloomington, Ind., 1986).

100. *Gazette*, January 13, 1876; *E-G Sesqui*, C-32, F-3.

101. *Gazette*, March 16, 1871; *Eagle*, April 11, 1898.

102. See E. Anthony Rotundo, *American Manhood: Transformations of Masculinity from the Revolution to the Modern Era* (New York, 1993), especially pp. 200–203, and Lewis Atherton, *Main Street on the Middle Border* (1954; reprint, Bloomington, Ind., 1984), pp. 186–90.

103. *Gazette*, January 2, 1868, February 24, 1876, September 12, 1896; *Eagle*, April 27, 1898; *E-G*, January 24, 1996.

104. *Gazette*, December 30, 1869, January 6, 1870.

105. Ibid., December 24, 1874.

106. *Eagle*, July 2, 1892.

107. *Gazette*, December 5, 1867, March 19, 1868, February 4, 1869, September 29, 1870, February 9, 1871, February 1, 1872, March 25, 1880.

108. Ibid., June 20, 1872.

109. *E-G Sesqui*, E-34.

110. Ibid., H-27, 34.

111. *Gazette*, March 10, 1870, July 16, 1874.

112. *E-G Sesqui*, I-4.

113. *Gazette*, April 11, 1867, May 19, 1870, November 30, 1871, February 14, 1878; *Eagle*, August 13, 1898.

114. *E-G Sesqui*, G-18.

115. Ibid., H-4.

116. *Gazette*, August 26, 1896.

117. Jedlicka, "Lancaster's Street Railway System," p. 6.

118. Anonymous, "The Hillside Hotel: A Love Affair," *FHQ*, Winter 1992, pp. 2–5. This article was, in turn, based upon an account of the hotel written in 1946 by one of its long-time residents, Bess Boerstler Swinnerton. See also Ebbert, *Lancaster and Fairfield County*, pp. 155–57.

119. *Gazette*, March 22 and May 31, 1866; *Eagle*, August 3, 1898; David Schiltz, "Bicycling in Sugar Grove and Lancaster in the 1890s," *FHQ*, Fall 1993, pp. 5–6, 8.

120. *Gazette*, September 13, 1866, May 14, 1868, December 24, 1868, December 10, 1874. On the role of local newspapers in creating a sense of community, see Sally Foreman Griffith, *Home Town News: William Allen White and the Emporia Gazette* (New York, 1989). See also William Allen White, *Autobiography* (New York, 1946).

121. *E-G Sesqui*, C-26.

122. Council Minutes, February 1, 1890.

123. Ibid., February 11, 1884.

124. Charles Drinkle, "As I Recall It," p. 5. This was a talk that Drinkle delivered before the Symposium Club in 1956. I am indebted to his daughter, Mary Alice Drinkle Kuhn, for sharing a typed version of this presentation.

125. *E-G Sesqui*, H-19.

126. *Gazette*, May 30, 1867.

127. Ibid., August 8, 1867.

128. *Eagle*, June 9, 1892.

129. *Gazette*, July 27, 1876; Drinkle, *Architecture and Arts*, p. 60.

130. *Gazette*, July 27, 1876.

131. Council Minutes, October 27, 1871.

132. *Gazette*, November 2, 1871. This account was reprinted by the *Gazette* from the *Cincinnati Commercial*, October 28, 1871.

133. Wiseman, *Centennial History*, pp. 118, 125, 156.

134. Ruth Drinkle, "Fairfield Society—A Social Century," *FHQ*, Winter 1981, pp. 4–6; Wiseman, *Centennial History*, pp. 106, 111–15.

135. Wiseman, *Centennial History*, pp. 278, 290, 292, 300, 355; Ebbert, *Lancaster and Fairfield County*, p. 120; *Gazette*, December 21, 1881; "The Peters Family Genealogical Record (privately published, 1930), private collection of Caroline Peters Rockwood.

136. Because Germany was not unified until 1870, German-speaking residents in Lancaster hailed from a number of kingdoms, states, principalities, and other political entities that would later compose Germany.

137. Census figures and related information here and in the following paragraphs are from the Eighth Census of the United States, 1860, and the Tenth Census of the United States, 1880.

138. Ibid. In 1860, the only foreign-born person in Lancaster who did not come from any of these countries put himself down as Swiss. In 1880, the category of "other" nationalities was made up of 5 from Hungary, 2 from Portugal, 2 from Russia, 2 from Italy, and 1 from Belgium. Only the 5 Hungarians and the 2 Italians did not come from northern and western Europe.

139. Ibid.

140. Ibid.

141. Knepper, *Ohio and Its People*, p. 188.

142. *Gazette*, November 2, 1871; *E-G*, March 1, 1996.

143. *Gazette*, July 22, 1869, January 27, 1870, February 24, 1870, January 27, 1876, December 17, 1896; *Eagle*, July 15, 1869. For a wider perspective on local segregation, see David A. Gerber, *Black Ohio and the Color Line, 1860–1915* (Urbana, Ill., 1976).

144. *Gazette*, January 27, 1870.

145. Ibid.

146. Jo Libert, "A Monumental Omission," *FHQ*, Fall 1982, pp. 2–4; Patricia Brown, "The Sherman Cannon," *FHQ*, Summer 1991, pp. 2–3. According to Libert, the local GAR actually raised $25,000 for a permanent monument, but none of the funds were ever expended for that purpose.

147. For a wider view of regional politics during the latter half of the nineteenth century, see Paul Kleppner, *The Cross of Culture: A Social Analysis of Midwestern Politics, 1850–1900* (New York, 1970), and Cayton and Onuf, *Midwest and the Nation*, pp. 92–102.

148. *Gazette*, August 9, 1866, October 14, 1866, February 21, 1867.

149. Ibid., November 26, 1868, November 28, 1872.

150. Ibid., November 11, 1880.

151. Ibid., October 15, 1884, November 8, 1884; Jo Libert, "James Gillespie Blaine," *FHQ*, Summer 1997, pp. 2–6.

152. *Gazette*, October 16, 23, 1896.

153. *Eagle*, November 4, 1896.

154. *Gazette*, November 10, 1888, November 9, 1892.

155. Ibid., April 27, 1871.

156. Ibid., May 4, 1871.

157. Ibid.

158. Ibid., July 6, 1876.

159. Ibid., November 9, 1898.

160. *Eagle*, April 25, 26, 28, 1898.

## Chapter Four

1. *Eagle*, January 1, 1900.

2. Experts debated in 1900, as they have since, over whether the twentieth century officially began in 1900 or 1901. But for most individuals the new-sounding number, 1900, seemed to settle the matter.

3. Goslin Notebooks, vol. 7, FCDL; *Gazette*, March 23, 1900.

4. *Eagle*, June 20, 1900.

5. This was Ebbert, *Lancaster and Fairfield County*, as cited earlier.

6. J. A. Bownocker, "The Bremen Oil Field," *Geological Survey of Ohio*, Fourth Series, Bulletin 10, Columbus Ohio, October 1910.

7. *E-G Sesqui*, E-14.

8. Dwight Barnes, "Chamber of Commerce Reaches Century Mark," *E-G*, July 15, 1998.

9. For a good list and brief account of these industries, including the dates of their founding, see Ebbert, *Lancaster and Fairfield County*, pp. 170–88.

10. *Gazette*, March 2, 1900.

11. Ebbert, *Lancaster and Fairfield County*, p. 172.

12. *Eagle*, September 10, 1900.

13. Ebbert, *Lancaster and Fairfield County*, p. 173; *E-G Sesqui*, A-7.

14. "This is America: Portrait of a City," *Forbes*, November 15, 1947, pp. 56–59, 108, 110, 112.

15. *National Cyclopedia of American Biography*, 59:325–26; John L. Gushman, "Living Glass: The Story of the Anchor Hocking Glass Corporation," pamphlet published by the Newcomen Society (New York, 1965). On Maher and Collins, see Dwight Barnes, "Maher Leaves Legacy of Park," *E-G*, June 26, 1996.

16. "Tycoon Isaac J. Collins," *Forbes*, November 15, 1947, p. 110.

17. *E-G Sesqui*, E-14, 30.

18. Ibid., E-12.

19. Andriot, *Population Abstract of the United States*, 1:614, 620.

20. These new models had been made as electric streetcars, unlike Lancaster's first trolleys, which were converted horsecars. See *Eagle*, November 23, 1915.

21. Ibid., July 28, 1904; Goslin, *Crossroads and Fence Corners*, 2:79. See also Jane Holtz Kay, *Asphalt Nation: How the Automobile Took Over America and How We Can Take It Back* (New York, 1997), p. 152, and Kenneth T. Jackson, *Crabgrass Frontier: The Suburbanization of the United States* (New York, 1985), p. 122.

22. Virginia Mowry (Mrs. Perrin) Hazelton, telephone interview by author, June 21, 1997. The aunt who was nearly electrocuted by the third rail was Elizabeth Mowry (Mrs. Walter F.) Miller.

23. *E-G Sesqui*, G-39.

24. Ibid., F-6.

25. Council Ordinances, June 22, 1903.

26. Council Ordinances, December 27, 1909.

27. *Gazette*, July 7, 1904; *E-G Sesqui*, F-11.

28. Council Ordinances, August 13, 1912.

29. See James Flink, *America Adopts the Automobile, 1895–1910* (Cambridge, Mass., 1970), and Atherton, *Main Street*, pp. 237–40.

30. *Gazette*, March 21, 1917, January 5, 1918.

31. Ibid., May 7, 1920.

32. For a full account of this trip, see David R. Contosta, "Westward Ho with the Hazelton Family: Summer 1923," *FHQ*, Summer 1994, pp. 2–7.

33. *E-G Sesqui*, C-12.

34. Ibid., A-20, B-35, G-20, I-9, 13, 22.

35. Drinkle, *Architecture and Arts*, p. 53.

36. *Eagle*, October 6, 1908.

37. *E-G Sesqui*, H-31. For a further exploration of downtowns much like Lancaster's during this period, see Santmyer, *Ohio Town*, pp. 25–50.

38. For additional commentary on small-town housing during this period, see Santmyer, *Ohio Town*, pp. 53–80.

39. Dwight Barnes, "The Artie Thomas Store," *E-G*, December 29, 1992.

40. For further descriptions of this area, see Goslin, *Crossroads and Fence Corners*, 1:76; 2:5, 79–82.

41. Council Ordinances, August 14, 1905.

42. Such was the case on Park Street, in the North End, where this author, his mother, and her siblings grew up. Concerning the belief in a classless society among small-town Midwesterners, see Atherton, *Main Street*, pp. 100–105.

43. *Eagle*, September 14, 1900.

44. *E-G Sesqui*, I-28–29.

45. Knepper, *Ohio and Its People*, p. 322.

46. *Gazette*, February 15, 1917; *E-G Sesqui*, G-29, I-28.

47. *Gazette*, October 27, 1924.

48. Ibid., October 23 and 29, 1924.

49. Ibid.

50. Ibid., November 4, 1924.

51. Ibid., November 5, 1924.

52. *Eagle*, November 2 and 5, 1927, November 6, 1929; *Gazette*, November 2 and 9, 1927.

53. *E-G Sesqui*, I-26.

54. *Gazette*, July 26, 1912; Herbert M. Turner, "A Brief History of the Lancaster and Fairfield County Y.M.C.A," FCDL.

55. Drinkle, "As I Recall It," pp. 4–5.

56. *Gazette*, October 29, 1924.

57. *E-G Sesqui*, F-15, H-17, K-32. On the proliferation of clubs in Midwestern towns during the early twentieth century, see Atherton, *Main Street*, pp. 290–93.

58. *E-G Sesqui*, I-8. A good photograph of the decorated tower and intersection appeared on the cover of the summer 1981 issue of *FHQ*. An excellent general history of this organization is Stuart McConnell, *Glorious Contentment: The Grand Army of the Republic, 1865–1900* (Chapel Hill, N.C., 1992).

59. *E-G Sesqui*, E-6.

60. Ibid., A-22, K-32.

61. *Eagle*, October 6, 1908; Goslin, *E-G*, "Nature Notes," November 10, 1984.

62. *E-G Sesqui*, E-4.

63. Jean Rodabaugh, "Lancaster Country Club, 1909–1959," courtesy of Lancaster Country Club.

64. On the country club movement in the United States, see Baltzell, *The Protestant Establishment*, pp. 355–62. For the country club movement in Midwestern towns, see Atherton, *Main Street*, pp. 293–95.

65. Goslin, *Crossroads and Fence Corners*, 2:192.
66. *E-G Sesqui*, A-4.
67. On the establishment of the national DAR, see Karal Ann Marling, *George Washington Slept Here: Colonial Revivals and American Culture, 1876–1986* (Cambridge, Mass., 1988), pp 95–97.
68. On this matter, see Atherton, *Main Street*, p. 294, and Stuart M. Blumin, *The Emergence of the Middle Class: Social Experience in the American City* (New York, 1989), pp. 304–10.
69. *Eagle*, October 3, 1908. On lineage societies as a whole, see Baltzell, *Protestant Establishment*, pp. 114–16.
70. *Gazette*, November 16, 1902.
71. *Eagle*, October 3, 1908.
72. *Who Was Who in America*, vol. 3, 1951–60, p. 235.
73. *E-G Sesqui*, F-39.
74. See Dwight Barnes's articles on local wrestling in *E-G*, June 4 and 11, 1997.
75. *E-G Sesqui*, H-34.
76. Ibid., C-29.
77. A brief historical account of movie houses in Lancaster appeared in *E-G*, June 7, 1950.
78. Dwight Barnes, "When 'The Hip' Was Hot," *E-G*, July 16, 1997.
79. *E-G Sesqui*, F-17.
80. Bill Shea, "A Golden Gale Tradition," *E-G*, September 29, 1997; *Eagle*, October 3, 1908.
81. *Eagle*, October 28, 1932.
82. Ibid., October 31, 1925; *Mirage*, 1926, p. 97.
83. See, for example, *Eagle*, November 5, 1900.
84. *Gazette*, August 22, 1912. For a photograph of this event, see the front cover of the Fall 1979 issue of *FHQ*.
85. *Columbus Dispatch*, July 8, 1929; *E-G Sesqui*, E-8.
86. Bill Blackbeard, ed., *R. F. Outcault's The Yellow Kid: A Centennial Celebration of the Kid Who Started the Yellow Kid* (Northhampton, Mass., 1995); *DAB*, 14:112; Zane L. Miller to author, March 23, 1998.
87. Armstrong, *Buckeye Lake*, pp. 59–60.
88. Ibid., pp. 62–63; *Gazette*, November 3, 1908.
89. Armstrong, *Buckeye Lake*, p. 61; *Eagle*, June 2, 1900.
90. *Gazette*, January 14, 1904.
91. Braig, *My Buckeye Lake*, pp. 28–32.
92. Ibid., pp. 32–36, 52–61.
93. Armstrong, *Buckeye Lake*, p. 64; Braig, *My Buckeye Lake*, pp. 38–40.
94. *E-G Sesqui*, I-38.

95. Virginia Fetters, "Buckeye Lake: Those Were the Days My Friend," *FHQ*, Fall 1981, p. 6.

96. See ibid. for an excellent remembrance piece about the lake.

97. For more on the grocery boat, see ibid. See also Russel Bowers, interview by Ruth Drinkle, c. 1980, FHA Oral History Project, FCDL. Bowers was the proprietor of the grocery boat that operated out of Millersport.

98. For a list and discussion of these places, see the article by Charles Goslin in *E-G Sesqui*, I-27.

99. *Eagle*, November 5, 1932.

100. *Gazette*, June 16, 1904.

101. Ibid., June 16, 1904. In 1912 the city council passed legislation that prohibited the use of obscene or licentious language in front of a female. The maximum fine for such an offense was $200. See Council Ordinances, July 24, 1922.

102. *E-G Sesqui*, E-33.

103. Despite the charges, Layton was hired that fall as superintendent of the public schools in Altoona, Pennsylvania. It is unknown whether the Altoona board knew of the events involving Layton the previous spring in Lancaster. See *Gazette*, May 3, 4, 18, and 19, June 5, 16, and 20, August 3, 8, and 9, 1917.

104. Council Ordinances, January 22, 1906.

105. Ibid., January 11, 1909.

106. Ibid., February 26, 1912, April 10, 1916.

107. Ibid., April 13, 1914.

108. Ibid., February 26, 1912.

109. This theme is explored in Maureen Ogle, "Beyond the Great City: Finding and Defining the Small City in Nineteenth-Century America," in Joseph Rishel, ed., *American Cities and Towns* (Pittsburgh, 1992), pp. 48–66.

110. See Atherton, *Main Street*, pp. 217–22.

111. Council Minutes, October 3, 1887, September 2, 1889, February 26, 1890, August 9, 1897.

112. Ibid., September 27, 1897.

113. Ibid., June 14, 1886; Council Ordinances, September 9, 1912.

114. Council Ordinances, October 26, 1908.

115. Council Minutes, February 25, 1884, August 23, 1886.

116. Ibid., December 12, 1898.

117. For further insights, see Dominick Cavallo, *Muscles and Morals: Organized Playgrounds and Urban Reform* (Philadelphia, 1981).

118. Goslin, *Crossroads and Fence Corners*, 2:76.

119. Wiseman, *Centennial History*, pp. 278–79.

120. On the Rising gift and the early years of the park, see Virginia Fetters, "Rising Park: The Early Years," *FHQ*, Spring 1991, pp. 2–5. The *FHQ* for Spring 1993, p. 7, published excerpts, edited by Jo Libert, from a packet of letters written in 1908

to Philip Rising about purchasing the property and its donation to the city. See also the seventy-fifth anniversary feature about the park in *E-G*, May 14, 1984. An additional account of Rising Park appears in a pamphlet put out by the Lancaster Park Commission entitled "History of Lancaster's Parks" (n.d., but probably around 1990), pp. 2, 6–13.

121. Council Ordinances, December 28, 1922.
122. Ibid., June 8, 1936.
123. *Eagle*, March 6, 8, 21, 27, August 27, September 5 and 27, 1919; August 9, September 13, 1921.
124. This information on the Howe sisters and the Fresh Air Camp is taken from Fannie Howe's obituary in *E-G*, January 30, 1959.
125. On this connection between urban settlement houses and such activities as summer camps and visiting nurse organizations, see Allen F. Davis, *Spearheads for Reform: The Social Settlement and the Progressive Movement, 1890–1914* (New York, 1967).
126. *Eagle*, October 5, 1908.
127. Ibid., November 7, 1908.
128. Ibid.
129. Ibid., October 3, 1908.
130. *Gazette*, December 26, 1917.
131. Ibid., November 2, 1917, January 23, 1918.
132. *Eagle*, November 6, 1918.
133. Ibid., October 6, 1908.
134. Dwight Barnes, "The Bottom Drops Out," *E-G*, February 26, 1997.
135. Ibid.
136. *Eagle*, October 13, 1928.
137. *Gazette*, July 18, 1932.
138. Ibid., November 8, 1933.
139. Ibid., August 22, 1912, July 30, 1914.
140. *E-G Sesqui*, A-4.
141. Ibid.
142. Elizabeth Noecker to author, November 18, 1997.
143. Grace Ray Moon, "Fairfield Garden Club, 1924–1989," FCDL; *E-G*, August 13, 1997; Grace Ray Moon to author, August 28, 1997.
144. *E-G*, October 27, 1973; Council Ordinances, November 10, 1913, June 8, 1914.

## Chapter Five

1. *Eagle*, July 30, 1914.
2. *Gazette*, April 2, 1917.
3. Ibid., April 4, 1917.

4. Ibid., April 7, 1917.

5. Knepper, *Ohio and Its People*, p. 245.

6. A good summary of the local experience with World War I is Virginia Fetters, "Fairfield County in World War I," *FHQ*, Winter 1987, pp. 2–7, and Spring 1987, pp. 2–6. See also Van A. Snider, *Fairfield County in the World War* (Lancaster, Ohio, 1926).

7. *Gazette*, November 14, 1918.

8. Fetters, "World War I," Winter, pp. 4–5.

9. *Eagle*, November 8, 1918.

10. Ibid., November 12, 1918.

11. Fetters, "World War I," Spring, p. 6.

12. One of the best general histories of the Klan remains David M. Chalmers's *Hooded Americanism: The History of the Ku Klux Klan* (New York, 1981). For Chalmers's account of the Klan in Ohio, see pp. 175–97.

13. Knepper, *Ohio and Its People*, pp. 365–66; Ronald E. Marec, "The Fiery Cross: A History of the Ku Klux Klan in Ohio, 1920–1930" (master's thesis, Kent State University, 1967), pp. 14, 20–28, 38. See also John F. Marszalek, "The 1920s Ku Klux Klan in the Midwest," *Timeline*, March–April, 1994, pp. 3–20.

14. Marec, "Klan in Ohio," p. 50.

15. Ibid., pp. 74–75; Braig, *My Buckeye Lake*, pp. 48–50. The location of Stephenson's cottage at the lake is unknown. After a search in local records, author Donna Fisher Braig was unable to locate where it might have been. See *My Buckeye Lake*, p. 50.

16. *Eagle*, October 27, 1924.

17. *Gazette*, October 27, 1924.

18. Hubert Eyman Sr., interview by Ruth Drinkle, May 27, 1981, FHA Oral History Project, FCDL; *Gazette*, November 7, 1923, November 5, 1924; *Eagle*, November 6, 7, and 8, 1923, November 5, 1924.

19. Marec, "Klan in Ohio," pp. 86–87.

20. Ibid., pp. 168–80; Marszalek, "Klan in the Midwest," p. 11.

21. Fourteenth Census of the United States, 1920; Twelfth Census of the United States, 1900; Tenth Census of the United States, 1880; Eighth Census of the United States, 1860.

22. Holly Saunders, interview by author, August 20, 1997.

23. Kenneth Saunders, interview by author, August 20, 1997. Saunders's account of discrimination in restaurants and the movie theater was confirmed by several long-time white residents who did not wish to be identified.

24. Ibid.

25. Even in the late 1990s this expression is not unknown among some older white residents.

26. Agnes Moio, "Italian Immigration in Fairfield County," *Fairfield Trace* [a genealogical newsletter], Fall 1987, p. 65, FCDL.

27. Paul Pulsinelli, telephone interview by author, January 3, 1998.

28. For an account of Lancaster's Jewish community, see Virginia Fetters, "Congregation B'nai Israel," *FHQ*, Spring 1986, pp. 2–3, 6.

29. Fourteenth Census of the United States, 1920.

30. Helpful in illuminating the experience of Lancaster's Jewish community is Ema Morawska's *Insecure Prosperity: Small-Town Jews in Industrial America, 1870–1940* (Princeton, 1996).

31. *E-G Sesqui*, D-36.

32. *Gazette*, July 18, 1932.

33. *E-G Sesqui*, K-26, 31.

34. Dwight Barnes, "Depression Takes its Toll on Area," *E-G*, March 5, 1997.

35. Andriot, *Population Abstract*, 1:614.

36. Knepper, *Ohio and Its People*, p. 368.

37. Virginia Fetters, "Brother Can You Spare a Dime?" *FHQ*, Summer 1982, pp. 2–3.

38. Barnes, "Depression Takes its Toll."

39. Council Minutes, November 25, 1935.

40. Fetters, "Brother Can You Spare," pp. 3–4; Council Ordinances, August 26 and September 9, 1935, June 22, 1936, July 12, 1937, August 8, 1938, February 1 and May 8, 1939. Funds for a sanitary sewer system also came from the Federal Emergency Relief Administration (FERA). See Council Ordinances, December 10, 1934. On earlier pressure to build a municipal sewage treatment plant, see *Gazette*, April 17, July 13, September 9, 1919.

41. Fetters, "Brother Can You Spare," pp. 3–4.

42. For a personal account of the Depression in rural Fairfield County, see Mary Elizabeth Thomas Soliday, *Through Three Wars and a Depression* (New York, 1974).

43. Barnes, "Depression Takes its Toll."

44. *Gazette*, October 4, 1934; *E-G*, September 4, 1936.

45. Fetters, "Brother Can You Spare," p. 4.

46. See Ibid.

47. *E-G Sesqui*, E-36.

48. *Gazette*, March 12, 1934.

49. Ibid., March 9 and 20, 1934, August 24, 1934.

50. *Eagle*, September 2, 1934.

51. Ibid., September 5, 1934.

52. *Gazette*, September 4, 5, 6, 15, 1934; *Eagle*, September 19, 1934.

53. *Gazette*, September 6, 10, 11, 13, 17, 26, 28, and 29, 1934; *Eagle*, September 10, 13, and 28, October 9, 1934.

54. "Free Enterprise—In Terms of a Town," *Forbes*, November 15, 1947, p. 100; *E-G*, February 22, 1957.

55. *Eagle*, September 21, 1934.

56. Ibid., September 24, 1934.

57. *Gazette*, September 25, 1934.

58. Ibid., September 20, 1934; *Eagle*, September 20, October 3, 1934. In a September 25 article in the *Gazette*, the businessmen declared that they were not trying to punish the strikers, but rather to protect themselves from losing money and the business community in general from losing its reputation for sound judgment.

59. For another of these front-page editorials by Beach, see *Gazette*, April 18, 1934.

60. *Eagle*, September 15, 1934.

61. *Gazette*, October 9, 1934.

62. "In Terms of a Town," p. 61; *Eagle*, September 21, 1934.

63. Tom Joyce, quoted in "In Terms of a Town," p. 61.

64. *Gazette*, March 13, 21, 23, and 24, 1934, May 22, 1934, June 7, 8, and 15, 1934.

65. Lancaster's first Labor Day observances took place in 1903. See *E-G Sesqui*, H-31.

66. *E-G*, September 4, 1934.

67. Ibid., September 3 and 5, 1936.

68. *E-G Sesqui*, D-16.

69. *Eagle*, October 2, 1934; *Gazette*, October 22, 1934.

70. *E-G*, March 11, 1936.

71. "In Terms of a Town," pp. 74–75, 118.

72. *Who Was Who in America*, vol. 7, 1977–81, p. 503; Charles Sawyer, *Concerns of a Conservative Democrat* (Carbondale, Ill., 1968), pp. 55–56. Obituaries of Sawyer may be found in the April 9 issues of *E-G*, the *Columbus Dispatch*, and the *Cincinnati Enquirer*, among others.

73. A lengthy obituary of Kerr may be found in *E-G*, May 11, 1953.

74. "In Terms of a Town," p. 118.

75. A history of the orchid award appears in *E-G*, June 10, 1987.

76. See, for example, Gordon F. Lewis, "The Backgrounds and Careers of Small Businessmen in Lexington, Kentucky," in Edward Pessen, ed., *Three Centuries of Social Mobility in America* (New York, 1974), pp. 209–21.

77. *E-G*, October 28, 1936.

78. "In Terms of a Town," pp. 56–58, 108. See section D of *E-G Sesqui* for an account of Anchor Hocking, which, as might be expected, is written from the company's point of view, as was the story on the company in *E-G*, June 3, 1940.

79. Dwight Barnes, "Depression Era Fades in County," *E-G*, March 19, 1997.

80. Ibid.

81. *E-G Sesqui*, A-28.
82. Ibid., E-11, 22.
83. Ibid., A-37.
84. Barnes, "Depression Era Fades."
85. Patricia Brown, "City Buses," *FHQ*, Spring 1992, pp. 4–7.
86. For a brief account of this supposed conspiracy by General Motors, see Howard Kunstler, *The Geography of Nowhere: The Rise and Decline of America's Man-Made Landscape* (New York, 1993), pp. 91–92, and Kay, *Asphalt Nation*, pp. 212–14. In any case, some three hundred tons of trolley rails had been torn from the streets by the end of 1939 and were put up for bid to scrap metal dealers. See Council Ordinances, December 11, 1939.
87. *E-G*, June 3, 1940, A-21.
88. *Eagle*, July 24, 1929; *E-G*, June 3, 1940, B-4, D-14; Jo Libert, "'Tella' A Sequel," *FHQ*, Summer 1992, p. 5.
89. *E-G*, June 3, 1940, A-36.
90. Ibid., A-9, 40.
91. Ibid., March 29, 1998.
92. Ibid., June 3, 1940, A-7, 18, 20, 24, 26, B-8. See also *E-G*, June 4, 5, and 6, 1940.
93. Andriot, *Population Abstract*, 1:613–17.
94. Ibid., pp. 618–23.
95. Ibid., p. 620.
96. Mary Alice Drinkle Kuhn to author, November 6, 1997.
97. *E-G Sesqui*, H-22.
98. *Gazette*, November 9, 1900, November 10, 1904, November 4, 1908, November 6, 1912, November 8, 1916, November 3, 1920; *Eagle*, November 3, 4, and 6, 1908, November 4, 1920.
99. *Gazette*, November 1 and 5, 1924; *Eagle*, November 8, 1924.
100. *Gazette*, November 8, 1928.
101. *Eagle*, November 5, 1928.
102. *Gazette*, November 9 and 11, 1932.
103. Ibid., November 4, 1932.
104. Ibid., November 4, 1932.
105. Ibid., November 5, 1932.
106. *Eagle*, October 26, 1932. See also Ibid., November 5, 1932.
107. *E-G*, November 4, 1936.
108. Ibid., November 6, 1940.
109. *Eagle*, November 4, 1925, November 6, 1929, November 4, 1931; *Gazette*, November 4, 1931, November 8, 1933, November 6, 1935; *E-G*, November 8, 1939, November 5, 1941.
110. *Gazette*, November 9, 1900, November 10, 1904, November 6, 1912, Novem-

ber 8, 1916, November 3, 1920, November 5, 1924, November 8, 1928, November 11, 1932; *Eagle*, November 6, 1908, November 8, 1924, November 5, 1928; *E-G*, November 4, 1936, November 6, 1940, November 8, 1944.

111. *Eagle*, October 11, 1928.
112. *E-G*, August 26 and September 6, 1939, November 5, 1941.
113. Also see the editorials in *E-G*, December 9 and 11, 1941.
114. Ibid., December 12, 1941.
115. Ibid., May 30, 1946.
116. See ibid., May 30, 1947, for an account of Hazelton's wartime file of local residents in World War II.
117. This information comes from a number of issues of the *E-G* during 1943. See also Council Ordinances, February 17, October 10, 1943.
118. Council Ordinances, April 13, 1942.
119. Ibid., November 22, 1943.
120. *E-G*, August 29, 1944.
121. Ibid., October 6, 1944.
122. Ibid., June 6, 1944.
123. Just six days after Pearl Harbor, a group of Lancaster businessmen called a "mass meeting" to collect signatures on a petition to Washington to utilize the Godman plant for a war-related purpose. See *E-G*, December 13, 1941.
124. Ibid., August 15, 1945.

## Chapter Six

1. For many Americans, wherever they might be living, this was also a heady time. See William L. O'Neill, *American High: The Years of Confidence, 1945–1960* (New York, 1986).
2. In this chapter I have drawn upon some of the insights developed in a yet unpublished memoir about growing up in Lancaster during the postwar period, written in collaboration with Philip M. Hazelton.
3. *E-G*, May 29, 1947, June 2, 3, 4, 1947.
4. Ibid., June 4, 1947.
5. Ibid., June 16, 1947.
6. Ibid., June 5, 9, 16, 19, 20, 23, 1947; *Columbus Citizen*, June 5, 1947; *Ohio State Journal*, June 6 and 14, 1947; *Zanesville News*, June 8, 1947; *Columbus Dispatch*, June 13, 1947; *Columbus Star*, June 14, 1947; *Akron Beacon Journal*, June 22, 1947; *Columbus Sunday Dispatch Magazine*, July 13, 1947.
7. One who made a lasting acquaintance with Ives was then *Eagle-Gazette* associate editor, Perrin "Pel" Hazelton. Virginia Hazelton, interview by author, May 1997.

8. The author was fortunate enough to find an hour-by-hour schedule of these events, put together by the local "Premiere Committee," in the personal papers of the late Perrin Hazelton. Press coverage of the premiere appeared in E-G, May 25 and 26, 1947.

9. Kerr played the part of Ohio's governor, who awarded the "Governor's Cup" to the winner of the horse race.

10. E-G, June 13, 14, 15, 1998.

11. A day-by-day schedule of sesquicentennial events appeared in E-G, June 2, 1950.

12. Ibid., June 5, 1950.

13. Ibid., June 2 and 6, 1950.

14. Ibid, June 7, 1950.

15. Ibid., June 6, 1950.

16. Ibid., March 20, 1950.

17. Ibid., June 8 and 9, 1950.

18. Ibid., June 5 and 10, 1950.

19. Ibid., June 8 and 12, 1950.

20. Ibid., June 12, 1950.

21. Ibid., June 15, 1950.

22. Ibid., June 6, 1950.

23. Ibid.

24. Ibid.

25. E-G Sesqui, A-1, 2.

26. Ibid., A-24.

27. Christopher Winans, *Malcolm Forbes: The Man Who Had Everything* (New York, 1990), p. 37.

28. Malcolm Forbes, "In Terms of a Town," p. 49.

29. Ibid.

30. Ibid., p. 53.

31. Ibid., p. 54.

32. Ibid.

33. Ibid., p. 55.

34. Ibid., p. 74.

35. Ibid., p. 100.

36. Ibid., pp. 53, 106.

37. E-G, June 13, 1947; E-G Sesqui, E-36.

38. E-G Sesqui, E-2; E-G, February 26, 1957.

39. E-G Sesqui, I-22, K-34.

40. Ibid., F-17; E-G, March 30, 1979, March 28, 1980; "Era of Erickson," *Columbus Dispatch Sunday Magazine*, October 24, 1971, pp. 8–13; Romona C. and Franklin

H. Knower, *Erickson Freehand Glass, 1943–1961* (New York, 1971).

41. *E-G*, "Highlights of 1955," December 31, 1955; February 27, 1957; "Top '57 News," December 31, 1957.

42. *E-G Sesqui*, A-30.

43. "In Terms of a Town," pp. 72–74, 114, 116.

44. Eva Friesner, interviewed by Ruth Miller, April 28, 1981, FHA Oral History Project, FCDL.

45. "In Terms of a Town," pp. 74–78.

46. *E-G Sesqui*, B-38, G-30.

47. Dwight Barnes, "Maher Leaves Legacy of Park," *E-G*, June 26, 1996.

48. *E-G Sesqui*, H-9.

49. Ibid., H-31.

50. *E-G*, "Highlights of 1955," December 31, 1955; "Local '56 News," December 31, 1956; "Top '57 News," December 31, 1957.

51. Andriot, *Population Abstract*, 1:620.

52. Ibid., 1:614.

53. *E-G*, June 12, 1950.

54. *Mirage*, 1954, p. 60; 1955, p. 6; 1968, p. 13.

55. *E-G*, March 4, 1953, May 5, 1954.

56. *E-G*, "Local '56 News," December 31, 1956; "Top '57 News," December 31, 1957.

57. See the year-end news summaries in *E-G* from this period.

58. *Mirage*, 1960, p. 13.

59. *E-G*, November 3 and 7, 1956.

60. *E-G*, "Area News during 1962," December 31, 1962.

61. Braig, *My Buckeye Lake*, pp. 91–100.

62. *E-G*, "Area News during 1962," December 31, 1962; "Highlights of 1955," December 31, 1955.

63. Jack Furniss, telephone interview by author, January 4, 1998; *E-G*, April 27, 1998.

64. *E-G*, "Looking Back on 1954," December 31, 1954; "Highlights of 1955," December 31, 1955; "Top '57 News," December 31, 1957; "Looking Back on 1958," December 31, 1958. See also *E-G*, December 29, 1953.

65. This author recalls such a pedestrian world for youngsters in Lancaster that lasted into the early 1960s. This theme is also discussed by Thomas Hylton in *Save Our Land, Save Our Towns: A Plan for Pennsylvania* (Harrisburg, Penn., 1995), pp. 12–13.

66. Grant became society editor in 1948 and remained in that position until she died in 1959. See *E-G*, September 19, 1959.

67. Ibid., September 11, 1959. For a history of this group, see *E-G Sesqui*, F-10.

68. *E-G*, February 18, 1957; Mary Ellen "Spec" Reed, telephone interview by author, January 10, 1998.

69. Dwight Barnes, "Old Bill Bailey's," *E-G*, August 5, 1998.

70. *E-G Sesqui*, K-28, 39.

71. On crime during this period, including the Geer case, see the year-end summaries of news in *E-G*, as cited in note 62 above.

72. Ibid., June 8, 1955.

73. Quoted in Dwight Barnes, "Local Inventor Lived Interesting Life," *E-G*, December 11, 1996.

74. Quoted in Davidson's obituary, *E-G*, August 20, 1957.

75. Armand Romano, "Henry Weaver Davidson: Inventor, Philosopher, Prophet," *Fairfield Monthly*, October 1984, pp. 30–32. Romano's article is the fullest account of Davidson. See also Barnes, "Local Inventor."

76. See year-end news summaries in *E-G* for these years, as cited above.

77. See, for example, *E-G*, May 28, 1947.

78. *E-G*, May 27, 1946.

79. On the role of parades and other patriotic symbols in building a sense of community, see John Bodnar, *Bonds of Affection: Americans Define Their Patriotism* (Princeton, 1996).

80. *E-G*, June 26, 1950; Patricia Brown, "The Korean War," *FHQ*, Winter 1997, pp. 1–5.

81. *E-G*, June 15, 1955.

82. Ibid., July 9, 1953

83. Ibid., "Looking Back on 1954," December 31, 1954.

84. Ibid.

85. Ibid., July 22, 1948.

86. *E-G Sesqui*, B-22, I-32; *E-G*, January 22, 1937.

87. Patricia Brown, "The Big Snow of 1950," *FHQ*, Winter 1991, pp. 2–5.

## Chapter Seven

1. Clarence E. Miller, interview by author, August 18, 1997.

2. *E-G*, July 23, 1964, March 11 and 25, 1965, April 29, 1965, June 13, 1965, November 19, 1966; Goslin Notebooks, vol. 7, FCDL; Miller interview, August 18, 1997.

3. *E-G*, October 13, 1954, October 23, 1958, December 31, 1959. See also the year-end reviews in ibid., December 31, 1958, December 31, 1959, December 30, 1960, December 30, 1961, and December 31, 1962; Miller interview, August 18, 1997; Leonard Hajost, interview by author, August 21, 1997.

4. Kay, *Asphalt Nation*, pp. 221–45.

5. For an informative article on the effects of the 1954 tax code on the rush to

put up shopping centers and malls during this period, see Thomas W. Hanchett, "U.S. Tax Policy and the Shopping Center Boom of the 1950s and 1960s," *American Historical Review,* October 1996, pp. 1082–110.

6. Before 1948 the road was known as Front Street and before that as First Street. See Dwight Barnes, "Historical Story Updates for '97," *E-G,* December 10, 1997, and Council Ordinances, May 27, 1957.

7. On Hannan, see *E-G Sesqui,* K-30.

8. *E-G,* January 30, 1959, October 19, 1960, and the year-end summary in ibid., December 30, 1960; Miller interview, August 18, 1997.

9. Both were based on a novel by James Michener called *Tales of the South Pacific.*

10. Dwight Barnes, "Tiki Lanes Enters its 35th Year," *E-G,* April 2, 1997. See also ibid., November 9, 1973, and Council Ordinances, September 9, 1970.

11. See *E-G* year-end summaries, December 31, 1956, December 31, 1958, December 31, 1959, December 30, 1960, December 31, 1962.

12. Ibid., October 28, 1960.

13. Ibid., March 28, 1962, December 13, 1963.

14. Ibid., September 1, 1961, November 14, 1971.

15. Ibid., September 9, 1963.

16. Ibid., March 30, 1982, September 11, 1998.

17. Jackson, *Crabgrass Frontier,* pp. 203–18; Kunstler, *The Geography of Nowhere,* pp. 102–4; Richard Moe and Carter Wilkie, *Changing Places: Rebuilding Community in the Age of Sprawl* (New York, 1997), pp. 48–54.

18. *Upclose 1990 Census Sourcebook,* vol. 3, Midwest, p. 276.

19. *E-G Sesqui,* A-13; *E-G,* April 11, 1995, September 8, 1997.

20. *E-G,* April 16, 1953, July 27, 1954.

21. The city council established official procedures for developers seeking approval of subdivisions in 1954. See Council Ordinances, October 26, 1954.

22. Codified Ordinances of the City of Lancaster, Ohio, Complete to October 25, 1992, Section 11, Planning and Zoning, chapter 1151, FCDL; Dave Darfus, Lancaster City Code Administrator, telephone interview by author, January 12, 1998.

23. Kunstler, *Geography of Nowhere,* pp. 169–70.

24. Codified Ordinances, Lancaster Ohio, chapter 1151. On the history of zoning in the United States and some of its negative consequences for the pedestrian, see Barry Cullingworth, *Planning in the USA: Policies, Issues and Processes* (New York, 1997), pp. 56–89; Hylton, *Plan for Pennsylvania,* p. 81; Kay, *Asphalt Nation,* pp. 295–301.

25. Patricia Brown, "City Buses," *FHQ,* Spring 1992, pp. 6–7; *E-G,* March 28, 1969.

26. *E-G,* January 2, 1950.

27. C. J. Cross, "Seeing Stars and Movies," *E-G*, August 9, 1996; "Lancaster's Original Cruise In," *FHQ*, Fall 1998, p. 2; *E-G Sesqui*, F-15.

28. Dwight Barnes, "Jimmy's," *E-G*, March 13, 1996.

29. Kay, *Asphalt Nation*, pp. 247–50.

30. *Columbus Citizen-Journal*, February 14, 1968.

31. Tom and Esther Alfred, interview by Virginia Fetters, July 31, 1981, FHA Oral History Project, FCDL.

32. *E-G*, October 7, 1959. A photograph in the *E-G* for September 18, 1960, showed such a downtown mall in Middletown, Ohio.

33. *E-G*, October 12 and 15, 1960; year-end summary in ibid., December 31, 1959.

34. Francaviglia, *Main Street Revisited*, pp. 145–67.

35. *E-G*, August 23, 1957, August 19, 1972.

36. *E-G*, June 2, 1962.

37. Ibid., March 29, April 13 and 26, May 6, 1971, September 1, 1972.

38. Mary Alice Drinkle Kuhn to author, November 6, 1997.

39. Drinkle's obituary appeared in the *E-G*, April 26, 1993.

40. Pat Brown, "The Way It Was . . . Ruth Drinkle," *FHQ*, Winter 1993, pp. 6–7; Kuhn to author, November 6, 1997. The author has also drawn upon the many conversations that he had with Ruth and Charles Drinkle in their Lancaster home during the 1970s and early 1980s.

41. Wiseman, *Centennial History*, pp. 332–33. Kuhn to author, November 6, 1997. On Charles Drinkle, see *E-G*, May 8, 1991.

42. Brown, "The Way It Was," pp. 2–4; Jack Furniss, telephone interview by author, January 4, 1998; Caroline Peters Rockwood to author, August 28, 1998.

43. Brown, "The Way It Was," p. 2.

44. On Goslin, see *E-G*, June 25, 1985, April 26, 1986, January 23, 1988, April 20 and 22, 1990.

45. Drinkle, *Architecture and Arts*, p. 85.

46. Ebbert, *Lancaster and Fairfield County*.

47. *E-G*, October 13, 1936.

48. Fairfield County Commissioners, "Six Fairfield County Tours" (Lancaster, 1955), FCDL.

49. Dorothy Ent [Coleman], "Architectural Development of Early Lancaster, Ohio" (master's thesis, Ohio State University, 1945). On Coleman, who died in 1994, see Dwight Barnes, "Ent Coleman's Legacy Lives On," *E-G*, June 21, 1995.

50. Virginia Fetters, "The Mumaughs of Main Hill," *FHQ*, Fall 1990, pp. 2–5; Drinkle, *Architecture and Arts*, p. 5.

51. Mary Alice Drinkle Kuhn, telephone interview with author, August 3, 1998; Caroline Peters Rockwood to author, August 10, 1998. Well into adulthood, this

author himself heard older members of the preservation community in Lancaster criticize Collins for his destruction of the Effinger House.

52. *E-G*, December 9, 1978. This author wrote a preface to both the 1978 and 1994 editions of *Architecture and Arts*.

53. Laura E. Kerr, *Campfire to Courthouse: An Early History of Fairfield County, Ohio* (Lancaster, 1981), illustrated by Betty Arnsbarger. In 1984 Kerr published a short history of William T. Sherman and family, again under the aegis of the Fairfield Heritage Association, entitled *William Tecumseh Sherman: A Family Chronicle*.

54. Virginia Fetters, "From Campfire to Courthouse," *FHQ*, Spring 1981, p. 4.

55. Ruth Drinkle, "Oral History Project," in *FHQ*, Spring 1981, p. 7.

56. On the tea room and gift shop, see *E-G Sesqui*, A-28.

57. *Columbus Dispatch Magazine*, April 29, 1973; Drinkle, *Architecture and Arts*, pp. 63–70; "The Maccracken Family Silver Returned to the Georgian," *FHQ*, Winter 1998, p. 2.

58. Jo Voss, "Sherman House," *FHQ*, Spring 1981, p. 6; "Heritage Takes Over Sherman House," *FHQ*, Summer 1982, p. 5; "Sherman House Dedication," *FHQ*, Summer 1983, pp. 4–6; *E-G*, December 26, 1962; Council Ordinances, November 12, 1945, March 25, 1946, November 28, 1949, November 9, 1981.

59. *E-G Sesqui*, I-2; "The Herbert M. Turner Pioneer Collection" (brochure); Hajost interview, August 21, 1997. Although the Fairfield County Historical Society had not been officially disbanded at the time of this writing, it had again become a moribund organization.

60. Many other American communities have not been so fortunate. For further insights into conflicting popular views of the local past, see John Bodnar, *Remaking America: Public Memory, Commemoration, and Patriotism in the Twentieth Century* (Princeton, 1992). For a case study of a particularly sharp dispute over how to interpret a community's past, see Contosta, "Philadelphia's 'Miniature Williamsburg,'" *Pennsylvania Magazine of History and Biography*, October 1996, pp. 283–320.

61. Council Ordinances, October 25, 1965; *E-G*, October 26, 1965.

62. *E-G*, July 1 and 6, 1976.

63. Jo Voss, "Preservation Power," *FHQ*, Winter 1979, p. 5; Edward Rutherford, telephone interview by author, January 10, 1998.

64. Goslin, *Crossroads and Fence Corners*, 1:58, 2:45. The Fairfield County Visitors and Convention Bureau, in conjunction with a number of volunteers, produced a guided walking tour of Lancaster, available on both audiotape and in print, entitled "A Walk Through Lancaster's Square 13," 1992, with the script by Jo Voss of the Fairfield Heritage Association.

65. C. J. Cross, "Architecture Builds Up Historic District," *E-G*, October 25, 1995.

66. C. J. Cross, "Groups Continue to Preserve Historic Area," in ibid.; Codified Ordinances, Lancaster, Ohio, chapter 1327, Historic Preservation.

67. This report was entitled "Handbook for Main Street Lancaster, Ohio," FCDL; Hajost interview, August 21, 1997.

68. "Handbook for Main Street," p. 3.

69. Ibid., p. 5.

70. Ibid., p. 4.

71. Ibid., p. 23. See also *E-G*, March 21, 1978.

72. *E-G*, May 2 and 18, 1978; Joseph G. Madonna, "Development Plan and Program, Central Business District, Lancaster, Ohio, August 29, 1978," FCDL; Hajost interview, August 21, 1997.

73. *E-G*, May 11, 1978.

74. Voss, "Preservation Power," pp. 4–5.

75. The last year that the Charles P. Wiseman Company appeared in Polk's *City Directory* for Lancaster was 1960. See also year-end summary, *E-G*, December 30, 1960; Jack Furniss, interview by author, August 15, 1997; Betty Baughman, telephone interview by author, January 10, 1998.

76. *E-G*, July 3, 1965, August 5, 1965, February 3, 1984.

77. Dwight Barnes, "Reed's Prescribe to Lancaster," *E-G*, August 30, 1995; and *E-G*, February 3, 1984. The last year that a listing for the Lyric Theater appeared in Polk's *City Directory* for Lancaster was 1980. The Broad Theater had closed about 1957. See Larry McMurtry, *The Last Picture Show* (New York, 1966).

78. Gene Ash, telephone interview by author, January 16, 1998; "The Year That Was," 1985 and 1986, *E-G*, December 30, 1989.

79. Gene Ash to author, February 17, 1998.

80. *E-G*, November 27 and 28, 1989.

81. Ibid., May 12, 1970; Veronica Martin, Ohio Governor's Office of Veterans Affairs, telephone interview by author, January 13, 1998. Martin did not have a count of those from Fairfield County who had lost their lives in Vietnam, nor did the Fairfield County Veterans Affairs Office or the American Legion, Fairfield Post 11, when the author spoke with them by telephone on January 13, 1998.

82. *E-G*, May 9, 1970.

83. Ibid., November 2, 3, 6, 9, and 10, 1973, December 1, 1973, February 16, 1974.

84. Ibid., January 27, 28, 29, and 30, 1978.

85. Ibid., April 29, June 15, 1965, November 4, 1966, February 23, 1973.

86. Ibid., August 10, 1994; *Columbus Dispatch*, May 18, 1965.

87. *E-G*, December 28, 1989.

88. Ibid., December 5 and 29, 1989.

89. Ibid., July 1 and 7, 1987.

90. It is also interesting to recall that Muncie and Lancaster prospered after discoveries of natural gas in both communities attracted glass and other successful industries to town.

91. Ash to author, February 17, 1998. The city library had been transferred to Fairfield County in 1960. See Council Ordinances, April 11, 1960.

92. Last Will and Testament of I. J. Collins, dated June 9, 1972; Charles E. Reed, Esq., to author, November 14, 1997.

93. Clarence E. Miller, interview by author, August 18, 1997.

94. Edward Rutherford, telephone interview by author, January 10, 1998.

95. *E-G*, September 4, 1991.

96. "Lancaster and Fairfield County: Buyers Guide and Membership Directory, 1996–97," Lancaster Fairfield County Chamber of Commerce, p. 9.

97. "Lancaster Fairfield County Community Profile," Lancaster Fairfield County Chamber of Commerce, 1997.

98. For a fascinating historical and social analysis of the shopping mall in general, see Kenneth T. Jackson, "All the World's a Mall: Reflections on the Social and Economic Consequences of the American Shopping Center," *American Historical Review* (October 1996): 1111–21.

99. Rutherford interview, January 10, 1998.

100. *Columbus Dispatch*, January 27 and November 15, 1986; *E-G*, January 22 and 27, February 21, June 14, 1986; Council Ordinances, August 24, 1987.

101. Art Wallace, interview by author, August 20, 1997.

102. Rutherford interview, January 10, 1998. Franklin B. Melick, Director, Lancaster Community Development Department, agreed with Rutherford, in an interview by the author on July 14, 1998, that the River Valley Mall was attracting shoppers from the southern fringes of Columbus.

103. Wallace interview, August 20, 1997; Council Ordinances, June 26 and September 11, 1995.

104. Joel Garreau, *Edge City: Life on the New Frontier* (New York, 1991), pp. 6–7.

105. Ibid., pp. 425–26.

106. This estimate was provided to the author by the Lancaster Chamber of Commerce in a telephone interview with Kathy Kohl, January 8, 1998.

107. These figures are taken from a document entitled "U.S. 33 Lancaster Bypass: City of Lancaster Perspective," compiled by Franklin B. Melick, Director of Lancaster's Community Development Department. According to this document, peak traffic counts going north on Route 33 were as follows: 1954—6,796; 1964—11,240; 1986—22,120; and 1998—50,290.

108. Wallace interview, August 20, 1997; *E-G*, January 14, 1995, June 28, 1995, July 24, 1997.

109. Melick interview, July 14, 1998; Peter Rockwood, interview by author, July 13, 1998; *E-G*, December 14 and 15, 1997; January 5, 1998.

110. *Pickerington and Violet Township: Community Guide and Membership Directory* (n.d.), p. 3; "Pickerington's Special Details," pp. 3–4. Both of these publications are distributed by the Pickerington Chamber of Commerce. James W. Jim Reed, interview by author, August 11, 1997.

111. *E-G*, September 24, 1997.

112. Reed interview, August 11, 1997.

113. These figures were published by the Ohio State Extension, Fairfield County Office, July 1994.

114. *E-G*, August 22 and 25, October 12 and 13, December 5 and 10, 1997. See also Moe and Wilkie, *Changing Places*, pp. 246–47.

115. *Ohio Metropolitan Areas and County Populations* (Columbus, Ohio, 1994), Table A-1, Population Counts and Estimates, by County: 1970–94.

116. *Upclose 1990 Census Sourcebook*, vol. 3, Midwest, p. 276.

117. Ibid.; Andriot, *Population Abstract*, 1:620; Kohl interview, January 8, 1998.

118. Bureau of the Census, 1990 Census of Housing: Population and Housing Characteristics for Census Tracts and Block Numbering Areas, Columbus PMSA, Tracts 316, 319, 323; Melick interview, July 14, 1998; *E-G*, September 20, 1998.

119. *E-G*, November 6 and December 17, 1997, March 28, 1998.

120. Ibid., March 18, 1998.

121. Ibid., February 28, 1987, March 5, 1995, December 28, 1993, June 20, September 23, October 5, 6, 20, and 30, 1997, January 15 and 20, April 21, May 19, June 23, 1998; Melick interview, July 14, 1998.

122. Pierce Lewis, "The Galactic Metropolis," in George Macinko and Rutherford H. Platt, eds., *Beyond the Urban Fringe: Land Uses of Nonmetropolitan America* (Minneapolis, 1983), pp. 23–49.

123. For a discussion of this phenomenon in other towns, see Esther Romeyn and Jack Kugelmass, "Community Festivals and the Politics of Memory: Postmodernity in the American Heartland," in Bertens and D'haen, eds., *Small Town in America*, pp. 196–216.

124. *E-G*, August 16, 1997.

125. Ibid., September 25 and 27, 1997.

126. Ibid., October 13, 1997.

127. Lancaster Festival, 1997 (program); *E-G*, July 31, 1988, August 1, 1997, February 13, 1998.

128. *E-G*, June 26 and September 24, 1997, April 15, 1998.

129. For example, see ibid., January 22, 1998.

130. Phyllis Kuhn, "Sherman to be Honored With Statue," *FHQ*, Winter 1998, pp. 5–6.

## Conclusion

1. Hylton, *A Plan for Pennsylvania*, p. 109. Many of the proposals in this book for saving land and towns in Pennsylvania could be adapted for Lancaster.

2. Moe and Wilkie, *Changing Places*, pp. 217–18.

3. Such discussions were being initiated in 1997 and 1998 by the townships to be affected, but the nature and results of these discussions were unclear at the time of this writing. See *E-G*, December 14, 1997, January 5 and 28, 1998, April 22, 1998. See also Kay, *Asphalt Nation*, pp. 285–94; Moe and Wilkie, *Changing Places*, pp. 143, 219–20.

4. Kay, *Asphalt Nation*, pp. 303–21.

5. Hylton, *Plan for Pennsylvania*, pp. 86–88.

6. Such ideas were part of a proposed new code: City of Lancaster, Proposed Planning and Zoning Code, Draft Copy, February 15, 1996, pp. III-10, 25. See also *E-G*, August 29, September 4, and October 3, 1997, May 14 and July 26, 1998.

7. Proposed Planning and Zoning Code, III-28–30. See also Kay, *Asphalt Nation*, pp. 323–31, and Hylton, *Plan for Pennsylvania*, pp. 78–80.

8. Moe and Wilkie, *Changing Places*, pp. 66–68, 240–44; John Hale, "From the Editor," *FHQ*, Winter 1998, p. 6.

9. Hylton, *Plan for Pennsylvania*, pp. 102–3.

# Bibliographic Essay

THERE ARE A NUMBER of works that help to place Lancaster into the wider context of American towns and small cities. These include Sherwood Anderson, *Home Town* (New York, 1940); Stuart Blumin, *The Emergence of the Middle Class: Social Experience in the American City, 1760–1900* (New York, 1989); Grady Clay, *Close-Up: How to Read the American City* (Chicago, 1980); Richard V. Francaviglia, *Main Street Revisited: Time Space, and Image Building in Small-Town America* (Iowa City, Iowa, 1996); Walter Holbling, "From Main Street to Lake Wobegon and Half-Way Back: The Mid-West Small Town as a Literary Place in Twentieth-Century U.S. Literature," in Hans Bertens and Theo D'haen, eds., *The Small Town in America* (Amsterdam, 1995), pp. 97–108; Howard Gillette Jr. and Zane L. Miller, *American Urbanism: A Historiographical Review* (New York, 1987); Dwight W. Hoover, "Social Science Looks at the Small American Town," in Bertens and D'haen, eds., *Small Town in America*, pp. 19–29; Kenneth Jackson, *Crabgrass Frontier: The Suburbanization of the United States* (New York, 1985); Richard Lingerman, *Small-Town America: A Narrative History, 1920–Present* (Boston, 1980); Margaret Marsh, "Reconsidering Suburbs," *Pennsylvania Magazine of History and Biography*, October 1988, pp. 576–605; Maureen Ogle, "Beyond the Great City: Finding and Defining the Small City in Nineteenth-Century America," in Joseph F. Rishel, ed., *American Towns and Cities* (Pittsburgh, 1992); David Plowden, *Small Town America* (New York, 1994); Page Smith, *As a City on a Hill: The Small Town in American History* (New York, 1966); Michael Southworth and Eran Ben-Joseph, *Streets and the Shaping of Towns and Cities* (New York, 1997); Arthur J. Vidich and Joseph Bensman, *Reflections on Community Studies* (New York, 1964); and Richard Wade, *The Urban Frontier: The Rise of Western Cities, 1790–1830* (1959; reprint, Chicago, 1996).

Informative studies of actual towns and small cities include Lewis Atherton, *Main Street on the Middle Border* (1954; reprint, Bloomington, Ind., 1984); Michael Birkner, *A Country Place No More: The Transformation of Bergenfield, New Jersey, 1894–1994* (Rutherford, N.J., 1994); Stanley Buder, *Pullman: An Experiment in Industrial Order and Community Planning, 1880–1930* (New York, 1967); Richard O. Davies,

*Main Street Blues* (Columbus, Ohio, 1998), a study of Camden, Ohio; Robert R. Dykstra, *The Cattle Towns* (New York, 1968); Michael H. Frisch, *Town into City: Springfield, Massachusetts, and the Meaning of Community, 1840–1880* (Cambridge, Mass., 1972); Carol O'Connor, *A Sort of Utopia: Scarsdale, 1891–1981* (Albany, N.Y., 1983); Helen Hooven Santmyer, *Ohio Town* (Columbus, Ohio, 1962), which is about Xenia, Ohio; and Alexander von Hoffman, *Local Attachments: The Making of an American Urban Neighborhood, 1850 to 1920* (Baltimore, Md., 1994). A number of titles from earlier periods appear in the introductory chapter of this book.

Previously published histories or historical materials about Lancaster and Fairfield County are as follows: Edward S. Ebbert, *Lancaster and Fairfield County, Ohio* (Lancaster, Ohio, 1901); Hervey Scott, *A Complete History of Fairfield County, Ohio* (Columbus, Ohio, 1877); George Sanderson, *A Brief History of the Early Settlement of Fairfield County* (Lancaster, Ohio, 1851); Norris Schneider and Clair C. Stebbens, *Zane's Trace: The First Road in Ohio* (Zanesville, Ohio, 1973); C. M. L. Wiseman, *Centennial History of Lancaster, Ohio, and Lancaster People* (Lancaster, Ohio, 1898), and *Pioneer Period and Pioneer People of Fairfield County, Ohio* (1901; reprint, Columbus, Ohio, 1984); and Herbert M. Turner, *A History to Remember: The Story of the Settlement of the Upper Hocking Valley* (Lancaster, Ohio, 1976). Helpful in understanding the natural history of the area is Edward W. Wolfe et al., *Geology of Fairfield County* (Columbus, Ohio, 1962). "A Bibliography of Printed Materials about Fairfield County, Ohio and Fairfield Countians" (1981) is available at the Fairfield County District Library (FCDL) in Lancaster. Also helpful is Joyce Harvey, "Bibliography of Selected Materials in the Historical Collection" (n.d.), FCDL.

Although not a history in the traditional sense, the Sesquicentennial Edition of the *Lancaster Eagle-Gazette*, published June 3, 1950, offers a trove of historical information about Lancaster and Fairfield County that appears nowhere else. It includes a bibliography of Lancaster and Fairfield County (p. H-34). Most of this history was compiled and written by then associate editor of the *Lancaster Eagle-Gazette*, Perrin "Pel" Hazelton.

Charles R. Goslin, a local naturalist and historian, has left a large body of material that illuminates the history of Lancaster and Fairfield County. For thirty-five years, beginning in 1953, Goslin published a newspaper column entitled "Nature Notes" that appeared in the *Lancaster Eagle-Gazette* every Saturday. The best of these were collected and published in two volumes entitled *Crossroads and Fence Corners: Historical Lore of Fairfield County* (Lancaster, Ohio, 1976, 1980). These works are supplemented by the eight volumes of Goslin's notebooks at the FCDL in Lancaster. There is another large collection of Goslin manuscript material at the library of Ohio University–Lancaster.

Dozens of insightful articles have appeared in the *Fairfield Heritage Quarterly*, published since 1979 by the Fairfield Heritage Association, the local historical and historic preservation society. The titles of such pieces and their authors appear in the notes.

In addition to publishing the quarterly, the Heritage Association conducted an ambitious oral history project in the early 1980s, typed transcripts of which are available, in three large binders, at FCDL. In addition to these, this author has conducted a number of interviews, the subjects and dates of which can be found in the notes.

Information on the population and people of Lancaster may be found in the federal manuscript census schedules, those from 1860, 1880, 1900, and 1920 having been used for this study. In addition to these, census information for Lancaster appears in John L. Andriot, ed., *Population Abstract of the United States*, 2 vols. (McLean, Va., 1983); *General Population Characteristics, Ohio, 1970 Census of Population* (Washington, D.C., 1971); *1980 Census of Population and Housing, Census Tracts, Columbus, Ohio Standard Metropolitan Statistical Area* (Washington, D.C., 1983); *1990 Census of Housing: Population and Housing Characteristics for Columbus Ohio Standard Metropolitan Statistical Area* (Washington, D.C., 1992); *Ohio Metropolitan Areas and County Populations* (Columbus, Ohio, 1994); "Lancaster/Fairfield County Community Profile," Lancaster/Fairfield Chamber of Commerce, 1997; and Polk's *City Directory* of Lancaster (various years). An extensive list of early residents of Lancaster and Fairfield County is found in Patsy Kishler, "Who, What, When, and How of Immigration to Fairfield County, Ohio." A copy of this may be found in FCDL. Accounts of high-profile Lancastrians appear in various volumes of *Who's Who in America*, *Who Was Who in America*, *The Dictionary of American Biography*, and the *National Cyclopedia of American Biography*. Several of the nineteenth-century histories of Lancaster and Fairfield County, listed above, contain extensive biographical entries on local residents.

The local newspapers are essential sources for Lancaster and Lancastrians. The most important of these are the *Eagle*, established in 1807, and the *Gazette*, founded in 1826. These two newspapers, often at odds with one another over politics and other issues, merged in 1936 to form the *Lancaster Eagle-Gazette*, which continues to publish a daily newspaper. These newspapers form a central source for each of the chapters in this book, as the notes reveal. Several of the Columbus newspapers have also covered Lancaster events and people over the years, among them the *Ohio State Journal*, the *Columbus Dispatch*, the *Columbus Citizen*, and the *Columbus Citizen-Journal*. *Forbes* magazine carried an extensive and revealing story on Lancaster in its issue for November 15, 1947. On the role played by hometown newspapers, see Sally Foreman Griffith, *Home-Town News: William Allen White and the Emporia Gazette* (New York, 1989), and William Allen White, *Autobiography* (New York, 1946).

The ordinances and minutes of the Lancaster City Council proved to be very important sources, not only about local government but also about various individuals and events in the life of the town. Such records begin in 1859. Until the early twentieth century, the minutes and ordinances appeared together in the same volumes. After that they were set down in separate volumes.

Among pertinent studies of Ohio and of the Midwest are Andrew R. L. Cayton and Peter S. Onuf, *The Midwest and the Nation* (Bloomington, Ind., 1990); Henry Howe, *Historical Collections of Ohio* (Cincinnati, Ohio, 1908); Graham Hutton, *Midwest at Noon* (Chicago, 1946); Robert Leslie Jones, *History of Agriculture in Ohio to 1880* (Kent, Ohio, 1983); George W. Knepper, *Ohio and Its People* (Kent, Ohio, 1989); Lawrence J. Marzulli et al., *The Development of Ohio's Counties and Their Historic Courthouses* (Columbus, Ohio, n.d.); James Shortridge, *The Middle West: Its Meaning in American Culture* (Lawrence, Kans., 1989); and Clair C. Stebbens, *Ohio's Court Houses* (Columbus, Ohio, 1980).

On the architecture, furniture, and decorative arts of Ohio and the region, there are Richard V. Campen, *Ohio: An Architectural Portrait* (Chagrin Falls, Ohio, 1973); I. T. Frary, *Early Homes of Ohio* (New York, 1970); Donald A. Hutslar, "The Log Architecture of Ohio," *Ohio History*, Summer–Autumn 1971, pp. 172–269; Rexford Newcomb, *Architecture in the Old Northwest* (Chicago, 1950); Frank J. Roos Jr., "An Investigation of the Sources of Early Architecture in Ohio" (Ph.D. diss., Ohio State University, 1939); Catherine McQuaid Steiner and Bruce E. Steiner, *High Style and Vernacular: Ohio Furniture, Decorative Arts, and Craftsmen, 1800–1850* (n.p., 1988); and Charles Morse Stoltz, *The Early Architecture of Western Pennsylvania* (1936; reprint, Pittsburgh, 1996).

Concentrating on architecture, furniture, and the decorative arts in Lancaster itself are David R. Contosta, "Origins of Early Domestic Architecture in Lancaster, Ohio," *The Old Northwest*, Fall 1981, pp. 201–16; Ruth Drinkle, *Heritage of Architecture and Arts in Fairfield County, Ohio*, 2d ed. (Lancaster, Ohio, 1994); Dorothy Ent [Coleman], "Architectural Development of Early Lancaster, Ohio" (master's thesis, Ohio State University, 1945); and Whitney B. Tussing, "Early Housing in Lancaster, Ohio, 1800–1845" (master's thesis, Miami University, 1986). Of these works, Drinkle's is the most extensive and the most lavishly illustrated.

Works on American architectural and artistic styles that are helpful in interpreting Lancaster designs include Alan Axelrod, ed., *The Colonial Revival in America* (New York, 1985); David R. Contosta, "Philadelphia's Miniature Williamsburg: The Colonial Revival and Germantown's Market Square," *Pennsylvania Magazine of History and Biography*, October 1996, pp. 283–320; David P. Handlin, *The American Home: Architecture and Society, 1815–1915* (Boston, 1979); Donald A. Hutslar, *The Architecture of Migration: Log Cabin Construction in the Ohio Country, 1750–1850* (Athens, Ohio, 1986); Walter C. Kidney, *The Architecture of Choice* (New York, 1974); Calder Loth and Julius Trousdale Sadler Jr., *The Only Proper Style: Gothic Architec-*

*ture in America* (Boston, 1975); Karal Ann Marling, *George Washington Slept Here: Colonial Revivals and American Culture, 1976–1986* (Cambridge, Mass., 1988); and Kathleen Mahoney, *Gothic Style: Architecture and Interiors from the Eighteenth Century to the Present* (New York, 1995).

Helpful in reconstructing Lancaster's pioneer period are Randall Buchman, ed., *The Historic Indian in Ohio* (Columbus, Ohio, 1976); Andrew R. L. Cayton, *The Frontier Republic: Ideology and Politics in the Ohio Country, 1780–1825* (Kent, Ohio, 1986); Randolph Downes, *Frontier Ohio, 1788–1803* (Columbus, Ohio, 1935); John Jackel, *Images of the Ohio Valley: A Historical Geography of Travel* (New York, 1977); Richard Lyle Power, *Planting Corn Belt Culture: The Impress of the Upland Southerner and Yankee in the Old Northwest* (Indianapolis, 1953); John W. Reps, *Town Planning in Frontier America* (Columbia, Mo., 1980); and Erminie Wheeler-Voegelin and Helen Hornbeck Tanner, *Indians of Ohio and Indiana Prior to 1795*, 2 vols. (New York, 1974).

Historical context for Lancaster's canal- and railroad-building era appears in Carl Abbott, *Boosters and Businessmen: Popular Economic Thought and Urban Growth in the Antebellum Middle West* (Westport, Conn., 1981); Jack Gieck, *A Photo Album of Ohio's Canal Era, 1825–1913* (Kent, Ohio, 1988); Carter Goodrich et al., *Canals and American Economic Development* (New York, 1961); Harry N. Scheiber, *Ohio's Canal Era: A Case Study of Government and the Economy, 1820–1861* (Athens, Ohio, 1969); Ronald E. Shaw, *Canals for a Nation: The Canal Era in the United States, 1790–1860* (Lexington, Ky., 1990); George R. Taylor, *The Transportation Revolution, 1815–1860* (New York, 1968); and Frank Wilcox, *The Ohio Canals* (Kent, Ohio, 1969). Especially pertinent to railroads in Lancaster is Ivan M. Tribe, "Dream and Reality in Southern Ohio: The Development of the Columbus and Hocking Valley Railroad," *Old Northwest*, Winter 1978, pp. 337–57.

Works that give background for the Civil War period in Lancaster are Bernard Bailyn, *The Origins of American Politics* (New York, 1967); Lee Benson, "Ethnocultural Groups and Political Parties," in Felice A. Bodadio, ed., *Political Parties in American History, 1828–1890* (New York, 1974); Jack J. Detzler, "The Religion of General William Tecumseh Sherman," *Ohio History*, Winter 1966, pp. 26–34; Jeanne Innis, "Underground Railroad," *Zane Monthly*, April 1983, pp. 18–19; John H. Fenton, *Midwest Politics* (New York, 1966); Byron D. Fruehling and Robert H. Smith, "Subterranean Highways of the Underground Railroad in Ohio: An Architectural, Archaeological, and Historical Critique of Local Traditions," *Ohio History*, Summer–Autumn 1993, pp. 98–117; Robert S. Harper, *The Ohio Press in the Civil War* (Columbus, Ohio, 1964); Daniel Walker Howe, *The Political Culture of the American Whigs* (Chicago, 1979); Frank L. Klement, *The Copperheads in the Middle West* (Chicago, 1960), and *The Limits of Dissent: Clement L. Vallandingham and the Civil War* (Lexington, Ky., 1970); Paul Kleppner, *The Cross of Culture: A Social Analysis of Midwestern Politics, 1850–1900* (New York, 1970); Stephen E. Maizlish, *The Tri-*

umph of Sectionalism: The Transformation of Ohio Politics, 1844–1856 (Kent, Ohio, 1983); Donald J. Ratcliffe, "Politics in Jacksonian Ohio," Ohio History, Winter 1979, pp. 5–36; Henry Wilbur Siebert, The Mysteries of Ohio's Underground Railroads (Columbus, Ohio, 1951); Henry H. Simms, Ohio Politics on the Eve of Conflict (Columbus, 1964); John B. Weaver, "Ohio Republican Attitudes Towards Nativism, 1854–1855," Old Northwest, Fall 1983, pp. 289–306; and Grady Wood, The Hidden Civil War: The Story of the Copperheads (1942; reprint, New York, 1964).

Helpful biographies of Lancaster's most famous son and Civil War hero, William Tecumseh Sherman, are Michael Fellman, Citizen Sherman (New York, 1995); Stanley P. Hirshson, The White Tecumseh: A Biography of William Tecumseh Sherman (New York, 1997); John F. Marszalek, Sherman: A Soldier's Passion for Order (New York, 1993); and James M. Merrill, William Tecumseh Sherman (Chicago, 1971).

Of assistance with the Victorian period are Jacques Barzun, Classic, Romantic, and Modern (Chicago, 1961); Richard D. Brown, Modernization: The Transformation of American Life (Prospect Heights, Ill., 1988); David R. Contosta, Henry Adams and the American Experiment (Boston, 1980); David A. Gerber, Black Ohio and the Color Line, 1860–1915 (Urbana, Ill., 1976); Daniel Walker Howe, ed., Victorian America (Philadelphia, 1976); Paul Kleppner, The Cross of Culture: A Social Analysis of Midwestern Politics, 1850–1900 (New York, 1970); Stuart McConnell, Glorious Contentment: The Grand Army of the Republic, 1865–1900 (Chapel Hill, N.C., 1992); Colleen McDannell, The Christian Home in Victorian America, 1840–1900 (Bloomington, Ind., 1986), and Material Christianity: Religion and Popular Culture in America (New Haven, Conn., 1995); W. J. Rorabaugh, The Alcoholic Republic: An American Tradition (New York, 1979); Anthony E. Rotondo, American Manhood: Transformations of Masculinity from the Revolution to the Modern Era (New York, 1993); Thomas J. Schlereth, Victorian America: Transformations in Everyday Life (New York, 1991); and Rubin F. Westin, ed., Blacks in Ohio History (Columbus, 1976).

Helpful in viewing Lancaster life during the first half of the twentieth century in a broader framework are a number of titles: E. Digby Baltzell, The Protestant Establishment: Aristocracy and Caste in America (New York, 1964); Dominick Cavallo, Muscles and Morals: Organized Playgrounds and Urban Reform (Philadelphia, 1981); Ernst A. Breisach, American Progressive History: An Experiment in Modernization (Chicago, 1993); David M. Chalmers, Hooded Americanism: The History of the Ku Klux Klan (New York, 1981); Robert M. Crunden, Ministers of Reform: The Progressives' Achievement in American Civilization, 1889–1920 (New York, 1982); Allen Davis, Spearheads for Reform: The Social Settlement and the Progressive Movement, 1890–1914 (New York, 1967); Eldon J. Eisenbach, The Lost Promise of Progressivism (Lawrence, Kans., 1994); James Flink, America Adopts the Automobile, 1895–1910 (Cambridge, Mass., 1970); John W. Jeffries, War-Time America (Chicago, 1997); David M. Kennedy, Over Here: The First World War and American Society (New York, 1980);

Marc Raphael Lee, *Jews and Judaism in a Midwestern Community: Columbus, Ohio, 1840–1975* (Columbus, 1979); Gordon F. Lewis, "The Backgrounds and Careers of Small Businessmen in Lexington, Kentucky," in Edward Pessen, ed., *Three Centuries of Social Mobility in America* (New York, 1974), pp. 209–21; Ronald E. Marec, "The Fiery Cross: A History of the Ku Klux Klan in Ohio, 1920–1930" (master's thesis, Kent State University, 1967); John F. Marszalek, "The 1920s Ku Klux Klan in the Midwest," *Timeline*, March–April 1994, pp. 3–20; Ema Morawaska, *Insecure Prosperity: Small-Town Jews in Industrial America, 1870–1940* (Princeton, 1996); William L. O'Neill, *The Progressive Years: America Comes of Age* (New York, 1975); Landon Hoyt Warner, *Progressivism in Ohio, 1897–1917* (Columbus, Ohio, 1964); Marta Whitlock, ed., *Women in Ohio History* (Columbus, Ohio, 1976); and Allan M. Winkler, *Home Front U.S.A.* (Arlington Heights, Ill., 1988).

For Lancaster and vicinity during the early decades of the twentieth century, there are Kyle W. Armstrong, *An Appreciation of Buckeye Lake* (Coshocton, Ohio, 1952); Bill Blackbeard, ed., *R. F. Outcault's Yellow Kid: A Centennial Celebration of the Kid Who Started the Yellow Kid* (Northampton, Mass., 1995); J. A. Bownocker, "The Bremen Old Field," in *Geological Survey of Ohio*, Fourth Series, Bulletin 10 (Columbus, Ohio, October 1910); Donna Fisher Braig, *My Buckeye Lake Story: A Memorable History of "The Playground of Ohio"* (Millersport, Ohio, 1997); David R. Contosta, "Westward Ho with the Hazelton Family: Summer 1923," *FHQ*, Summer 1994, pp. 2–7; John L. Gushman, "Living Glass: The Story of the Anchor Hocking Glass Corporation," Newcomen Society (New York, 1965); "Lancaster Municipal Gas Works, 1888–1988" (Lancaster, Ohio, 1988); Charles Sawyer, *Concerns of a Conservative Democrat* (Carbondale, Ill., 1968); Agnes Moio, "Italian Immigration in Fairfield County," *Fairfield Trace*, Fall 1987, p. 65; Mary Elizabeth Thomas Soliday, *Through Three Wars and a Depression* (New York, 1974); and Van A. Snider, *Fairfield County in the World War* (Lancaster, Ohio, 1926).

Adding depth to Lancaster's post–World War II experience are John Bodnar, *Bonds of Affection: Americans Define their Patriotism* (Princeton, 1996); David Halberstam, *The Fifties* (New York, 1993); Douglas T. Miller, *On Our Own: Americans in the Sixties* (Lexington, Mass., 1996); and William L. O'Neill, *American High: The Years of Confidence, 1945–1960* (New York, 1986). On Malcolm Forbes, who launched his publishing career in Lancaster, see Christopher Winans, *Malcolm Forbes: The Man Who Had Everything* (New York, 1990). Fairfield County's famous glassblowing firm is chronicled in Ramona C. Knower and Franklin Knower, *Erickson Freehand Glass, 1943–1961* (New York, 1971). The best article on Henry Weaver Davidson is Armand Romano, "Henry Weaver Davidson: Inventor, Philosopher, Prophet," *Fairfield Monthly*, October 1984, pp. 30–32. The author has also drawn inspiration for this period from a yet unpublished memoir of growing up in postwar Lancaster, written in collaboration with Philip M. Hazelton.

For insight into how Lancaster's physical fabric has been shaped during the latter half of the twentieth century by powerful forces in American culture, see John Bodnar, *Remaking America: Public Memory, Commemoration, and Patriotism in the Twentieth Century* (Princeton, 1992); Barry Cullingsworth, *Planning in the USA: Policies, Issues, and Processes* (New York, 1997); Joel Garreau, *Edge City: Life on the New Frontier* (New York, 1988); Thomas W. Hanchett, "U.S. Tax Policy and the Shopping-Center Boom of the 1950s and 1960s," *American Historical Review*, October 1996, pp. 1082–110; Jane Kay Holtz, *Asphalt Nation: How the Automobile Took Over America and How We Can Take It Back* (New York, 1997); Thomas Hylton, *Save Our Land, Save Our Towns: A Plan for Pennsylvania* (Harrisburg, Penn., 1995); Kenneth T. Jackson, "All the World's a Mall: Reflections on the Social and Economic Consequences of the American Shopping Center," *American Historical Review*, October 1996, pp. 1111–21; Howard Kunstler, *The Geography of Nowhere: The Rise and Decline of America's Man-Made Landscape* (New York, 1993); Peter O. Muller, *Contemporary Suburban America* (Englewood Cliffs, N.J., 1981); Richard Moe and Carter Willkie, *Changing Places: Rebuilding Community in the Age of Sprawl* (New York, 1997); Esther Romeyn and Jack Kugelmass, "Community Festivals and the Politics of Memory: Postmodernity in the American Heartland," in Bertens and D'haen, eds., *The Small Town in America*, pp. 196–216; Pierce Lewis, "The Galactic Metropolis," in George Macinko and Rutherford H. Platt, eds., *Beyond the Urban Fringe: Land Uses of Nonmetropolitan America* (Minneapolis, 1983), pp. 23–49.

Proposals to vitalize Lancaster's downtown are Joseph G. Madonna, "Development Plan and Program, Central Business District, Lancaster Ohio," August 29, 1978; "Lancaster Comprehensive Downtown Revitalization Plan," 1994. Both of these studies are available at the FCDL.

# Index

Abolitionism, 57
African Americans, 15–16, 23, 237; and Burnt Corkers, 223–24; celebrate centennial of American independence, 123; and Civil War, 64; and Emancipation Proclamation, 65; mob violence against, 57–58; as percentage of population, 119–20, 173–74, 237; prejudice against, 65; segregation at Miller Park swimming pool, 174; segregation in residence, 120; segregation in restaurants, 174; segregation in schools, 96–97; social activities, 120; underground railroad, 58–59
African Methodist Episcopal (AME) Church, 16, 119
Air show (1912), 150–51
Air travel, 151
Akron, 18
Albert, Cy, 217
Alcohol: early problems with, 106–7; crusade against, 107–8; local production, 77, 106; prohibition, 161–63; regulation of sales, 107, 156; sanitarium for alcoholics, 107; Washington Temperance Society, 107
Alfred, Thomas, 241
Allegheny Quarry, 89, 127
Alleys, 22
Alspach, Bert, 172
Alt, Russell, 211
Alten, Henry, 77
Alten's Foundry, 77, 213, 255
Amanda, 29
American Electric Power (AEP), 257–58
American Legion, 136, 145, 207
American Literary Club, 164
American Party, 56

Anchor Cap Company, 128
Anchor Hocking: acquisition by Newell Company, 255–56; aerial photo of Plant 1, 255; downsizing in 1980s, 255–58; expansion in 1960s, 231; *Forbes* criticism of, 213–14; merger of Anchor Cap Co. and Hocking Glass, 188; offices in downtown Lancaster, 188–89; role in Hotel Lancaster, 190–92. *See also* Collins, Isaac J.
Annexation, of housing developments, 72, 80, 239
Anti-Catholicism, 56–57, 67–68, 171
Anti-Semitism, 175–76
Antislavery, 57
Arab oil boycott, 254
Architecture: Colonial influences, 29; Colonial Revival, 129, 136–37, 140, 147, 188–89, 192; destruction of, 242–43, 253; Federal style, 29, 41–42, 135, 139, 243, 247; Georgian influences, 29; Greek Revival style, 41–42, 139, 247; Italianate style, 82–83, 86, 243; Mansard style, 92, 243; Neoclassical, 29, 135; New England influences, 27–29; Pennsylvania influences, 25–27; preservation of, 243–53, 266–67, 273; regional origins of, 23–29; Renaissance Revival, 86–87; Romanesque style, 89, 92, 103; Roman Revival, 135; southern influences, 24–26; Virginia influences, 24
Arnsbarger, Betty, 247
Asiatic cholera, 45
Athens, Ohio, 38, 79, 236
Athletic Club, 136, 145
Automobiles: and decentralization, 269; first appearance in Lancaster, 131–34; and suburbanization, 230–63
Avondale development, 137

321

# INDEX

Baby boom, 218
Baltimore Pike, 74
Bandstand, Zane Square, 250
Bank Holiday (1933), 178
Bank One, 81
Baseball, 115–16, 149
Baughman, Leo, 253
Bauman, Andy, 87–88, 92, 118
Beach, Clark, 182–83, 185
Beck, Ralph, 211
Becker, Ernest, 77, 118
Becker Brewing Co., 77, 106, 125, 127
Beck's Knob, 154
Beecher, Philemon, 46–47
Beiter and Flege's Drug Store, 217
Belhorn, William, 169–70
Ben Butterfield Post, Grand Army of the Republic (GAR), 110, 120
Betz, Philip, 115
Bicentennial of the United States (1976), 249–50
Bicycling, 111–12
Big Bear supermarket, 189
"Big snow" of 1950, 229–30
Bishop Fenwick High School, 236. See also St. Mary School
Bismark Beer, 77
Blacks. See African Americans
Blaine, James G., 121–22
Blizzard of 1978, 254
B'nai Israel Synagogue, 176
Board of Trade, 98, 126–27
Bodenheimer, William, 19
Boeger, Carl, 207
Boerstler, George M., 108
Boy Scouts, 144, 160, 168–69
Boys' Industrial School (BIS), 98–99, 130, 146, 154–55, 225, 255
Branch campus. See Ohio University–Lancaster
Brasse, John T., 47
Bremen, 126–27, 215, 266
Bremen oil boom, 126–27
Brenner, William G., 160
Brick paving, streets and sidewalks, 157, 208
Brock-Utley House, 82
Brough, John, 47
Brown, Edward Merion, 116
Brown, J. E. (Jack), 218–19

Brown, Merrit H., 211
Bryan, William Jennings, 106, 122
Buckeye Lake, 151–54, 222; and Ku Klux Klan, 171–72. See also Buffalo Swamp; Licking Reservoir
Buckeye Lake Park, 152–53
Buckeye Lake Yacht Club, 153
Buffalo Swamp, 151. See also Buckeye Lake; Licking Reservoir
Building associations, 80–81
Burnt Corkers, 223–24
Buschmeyer, Frederick, 158–60
Busses: arrival of, 190–91; end of local service, 240
*Buster Brown* comic strip, 151
Butler, Ellwood, 211
Bypasses. See Highway bypasses; *and individual route numbers*

Camp Anderson, 60
Campground, Methodist, 105–6, 131
Camp Ki-Y-Ro, 144
Canals: construction, 34–39; demise, 72, 152; effects of, 39–40, 49–50; excursions on, 45; water power for mills, 40; water supply for Lancaster, 102–3
Canal Winchester, 131
Candlelight Ball, 224
Carpenter, Emanuel, Jr., 16, 22
Carpenter, Emanuel, Sr., 15, 21
Carpenter Addition, 22–23, 44, 137
Carroll, 38, 131
Catholics: opposition to, 56–57, 67–68; schools, 97–98, 171–72, 234–36; suburban parishes, 233–34
Cedar Heights School, 139
Census. See Population
Centennial of Lancaster (1900), 125–26
Centennial of the United States (1876), 123
Central Labor Union, 179–80
Chamber of Commerce, 127
Chesapeake and Ohio Railroad, 71
Children's Home, 98
Chillicothe, compared to Lancaster, 14, 18, 24, 39, 49, 51, 79, 193
Chillicothe Turnpike Co., 18, 37, 39
Christmas Rocks, 113, 154
Cincinnati, 193
Cincinnati, Wilmington, and Zanesville Railroad, 50, 70

# INDEX

323

Cinema. *See* Movie theaters
Circleville, compared to Lancaster, 16, 29, 37, 39, 49, 50–51, 66, 79, 193
City Drive-In, 240
City Federation of Women's Literary Clubs, 163
City Hall: first, 52, 86, 94; second, 88–90, 94
Civilian Conservation Corps (CCC), 178
Civil War: as experienced by local residents, 53–68; last surviving veterans, 226; local memory of, 267–68; southern origins of residents, 15, 54–55, 66
Civil War monument, 120–21
Clark, P. L., 146
Claspill, Robert, 19
Class. *See* Social class/stratification
Clay, Henry, 56
Cleveland, 18, 193
Clock Restaurant, 217
Coal: 45; mines in Hocking County, 45, 71; used for fuel, 45
Cobb, Henry Ives, 89
Cold Spring Hill, 12, 38, 40, 232
Cold Spring Reservoir, 40, 72, 232
Cold War, 227–28
Coleman, Dorothy Ent, 246
Coliseum, failure to construct, 222
Collins, Isaac J.: background, 128–29; death, 256; and demolition of Effinger House, 191, 246; described in *Forbes* magazine, 211; and downtown office of Anchor-Hocking, 188; and *Eagle-Gazette*, 185; and election of 1932; founder of Hocking Glass, 128–29; and Hotel Lancaster, 191; residence, 139. *See also* Anchor Hocking Glass; Hocking Glass
Collins, Lillian (Mrs. Isaac J.), 128
Colonial Revival architecture and influences, 29, 129, 136–37, 140, 147, 188–89, 192
Columbus, xv, 16–18, 29, 49–51, 79, 193; expansion toward Pickerington, 262–63; Lancaster as edge city to, 260–62; railroad connections to, 71; relation to Buckeye Lake, 152–53; Route 33 as highway to, 231; telegraph connection to, 50
Columbus, Buckeye Lake, and Newark Traction, 152. *See also* Interurban rail lines
Community identity: and "big snow" of 1950, 229; and Buckeye Lake, 154; downtown as symbol of, 134–36, 201, 230, 273;

erosion of, 236, 269; and flood of 1948, 228; and football, 220; and *Forbes* magazine feature on Lancaster, 210–14; and galactic metropolis, 266; and *Green Grass of Wyoming*, 205; and historic preservation, 273; and movies, 149; and Orchid Award, 187; and pedestrian scale of town, 217, 273; rites of, 68; schools as reinforcement for, 98; Victorian period, 124; and walking town, 217, 236; weakened by exclusive clubs, 147. *See also* Parades; Sesquicentennial
Compulsory education law, 140
Conservatism, 54–55, 64, 196–97, 270–71
Consumer's Carbon Co., 128
Contosta, Betty J. Mowry, 199
Contosta, Miles R., 199
Cook, Lewis, 210
Copperheads, southern sympathizers in Civil War, 66–68, 267
Cornell, Benjamin, 37
Council, city and village, 32, 106–7
Council of National Defense, World War I, 169
Country Club, 144–46, 155
Courthouse: first, 23–24, 85–86; second, 85–86
Courtright, Thurman T., 149
Cox-Hunter-Welsh House, 42
Creed, John M., 47, 82, 107
Creed-Tallmadge-Nusser House, 82–83
Crime, 31, 115–16, 155–56, 224
Crystal Ball Room, Buckeye Lake Park, 153
Crystal Pool, Buckeye Lake Park, 153

"Darling Nelly Gray," 58
Daughters of the American Revolution (DAR), Elizabeth Sherman Reese Chapter, 147, 165
Davidson, Henry Weaver, 225–26
Dayton, 18
Deeds Mill, 127
Deep Cut, 37, 39–40. *See also* Buckeye Lake
Deitrich, Jacob, 15
Delancy, Edward, 146
Democratic Party: Civil War, 64–68; Depression, 195–96; and Ku Klux Klan, 172–73; majority party in Lancaster and Fairfield County, 54–55, 121–22; majority status lost, 122, 196–97; and Prohibition,

Democratic Party (*continued*)
  162–63; states' rights party, 54, 122, 196–97; supported by *Eagle*, 55–57, 195
Denny, J. L., 140
Depression (1930s), 177–97
DeVol-Dallow-Anchor Hocking House, 42–43
Diamond Power Specialty Corporation, 214, 218, 250
Diamond Unity Management Club, 250
Dickey, Edmund, 130
Disneyland, 242
Douglas, Lloyd C., 147–48
Downtown Area Rehabilitation Effort (DARE), 252
Downtown Business Association, 251
Downtown Lancaster: and the automobile, 134; busses in, 190–91; community center, 134–36; decline of, 236, 242–43, 253; description, by *Forbes* magazine, in 1947, 212–13; description in 1880s, 84–85; description in 1950s, 217; first electric lighting, 157; gas lamps, 45; parade route, 59–61, 68, 141, 169–70, 172, 190, 200, 220, 226, 236; paving of, 157; pedestrian scale of, 241; revitalization of, 251–53, 264–65, 273; trolleys in, 93; view in 1846, 44; wooden construction prohibited in, 156. *See also* Main Street
Dreamland movie theater, 149
Drinkle, Charles, 144, 194, 244–45
Drinkle, Henry Clay, 194
Drinkle, Ruth Wolfley, 243–47
Drive-in movies, 240
Dungan, Rev. Irvine L., 168
Durdin, L. C., 238–39
Dust storm (1934), 178

*Eagle*: and Civil War, 64–67; early advertisements in, 19; and Godman Shoe strike, 182; merger with *Gazette*, 185–88; supporter of Democratic Party, 55, 195
*Eagle-Gazette*: anti-union, 187–88; criticized by *Forbes* magazine, 213; favorable view of Anchor Hocking, 187; merger with *Eagle*, 185–88; Orchid Award, 187; Parade of Progress Edition (1940), 193; Sesquicentennial Edition (1950), 209–10. *See also* Kerr, R. Kenneth; Sawyer, Charles
Eagle Machine Works, 73
Eagle Park, 150
Eagles Lodge, 144
East End, 137, 139
East End Natural Gas Co., 75
Eastern Addition, 42
Eastland Shopping Mall, Columbus, 241
East Main Street, as shopping strip, 232
East School, 95, 139, 168
Eck, Charles, 180
Edge city, 6, 259–63, 265–66
Effinger, Michael, 58, 145
Effinger, Samuel, 16, 19, 26–27, 47, 58
Effinger House, 26–27, 58, 135–36; demolition of, 191, 246
Elections: 1860, 59; 1864, 67; 1868–96, 121–22; 1899–1944, 194–96
Electricity, first available in Lancaster, 157
Elks Club, 144, 150
Elmwood Cemetery, 100
Emancipation Proclamation, local reaction to, 64–65
Emanuel Lutheran Church, 105, 176
Engine House I, 103
English Lutheran Church, 42, 102
"Epic of Standing Stone" (1950), 208–9
Epstein Shoes, 176
Epsy, Josiah, 18
Equitable Federal Savings and Loan, 81, 253
Erickson, Carl, 215
Erickson, Steve, 215
Ericksonware, 215
Etta Kett Day, 193, 206
Ewing, Hugh, 47
Ewing, Maria Boyle (Mrs. Thomas), 62, 121
Ewing, Mary Eleanor, 116
Ewing, Philemon B., 116
Ewing, Thomas: death, 117; foster father of William T. Sherman, 62; political career, 46; residence, 25–26; speech at groundbreaking for Ohio and Erie Canal, 37; wealthy investor and entrepreneur, 71
Ewing, Thomas, Jr., 47
Ewing House, 25–26
Eyman, Hubert, Sr., 172–73

Fair. *See* Fairfield County Fair
Fairfield County, 14, 16–17; boundaries of, 32; establishment of, 31–32; purchase of railroad stock, 50

Fairfield County Agricultural Society, 52, 511. *See also* Fairfield County Fair; Fairgrounds
Fairfield County District Library, 27, 138, 256. *See also* Public Library
Fairfield County Fair, 52–53, 93, 109–11, 198, 220–21, 266
Fairfield County Historical Society, 249
Fairfield County Infirmary, 99–100
Fairfield County Orphans Home, 98
Fairfield Federal Savings and Loan, 81, 145, 253
Fairfield Garden Club, 164–65, 198
Fairfield Heritage Association, 243–49
*Fairfield Heritage Quarterly*, 247
Fairfield Homes, 238
Fairfield Industries, 180
Fairfield National Bank, 118, 134, 159
Fairfield Paper and Container Co., 130. *See also* Gaylord Container Co.
Fairfield School for Boys (FSB), 255. *See also* Boys' Industrial School; State Farm
Fairgrounds: air show (1912), 150–51; Bicentennial of U.S., 250; Camp Anderson in Civil War, 60; Centennial of U.S., 123; coliseum proposal for, 222; and *Green Grass of Wyoming*, 203–4; grounds expanded, 111; historic buildings in, 249; horse racing by gaslight, 76; and Ku Klux Klan rally, 172; proposal to build a new Lancaster High School in, 234. *See also* Fairfield County Fair
Family Y (YMCA/YWCA), 222
Farmers and Citizens Bank, 135
Farmland, destruction of, 263, 270
Federal Housing Administration (FHA), 236–37
Federal style architecture, 29, 41–42, 135, 139, 243
Ferguson, William, 27
Ferguson-Furniss House, 27–28
Fire department, first professional force in 1893, 103
Fireworks prohibited, 156
First Church of Christ Scientist, 105
First Methodist Church, 105
First Presbyterian Church, 105, 107, 168, 223
Fisher, Jack, 211
Fisher, William V., 184–85, 188, 191–92, 236
Flat Rocks, 102, 154
Floods, 228–29

Flu (1918), 169
Football, Lancaster High School, 149–50, 220
Forbes, Malcolm, 210–11, 213
*Forbes* magazine, feature on Lancaster (1947), 210–14
Foreign-born residents, Lancaster and Fairfield County, 118–19, 173, 175–76
*Forest Rose*, 12, 158, 209
Forest Rose Avenue, 12
Forest Rose Beer, 13
Forest Rose Cemetery, 12, 100–102, 137, 154, 226
Forest Rose Flour, 13
Foster, Frederick A., 37
Foul language law suits, 156
Fountain: erected in Zane Square, 87–89; park around, 135; threat to demolish during World War II, 198
Fountain Committee, 87–88
Fountain Square. *See* Zane Square
Fourth of July celebrations, 29–30, 38, 45, 76, 123, 250
Franco-Prussian War, 123
Frankenberg Brothers, 127
Fresh Air Camp, 161
Friesner, Eva, 216
Froeble Study Club, 163
Frontier town, xv–xvi; Lancaster as, 9, 32
Front porches, 240, 269
Front Street, 21. *See also* Memorial Drive; Route 33
Fugitive Slave Act, 58
Fuller, Ruth B., 178
Fulton, Cyrus L., 192, 234
Fulton, Thomas C., 188
Fulton Field, 234
Furniss, John F., 245
Furniss, Marian, 245

Galactic metropolis, 266
Gallagher's Drug Store, 217
Gambling prohibited, 156
Garaghty, Michael, 48
Garaghty-Mumaugh House, 27, 245; bequest to the City of Lancaster, 246
Garden Club, 164–65, 198
Garreau, Joel, 259–60
Gaslight: illuminated arch, 76–77; street lamps, 76–77

# INDEX

Gates, James, 48
Gay-Fad Studios, 214
Gaylord Container Co., 215. *See also* Fairfield Paper and Container Co.
*Gazette*: anti-Catholic biases of, 56–57; and Civil War, 64–67; opposition to Godman strike, 182–83; purchased by Hocking Glass, 185; supporter of Republican Party, 64, 195; and Whig Party, 55–56
Geer, Constance, 224
Geer, Joseph, accused of murder, 224
General Mills, 231, 255
General Sherman Junior High School, 219
General Welfare Association, 177
Geology, of Lancaster and Fairfield County, 10–11
Georgian (Maccracken House), 24, 41–42, 58; restoration of, 247–49; as tea room and gift shop, 247
German influences in Lancaster and Fairfield County, 15, 18, 81, 118, 123, 168, 173
German Lutheran Church, 102
Getz, Albert, 77, 118, 127; Lancaster's last living Civil War veteran, 226
Getz Shoe factory, 77, 127, 189
Giani's Wine House, 45
Giesy, H. H., 60–61, 63, 145
Glaciers, 10–11
Glassco, 185
Glimcher, David, 258
Godman, Henry C., 127
Godman Shoe factories, 127, 189, 199, 214; strike in 1934, 180–83, 209
Goetz, Caroline Bauman, 113–14
Goetz, Von S., 146
Goetz, William, 113–14
Good, Edward B., 128
Gorsuch, Frank, 238
Goslin, Charles, 245–47
Government regulation, opposition to, 54–55, 64, 196–97, 270–71
Grace Reformed Church, 105; move to suburbs, 234
Grand Army of the Republic (GAR), 144–45, 169; encampment in Lancaster (1902), 145
Grant, Juanita, 223
Greek Revival architecture, 41–42, 139
Greene, Jacob, 37
Greenfield Volunteers, 30

*Green Grass of Wyoming*, 201–5
Griffey, C. H., 179
Griggs, Charles, 207, 226
Ground Observer Corps, 227
Growth boundaries, 270–71
Grubb, Joseph, 48

Hanby, Benjamin, 58
Hanby, Rev. William, 58
Hannan, Kelly, 232
Hansel, George, 180
Harbor Hills, Buckeye Lake, 153
Harrison, Avery, 253
Harrison Avenue shopping district, 138
Hartman, Absalom, 194
Hatcher, Fred, 207
Hazelton, Henson M., 133–34
Hazelton, Lillian P., 133
Hazelton, Perrin (Pel), 133–34, 197–98, 206–7, 210
Hazelton, Virginia Mowry, 207
Heiston, Lewis N., Fairfield County's last surviving Civil War veteran, 227
Herman Manufacturing, 189, 213
Hickle, George M., 146
Hickle's department store, 215–16; closing of, 253
Hickson, Dean, 156
Highway bypasses, proposed, 231, 241, 262, 271
Hillside Hotel, 112–14; demolished, 243
Hippodrome movie theater (later the Liberty), 148–49
Historical consciousness, 125–26, 205–11, 243–50, 266–68
Historic Lancaster District, 250–52
Historic preservation, 243–53, 266–67, 273
Hocking Glass: establishment of, 128–29; fire of 1924, 177; Glassco activities, 185; Depression, 179; Italians attracted by jobs at, 175; purchase of *Gazette*, 185; sponsorship of Labor Day Picnic, 184; support from *Eagle-Gazette*, 187; unionization of, 183–84; and West Side, 137–39. *See also* Anchor Hocking Glass; Collins, Isaac J.
Hocking Hills: beauty of, 102, 222; and Civilian Conservation Corps, 178; railroad excursions to, 71
Hocking River/Valley: boundary to West Side, 138; and canal, 38, 40, 45; flooding

# INDEX

of, 228–29; ice skating on, 144; as industrial corridor, 84; swimming in, 144; as transportation corridor, 10
Hocking Valley Bank, 49, 76, 134
Hocking Valley Bridge Works, 73, 127
Hocking Valley Canal, 38–40, 45, 82
Hocking Valley Manufacturing, 73, 76, 127, 213
Hocking Valley Railroad, 70–73, 79, 271; excursions into Hocking Hills, 72; local investors in, 71
Homeownership, 212
Hooker Station, 131
Hop Company, 79; land used for new housing, 79–80
Horsecars, 92–93
Hospital, Ewing Street, 165
Hospital, Park Street, 164–65
Hotel Lancaster, 27, 190–91; and *Green Grass of Wyoming*, 203–5
Hotel Martens, 92, 135; demolished, 243
House, W. H., 146
Housing developments, 22–23, 72, 79, 81–84, 137–39, 212, 238–40, 262
Howe, Fannie, 161
Howe, Flora, 161
Howe, Mark, 31
Howe, Samuel, 31
Howe's Academy, 30–31, 122
Huffer-Durdin Addition, 239
Hunter, Hocking, 47, 68, 117
Hunter, Joseph, 16
Hutsler, Donald, 226
Hutsler, Sam, 202, 226
Hyde, Simon, 58

Incorporation of Lancaster: as city (1851), 51; as village (1831), 32
Indians. *See* Native Americans
Industrial parks, 231, 258
Industrial revolution, 127
Industry, 40, 84, 125–30, 212–15, 255–56
Influenza epidemic (1918), 169
International Order of Odd Fellows, 110
Interstate Route 70, 49, 263
Interurban rail lines, 130–31, 146, 152, 271
Irish, in Lancaster, 118
Irvin, William W., 47
Irving Drew Shoes, 189, 213, 231
Italianate architecture, 82–83, 86–87, 243

Italians, in Lancaster, 175

J. A. Arney Foundry and Machine Shop, 73
Jacob's Ladder, 114, 154
Jerry Maher's restaurant and bar, 149–50, 217
Jessup, Virginia, 204
Jews, in Lancaster, 175–77
Jimmy's Drive-In, 240–41
Joyce, Thomas, 179, 183–84, 211
Judson, A. M., 178
Jurgensmier, Gotlieb (Jergy), 116
Juvenile delinquency, 116, 144, 225

Kelly and Bush Ice Cream Saloon, 45
Kerr, Laura, 247
Kerr, R. Kenneth: and *Eagle-Gazette* merger, 185–87; and flood of 1948, 228; and *Forbes* magazine, 211; *Green Grass of Wyoming*, 201–5; and Hotel Lancaster, 192; Lancaster booster, 186; and Sesquicentennial Edition of *Eagle-Gazette*, 209–10
Kinkead Hill, 161
Kiwanis Club, 144–45
Knights of Pythias, 110
Korean War, 227
Kridelbaugh, John E., 19
Kreider, M. Z., 107
Kuhn, Mary Alice Drinkle, 243
Ku Klux Klan: Lancaster and Fairfield County, 170–73; and local politics, 172–73, 194; rally in Lancaster (1924), 172

Labor Day, 184
Labor unions, 179–85
Ladies' Benevolent Society, 109
Lake Breeze Hotel, Buckeye Lake, 152
Lancaster: early government, 32; incorporation as city (1851), 51; incorporation as village (1831), 32; origin of name, 15, 21. *See also* Downtown Lancaster; Main Street
Lancaster, Pa., and Lancaster, Ohio, 15, 20
Lancaster Academy, 30, 87
Lancaster Athletic Club, 136, 145
Lancaster bar (legal profession), 45–47
Lancaster Country Club, 144–46, 155
Lancaster Drug Store, 44
Lancaster Electric Light Company, 157
Lancaster Electric Railroad, 93
Lancaster Electro Plating, 214, 231

Lancaster Festival, 266
Lancaster Glass, 215, 231. *See also* Lancaster Lens
Lancaster Guards, 59–60
Lancaster Gun Club, 110
Lancaster High School: addition of 1931, 142; after-school soda fountains, 217; assault on principal by superintendent, 156; community identification with, 143–44; early years of, 95–96; football, 149–50, 220; girls smoking at, 116; Homecoming, 220; move to Route 37 location, 234–35; Mulberry Street building, 140–42; nostalgia about, 143–44; rally at U.S. declaration of war (1917), 168; unsuccessful campaign for new high school in 1920s, 141–42
Lancaster Hop Co., 79
Lancaster Institute, 47
Lancaster Iron and Shovel Works, 73
Lancaster Lateral Canal, 37–41, 45, 47
Lancaster Lens, 129–30, 183, 213, 215. *See also* Lancaster Glass
Lancaster Literary (women's club), 109
Lancaster Military Band, 123
Lancaster Mould Company, 213
Lancaster National Bank, 135
Lancaster Natural Gas Company, 75–77
Lancaster Ohio Bank, 18, 37, 46, 48
Lancaster Street Railroad (horsecars), 92–93
Lanz, Charles, 250
Last Chance Saloon, 162
"Last Round Up," of trolleys, 190
Lawyers, early, 45–47
Layton, S. H., trial for assault, 156
Licking Summit, 37, 39
Licking Reservoir, 37. *See also* Buckeye Lake; Buffalo Swamp
Lincoln, Abraham: criticized by *Eagle*, 64; denounced as dictator, 64, 66; mourning at death of, 68
Lithopolis, 16, 29
Little Italy, Lancaster, 175
lodges, for men, 108–9, 144–45
Logan, 16
Loroco Industries, 213
Lyric movie theater, 149; as "last picture show" downtown, 253

Maccracken, Samuel F., 19, 37, 41–42, 47, 247–49

M'Crellis, Elizabeth, 31
M'Crellis, Thomas, 31
McIntire, John B., 13
McNaughton, Roy, 173
McNeil, Robert, 47–48
McNeil-Peters-Reynolds House, 82
Madonna, Joseph C., 252
Madonna Planning Report, 252
Maher, Jerry, 128, 149, 150, 217; friend of I. J. Collins, 128
Main Street: description in 1920s, 134–35; parade route, 59–61, 68, 76, 122–24, 141, 169–70, 172, 190, 200, 220, 226, 236; paving of, 157; untidy appearance in 1874, 86–87. *See also* Downtown Lancaster
Majestic movie theater, 149
Mansard style in architecture, 92, 243
Mansfield, 18
Manson's, 253
Maple Street Addition, 80–81
Marietta, 49
Market House: first, 20, 52, 88; second, 135, 176
Martens, Charles, 92
Martens, McClelland, 92, 146
Martin, Emilie, 245
Martin, George, 245
Martin, John D., 47, 63, 71–72
Masonic Lodge, 110
Masonic Temple, 108
Mast, Jimmy, 240
Matlack, Samuel, 25
Matlack-Burns-Roche House, 42
Matlack House, 25
Medill, William, 47, 117
Melish, John, 18
Memorial Day, 226–27
Memorial Drive, 40; congestion on, 262; as corridor through edge city, 258; named in 1948, 232. *See also* Route 33
Methodist Campground, 105–6, 131
Methodist Church: First Methodist Church, 105; Sixth Avenue Methodist Church, 138
Middle Atlantic states, influences on Lancaster and Fairfield County, 14–15
Midland Screw Corp., 215
Miesse, Gabriel, 151
Miller, Clarence E., 231, 256
Miller, Fred, 180

# INDEX

329

Miller, Frederick, 160
Miller, Marilyn, 211–12, 216–17
Miller Park, 160, 184
Millersport, 39–40, 266
Millersport Sweet Corn Festival, 266
Minority population, 237. *See also* African Americans; Foreign-born residents
Mithoff, George, 71
Mithoff, Theodore, 75–76, 118
Mithoff House, 76
Mokena Mill, 127
Monticello, lost village of, 39–40
Moore, Charles E., 181
Moose Lodge, 144
Morgan's Raiders, panic in Lancaster over, 61
Mount Pleasant, 10, 12, 52, 60, 102, 137, 150, 158, 222
Mount Pleasant Guards, 110, 124
Mount Pleasant Natural Gas Co., 75
Movie theaters: clergy against Sunday movies, 149; effects on traffic patterns, 149; list of, 148–49; premier of *Green Grass of Wyoming*, 204–5; in World War II, 198
Mulberry Hill, 84, 129, 264
Mumaugh House. *See* Garaghty-Mumaugh House
Mumaugh, John R., 71, 246
Mumaugh, Mary Francis (Fannie), 246
Muncie, Indiana, 2; compared to Lancaster, 256
Municipal Gas Works, 76–77, 88

National Recovery Administration (NRA), 184
National Road, 49
Native Americans, 11–12
Nativism, 57
Natural gas, discovered at Lancaster, 74–76
Nelsonville, 45, 71
Newark: compared to Lancaster, 29, 37, 39, 41, 49, 51, 79, 86, 193; connections to Buckeye Lake, 153; as football rival, 150
New Deal, local criticism of, 209
New England states, influences on Lancaster and Fairfield County, 14–15, 27, 54
New Lancaster, 15, 21
New Straitsville, 72
Noble, John W., 19, 47–48

North End, 131, 137, 139, 161, 219
North Field, 150, 220
North School, 94–97, 139, 150, 208
Northwestern Addition, 42
Northwest Ordinance of 1787, 16
Northwest Territory, 31
Numbering of houses and buildings required, 157

*Ohio Adler, Der*, 15, 18. *See also Eagle;* German influences
Ohio Flint Glass, 128, 137
Ohio Stage Co., 44
Ohio University–Lancaster: establishment of, 236–37; and Lancaster Festival, 266; Turner collection of pioneer artifacts, 249
Oktoberfest, Bremen, 266
Old Bill Bailey's, 224
"Old Man Himself" (gas well), 76
Olds, Edson B., 66–68, 209, 267
Opera House, 91–92, 111–12, 147–48
Orchid Award (*Eagle-Gazette*), 187
Orman, Henry, 86
Osbourne, Lillie Bookwalter, 245
Osbourne, Milton, 245
Outcault, Mary Jane Martin, 151
Outcault, Richard Fenton, 151

Palace movie theater: and "big snow" of 1950, 229; building of, 149; robbery of 1932, 155; world premier of *Green Grass of Wyoming*, 204–5
Panic of 1837, 48–49
Panic of 1857, 51
Panic of 1893, 77–79
Parade of Progress (1940), 192–93; compared to Sesquicentennial of 1950, 206
Parades, 59–61, 68, 76, 88, 111, 122–24, 141, 169–70, 172, 190, 193, 200, 205, 220, 226, 236
Parks, 157–60, 271–72
Park Street Hospital, 164–65
Paving of streets, 157
Pennsylvania, influence on Lancaster and Fairfield County, 25–27
Pennsylvania Railroad, 50, 70, 79
Peter, Herman, 115
Peters, Dorothy Bell Whiley, 234
Peters, Emma Idelle Rising, 118

INDEX

330

Peters, Henry B., 118, 127, 145–46, 245
Peters, Henry Charles, 234
Peters, Philip Rising, 146, 211, 234
Philadelphia, Pa., influences on Lancaster, 20–22, 54
Phillips, J. J., 141
Phoenix Hotel, 44
Pickerington, 29; as edge city, 263; rapid growth of, 262
Pier Ballroom, Buckeye Lake, 153
Pioneer Addition, 138
Pioneer artifacts, Turner Collection, 249
Planning reports, on downtown, 251–52
Plan of Lancaster (original), 9, 20–23
Plaza Shopping Center, 232
Police, rudimentary force established, 32
Police call boxes, 157
Politics, 54–57, 59, 121–22, 194–97; shift from Democrats to Republicans, 196–97. See also Conservatism; Democratic Party; Republican Party
Pollution, 269
Popular entertainments, 29–30, 111, 144, 147, 152–55, 220–24
Population, 18, 48–49, 51, 78–79, 130, 193, 212, 217–18, 237, 260, 263, 264
Poverty, 263–64
Presbyterian Church. See First Presbyterian Church
Prichard's Restaurant, 217
Princess movie theater, 149, 207
Prizefighting, 111–12
Progressive Businessmen's Association, 241
Prohibition, 161–63
Public Library, 89, 94. See also Fairfield County District Library
Public Square, 85–88, 120–21. See also Zane Square
Purcell, L. H., 156
Purvis, J. E., 126–27

Quota Club, 193

Race riot (1848), 57–58
Racial segregation, 96–97, 120, 174–75; not a cause of suburbanization in Lancaster, 237. See also African Americans
Racing by gaslight, at fairgrounds, 76
Railroads, 50–51, 70–73; passenger service discontinued (1949), 240; Union Station, 93–94
Rainbow Division, World War I, 168, 170
Ralston Purina, 255
Rat hunts, 111–12
Ray-O-Vac Battery, 189, 213
RBM, 214
RBM Building, 127, 180. See also Godman Shoe factories
Reber, John, 52
Reed and Walters Drug Store, 114, 253
Reed's Total Discount, 252–53
Reese, Mary Elizabeth Sherman, 118, 147
Reese, William J., 47–48, 118, 159
Reese-Mattox-Rockwood House, 42
Reese-Peters House, 25, 42, 116, 159; donated as decorative arts museum, 266–67
Regional influences, on Lancaster and Fairfield County. See Middle Atlantic states; New England states; Southern states
Regional planning, need for, 271
Religious denominations, 30, 105
Religious revivals, 30, 106
Repass, H. L., 168
Republican Party: and Civil War, 64–68; and election of 1860, 59; Gazette support for, 55, 57; and Ku Klux Klan, 172–73; local majority party, 194–97; local minority party, 121–22; and Prohibition, 192–93; and respectability, 197
Rinehart, Forest, 199
Rinehart, Ruth Contosta, 199
Rising, George P., 145
Rising, Philip, 118, 159–60
Rising Park, 158–60, 205
Riven Rock, 154
River Valley Mall, 258–62
Rock Mill Industrial Park, 258
Rockwood, Caroline Peters, 245
Roe, Eugene Oscar, 197
Romanesque architecture, 89, 92, 103
Roosevelt recession, 188–89
Rosebank development, 82–83, 205
Rosedale development, 238
Rotary Club, 144–45, 160
Route 22 (U.S.), 82, 98, 133; bypass proposed, 231, 241; development along, 231, 232
Route 33 (U.S.), 40; bypass proposed, 262, 271; commercial strip along, 232; "expressway," 231; River Valley Mall, 258

Route 37 (Ohio): high schools move to, 234–35; Ohio University–Lancaster, 236
Route 40 (U.S.), 49
Route 256 (Ohio), 263
Rural Electrification Administration (REA), 178
Rushville, 29, 58
Rutherford, Edward, 250, 257–58

St. Bernadette Roman Catholic Church, 234
St. John's Episcopal Church, 24, 42, 105
St. Mark Roman Catholic Church, 233
St. Mary Roman Catholic Church, 105, 116, 175, 233
St. Mary School, 97–98, 139, 142–43, 217. *See also* Bishop Fenwick High School; William V. Fisher Catholic High School
St. Peter's Lutheran Church, 95, 104–5
Salvation Army, 177
Sanderson, George, 16, 30, 48, 55, 106
Saunders, Holly, 174
Saunders, Kenneth, 174
Schofield, Elnathan, 37, 47
School bond issues: in 1920s, 141–42; in 1950s, 218–19, 234
Schools: Catholic schools, 97–98, 139, 142–43, 217, 236; community identification with, 143–44; consolidation of county schools, 219; Depression, 178, 189; early private schools, 30–31; expansion in 1950s and 1960s, 218–220; failed attempt to build new high school in 1920s, 140–42; half-day sessions, 218; nostalgia about, 97, 143–44; projected enrollments for 1998–2003, 264; public schools established, 31; racial segregation in, 96–97; suburban relocations, 234–36; during Victorian period, 94–98; and wartime harvests (1943), 198. *See also individual schools by name*
Scioto River, 14
Scioto Valley Traction Co., 130–31. *See also* Interurban rail lines
Screening committee, for African American residents, 174
Segregation. *See* African Americans; Racial segregation
Seifert, Myron T., 210
Selby, Joseph, 58

Sesler, Gail, 181
Sesquicentennial (1950), xvii, 205–10
Sesquicentennial Ball, 201
Sesquicentennial Edition of *Eagle-Gazette*, 209–10
Shaner, Charles, 180
Sharp Quarry, 127
Shaw's Restaurant and Inn, 27. *See also* Hotel Lancaster
Shelter House, Rising Park, 159
Sheridan Drive development, 232
Sherman, Charles Robert, 27, 46–47, 61–62
Sherman, Ellen Ewing (Mrs. William T.), 62–63, 117
Sherman, John, 27, 47, 117, 122
Sherman, Mary Hoyt, 61
Sherman, Rev. Thomas, S.J., 148
Sherman, William Tecumseh: birthplace, 27–28; childhood and youth, 61–62; Civil War general, 61, 63; commemorations of, 267; contrast to Edson B. Olds, 66–67, 267; death of, 117; in "Epic of Standing Stone," 209; foster child of Ewing family, 62; junior high school named for, 219; marriage to Ellen Ewing, 62–63; religious views of, 62–63; Sherman Armory, 67, 135, 168; statue of, 267; visit to Lancaster, Christmas 1863, 63
Sherman Armory, 135, 168; as exhibition hall, 193, 206
Sherman House, 27–28, 67; museum, 249
Sherman Light Guards, 110
Sherman-Sheridan Highway, 133
Sidewalks, mandated by council, 157
Sifford, Daniel, 42, 52
Sifford and Son Drug Store, 116
Sixth Avenue Methodist Church, 138
Skyview Cruise-In, 240
Slavery, attitudes toward, 57–59
Smith, Alice M. Stover, xvii
Smith, Benson D. (Ben), 224
Smith, Edson B. Olds, xvii, 67, 74, 76, 82, 110, 113, 145
Smith, Irvine, 245
Smith, Mary Peters (Petie), 245
Smith, Nelson, 58
Smith, Scipio (Scipio Africanus), 16, 58
Smith-Van Gundy House, 82
Soap Box Derby, 222
Social class/stratification: Buckeye Lake,

Social class/stratification (*continued*)
152–54; clubs and organizations, 47–48, 145–47, 155; family, 19, 118; historic preservation, 245, 249; income, 263–64; leisure time, 112–13; neighborhoods as basis for, 23, 41, 84, 137–39; occupation, 19, 46–48, 118–19; political respectability, 197; recreation, 112–15; schools, 139, 219; weddings, 116–17. *See also* Anti-Catholicism; Anti-Semitism; Racial segregation
Social Reading Club, 109
Society news, 155, 223
Southeastern Ohio Correctional Institution, 255. *See also* Boys' Industrial School; Fairfield School for Boys; State Farm
South End, 93, 100, 137, 139, 263
Southern states, influences on Lancaster and Fairfield County, 14–15, 24–25, 54, 171
South School, 94–96, 139
Spanish-American War, 123–24
Speed limits, 132–33
Spook Hollow, 246
Square 13, 250–51
Stafford, Joab A., 59–60
Stallsmith, John, 19
Stanbery, Henry, 46–47
Stanbery-Rising House, 42–43
Stanbery School, 140
Standing Stone Bank, 253
State Farm, 98–99. *See also* Boys' Industrial School; Fairfield School for Boys
States' rights, 59, 67, 122, 196–97
Steinman, Gotlieb, 48
Stratification. *See* Social class/stratification
Streets: illumination by electricity, 157; illumation by gas, 45; opening of, 72; trees, 137, 212, 271–72
Strip shopping centers, 232–33
Stuckey, W. H., 146
Stuck Mould Works, 213, 255
Sturgeon, Timothy, 19
Suburbia, 230–68; suburban sprawl, 263
Sugar Grove, 39, 144
Summerland Beach, Buckeye Lake, 153
Sunday, Billy, 106
Swimming Pool, Miller Park, 160; racial segregation of, 174

Tallmadge, Darius, 44, 82, 219
Tallmadge, T. W., 79
Tallmadge House, 44–45
Tallmadge School, 219
Tarhe, Chief, 12
Tarhe Town, 12
Tarhe Trail, Mount Pleasant, 158
Tax code, and shopping centers, 232
Telegraph, first service in Lancaster, 50
Telephone, first service in Lancaster, 157
Thomas Ewing Junior High, 219
Thomas grocery, 138
Tiki complex, 233
Tiki Swim Club, 233
Tobias, J. H., 135
Tobias, Lloyd, 135
Tobias, Roy, 135
Tobias Studio, 135
Townscape Report, 251–52
Town square. *See* Zane Square
Trinity Evangelical Church, 105
Trolleys, 93, 138; discontinuance of, 190; entertainments, 113–14; new purchases (1915), 130
Trout Building, 243
Turner, Herbert, 208, 246, 249
Turner, James, 31
Turnpikes, 73–74
Twentieth century, beginning of celebrated in Lancaster, 125
Twentieth Century Fox, 201–5

Union Station, 93–94
United Brethren Church, 105

Van Trump, Philadelphus, 46
Veterans Administration (VA), 236–37
Victorian period, 69–124
Victory celebrations: Civil War, 61, 68; Spanish-American War, 123–24; World War I, 169–70; World War II, 200
Vietnam War, 245
Vlerebome, Arthur, 245
Vlerebome, Mary Kathryn, 245
Von Stein, Fred, 202
Vorys, Isaiah, Sr., 26, 245

Wacker, Gail, 232–33
Wages in the 1940s, 212
Walking town, 40–41, 44, 81, 217, 223, 269–70, 272–73
Washington's birthday celebration (1833), 30

Washington Temperance Society, 107
Waterworks, 101–3
Waterworks Hill, 103
Weapons control (1909), 156
Webb, Nimrod, 63
Wenger, Paul, 219
West Allen Street Addition, 80
Westerman Boiler and Tank Works, 127
West Side, 30, 137–39, 141, 144, 219, 231; aerial photo, 255; flood of 1948, 228
Wetzler, Thomas, 118
Wheeling Hill, 40, 84, 264
Whig Party, 55–56
Whiley, C. B., 146
White, James, 48
White Columns. *See* Lancaster Athletic Club
WHOK Radio, 224, 229
Williamsburg, as inspiration for historic preservation, 213
Williamson, Foster, 179
William V. Fisher Catholic High School, 236. *See also* St. Mary School
Wiseman, Charles P., 215
Wiseman, Thomas, 211, 215–16, 253
Wiseman's department store, 215–16; closing of, 253
Woltz, Jesse, 19–20
Women's baseball, 116
Women's Christian Temperance Union, 107
Women's clubs/organizations, 87–88, 107, 109, 163–65, 169, 193, 223–24
Women's Liberty Loan Committee, 169
Women's Relief Corps, 109
Women's suffrage, 163
Wooden construction prohibited in downtown, 156
Work, Joseph, 19, 48
Works Progress Administration (WPA), 178, 209

World War I, 167–70
World War II, 197–200
Wrestling, 148
Wright, Rev. John, 47
Wyandot people, 11–12, 158

Xenophobia, 56, 171, 194

*Yellow Kid*, 151
Young Men's Christian Association (YMCA), 222
Young Women's Christian Association (YWCA), 144, 222

Zane, Ebenezer, 13, 14, 250
Zane, John, 14–15
Zane, Jonathan, 13
Zane, Noah, 14–15
Zane Square: bandstand, 250; William Jennings Bryan speaks from, 122; description in early twentieth century, 135–36; description, in *Forbes*, in 1947, 213; fountain placed on, 87–88; German howitzer placed on (1926), 136; old courthouse removed, 85; Philadelphia as model for, 20; Sherman statue, 267; temporary Civil War monument, 120–21; Zane Square Festival, 266
Zane Square Festival, 266
Zane's Square Mile, 21
Zane's Trace, 13–14, 17–18, 39, 46, 133
Zanesville, compared to Lancaster, 14, 18, 29, 49, 79, 193; as football rival, 150
Zoning: commercial establishments and residences mixed in period before zoning, 81; need for zoning reform, 272; setbacks from street, 240; zoning code not pedestrian friendly, 240

## Urban Life and Urban Landscape Series
Zane L. Miller, General Editor

The series examines the history of urban life and the development of the urban landscape through works that place social, economic, and political issues in the intellectual and cultural context of their times.

Cincinnati, Queen City of the West: 1819–1838
Daniel Aaron

Proportional Representation and Election Reform in Ohio
Kathleen L. Barber

Fragments of Cities: The New American Downtowns and Neighborhoods
Larry Bennett

The Lost Dream: Businessmen and City Planning on the Pacific Coast, 1890–1920
Mansel G. Blackford

Planning for the Private Interest: Land Use Controls and Residential Patterns in
    Columbus, Ohio, 1900–1970
Patricia Burgess

Cincinnati Observed: Architecture and History
John Clubbe

Suburb in the City: Chestnut Hill, Philadelphia, 1850–1990
David R. Contosta

Main Street Blues: The Decline of Small-Town America
Richard O. Davies

The Mysteries of the Great City: The Politics of Urban Design, 1877–1937
John D. Fairfield

The Poetics of Cities: Designing Neighborhoods That Work
Mike Greenberg

History in Urban Places: The Historic Districts of the United States
David Hamer

Getting Around *Brown:* Desegregation, Development, and the Columbus Public Schools
Gregory S. Jacobs

Building Chicago: Suburban Developers and the Creation of a Divided Metropolis
Ann Durkin Keating

Silent City on a Hill: Landscapes of Memory and Boston's Mount Auburn Cemetery
Blanche Linden-Ward

Plague of Strangers: Social Groups and the Origins of City Services in Cincinnati, 1819–1870
Alan I. Marcus

Changing Plans for America's Inner Cities: Cincinnati's Over-The-Rhine and Twentieth-Century Urbanism
Zane L. Miller and Bruce Tucker

Polish Immigrants and Industrial Chicago: Workers on the South Side, 1880–1922
Dominic A. Pacyga

The New York Approach: Robert Moses, Urban Liberals, and Redevelopment of the Inner City
Joel Schwartz

Designing Modern America: The Regional Planning Association and Its Members
Edward K. Spann

Hopedale: From Commune to Company Town, 1840–1920
Edward K. Spann

Visions of Eden: Environmentalism, Urban Planning, and City Building in St. Petersburg, Florida, 1900–1995
R. Bruce Stephenson

Welcome to Heights High: The Crippling Politics of Restructuring America's Public Schools
Diana Tittle

Washing "The Great Unwashed": Public Baths in Urban America, 1840–1920
Marilyn Thornton Williams

www.ingramcontent.com/pod-product-compliance
Lightning Source LLC
Chambersburg PA
CBHW020121240426
43673CB00038B/547